THE POLITICS OF
MASSACHUSETTS EXCEPTIONALISM

THE POLITICS OF
MASSACHUSETTS EXCEPTIONALISM

REPUTATION MEETS REALITY

EDITED BY

Jerold Duquette and **Erin O'Brien**

University of Massachusetts Press

Amherst and Boston

ISBN 978-1-62534-667-4 (paper); 668-1 (hardcover)

Designed by Deste Roosa
Set in Adobe Garamond Pro and Clarendon
Printed and bound by Books International, Inc.

Cover design by John Barnett | 4eyesdesign.com
Cover photos: (top left) George Rizer, *Annual St. Patrick's Day politico breakfast,* March 16, 1974. The Boston Globe via Getty Images; (top right) *African American students board school bus outside South Boston High School, on first day of court-ordered busing program,* September 12, 1974. AP Photo; (bottom left) Steven Senne, *Demonstrators protest COVID-19 restrictions in front of the Statehouse in Boston,* May 4, 2020. AP Photo; (bottom right) Steven Senne, *U.S. Senator Elizabeth Warren (D-MA) jokes with audience with State Senator Linda Dorcena Forry at annual St. Patrick's Day breakfast,* March 20, 2016. AP Photo.

Library of Congress Cataloging-in-Publication Data
Names: Duquette, Jerold J., 1968– editor. | O'Brien, Erin E., editor.
Title: The politics of Massachusetts exceptionalism : reputation meets
    reality / edited by Jerold Duquette & Erin O'Brien.
Description: Amherst : University of Massachusetts Press, [2022] | Includes
    bibliographical references and index.
Identifiers: LCCN 2021054476 (print) | LCCN 2021054477 (ebook) | ISBN
    9781625346681 (hardcover) | ISBN 9781625346674 (paperback) | ISBN
    9781613769454 (ebook) | ISBN 9781613769461 (ebook)
Subjects: LCSH: Political parties—Massachusetts. | Political
    participation—Massachusetts. | Exceptionalism—Massachusetts. |
    Massachusetts—Politics and government.
Classification: LCC JK3116 .P65 2022 (print) | LCC JK3116 (ebook) | DDC
    324.29744—dc23/eng/20220206
LC record available at https://lccn.loc.gov/2021054476
LC ebook record available at https://lccn.loc.gov/2021054477

British Library Cataloguing-in-Publication Data
A catalog record for this book is available from the British Library.

To Jerry Mileur
JD

For all the outsiders
EO'B

CONTENTS

ACKNOWLEDGMENTS

Three decades ago, UMass Amherst professor Jerry Mileur envisioned a volume like this one authored by UMass political science graduate students. As one of those graduate students, I long regretted our failure to make Professor Mileur's vision a reality. With this volume I have put that regret to rest. In 2011, Maurice Cunningham, Peter Ubertaccio, and I started a blog called *MassPoliticsProfs* in order to bring a novel perspective to the day-to-day coverage and analysis of Massachusetts politics by marrying our love of and experience in practical politics with our political science scholarship. Over the past decade, our ranks have more than doubled and our blog has gained a loyal following. This volume is a work of the *MassPoliticsProf* and a testament to our distinctive approach to understanding and explaining Massachusetts politics. Six of the seven *MassPoliticsProfs* contributors authored chapters here and the seventh provided invaluable critique of the manuscript. This volume never would have seen the light of day, however, without the brilliance and herculean efforts of one *MassPoliticsProf* in particular. If Erin O'Brien had not signed on as my coeditor, this volume would still be just a great idea. Thanks too must go to our acquisitions editor at UMass Press, Brian Halley, for sharing our belief in the value of this project, and to production editor Rachael Deshano for her patient guidance and assistance. Finally, I must thank my wife, Kara, and my children, Deirdre, Jerold, Bridget, and Francis, whose love and support sustain me.

JD

I deplore "networking." I love talking politics, analyzing politics, working to make change, and I insist on considerable fun along the way. In Massachusetts, I've joined with a merry band of academics (like the contributors to this volume), valued UMass Boston colleagues, students, students now influential practitioners of politics, and dedicated journalists who share these passions. I am impressed by your commitments to making Massachusetts more equitable, transparent, and understood from the perspective of *all* its inhabitants. . . . Holy smokes—I have a network! It grew via substance and goodwill. I value it deeply. I owe particular thanks to my hiring chair and wonderful friend Elizabeth Bussiere for being integral in bringing me to

UMass Boston, an institution I love, and keeping me within shouting distance of sanity. Thanks too to our editor at the University of Massachusetts Press, Brian Halley, and his team for shepherding this project to completion. Jane JaKyung Han is a true hero of this book. Thank you for your tireless research assistance, technical acumen, and zoom catch-ups. Your professionalism and dedication during sometimes very trying circumstances leave me in awe. Tremendous gratitude goes to Callie Crossley as well. Callie was the first person in Boston media to invite me on her NPR show and truly embrace my voice—so many opportunities and connections sprang from that initial invite. Thank you. Making lists is dangerous because you always accidentally leave someone out, so sincere appreciation to the journalists, camera people, and producers who value having my PoliSci voice in the mix. You know who you are. And, to show I've really become a Bostonian, you know who you are not! ;)

This "Bostonian with Buckeye flair" has found a home in Massachusetts.

EO'B

THE POLITICS OF
MASSACHUSETTS
EXCEPTIONALISM

MASSACHUSETTS EXCEPTIONALISM
AS IDENTITY AND DEBATE

Jerold Duquette and Erin O'Brien

What is so special about state government and politics in Massachusetts? What, if anything, makes Massachusetts politics stand out from that of its forty-nine peers or from national politics? Are the claims of exceptionalism, of Massachusetts' special and instructive place in American history and politics, justified? If so, does this instructiveness come from the state's example of exceptional virtue or exceptional vice? Is it an example of "how to" or "how not to"? The animating questions of this volume revolve around *exceptionalism*, an idea of debatable properties but indisputable gravitational pull in Massachusetts and American history and politics. The contributors to this volume are united by a twofold understanding of exceptionalism. On the one hand, we look to institutional arrangements, functioning, and relationships. Here, many aspects of the state's historical and institutional development are exceptional, which is to say "unique" when compared to other American states and to the national government. On the other hand, and more normatively, on the question of whether Massachusetts is "exceptionally virtuous," the case for Massachusetts exceptionalism, is at best a mixed bag. Taken together, the chapters in this volume provide a frank assessment of the commonwealth's exceptionalism from the perspective of institutional dynamics as well as diversity, voice, and policy innovation. Each contributor to this volume puts a key element of the commonwealth's political system to the test in order to determine whether Massachusetts' reputation and understanding of itself as exceptionally different or exceptionally virtuous—or both—are supported by the evidence.

The machinery, transactional, and individualistic elements of Massachusetts political culture operate according to the logic and design of the U.S. Constitution more closely than any other state, better even than the national government framed by that constitution, which is now the second oldest democratic constitution in the world. (Can you guess which one is the oldest? That's right, "Massachusetts.") Exceptionally durable fidelity to the Madisonian notion of individualistic, self-interested political competition has enabled the Bay State to weather national political transitions and transgressions without destabilizing fallout for centuries. Even now, as bitter partisan culture wars swallow up democratic politics and processes in Washington, DC, and state capitols across America, life on Beacon Hill remains an exceptionally nonpartisan affair. Democrats who dominate at the Massachusetts State House generally work hand in hand with Republican governors. Of course, exceptional stability also has downsides. Several contributors to this volume vividly illustrate that avoidance of destabilizing change can also mean avoidance of necessary and positive change. Change-resistant institutions and cultural norms have unquestionably preserved and protected unjustifiable power imbalances in Massachusetts government and politics. In stark contrast to its progressive national reputation, the Bay State is home to many of the most egregious examples of social, economic, and political inequality in America.

Massachusetts exceptionalism then is real, but complicated. Its centrality to the state's founding and understanding of its own reputation today make exceptionalism a powerful analytical lens through which to scrutinize and evaluate government and politics in the Bay State. Exceptionalism is a lens that brings the good, the bad, and the ugly of Massachusetts' government and politics into sharp relief.

Two historical facts provide a springboard for assessments of Massachusetts' exceptionalism in the chapters that follow. Both are facts no other American state can marshal to distinguish itself. Both make comparisons between Massachusetts and American national government and politics irresistible in the present undertaking. First, the concept of exceptionalism itself in American and Massachusetts politics can be traced to the same moment, the same author. Several of the contributors to this volume highlight the significance of John Winthrop's 1630 promise to make the Massachusetts Bay Colony a model of Christian charity for the world and the parallel development of Massachusetts and American political thought. Second, the Massachusetts Constitution of 1780, more than those of any of its peers at the time and alone among them today, served as the principal model on which the framers of the U.S. Constitution relied for their handiwork. This philosophical and constitutional seniority has had an unmistakable impact on Massachusetts' reputation and self-sense of exceptionalism.

Firmly ensconced in the state's identity, exceptionalism attaches effortlessly to the long line of Massachusetts citizens who took for granted their rightful place on the national political stage. Yet the state's reputation for excessive self-regard is well worn nationally as Massachusetts ranks as the "snobbiest" state in the nation (Cote 2021) and as only the thirty-first best state by fellow Americans (Gartsbeyn 2021). They don't call us "Massholes" for nothing! Nevertheless, within the state, exceptionalism provides narrative cover for stubborn contradictions between reputation and reality in the commonwealth even today. In Massachusetts, old-school politics—which is to say wait your turn, establishment-friendly politics—wears a cloak of respectability to many in part because it is literally the oldest school of politics in America.

Today, in the wake of Donald Trump's presidency, Americans are more divided, distrustful, and cynical than ever before. By the time Joe Biden took the oath of office on January 20, 2021, following the January 6 attack on the U.S. Capitol by Trump supporters, there was little doubt that American politics had become incredibly toxic. Yet Massachusetts-based pollster and political analyst Steve Koczela took the occasion to highlight evidence point-ing to the comparative nontoxicity of Massachusetts' politics:

> POLITICS IS NOT all toxic. Here in Massachusetts, voters hold political leaders in very high regard. The state legislature [*sic*] has climbed to 65 percent approval in a poll we released last week, the highest we have seen in our polling going back over a decade. Gov. Charlie Baker sports a 73 percent approval rating and has been in the 70s and 80s for most of his term. Taken together, we have what may be the most popular governor and the most popular legislature in the country. . . . Putting the two together shows how much of an outlier Massachusetts truly is. Maryland—another blue state with a moderate Republican governor—is the only other state that comes close. (2021)

Massachusetts-based political journalist Adam Reilly, in a Twitter response to Koczela's polling data, theorized that it "reflects both genuine substantive approval, and also a *very Massachusetts tendency to assume things are great just because they're from Massachusetts*" (2021; emphasis added). Koczela's positive assessment and Reilly's rebuttal reflect both the durability and the contesta-bility of the state's long love affair with exceptionalism. Several contributors to this volume, via their empirical analyses, find that this admiration for the commonwealth's political institutions and actors is not universally shared even within the state's borders. In communities disproportionally alienated from access to political and economic power in the state, such as people of color and immigrants, this sanguinity, noted by Koczela and subtly mocked by Reilly, is a cruel reminder of the gap between reputation and reality that powers and protects inequality and discrimination in Massachusetts. This tension between reputation and reality runs through all of the analyses in this volume.

Average Bay State voters are not now, nor have they ever been, outraged by career politicians engaging in transparently transactional politics because they want their representatives to be powerful and expect them to use that power on behalf of their constituents (Duquette 2020). As Professor Ubertaccio shows in chapter 3 and Professors Ubertaccio and Cunningham show in chapter 7, Massachusetts voters do not punish politicians for having national aspirations, for political careerism. In the same breath, several contributors to this volume show how the tension between political insiders and outsiders plays when Bay State pols seek higher office. Congresswoman Ayanna Pressley, Attorney General Maura Healey, State Senator Sonya Chang-Díaz, Boston City Councillor Andrea Campbell, and Boston mayor Michelle Wu are all successful progressive politicians working their way up the political career ladder. They do so by marrying outsider, antiestablishment policy priorities with establishment-friendly résumés that distinguish them from antiestablishment progressives, such as Alexandria Ocasio-Cortez or Tahirah Amatul-Wadud, the civil rights attorney and activist easily defeated by Congressman Richie Neal on the same day Councilwoman Pressley upset Mike Capuano en route to the U.S. House of Representatives. Though the commonwealth does have "a [long] tradition of moralistic activism and reform that has made and remade America," the practice of elective politics and public policy making in the state is decidedly individualistic and transactional (Mileur 1997, 77). Bay State politics is passionate, but it is not the passion of the preacher or the profit; it is the passion of the player, the competitor, engaged on behalf of her constituents in a blood sport, not a holy war.

The political memoir of former senate president Billy Bulger, whose eighteen-year rule of the senate from 1978 to 1996 remains the longest in state history, is filled with colorful stories about his bouts with competitors for power and policy in the blood sport of Bay State politics. In it, Bulger openly celebrates the old-school, nonideological, and transactional nature of Massachusetts politics, as well as the unchecked power of insiders at the statehouse. In Governor Bill Weld, Bulger had a particularly skilled opponent with whom he fought hard, but never let disagreement come between two of the "big three" who then ruled the statehouse. Speaking at the 1993 St. Patrick's Day breakfast (an annual political-insider lovefest described in this volume by Professor O'Brien in chapter 1), Weld deftly and humorously

illustrated his relationship with Bulger. He assured the crowd he was una-
fraid to publicly state his position on his frequent nemesis "William Michael
Bulger," a position Weld stated in part as follows:

> If you mean the sultan of South Boston, the suzerain of the statehouse, the
> tyrant who terrorizes the goo-goos and suckles the suspect, the Napoleonic
> oppressor whose fast gavel denied every citizen a vote on term limits and
> basic rights, . . . the very man who thwarts everything that is good and
> right and pure about Massachusetts, then certainly I am against him. . . .
> But if, when you say "Billy Bulger," you mean the learned leader of his
> esteemed chamber, the sage whose single words steer his colleagues back
> from the wayward path, the saint of East Third Street, . . . the champion
> of the working man and the guardian of the widowed, . . . the brave Latin
> scholar and philosopher who resists the evils of television and the *Boston
> Globe*, . . . then certainly I am for him. . . . This is my stand. I will not
> retreat from it. (Bulger 1996, 271–72)

The relationship between Democrats and Republicans at the Massachusetts
State House, examined in this volume by several contributors, could not be
more different than in Washington or in state capitols around the country.
Despite the frequent presence of Republican governors and a Democratic
legislature whose veto-proof majority has gone unchallenged for three decades,
interparty and interbranch relations on Beacon Hill are far more cooperative
than combative. The legislative supremacy included in the designs of both the
Massachusetts and the U.S. Constitutions, a distant memory on Capitol Hill,
remains alive and quite well on Beacon Hill where the governor is but one of
three who set the agenda at the statehouse. The governor, senate president,
and Speaker of the house, known as "the big three," steer the ship of state
together, an arrangement that gives the legislature two hands on the wheel
to the governor's one. Though competitive, twenty-first-century Democratic
legislative leaders and Republican governors routinely choose incrementalism
over incivility, accommodation over confrontation.

As you will read in detail in Professor O'Brien's chapter 1, the primary
cleavage in Massachusetts government and politics, reflected in the state's
economy as well, is between insiders and outsiders, incumbents and challengers, haves and have-nots. Division by party and ideology are subordinated
or channeled away from the halls of state government where interest-based
bargaining is the coin of the realm. Issues or conflicts that threaten "politics

as usual" are routinely deflected away from the day-to-day work on Beacon Hill—much to the chagrin of those perceived to threaten "the way we have always done things." As Professors Duquette and Cunningham explain in chapter 9 of this volume, when issues that threaten comity at the statehouse cannot be left to local governments, or kicked down the road, they can be sent directly to the ballot, where opposing pressure groups can duke it out in the public square without putting legislative leaders or the governor in harm's way. Even when they cannot be deflected, potentially disruptive issues can be slowed and moderated. When the murder of Blacks by police in America finally found resonance in America's national political narrative in the summer of 2020, pressure to bring urgent and comprehensive change to the commonwealth did not topple "politics as usual" on Beacon Hill. The governor, senate president, and Speaker of the house had little difficulty delaying significant police reform and subjecting it to the same interest-based bargaining approach they use on less urgent and less visible policy-making imperatives. As Professors O'Brien and Jiménez make clear in chapters 10 and 11, the persistent underrepresentation of people of color, immigrants, and women in the statehouse often allows what most Americans see as the most progressive state in the Union to talk the talk without having to walk the walk.

Our scholarly examination of "Massachusetts exceptionalism" highlights the places where the label is accurate and where it is inaccurate. We name the tensions that define Massachusetts politics, if not its political rhetoric. The commonwealth was the center of abolition as well as the locale of busing riots. No other state is as dense with institutions of higher learning and medical research, yet the state's initial COVID-19 vaccination rollout was near last in the nation. The first two approved vaccines in the United States were developed by Moderna and Pfizer. "Moderna's headquarters" are literally in the "heart of Cambridge" and "less than a quarter-mile away is an outpost for Pfizer," but the Massachusetts city in which they are located, far too emblematically of Massachusetts, had no vaccination sites ready as both companies delivered their vaccines to states far more prepared to receive them (Krueger 2021). Massachusetts has and is seeing significant demographic change, as we document, but this has not yet been married with meaningful shifts in political influence. The Bay State is a place where the sweeping rhetoric of the Kennedys, and the state's influence on the national stage, has not translated into another Bay Stater in the White House—despite many recent attempts from Democrats and Republicans rooted here. Massachusetts is a model of bipartisanship between the Democratic state legislature and Republican governors but also a model of old-school, transactional, establishment-protective politics where new blood and new voices are routinely stifled at the statehouse. By making these tensions evident, this volume allows the reader to draw informed conclusions about where precisely, if at all, Massachusetts is exceptional. In this volume, the "city on the hill," "the HUB," and "the Cradle of Liberty" get both earned reverence and earned critique. While your "cousin from Boston" may not like the entire ride, your professors from Massachusetts think it is worth the journey.

Plan of the Book

Each of the contributors to this volume focuses on a different piece of the Massachusetts exceptionalism puzzle, employing methodologies best suited to their subjects. We address political culture(s), local and regional government and politics, Massachusetts on the national stage, institutions, political parties, voter access and political participation, the initiative and referendum process, Latinx politics and representation, and the slow incorporation of women and women of color into elite elected positions in the commonwealth. Our methodologies reflect the variance in the field—historical analysis, textual analysis, interviews, and statistical analysis—but uniformly focus on how well the realities of Massachusetts government and politics live up to the state's sense of exceptionalism.

In part 1, Professors O'Brien, Jenkins, and Ubertaccio provide crucial historical, political, social, and economic context for the studies that follow. The authors note the national influence Massachusetts plays in electoral politics while also highlighting the state's bias toward Boston and the resulting regional inequities. Massachusetts is comparatively affluent, the most educated state in the Union, yet deeply unequal along the considerations of race, gender, ethnicity, and region.

In part 2, Professors Jenkins, Duquette, and Friedman focus on the history and development of the commonwealth's three branches of government, finding that all three are strongly and consistently shaped by the state's philosophical and constitutional seniority, both of which have made Massachusetts a model for its peers at crucial junctures in American history. Professors Jenkins and Duquette both see the endurance of legislative supremacy at the statehouse as exceptional, while Friedman emphasizes the Supreme Judicial Court's exceptional fidelity to the Madisonian notion of an independent judiciary in a separated-powers scheme. All three studies illustrate the exceptional consistency between the intentions of America's and Massachusetts' constitutional framers and the institutional development of state government in the commonwealth.

Part 3 finds Professors Ubertaccio, Cunningham, O'Brien, and Duquette pointing the exceptionalism lens at the practice of politics beyond the statehouse's golden dome. The history and practice of partisan and interest group politics, one hundred years of (somewhat) direct citizen access to lawmaking on the ballot, and the state's improving record on citizen access to the ballot box are examined and evaluated. In the chapter on ballot measures, we witness regression from democratic ideals via the ways in which those levers can be used to funnel dark money and to insulate elected officials from public accountability. On voter access, the Bay State has made improvements in the past decade when it comes to the ease with which residents can cast their legal ballots. Turning to government accountability, Massachusetts is decidedly unexceptional, following national trends, but when it comes to voter access policies, the commonwealth is increasingly a model for statehouses moving in the opposite direction.

Finally, in part 4, Professors Jiménez and O'Brien marshal both original and existing statistical data to evaluate the commonwealth's political and policy-making record on issues of diversity. By illuminating the place and progress of the state's Latinx community, women, and women of color in the commonwealth, Jiménez and O'Brien ground all the volume's assessments of Massachusetts exceptionalism in hard data, allowing readers to focus on the prospects of bridging the gap between the state's high opinion of itself and the tangible consequences of Beacon Hill politics for all of the state's residents.

The Chapters

In chapter 1, Professor O'Brien describes the social and economic contexts in which contemporary Massachusetts politics plays out, arguing that "while it is fairly easy to delineate the structural features and conditions that define the commonwealth's political landscape, classifying Massachusetts' political culture is both a popular sport and one where no clear winning take has emerged." O'Brien cautions that debate about whether Massachusetts' political culture is exceptional can conceal as much as it illuminates. Her statistical portrait provides a clear picture of Massachusetts residents today and their real-life social, economic, and political circumstances. She finds that while the state's knowledge economy is forward looking and has produced great affluence, its less well-publicized impact has been the increase of economic inequality in the state. O'Brien emphasizes Massachusetts' well-earned reputation for racism and inequality. As one Black Bostonian put it, "When I see stories of police brutality, not just on the news but from personal acquaintances, across the country, I think to myself that despite its liberal reputation, Boston is no different. Perhaps this city is just better at maintaining that illusion. Down South, racism is much more overt and direct. But in the liberal North, it's buried beneath macroaggressions and couched in progressive language" (Gray 2020). O'Brien details the impact of shifting residential patterns and demographic changes in the state's population that have accompanied the transition to a knowledge-based economy. An increasingly diverse population means an increasingly diverse electorate, which is transforming the political, as well as the economic, playing field. Professor O'Brien rounds out her contextual portrait by factoring in the cultural impact of Democratic Party dominance in the state's politics. Finally, she provides insights into Massachusetts political culture in the voice of political scientists as well as current political practitioners. She first introduces the pathbreaking work of Professor Edgar Litt, whose typology of Massachusetts political culture is utilized by several of the contributors to this volume, as well as the interstate political culture classification framework of Professor Daniel Elazar. The work of these two scholars has framed inquiry and discussion of Massachusetts political culture for more than fifty years.

In chapter 2, Professor Jenkins calls our attention to one of the paradoxes of Massachusetts' historical consciousness and its contributions to America's philosophical and constitutional foundations. Here in the birthplace of democratic local self-government where the town meeting remains the most common form of local government, local governments have little independent power. Instead, the state legislature jealously guards its turf and its resources, leaving the state's cities and towns little ability to exercise the powers granted to them under the state's home-rule statute. The large concentration of the population in the Boston area contributes to another unenviable element of Massachusetts politics, the significant advantages of the city of Boston and its immediate neighbors when it comes to the attention and resources of state government. The cities and towns of western and southeastern Massachusetts have long been used to fighting an uphill battle for political clout at the statehouse. Though Professor Jenkins reports some progress, when it comes to local government power and regional political clout, Massachusetts is not walking the exceptionalism walk.

In chapter 3, Professor Ubertaccio argues that the sons and daughters of Massachusetts have always made exceptional leadership contributions to American national government and politics but that in recent presidential election cycles campaigns for the nation's top office have not gone well for Massachusetts' politicians. The commonwealth's unique connections to the nation's philosophical and constitutional foundings helped shape the state's very historically conscious political culture, a culture that has always nurtured and rewarded personal political ambition and treated successful politicians like celebrities. Though the now famous Broadway musical lyric was delivered by Virginian George Washington, Professor Ubertaccio's analysis makes clear that "history has its eye on us" is a sentiment that was already deeply embedded in Massachusetts hearts and minds when the first shots of the American Revolution were fired on Massachusetts soil. The commonwealth's exceptional place on the national political stage, in presidential politics and congressional leadership especially, has survived into the twenty-first century, according to Professor Ubertaccio, because Massachusetts is home to the colleges and universities from which a disproportionate number of America's aspiring presidents, senators, and representatives are graduates. Ubertaccio argues that the state's vibrant intellectual and media culture, along with its proximity to New Hampshire, will continue to light the path between Massachusetts and Washington though the presidency eludes.

In chapter 4, Professor Jenkins argues that the exceptional endurance of legislative supremacy on Beacon Hill explains a great deal about Massachusetts government and politics. The leaders of the state senate and house of representatives in Massachusetts exert enormous control over the policy-making process. While being "exceptionally old school" may evoke nostalgia for some, Jenkins highlights the dangers of putting "going along to get along" above policy innovation. While the state senate has in recent years become more open to the policy innovations necessary to meet the governing challenges of the twenty-first century, "the exceptional concentration of power in . . . the hands of the Speaker of the house" continues to place the imperatives of electoral politics ahead of effective and responsive governance in the commonwealth.

In chapter 5, Professor Duquette traces the history of executive leadership in Massachusetts from John Winthrop to Charlie Baker, demonstrating that the endurance of legislative supremacy in the commonwealth, in sharp contrast to Washington and state capitols across America, makes the Massachusetts governorship an exceptional example of the road not traveled by presidents and fellow governors alike. For four hundred years, Massachusetts chief executives have navigated the central tension at the heart of America's democratic experiment, the tension between democratic accountability and efficient administration of government. Presidents and governors alike, responding to the increasing complexity of democratic governance in a changing world, gradually became the dominant actors in American government and politics, fundamentally distorting the relationship between executive and legislative power and purpose that was enshrined in the Massachusetts and U.S. Constitutions. The Massachusetts governorship, however, remains squarely grounded in an institutional scheme and a cultural tradition that remain true to the framers' intentions and designs. Massachusetts provides an exceptionally Madisonian model of executive leadership that has made occupants of the corner office at the Massachusetts statehouse leaders and innovators without becoming the center of the political universe in the state.

The theme of continuity amid change also animates the study of Massachusetts' Supreme Judicial Court and the state constitution it is charged with interpreting. In chapter 6, Professor Friedman describes the "provenance, framework, and historical importance" of the commonwealth's constitution as well as the history of the Supreme Judicial Court's role and relationship to the legislature and the governor. The ways that Massachusetts' highest court has mediated the inescapable tensions between itself and the state's political branches mark it as an exceptional model of American constitutional jurisprudence. Friedman finds particular exceptionalism in the continuity between John Adams' conception of separated government powers, the design of the three branches of government enshrined in the Constitution of 1780 he authored, and the prudence and care with which the Supreme Judicial Court preserves its intended place in and the integrity of the separation of powers in Massachusetts state government.

Litt's typology first introduced in chapter 1 reappears in Professors Cunningham and Ubertaccio's chapter 7, where they use it to delineate the role of political parties in Massachusetts government and politics. They explain that the state's electorate is not quite what outside observers suspect. While the percentage of registered Democrats has long been more than twice that of registered Republicans, both parties' totals are exceeded by unenrolled voters—those who choose not to register with either party. This comes as a surprise to many outside of Massachusetts. The recent success of Republican gubernatorial candidates, according to Cunningham and Ubertaccio, is not a product of strong party organizations in the state. Neither the Massachusetts Democratic nor its Republican Party organizations enjoy impressive influence over their nomination processes or the behavior of fellow partisans in office. Democratic dominance in the state legislature is aided by an ineffectual Republican state party organization and the hesitance of GOP governors to invest too much energy in increasing Republican ranks in the legislature for fear of threatening the harmony between the corner office and Democratic leaders on Beacon Hill. The real partisan battle in the commonwealth is within the Democratic Party, where progressives have long had a hard time breaking through. Recently, however, the election of young progressive candidates of color in the state suggests that change may be afoot, though, as Professors Cunningham and Ubertaccio stress, establishment political actors have never yielded power easily in Massachusetts and there is little sign that this enduring element of Massachusetts politics will change anytime soon.

In chapter 8, Professor O'Brien compares the Bay State's performance in administering elections with its state peers, finding that the commonwealth has only recently begun to put its money where its mouth is. Between 2008 and 2018, Massachusetts moved up from "a dismal thirty-second . . . to eleventh" in state rankings. Despite this progress, O'Brien finds that while registration and turnout rates are comparatively high in Massachusetts, they "fall short of the expectations set by high levels of socioeconomic status among Massachusetts residents." The good news is that Massachusetts has been exceptional of late in the area of voter access policy. The bad news is that substantial gaps in registration and voting remain along familiar lines of race and ethnicity. Professor O'Brien concludes that the state's updated election laws and nimble response to the challenges presented by the COVID-19 pandemic indicate that Massachusetts, though "late to the game," is on the comeback trail when it comes to improving voters' access to the ballot box, but important work remains.

In chapter 9, Professors Duquette and Cunningham explain the history and impact of the state's ballot initiative and referendum process, finding that it has long provided a participatory outlet for Massachusetts citizens but that it has also provided elected leaders at the statehouse with a convenient political pressure valve of sorts. Because the legislature has more control over the process by which measures make the state ballot than legislatures in other states, Beacon Hill leaders have been able to channel politically sensitive issues away from the conventional policy-making process and away from their reelection campaigns. One of the reasons Massachusetts legislative elections are among the least competitive in America is this ability to dispose of controversial issues in an ostensibly democratic way without giving fuel to potential reelection challengers. Duquette and Cunningham argue that the gap between the commonwealth's liberal vanguard reputation and its exceptionally establishment-friendly political reality is aided and abetted by the ballot initiative and referendum process, which in recent years has increasingly become a venue for well-financed special interests to stage dramatic, misinformation-filled campaigns designed to protect or advance their narrow interests. Thanks to the campaign finance deregulation unleashed by the U.S. Supreme Court's *Citizens United* decision in 2010, ballot measure campaigns have become particularly fertile ground for unscrupulous campaign tactics, including the abundant use of so-called dark money. The ability to finance highly deceptive media campaigns for or against a ballot measure without revealing the identities of the financiers has accelerated and intensified the dangers of the state's century-old ode to direct democracy. This makes an already undeliberate approach to policy making even less deliberative.

In chapter 10, Professor Jiménez describes the history and present place of Latinx communities in Massachusetts government and policy, detailing the dramatic and accelerating demographic changes in the commonwealth over the past half century as well as the diversity among Massachusetts' Latinx population. Jiménez finds that Latinx candidates for public office are more successful at the local level than in statewide elections but that this success has been "slow and halting." He emphasizes throughout the diversity among those placed under the umbrella label of "Latinx," how these communities are often located in different parts of the state, and how they do not necessarily mirror one another in policy priorities. Professor Jiménez uses statistical data to compare the progress of Latinx communities in Massachusetts to their counterparts in the northeastern region and around the country, finding that while "the lack of descriptive representation has not precluded policies Latinx have demanded," enactment of policy that adequately responds to community needs has been "uneven." Professor Jiménez does find progress in the political organization and mobilization of the state's Latinx communities but concludes that the commonwealth is far from the head of the class "in providing Latinx with affordable housing, educating Latinx children, and closing the wealth gap that has developed between Latinx and whites." Many of the "same structural barriers" that make Latinx communities in the state economically vulnerable also limit progress in increasing Latinx representation at the statehouse.

Professor O'Brien measures the progress of women in Massachusetts government and politics in chapter 11, the volume's final original study, finding the commonwealth "not so exceptional" in this regard. "When it comes to electing women, Massachusetts is best described as 'exceptionally poor' in New England and 'exceptionally average' among the fifty states." The hard data reveal yet another gap between the state's progressive reputation and its reality when it comes to women in public office. O'Brien explains that the state's poor record on electing women is related to the dominance of the Democratic Party at the statehouse. Single-party dominance is an artifact of uncompetitive elections. Without competitive elections, it is more difficult to elect political newcomers as the party need not reinvent itself, reinforcing the predominantly male and white composition of elective offices. Professor O'Brien sees this as particularly problematic in Massachusetts, where Democratic supermajorities in the state legislature serve only to increase the level of difficulty for aspiring officeholders. O'Brien concludes that policy changes that would make it easier for women to run for office, such as addressing the high cost of child care, would help "keep women in the [political] pipeline" and that "a Republican Party that is a threat at the ballot box would help substantially" when it comes to electing women and women of color.

Collectively, these chapters offer a comprehensive portrait of Massachusetts government and politics as well as a rich, clear-eyed, and nuanced assessment of where Massachusetts' exeptionalism does and does not match up with reality. Enjoy the ride!

WORKS CITED

Bulger, William M. 1996. *While the Music Lasts: My Life in Politics*. New York: Houghton Mifflin.

Cote, Jackson. 2021. "Massachusetts Ranked Snobbiest State in the Country; All New England States Land in the Top 10." *MassLive*, April 20, 2021. https://www.masslive.com/news/2021/04/massachusetts-ranked-snobbiest-state-in-the-country-all-new-england-states-land-in-top-10.html.

Duquette, Jerold. 2020. "Mass Politics in 2020: Still Exceptionally Establishment-Friendly after All These Years." *New England Journal of Political Science* 12, no. 1: 111–19.

Gartsbeyn, Mark. 2021. "'They're Intimidated by the Accent': Readers React to Middling Ranking of Massachusetts in 'Best State' Poll." *Boston.com*, April 19, 2021. https://www.boston.com/news/local-news/2021/04/19/readers-react-massachusetts-best-state-poll/.

Gray, Arielle. 2020. "Boston Prides Itself on Its Progressive Image. Let Me Tell You What I Know." WBUR, June 2, 2020. https://www.wbur.org/cognoscenti/2020/06/02/george-floyd-police-brutality-protests-arielle-gray.

Koczela, Steve. 2021. "Voters Hold Beacon Hill in High Esteem." *CommonWealth Magazine*, January 19, 2021. https://commonwealthmagazine.org/news-analysis/voters-hold-beacon-hill-in-high-esteem/.

Krueger, Hanna. 2021. "Phase 2 Vaccination Are Set to Begin Monday. But Many Cities and Towns Say They Have No Way to Make That Happen." *Boston Globe,* January 28, 2021. https://www.bostonglobe.com/2021/01/29/nation/state-says-phase-2-vaccinations -begin-monday-many-cities-towns-say-they-have-no-way-make-that-happen/?p1 =StaffPage.

Mileur, Jerome M. 1997. "Party Politics in the Bay State: The Dominion of Democracy." In *Parties and Politics in the New England States*, edited by Jerome M. Mileur. Amherst, MA: Polity Press.

Reilly, Adam (@reillyadam). 2021. "THEORY: This reflects both genuine and substantive approval." Twitter, January 20, 2021, 8:03 a.m. https://twitter.com/reillyadam?s=11.

PART I

Exceptionalism
in Political Context

CHAPTER I

MASSACHUSETTS POLITICS
Context and Culture

Erin O'Brien

The popularity of the blue state identity represents the most updated version of [the] long mythology of Massachusetts exceptionalism. Dating back to the Puritans christening of Boston as "the city on the hill" and claims that the city was the "birthplace of liberty" during the American Revolution and extending to the recent invocation of the "Massachusetts liberal" label, residents have frequently adopted various elements of the state's history and even appropriated criticisms as a means to distinguish themselves from the rest of the nation. By . . . emphasizing the ways that Massachusetts stood outside and above the rest of the nation, this discourse also makes exceptional the persistence of racial segregation in metropolitan Boston, the state's role in the tax revolt, [and] its strong tradition of moderate Republican politicians. (Geismer 2015, 15)

So opens Professor Lily Geismer's book *Don't Blame Us* on the role of affluent suburban liberals in the transformation of the national Democratic Party. She goes on to ponder "what issues and events this discourse [of Massachusetts exceptionalism] has magnified and what it has concealed" (2015, 15). This chapter examines this question as it relates to the context and culture(s) of Massachusetts politics. Readers will see that while it is fairly easy to delineate the structural features and conditions that define the commonwealth's political landscape, classifying Massachusetts' political culture is both a popular sport and one where no clear winning take has emerged. Nevertheless, one theme runs through all of these understandings of Massachusetts' political culture: exceptionalism.

Many treatments of Massachusetts' political culture stay true to the current that, while sometimes messy, it is "better here." Hogarty wrote in 2002 that "historically, Massachusetts can legitimately lay claim to many social and political innovations. It was the first state to have a written constitution with a separate Bill of Rights included; the first newspaper, the first public library,

Thanks to the more than twenty-six hundred Massachusetts politics professionals, reporters, analysts, organizers, and activists who weighed in from every ideological and regional corner of Massachusetts with their thoughts on what defines the state's political culture. Thanks also to Maurice Cunningham and Jerold Duquette for early scholarly resources on Massachusetts political culture.

the first college, and the first public high school were all founded here" (3). He goes on to write, though, that "most of all, it is a state with a dramatically contested past . . . cradle of liberty; the birthplace of the American Revolution; a hot bed of abolition that provoked the Civil War and eventually ended black slavery," while also being "a bastion of isolationism" and a "seedbed of McCarthyism" (2002, 3). Though Hogarty is not speaking explicitly about political culture, he is reflecting the fact that exceptionalism has always been deeply embedded in the culture (political and otherwise) of Massachusetts. It's the reason virtually every scholarly examination of Bay State politics includes acknowledgment of exceptionalism.

Contestation over Massachusetts political culture remains just as vigorous today, still organized around exceptionalism—for good or for bad. The Massachusetts "taste" for a Republican governor with strong Democratic majorities in the house and senate is bipartisanship personified for some and a glide path for corruption and policies that curtail political imagination to others. Administrative capture, when a state agency allows its mission to be co-opted by the governor or legislature, is a concern here as well. Some see Massachusetts as living the progressive expansionary ideal via abolition, being first among the fifty states in civil unions, and in bipartisan legislation enhancing transgender rights. Others look to how political power remains disproportionately the province of white men to the detriment of long-aggrieved minority communities—particularly Black Americans. To some, the better analytic distinction is "business as usual/insiders" versus "outsiders" unwilling to wait their turn and play by old norms. This insider-outsider distinction correlates with race and ethnicity—with outsiders more likely to be individuals of color. Cordial relationships between the occupant of the "corner office" and the legislature are the antidote for DC dysfunction, but, upon scratching the surface, some see Massachusetts politics as one where old-fashioned revenge rules the day.

Perhaps the most interesting take is that Massachusetts political culture is defined by a refrain familiar to many young adults: "Do as I say and not as I do." Here Massachusetts is exceptionally comfortable telling the other forty-nine states how to behave in policy but quick to abandon its bluest-of-blue label at home. One response is that this label has always obscured ideological differences among Massachusetts Democrats and the ways in which these differences make for ambivalences and tensions in its political culture and subsequent policy. Another response is that those who decry Massachusetts as wanting have too often not lived elsewhere and do not know how good they comparatively have it: glass half-full, glass half-empty.

The chapter that follows first provides the context within which Massachusetts politics and policy occur. These trends are largely uncontested. From there, we turn to Massachusetts political culture—both what the scholarship indicates and what activists and professional political observers in the state observe. That Massachusetts is exceptional is borne out. Whether this is for good or bad, an accurate description or exceptional in its denialism, or somewhere in between is for readers of this volume to decide.

Massachusetts Political Context

Political context is the field on which politics is played. Think of a professional American football field. Level, one hundred yards long, uniform width, clear white boundaries, field goal posts dead center, ten yards into the end zone: everywhere, no variation. Now consider Major League Baseball diamonds. The distance between the bases, as well as the mound and home plate, is always the same, but each stadium then embraces variation. At Boston's Fenway Park, a thirty-seven-foot, two-inch-tall left-field wall, "the Green Monster," intimidates hitters. At the New York Yankees' relatively new stadium, the configuration of the right-field wall is largely responsible for the park being known as a home-run derby (and, in Massachusetts, an abomination). Minute Maid Park, where the Houston Astros play, features a retractable roof that can literally alter the weather conditions on game day, and if a ball hits it in fair territory it is playable. The American states are a lot more like baseball parks than football stadiums in their uniqueness and particularities. Yes, all fifty states are playing the same game, governance, and playing it in accordance with the U.S. Constitution's republican mandate, but the context in which they do so differs, sometimes quite dramatically.

Four factors or trends define the context in which the game of Massachusetts politics plays out today: the affluence and vulnerability accompanying the state's knowledge economy, shifts in population density and demographic change, racism and racial politics, and a very persistent one-party political arena where Democrats are dominant.

KNOWLEDGE ECONOMY: AFFLUENCE AND VULNERABILITY

The first factor is considerable affluence, largely driven by investments in and reliance on the knowledge economy, coupled with significant economic inequality. According to 2018 Census data, the median income of Massachusetts' households is $86,345. This means that half of Massachusetts' households fall above and half below this income threshold. This figure is far higher than the U.S. average of $63,179 and the highest among the fifty states and DC. Relatively speaking, Massachusetts' poverty rate is low, 8.7 percent, as measured by federal poverty thresholds ($26,200 for a family of four in 2020). This positions Massachusetts within the top ten states for the lowest poverty rate.

These positive metrics are largely driven by the strength of Massachusetts' "knowledge economy" and the first-in-the-nation percentage of individuals with a college degree (Zeigler 2020). The two are mutually reinforcing so that Massachusetts is a force in high-tech innovation, higher education, science, biotech, health care, and related industries. Organizing around, and creating policies that foster, this "creative class" pays dividends in earnings and new development (Florida 2002, 2017). Growth in Massachusetts has been on a significant upswing. Long derided as "Taxachusetts," the commonwealth is now perceived as a good place to do business.

High income and comparatively low poverty rates mask considerable inequality, though. The commonwealth is sixth worst among the fifty states and DC for income inequality. The ratio of earnings for the top 1 percent of income earners to that of everyone else (the bottom 99 percent) is 30.9 (Sommeiller and Price 2018). And living in Massachusetts is expensive—high comparative income does not adequately compensate for the fact that the state has the fifth-highest cost of living among the fifty states (World Population Review 2020). Said differently, even though every other state in the Union has a lower median income than Massachusetts, in the vast majority of states the dollars earned go considerably further in covering basic costs. The commonwealth is the fourth most expensive state in which to buy a home (Hoffower and Brandt 2019), and median monthly rent for a one-bedroom apartment in Boston as of 2020 was $2,590—making it the third most expensive rental market in the country (Esajian 2020). Poor and middle-income individuals regularly cannot afford these housing costs and are forced out ("priced-out") of the most attractive locales in terms of schools, commute time, and safety. Those forced out are disproportionately people of color.

The high-paying, professionalized jobs that accompany Massachusetts' leadership in health care, high-tech, and higher education produce affluence that is the envy of governors across the country. This embrace of the "creative class"—especially in metro Boston—is credited with much of the strong economic fortune of the state (Geismer 2015). The transformation from industrial jobs to that of the "knowledge economy," and the service jobs that support the knowledge economy (restaurant, day care, entertainment, retail), creates vulnerabilities as well.

The fallout from COVID-19 illustrates this in stark fashion. Prior to the pandemic, Massachusetts ranked in the top ten, and usually top five, for thriving economies (Comen 2019; U.S. News and World Report 2020). An educated populace, high gross domestic product despite relatively small population, GDP growth, employment, and business growth all seemed to bode well for Massachusetts' embrace of the knowledge economy. However, as of June 2020, months into the pandemic, Massachusetts had the highest unemployment rate among the fifty states—a staggering 17.4 percent (Executive Office of Labor and Workforce Development 2020; Leung and Edelman 2020). Turns out that gearing toward the "knowledge economy" provides booms that bust. When those in the knowledge economy stay home, the supporting service jobs in retail, entertainment, household assistance, and related fields dry up. Low-income workers who were the most economically vulnerable before the pandemic felt the effects of COVID first, as their industries are largely dependent on knowledge workers' discretionary spending. Savings often went up for the creative class due to fear of the unknown—entertainment, travel, day care, and retail budgets declined with disastrous effects for those working in service industries. Thus, while knowledge economy workers drove much of the state's growth, they also fostered the very interdependencies that made Massachusetts uniquely ripe for COVID to disrupt labor markets. By June 2021, with full vaccination rates over 60 percent in Massachusetts, unemployment fell to 6.5 percent—still 3.5 points higher than the June 2019 prepandemic rate of 3.0 percent. The vulnerability of a "knowledge economy" remains exposed by COVID.

There are no easy answers as to whether policy makers should work to undo some of the reliance on economic growth models they championed in the past. However, to understand Massachusetts politics, one must know how these patterns of affluence, want, and vulnerability are inculcated and distributed.

POPULATION DENSITY AND DEMOGRAPHIC CHANGE

The faces of Massachusetts, and where residents are located in the state, have undergone significant transformation. These shifts constitute the second major set of factors that define Massachusetts' political context—the arena in which Massachusetts politics is played.

According to the most recent Census Bureau figures, Massachusetts' population grew by 7.37 percent from 2010 to 2020—the most of any New

England state. Digging deeper, we see that the growth in Massachusetts is concentrated in metro Boston and driven, in significant number, by new immigrants to the state (P. Johnson 2019; Dumcius 2018). Suffolk County, where Boston is located, saw an 11.8 percent increase in population over the period, whereas "the four counties that make up Western Massachusetts all lagged behind the state average for [population] growth, and in Berkshire and Franklin counties actually declined" (P. Johnson 2019). Counties that include metro Boston all saw increases over the state average. These population shifts feed the large shadow Boston casts over the state's (and region's) politics. Residents in western and central Massachusetts, and the Cape and islands, regularly feel that the governor's attention, and Beacon Hill's legislative agenda, is overly responsive to the needs of metro Boston at the expense of those living elsewhere in the state.

The face of Massachusetts has also changed—especially in major cities. As of 2020, the U.S. Census Bureau reports that 71.1 percent of the Massachusetts population identifies as white, 12.4 percent Latinx, 9 percent Black, 7.2 percent Asian, 0.5 percent American Indian, and 2.6 percent with two or more races. The same comparative data is not available for all groups in 1990. Available comparisons, however, demonstrate the ways in which Massachusetts is becoming more demographically diverse. The breakdown in 1990 looks markedly different: 87.8 percent white, 4.8 percent Latinx, 4.6 percent Black, and 2.4 percent Asian (Borges-Mendez 2005).

Boston metro is the primary, though not exclusive, hub of diversity in the state. Every county in Massachusetts is majority white—but Suffolk County where Boston is located. Here 46.1 percent of residents identify as white. The "percentage of non-white residents has increased in all 147 cities and towns in Greater Boston since 1990—during that time, the non-white population outside of Boston increased by 254 percent, compared with a 63 percent increase in the city. In fact, a number of communities that were 80 percent or more white in 1990 are now 'minority-majority'" (Melnik, Waterhouse, and Schuster 2019).

Hampden County, home to the state's third-largest city, Springfield, is the next most diverse county, with 64.8 percent of the county's residents identifying as white. This hints at how it is the urban cores across the state—cities like Lynn, Brockton, Lowell, Lawrence, Chelsea, Springfield, and, especially, Boston—that are most responsible for the commonwealth's increasing diversity.

Boston is particularly instructive when it comes to changes over time and the increasing eclecticism of Massachusetts. One way to measure diversity is to use the "diversity index," which "calculates the probability that two people chosen randomly will be different from each other. One practical way to use the diversity index would be asking something like: What are the chances that a person standing next to me on a random street corner will be of a different race?" (Schuster and Ciurczak 2018b). The advantage of this measure is that it pushes us to think of diversity in ways more than white/nonwhite and consider the diversities experienced by Blacks, Puerto Ricans, Cambodians, Vietnamese, and so forth. What is the likelihood of all Bostonians regularly interacting with individuals outside the racial or ethnic groups with which they identify? In 2017 Boston's diversity index was 70.2. Using this metric, Boston is the sixth most diverse major American city. In 1980 the score was considerably lower, at 50.7, and placed Boston but twenty-fifth among the fifty largest U.S. cities (Schuster and Ciurczak 2018b).

This suggests how Boston's increasing diversity is born of an array of experiences. Often these are immigrant ones. Population growth in the commonwealth is driven by immigration and the fact that birth rates exceed mortality rates. Countries of origin have changed over time. In 1990 the top-ten origin countries were, in descending order, Canada, Italy, Portugal, China, the Dominican Republic, Haiti, Ireland, Russia/former USSR, Greece, and England. As of 2017, the top ten also in descending order were China, Dominican Republic, Brazil, India, Haiti, El Salvador, Vietnam, Cape Verde, Columbia, and Guatemala (Melnik, Waterhouse, and Schuster 2019).

RACISM AND RACIAL POLITICS

Increased diversity has done little to disassociate Massachusetts, and especially Boston, with racism, though—especially anti-Black racism. *Saturday Night Live* head writer and coanchor of the long-running "Weekend Update" segment Michael Che personified this succinctly in a bit in advance of the 2017 Super Bowl featuring the New England Patriots versus the Atlanta Falcons. Che, who is Black, joked, "I just want to relax, turn my brain off, and watch the blackest city in America beat the most racist city I've ever been to." He spoke for many. That same year the *Boston Globe* commissioned a national survey and "found that among eight major cities, black people ranked Boston as least welcoming to people of color. More than half—54 percent—rated Boston as unwelcoming" (A. Johnson et al. 2017).

Racism, racial strife, racial inequity, and the ways in which class and ethnic identities blend are all key to understanding the context within which

Massachusetts politics is played. Yes, Massachusetts is personified by liberalism, and, yes, Massachusetts too has a reputation for racial tensions and racism. Both things are true, and this tension is both central to understanding how Massachusetts understands itself as well as a key source of disagreement in these assessments.

As a matter of representation, Massachusetts' diversity far exceeds the diversity of its officeholders. In 2021 all six statewide elected officers are white. Whites hold ten of the eleven congressional seats. Though people of color make up nearly a third of Massachusetts' population, "just 13 percent of state legislators are people of color" (Guerra-Agramonte and Schroeder 2020). No gains were made between the 2019–20 and the 2021–22 legislative sessions. Until 2021 Boston was just one of nine major American cities to not have a Black mayor (Walker et al. 2017). And, even then, Mayor Kim Janey, a Black female, was not popularly elected, having ascended from the city council presidency when Mayor Marty Walsh joined the Biden administration. She lost her mayoral election bid in September 2021, failing to get out of the primary. In fact, all five mayoral candidates on the primary ballot were people of color, but none of the three Black candidates running made it to the November 2021 general election that eventually saw Michelle Wu win Boston's top spot. Chapters 10 and 11 explore these trends in great detail.

These representational trends extend beyond electoral office. As of 2017, fewer than one in fifty senior business managers are Black in Boston, and "census data indicate that relatively few local companies are owned by black residents. . . . Boston's largest law firms have hundreds of partners, but few are black. . . . The data showed fewer than 1 percent of law partners at Boston law firms [in 2016] were black, up only slightly from 1997" (Walker et al. 2017).

Wealth and income inequality, as well as residential segregation, too define the context of Massachusetts politics. In Boston, "African Americans have a median net worth of $8, compared to white city dwellers, who have an average net worth of $247,500" (Hill 2017). Within Boston, "white household income is roughly two times as high as that for other racial/ethnic groups. These disparities close a bit when looking at all of Metro Boston" (Schuster and Ciurczak 2018a). Massachusetts and Boston, as we have seen, are becoming more diverse, and the diversity index has increased. But that does not necessarily mean neighborhoods are integrated. As Catherine Elton compellingly compiled, "Two-thirds of Boston's Black population live in one of three neighborhoods: Dorchester, Roxbury, or Mattapan" (2020). She goes on to note that "of the 147 municipalities that form the Greater

Boston area, 61 are at least 90 percent white and some are much whiter, according to 2017 data. Winchester and Hingham, for instance, recorded an estimated Black or African-American population no greater than 0.5 and 0.6 percent, respectively." Punctuating all this is that of the United States' "51 greater metropolitan areas with large Black populations, Boston ranks 15th for segregation" (2020).

Educational inequities beget the school-to-prison pipeline in Massachusetts as well. The nonpartisan Massachusetts Taxpayers Foundation found that "Massachusetts Hispanic and Black high school students drop out at a rate of 12.6 and 7.2 percent, respectively, while the dropout rate for whites is 3.2 percent," and that "Blacks and Hispanics graduate from college at a rate roughly 13 percent lower than the 77.6 percent rate for whites" (2021). Incarceration ratios for Blacks to whites and Hispanics to whites are higher in Massachusetts than in the United States (Massachusetts Taxpayers Foundation 2021).

Health-care inequities were on full display in the COVID crisis. At face value, Massachusetts' COVID death rates were fairly in line with the percentage of Asians, Blacks, Hispanics, and whites in the state's population (Ndugga et al. 2021). However, once adjusted for age,[1] dramatic differences emerged in Massachusetts. The age-adjusted death rate per 100,000 people in Massachusetts was 139.1 for Asians, an astounding 319.7 for Blacks and 334.9 for Hispanics, while 105.4 for whites (Brown 2021). Sonia Chang-Díaz, a state senator and candidate for the 2022 Massachusetts governorship, stated of the early vaccine rollout in February 2021, "You could not find a more textbook case study of structural racism if you tried. . . . Black, Latinx, and lower-income Bay Staters—those who are the most likely to get infected with coronavirus—are the least likely to have gotten a vaccine. This was an entirely predictable—and, indeed, predicted—problem" (DeCosta-Klipa 2021).

These numbers demonstrate that inequity regularly born of structural racism is part of the terrain that defines Massachusetts politics. They do not, however, fully capture the undercurrent, the contextual influence, the assumed, the known but seldom said, of racial division, differential power, and racism in the commonwealth.

Some of this is evident in the stories Massachusetts tells itself, in whom it reveres, how it remembers them, as well as whose history can even be recovered. Take John Winthrop, for example. His phrase of "city on the

---

1 As a group, whites in Massachusetts are significantly older than Blacks and Latinos. Older people died at much higher rates during COVID—hence the necessity to control for age.

hill" is quoted throughout this volume as it is bedrock to Massachusetts' "exceptional" political identity. An HBO series about "real Boston" makes the phrase its name. The orator who famously wished that the Massachusetts Bay Colony be that beacon, and who was its first governor, enslaved Africans, and was integral to making slavery legal in the colony. "Three years after the first shipment of enslaved Africans arrived on Massachusetts soil, [Winthrop] helped to write the first law in North America officially sanctioning the practice. The Massachusetts Body of Liberties in 1641 decreed there 'shall never be any bond slavery . . . *unless* it be lawful captives taken in just wars, and such strangers as willingly sell themselves or are sold to us.' Who could this formulation possibly leave out?" (Manegold 2010; emphasis added).

Winthrop's aspirations for Boston remain far more well known than his centrality to slavery. In a similar vein, the fact that Massachusetts was the first American colony to make slavery legal is far less known than its celebrated abolitionist influence. An accurate tale of Massachusetts and race features William Lloyd Garrison's *The Liberator* published in Massachusetts, the Boston Female Anti-Slavery Society, and Massachusetts as home to many free Blacks central in abolition. It is also the case that one of Massachusetts' most revered figures helped bring the practice here some two hundred years prior. This issue of what to emphasize when it comes to race in Massachusetts remains today.

For many, it is the violence of the 1970s busing era that so links Massachusetts with racism, violent racism. The state supreme court's ruling in *Morgan v. Hennigan* (1974) demanded that Boston integrate its schools to promote equal educational opportunity for Black students. The protests that followed, particularly in South Boston, are seared into the nation's memory— rocks, slurs, spit hurled at Black students' school buses. The violence got so bad that then mayor Kevin White declared a curfew and the National Guard was called in. High school–age white students in Southie largely boycotted going to integrated schools, and "a group of whites in South Boston brutally beat a Haitian resident of Roxbury who had driven into their neighborhood. A month later some Black students stabbed a white student at South Boston High. The school was shut down for a month" (Gellerman 2014). And the world watched. This gruesome chapter was but eleven years after the death of President John F. Kennedy and the racial liberalism he was associated with at the time. Which Massachusetts?

In short, race and contested views on whether Massachusetts is vanguard or villain have always been an undercurrent in Massachusetts politics. Some herald but the advancements, others but the places for significant improvement. Others are more nuanced. But to understand the playing field of Massachusetts politics is to understand the centrality of race, identity, whiteness and social class, and the limits of racial liberalism. Sometimes all this is discussed outright. Far more frequently, it is conveyed with an "insider/outsider" distinction—though many of those labeled "insiders" today rarely see themselves that way, as truly difficult Irish or Italian heritage immigrant stories define family histories and identities. The only place of agreement is that race, ethnicity, and social class are central to understanding Massachusetts politics, power, and policy.

PARTY POLITICS: DEMOCRATIC DOMINANCE

The final key contextual factor shaping Massachusetts politics involves party politics. It is not much of a party. But for the propensity to elect Republican governors in the modern era, Massachusetts is a one-party state when it comes to party in governance. Even where Republican successes are noteworthy—in winning the governor's office—there are notable Democratic exceptions, like Governors Michael Dukakis and Deval Patrick.

As of 2020, the Massachusetts delegation to Washington is entirely Democratic. The last Republican to represent Massachusetts in DC was Senator Scott Brown, who won a special election in 2010 to replace Senator Ted Kennedy (D) during a particularly tumultuous moment in the fight over Obamacare. Brown went on to lose to now senator Elizabeth Warren (D) in 2012. The last Republican elected to a full term representing Massachusetts ended his Senate service in 1978. On the House side, the last two Republicans to serve both lost their reelection bids in 1996.

At the statehouse, things are not much better for Republicans. As Professors Cunningham and Ubertaccio note in chapter 7:

> Democrats have been virtually unassailable, routinely holding between 32 and 36 seats in the 40-member senate. In 1990, the calamitous year for Democrats, Republicans took 16 state senate seats. In 1992 they lost 7 of them in a rout that produced veto-proof majorities in both chambers of the state legislature. The house has proven equally uncompetitive. In 2004 Governor Mitt Romney announced a "Romney Reform Team" of 131 Republican candidates. Other than the incumbents, they all lost. . . .

[I]n 2008 Republicans won just 16 House contests to the 160-member lower chamber including special elections. In 2010 they rebounded to win 32, dropping back to 31 in 2020.

As of January 2021, the Massachusetts State Senate has 37 Democratic senators and only 3 Republican senators. On the house side, Republicans fare a bit better—128 Democrats, 30 Republicans, 1 independent, and 1 vacancy. This amounts to 7.5 percent and 18 percent, respectively. This is a recipe for status-quo policy making and for corruption. A lack of competitive elections combined with single-party control is correlated with political corruption. Since 1996 three Massachusetts House Speakers have had to resign and been found guilty of felonies. In 2011 former state senator Dianne Wilkerson was convicted for taking bribes. State Representative Stephen Smith was convicted in 2013 for his part in a voter-fraud scheme. In 2018 the senate president resigned amid allegations that his husband had used their relationship to avoid consequences for inappropriate sexual advances. In February 2020, State Representative David Nangle was charged with twenty-eight counts of corruption.

TABLE 1.1. Percentage of Massachusetts Voter Enrollment by Political Party, 1950–2020

	DEMOCRAT	REPUBLICAN	UNENROLLED
1950	26.7	26.0	47.2
1960	29.7	24.1	46.1
1970	43.2	20.8	36.0
1980a	45.9	14.2	40.0
1990a	44.2	13.5	42.2
2000a	36.3	12.9	50.3
2010b	36.9	11.3	51.6
2020a	32.6	10.1	56.0

Data from Massachusetts Secretary of the Commonwealth, https://www.sec.state.ma.us/ele/eleenr/enridx.htm.

Note: Massachusetts consistently allowed for third-party registration in 1992. The percentage has yet to equal 1 percent of registered voters.

a February data for 1980, 1990, 2000, and 2020.
b August 2010 due to data omission in the original.

Most readers would understandably conclude that such significant Democratic dominance must mean that residents of Massachusetts identify as Democrats at near-exclusive rates. That is not the case. As chapter 8 spells out in considerable detail, "unenrolled" (the Massachusetts term for "independent") is the most popular choice for eligible voters in the commonwealth. When it comes to partisan identification, 56 percent of eligible voters identify themselves as "unenrolled" as of 2020 (see table 1.1). Democrats are second, with 32.6 percent of registered voters, and Republicans had but 10.1 percent of the electorate firmly in their corner. This third place showing for Republicans in Massachusetts has held since 1950 (Massachusetts Secretary of the Commonwealth).

This breakdown helps explain how progressive firebrand Elizabeth Warren and Republican governor Charlie Baker can both comfortably win reelection on the same ballot. The trends in partisan identification show that a majority of voters are not locked into one party, on paper at least.

Massachusetts Political Culture(s)

Scholars of Massachusetts political culture are few but significant in their influence. "Hot takes" by Massachusetts political activists, policy makers, party officials, and pundits on political culture are manifold but limited in impact. This section explicates both of their takes.

THE SCHOLARLY TAKES

The "granddaddy of them all" when it comes to analyzing Massachusetts political culture is Edgar Litt's classic and durable taxonomy introduced in his 1965 book, *The Political Culture of Massachusetts*. Tellingly, Litt saw Massachusetts political culture as "neither politically unique nor 'exotic' in its processes, corruption, or supposed alienation; rather, it can be understood only in historical perspective and in proximity to structural transformations in the American political economy" (1965). He posited that it is the interplay, and contestation, between four groups that defines Massachusetts political culture: managers, patricians, workers, and yeomen, as they were when Litt first conceived them.

The patricians, who count among themselves the "Puritan forefathers," first shaped Massachusetts' political culture (Litt 1965, 9). These individuals are cosmopolitan, the country-club Republicans. When governor, Mitt

Romney embodied patrician values. These elites "exercise large measures of private decision-making power. Radical change that would affect the power base, political positions, and welfare of the patricians is opposed or moderated. . . . [They] participate actively in politics through a loyal hardcore . . . [and support] civil liberties, civil rights, constitutional reform and urban and transportation measures designed to improve the political community" (Litt 1965, 10–11). Litt goes on to emphasize that doing so is not pure civic-mindedness—supporting or advancing these policies advances their own economic self-interest by promoting stability.

Contributing scholar to this volume Professor Cunningham summarizes that it was the "workers" in Litt's typology who "dislodged patrician supremacy" (2010). Workers were originally drawn from primarily European immigrants, and it was the Irish immigrants who came to symbolize worker ascendency in Massachusetts' political culture. They "lived in (but many have now fled) the cities, are Democratic and Catholic, and lower-to-middle class. Workers orient toward New Deal–style programs, though they are increasingly suspicious of social welfare spending, and are conservative on civil rights and civil liberties. Political patronage might not quite rise to a sacrament, but is considered the way the system works. Even in 1965 the workers' political power was contracting" (Cunningham 2010). Reagan Democrats and Obama-Trump voters in Massachusetts are very likely to fall into Litt's "worker" designation. As Litt writes, "It is their political style as underdog that merits the most attention" (1965, 18). It's family first, then neighborhood. It is not a politics of nationalism or internationalism; the solidarity of "people like us" is the orienting theme, and politics is a means to garner resources and advance "us."

"Real power, rising then and foremost now, is with the managers. Managers prize rationality, merit, and efficiency" (Cunningham 2010). They are described by Litt as middle-class "administrators and fee professionals," such as teachers, scientists, lawyers, advertisers, and aerospace engineers (1965, 21). They are whom Professor Lily Geismer more recently identifies as the suburban liberals in affluent communities who transformed the Democratic Party. They voice liberal views on civil rights and liberties but do so by advancing school integration into their suburban communities rather than reciprocal exchanges (Geismer 2017). Their now upper-middle-class identity advances "meritocratic priorities" and individualist economic values with prioritization of their immediate community (Geismer 2017, 6). This is the group within which we find "Warren-Baker voters," as both politicians speak to different aspects of their values. They are community oriented and liberal (if not always progressive) on civil rights and liberties while prioritizing fiscal responsibility, transparency, and coalition building in politics and policy. They prioritize professionalism and are liberal on social welfare—if done efficiently and without incentivizing bad behavior. Critics accuse them of NIMBYism ("not in my back yard") as it relates to affordable housing and busing.

Yeomen complete Litt's typology. Even in 1965, these rural residents had lost power, as the population and subsequent political power shifted from a mix of urban and rural to nearly exclusively the cities. Yeomen are "not likely to have a mellow view of the world, especially when they have few skills that are marketable in the national economy," according to Litt. Economic displacement breeds resentment. They form the "solid core of the Massachusetts Republican Party, and their views are reflected in the conservatism of the local weeklies" (Litt 1965, 12). As Professor Cunningham has updated for the modern era, think conservative talk radio (2010). Think too Reddit and conservative conspiracy groups like QAnon for a minority of yeomen. These are voters who form President Trump's core, immoveable base. They are disproportionately located in the rural towns of western Massachusetts as well as the trades-driven towns of the South Shore, such as Weymouth.

These actors drive the tensions undergirding Massachusetts politics. They are, of course, not "it," as Litt's typology offers little insight as to where activists, especially progressive activists drawn to causes like #BlackLivesMatter and #NoBoston2020, fit. Are they workers? Are they underdogs reminiscent of the Irish and other European immigrants working to upend the economic elites who prefer change only at the margins? This is plausible, but the progressive activists seeking to reshape Massachusetts politics draw too from the managers' commitment to process and transparency.

The beauty of Litt's typology, with important caveats above, is that it remains a helpful heuristic for understanding Massachusetts politics. If one understands political culture as nothing more than "blue/red," there is not much to say about Massachusetts. There is no analytic muscle in that simple dichotomy. But why did reformer Michael Dukakis first fail as governor (1975–79) only to win accolades for his governing style after he ran again and won (1981–91)? It's because the reformer Dukakis mellowed his tone and approach with the ascendant Democratic workers of the state legislature (Cunningham 2010). He went from pure manager technocrat to understanding the legislative worker impulses—pork, glad-handing.

Why does Massachusetts elect progressive firebrands like Congressman Barney Frank and Senator Elizabeth Warren as well as moderate Republican governors like Bill Weld, Mitt Romney, and Charlie Baker? It's because Democratic Party ties are not as strong among the suburban liberals as their managerial orientation. Both Frank and Warren are politicians who did more than talk—they are policy technocrats who could get deals made. This appeals to the managers, as does the fiscal responsibility of moderate Republican governors who are fiscally conservative but liberal on social issues like health-care access and abortion rights. What explains how Senator Ed Markey was able to beat back a Kennedy in the September 2020 Senate Democratic primary? Workers liked the goods Markey delivered, and activists saw Congressman Kennedy as a patrician.

Litt also helps explain a curious pattern in Massachusetts involving career pols and the state attorney general's office. The latter regularly presses and adjudicates corruption charges against state legislators and appointed officials who view the activities as hard-won political spoils and necessary constituent service. "These conflicts are built into Massachusetts," writes Professor Cunningham (2015), as reformers do not always get the transactional political values held by Massachusetts "workers."

The layered, intricate relationships between Massachusetts political players is another facet of Massachusetts' political culture that is of note (Hogarty 2002). All politicians, policy makers, and political actors work to build relationships, of course, but in Massachusetts, these relationships turn on decades, and sometimes centuries, of interplay as well as intergenerational transmission (Hogarty 2002). Massachusetts' political culture lived "the personal is political" long before the phrase was coined. Revenges and grudge matches play out in primaries and overlapping alliances in each election cycle. As one prominent political commentator and longtime newsman coined it, the political culture of Massachusetts' politics is "revenge."

Though Hogarty's assessment remains definitive, and Litt's classification of the state's political factions continues to facilitate acute description and analysis of Massachusetts' politics, the work of political scientist Daniel Elazar adds a very useful theoretical dimension as well. Elazar's tripartite classification of state-level American political culture into traditional, individualistic, and moralistic provides a wider lens that when pointed at Massachusetts brings greater clarity. Elazar sees Massachusetts as a mix of individualistic and moralistic political cultures.

Individualistic political cultures lead to politics being treated as a competitive arena in which politicians are expected to pursue their own self-interests in essentially the same manner as entrepreneurs in the private sector, with essentially the same type of positive implications for citizens and consumers. The Madisonian notion of politics as a "free market of ideas" is prized in individualistic political cultures. "From this perspective our political system, like our economy, is designed to function best when interests and individuals compete for power and profit" (Duquette 2005). Individualistic politics is a blood sport and one that Massachusetts workers and managers can find home within. But patricians and suburban liberals have faith! The moralism Elazar describes as also defining Massachusetts political culture is where "common-wealth" comes in. It puts the public interest above private interest and even condemns private gain from public service. In a moralistic political culture, good citizenship requires public service, which is understood as a duty and a sacrifice, not an opportunity, and certainly not a career.

Individualistic and moralistic predispositions provide a particularly useful framework for understanding the cleavages in contemporary Massachusetts politics. Without a competitive party system, most political conflict in Massachusetts happens outside of the left-right partisan, or ideological, narrative. Political contests in Massachusetts are much more likely to be framed as an insider-versus-outsider (read: moralistic insurgents versus the individualistic establishment) conflict (Duquette 2005).

While his characterization of practical politics in his native Boston as the "systematic organization of hatreds" gets far more attention, the historian Henry Adams' comparison to New England weather even more vividly illustrates the timeless and paradoxical nature of Massachusetts' political culture: "The violence of the contrast was real and made the strongest motive of education. The double exterior nature gave life its relative values. Winter and summer, cold and heat, town and country, force and freedom, marked two modes of life and thought, balanced like lobes of the brain" (1905, 7). Though not always explicitly, scholarly analyses of Massachusetts' politics that highlight its paradoxical political outcomes (including the recent tendency to elect Republican governors but Democrats down ballot) become clearer and more consistent when viewed through Elazar's individualistic/moralistic lens.

THE DOERS' TAKE

Unsurprisingly, most policy makers, activists, community leaders, and lobbyists are not immersed in the scholarly literature on Massachusetts' political culture—their loss. Informal interviews and social media engagement with more than twenty-six hundred political professionals, elected officials, reporters, volunteers, community organizers, and activists in the #mapoli crowd (the Twitter hashtag used for Massachusetts politics) provides additional insight. These are voices of those currently ensconced in Massachusetts' politics. Their insights do not always fit the formal definitions of "political culture" favored by political scientists, and Twitter is, thankfully, not a mirror of society. It is, however, a good way to tease out the range of perceptions about political norms in Massachusetts among current influencers.

The first theme that emerged is a familiar one—institutional respect. For good or for bad, those active in Massachusetts politics perceive "wait-your-turn politics" to still carry the day. Positively, this means, as one respondent said, that there is a "respect for history, tradition, decorum, and leadership." Seniority is respected: "There is a sense of respect that you are garnered the longer you stay in office, showing the power of incumbency." This creates stability and predictability in Massachusetts politics, which, from the perspective of the framers and those seeking to do business in Massachusetts, is a good thing. Substantial numbers of activists and observers, however, see this as a bad thing and one with particular ramifications for causes like racial justice. In the height of the Black Lives Matter movement, for instance, a police reform bill languished in committee. As one observer put it, Massachusetts does have "relatively progressive views (though not extremely so), but is *very* conservative in our approach. Before we leap, we look, and look again, and pass a referendum to look some more, and then wait for 5 other states to try it first, and then look one last time." Critics charge that change is slow in Massachusetts and that respect for institutions, incumbency, and seniority is to blame. Sonia Chang-Díaz, one of only two people of color serving in the Massachusetts State Senate in 2021, referenced the perceived complacency and slowness on Beacon Hill in her announcement video for a 2022 gubernatorial run. Highlighting her "legislative accomplishments in education funding and criminal justice reform," she stated, "Those wins didn't come easy. Beacon Hill insiders dragged their feet every step of the way, saying 'think smaller.' Instead, we fought unapologetically for the things working families actually need. . . . They said our ideas were impossible, we made them the law. The trouble is: that kind of urgency in our state government is still the exception rather than the rule. Too many leaders are more interested in keeping power than in doing something with it." The critique holds across party lines. As one former Republican state senator perceived it, Massachusetts provides "huge advantages for incumbents . . . [and] more power centralized in leadership than just about any other state." The safety incumbents enjoy makes them timid so that many see "a stifling sense of complacency among legislators, who know they won't lose their seats but are terrified of pissing off the wrong committee chair."

Legislators who reason as such are not necessarily wrong. When seniority and institutional norms are valued, violating them comes at a cost. The successful congressional Democratic primary challenges of Seth Moulton (2014) and Ayanna Pressley (2018) are exceptions to the rule. In Massachusetts, if you do not wait your turn, expect revenge, as "ego-driven grudges last for decades."

Former Boston mayor Thomas Menino held office from 1993 to 2014 and is famous in this regard—and representative to many well versed in Massachusetts politics. Boston city councilman Sam Yoon ran against Menino in the 2013 Democratic mayoral primary. Popular lore, and Yoon himself, reports that he was unhirable in Boston after coming up short in the race. Revenge and his willingness to call for change in Boston institutions were to blame, said Yoon: "It was subtle, but clear, that the fact I had run on a reform platform left some employers not willing to take a chance on me. . . . I knew there were risks involved for me in running against a 16-year incumbent, but I didn't know the degree that it would pervade the important institutions" (Ballou 2010). He moved to Washington, DC, to find employment. Tellingly, the cold shoulder Boston politics showed Yoon was blamed on Yoon not following the rules. The same article explains:

> Some analysts believe Yoon might have had a political future here if he had been more patient. Samuel R. Tyler, president of the Boston Municipal Research Bureau, said Yoon was the victim of a rushed timetable. "He suggested a different approach to running the city, a natural course for a candidate who has to convince voters he is a better choice. But I do think he could have taken a different approach by creating a résumé for himself on the City Council for more than two terms, and then running for mayor at a time of transition, which would enhance his chances and bolster his reputation.

Not waiting one's turn and, in so doing, violating the unwritten norms of Massachusetts politics comes with consequences. Revenge is real, and most political leaders abide by the rules even if they personally question them. A current Massachusetts political commentator aptly summarized, "There's internalization of that culture & fear of retaliation that keeps political folks in line & perpetuating it."

The culture of reprisal for stepping out of line, or "improperly" disrupting or disrespecting the webs of political relationships (Hogarty 2002), has a potential antidote in Massachusetts: humor. Humor alone is usually not enough, but pols gifted in intelligent one-liners who can laugh at themselves gain far more than "likability": they gain connections and, potentially, entrée if astute in Massachusetts' political culture. Humor is almost always appreciated in politics, but in Massachusetts it is so valued to be core to its political culture.

The most famous example of how humor is institutionalized in Massachusetts comes in the annual St. Patrick's Day breakfast in South Boston prior to the parade. It is a scene. Hundreds of politically connected neighborhood types greet a who's who of Massachusetts politicos each year. All Boston networks and New England Cable News carry it live. Anyone who is anyone elected usually shows up. After Ayanna Pressley won her congressional seat by ousting a sitting Democratic congressman, she greeted the crowd, midprogram, saying, "Perhaps you thought I was nervous, but I was just eager to get up here as I am not used to waiting my turn." Here she expertly uses one aspect of Massachusetts political culture, humor, to wink and nod at her abandonment of another: wait your turn. Senator Warren (D) "finished her [2018] monologue" with a similar conjuring but this time reminding the ambitious to be patient: "Reading what [Senator Warren] said were questions from residents, using it to rib one [fellow ascendant Massachusetts Democrat] who was not in the room [sic]. 'Senator Warren, why don't you just quit, resign now, and open up the seat for a new, young breed of Democrat,' Warren read, grimacing at the letter. 'Wow, that was a little harsh. But still, I always appreciate hearing from [sitting Democratic congressman] Seth Moulton'" (DeCosta-Klipa 2018). Moulton had been making noise regarding the age of the Democratic leadership in Washington at the time and strongly signaling his desire to move up the Massachusetts elected ranks.

Governor Mitt Romney forecast the next theme of insiders versus outsiders in his 2005 breakfast talk amid speculation he would run for president in 2008 (which he eventually did). As the *Atlantic* described at the time:

> The best one-liners at Romney's expense came from Romney. Standing at the podium to begin his remarks, he said, "Well, it's great to be here in Iowa this morning—whoops, wrong speech." He threw down a piece of paper and then continued. "Seriously, it's good to be here in Massachusetts.

I'm visiting for a few days." Everybody cracked up, and from that moment the room was his. He kept up a genuinely funny line of patter—much of it self-deprecating and based on his presumptive aspirations to higher office—for eight minutes; in comedy terms he killed. (Sample joke: As a Mormon, he said, "I believe that marriage should be between a man and a woman and a woman and a woman.") Not so long ago it would have been hard to imagine Mitt Romney—a Midwest-raised Mormon businessman—joking around with a bunch of Irish and Italian Democrats at a political backslapping session in Boston. (Pappu 2005)

The author correctly emphasizes the insider-outsider nature of political influence in Massachusetts and how it has correlated with the "worker" ascension of the Irish and Italians. How did Governor Romney, in part, close the gap? He did so through humor that was highly attuned to Massachusetts political culture. Not all liked Romney's jokes regarding Mormonism, but he was right that the line would serve him well him among the most influential in Massachusetts' political circles.

In Romney's remarks too we see that the humor of Massachusetts politics often leverages religion, race, and ethnicity—particularly whether one "fits" the Massachusetts prototype. Former Massachusetts congressman Barney Frank said of himself that he was "used to being in the minority as a left-handed Jew" (Weisberg 2009) and, in response to a Maryland Republican congresswoman declaring "'America to be a Christian nation' during an all-night debate over school prayer[,] Mr. Frank, who is Jewish, [and] was presiding as the speaker pro tem," responded, "Well, if this is a Christian nation, how come some poor Jew has to get up at 5:30 in the morning to preside over the House of Representatives?" (*New York Times* 2008).

Those immersed in Massachusetts politics and policy too highlight the division between insiders and outsiders signaled by Romney, Pressley, Warren, and Frank. In Boston this can mean the insiders who grew up in the city and those new to it. Though Massachusetts' economic engine, Boston remains a small town where a "small number of people and families . . . have a huge say." City council president Andrea Campbell, in making her bid for 2021 mayor official, repeatedly emphasized, "I know the pride and pain of being from the city of Boston." One of her key rivals, fellow councilwoman Michelle Wu, is from Chicago originally. Campbell's point of contrast was lost on no one versed in Massachusetts politics. Long-standing connections to the city, growing up in Boston, can make representation better, as individuals know the city's rhythms and have lived its problems. On the other hand, many activists and those not originally from the state perceive that a "Boston accent plus stories about high school sports [are] often a surrogate for actual accomplishments and knowledge." Another individual who works in Massachusetts politics summarized "the importance of being born in Massachusetts and/or Irish" in commonwealth politics. There is no doubt that Irish heritage runs deep in the state, especially Boston, and that it is central to the state's understanding of itself. This can be seen as the American Dream—the descendants of Irish immigrants, who were victims of extreme prejudices, have held considerable sway in commonwealth politics for decades. This emphasis, however, also leads to a feeling among significant activists, potential candidates, and those hoping to influence policy that "a defining theme/idea/norm" in Massachusetts political culture is "centering whiteness" and that it is "immersed even in the smallest political acts." The slow pace of change in the elected faces of Massachusetts is documented in chapter 8, and, as a former high-ranking Massachusetts government official states, there are "so many white dudes! Particularly at the strategy/campaign manager level."

This brings us to the last theme: ideological tensions among Massachusetts Democrats. Overwhelming Democratic majorities on Beacon Hill are well documented. But being a blue state does not mean an absence of ideological diversity within a party. As an example, some decry how "proud we are of our 'progressiveness' but when it comes to state government we really aren't that progressive in the State House." A vocal activist describes Massachusetts as offering a "breed of liberalism that believes in progress but wants nothing to change, combined with a Puritan holdover desire to fix all 49 other states instead of our own." Two others succinctly struck the same tone, "Think globally, NIMBY locally" and "Nimby liberalism. Full stop." In this telling, Massachusetts' political culture thrives on placing itself above the other forty-nine states and thinking it a model of liberalism while actually falling short in many realms—particularly racial justice. So Democrats are "pro workers rights but terrible on racial justice, suburban liberals [sic] fight for colorblind policies." This theme comes up repeatedly. One policy advocate explained that an "important aspect of Massachusetts political culture is that people believe that issues of race, bigotry, and discrimination don't exist here—but they do exist and they are very political. There's the problem of the discrimination, and the separate problem of not acknowledging it." Echoing this, Massachusetts' political culture involves an "unwillingness to challenge hierarchy and inability to honestly tackle racial issues . . . key weaknesses in a state that otherwise has many progressive and liberal features."

Single-party control and the power of incumbents are also linked to perceptions of regulatory or administrative capture. As one enraged Massachusetts politico put it when describing their perception that the governor and legislature have co-opted the notion of independent administrative oversight, "Absolute chickenshit-ery. Incapable of making decisions to benefit constituents. Gutless wonders. Regulatory capture prominent. Has no problem with using position of power to force agencies to go contrary to their mission statements." Another concurred that "regulatory capture in state agencies" is the norm. "The agencies (including transportation) have their decision already made and go through the motions with public comment periods and don't listen to stakeholders. Especially Environmental Justice populations: sacrifice zones." Other examples cited include the Baker administration's ineptitude on a natural-gas compressor station in the highly populous area where Weymouth and Quincy meet and the Massachusetts Bay Transportation Authority's constant inability to rein in inefficiencies and breakdowns on the T.

There are, of course, many who push back on these takes, arguing that democracy is compromise and the critics have unrealistic views of how fast political change can occur. Progressive activists also sometimes fail to take into account that many Massachusetts Democrats are moderate Democrats—no more, no less. Party dominance requires keeping these individuals in the fold, and absolutist positions do not do this. The progressive critique is also viewed as privileged by some. In this view, Massachusetts is wanting in its liberalism only if one has no real experience living in other states that are more wanting from the perspective of Democratic or left-leaning policy priorities. The grass is always greener.

From the Republican perspective, the idea that Massachusetts Democrats in the statehouse may not be so progressive is a good thing. On the one hand, Republican organizers see a "lack of accountability due to low competition and a massive incumbent advantage. [But] the Dems aren't as woke/insane as other states yet. . . . Maybe the lack of competition makes them feel more comfortable staying 'moderate.'" Another Republican commentator and former candidate for office agrees: "Entrenched Dems give lip service to progressive base while enacting very little (and correct IMO) of their leftist agenda." This is especially comforting when the Massachusetts GOP believes itself the victim of "media biases toward the center-left and left," as a different former GOP candidate voiced. He went on to cite the *Boston Globe* and NPR as guilty of liberal bias and to acknowledge the *Boston Herald* and radio stations WBZ and WEEI as opinion leaders that lean right—but offer less sustained, overt political reporting.

Conclusion

This chapter opened with the various labels that have signaled Massachusetts exceptionalism—"birthplace of liberty" and "Massachusetts liberal"—asking what these labels capture and miss about Massachusetts political culture (Geismer 2015, 15). The subsequent examination reveals that these labels, while rooted in real aspects of Massachusetts politics, do not capture the full, complicated, and contested nature of Massachusetts' political culture. It is for readers of the next ten chapters to decide, upon review, which descriptions best capture the unique mix that is Massachusetts politics and policy.

WORKS CITED

Ballou, Brian. 2010. "Yoon Looks to D.C. for New Start." *Boston.com*, June 29, 2010. http://archive.boston.com/news/local/massachusetts/articles/2010/06/29/yoon _looks_to_dc_for_new_start/.

Borges-Mendez, Ramon. 2005. "Urban and Regional Restructuring and Barrio Formation in Massachusetts: The Cases of Lowell, Lawrence, and Holyoke." PhD diss., Massachusetts Institute of Technology.

Brown, Karen. 2021. "COVID-19 Has Shown 'Ugly Truth' about Racial Disparities, but Gaps in Data Remain." New England Public Media, April 26, 2021. https://www.nepm.org/post /covid-19-has-shown-ugly-truth-about-racial-disparities-gaps-data-remain#stream/0.

Comen, Evan. 2019. "The States with the Best and Worse Economies." *USA Today*, July 6, 2019. https://www.usatoday.com/story/money/2019/07/06/jobs-gdp-unemployment -states-with-best-worst-economies/39651531/.

Cunningham, Maurice. 2010. "Identity Politics in the Race for Governor, Candidates Draw on Long-Established Traditions in Bay State Politics." *CommonWealth Magazine*, July 27, 2010. https://commonwealthmagazine.org/politics/identity-politics/.

———. 2015. "Massachusetts' Modern Organized System of Hatreds." *MassPoliticsProfs* (blog). http://blogs.wgbh.org/masspoliticsprofs/2015/11/13/massachusetts-modern -organized-system-hatreds/.

DeCosta-Klipa. 2018. "The Best Jokes and Jabs from Southie's St. Patrick's Day Breakfast." *Boston.com*, March 18, 2018. https://www.boston.com/news/local-news/2018/03/18 /south-boston-st-patricks-day-breakfast-jokes-2018/.

———. 2021. "Why One Massachusetts Lawmaker Says the State's Vaccine Rollout Is a 'Textbook Case Study of Structural Racism.'" *Boston.com*, February 26, 2021. https://www.boston.com/news/coronavirus/2021/02/26/sonia-chang-diaz-ma-vaccine -rollout-structural-racism/.

Dumcius, Gintautas. 2018. "Massachusetts Population Growing at Twice the Rate of Previous 10 Years, Fastest in Northeast." *MassLive*, December 19, 2018. https://www.masslive .com/news/2018/12/massachusetts-population-growing-at-twice-the-rate-of-previous -10-years-fastest-in-northeast.html.

Duquette, Jerold. 2005. "Massachusetts Politics in the 21st Century: Recognizing the Impact of Clashing Political Cultures." *New England Journal of Political Science* 1, no. 1: 209–24.

Esajian, J. D. 2020. "Rent Report: Highest Rent in US 2020." https://www.fortunebuilders .com/top-10-u-s-cities-with-the-highest-rents/.

Executive Office of Labor and Workforce Development. 2020. "Massachusetts Unemployment and Job Estimates for June 2020." Mass.gov, July 20, 2020. https://www.mass.gov /news/massachusetts-unemployment-and-job-estimates-for-june-2020.

Florida, Richard. 2002. *The Rise of the Creative Class*. New York: Basic Books.

———. 2017. *The New Urban Crisis: Gentrification, Housing Bubbles, Growing Inequality, and What We Can Do about It*. London: Bloomsbury.

Geismer, Lily. 2015. *Don't Blame Us: Suburban Liberals and the Transformation of the Democratic Party*. Princeton, NJ: Princeton University Press.

Gellerman, Bruce. 2014. "'It Was Like a War Zone': Busing in Boston." WBUR, September 5, 2014. https://www.wbur.org/news/2014/09/05/boston-busing-anniversary.

Guerra-Agramonte, Ashley, and Mitchell Schroeder. 2020. "Diversity, Competitiveness Remain Low in Mass. Politics." MassINC, November 25, 2020. https://massinc.org/2020/11/25 /diversity-competitiveness-remain-low-in-mass-politics/.

Hill, Selena. 2017. "Report: Blacks in Boston Have a Median Net Worth of $8, Whites Have $247k." Black Enterprise, December 13, 2017. https://www.blackenterprise.com /blacks-boston-median-net-worth-8/.

Hoffower, Hillary, and Libertina Brandt. 2019. "The Most Expensive and Affordable States to Buy a House, Ranked." *Business Insider*, July 5, 2019.

Hogarty, Richard. 2002. *Massachusetts Politics and Public Policy: Studies in Power and Leadership*. Cambridge, MA: MIT Press.

Johnson, Akilah, Todd Wallack, Nicole Dungca, Liz Kowalczyk, Andrew Ryan, and Adrian Walker. 2017. "Boston. Racism. Image. Reality." *Boston Globe*, December 10, 2017. https://apps.bostonglobe.com/spotlight/boston-racism-image-reality/series/image/

Johnson, Patrick. 2019. "Census Data Shows US Population Shifting South, West; Massachusetts Growth Concentrated around Boston." *MassLive*, April 21, 2019. https://www.masslive. com/news/2019/04/census-data-shows-us-population-shifting-south-west-massachu-setts-growth-concentrated-around-boston.html.

Leung, Shirley, and Larry Edelman. 2020. "Why Massachusetts Has the Highest Employment Rate in the Country." *Boston Globe*, September 13, 2020. https://www.bostonglobe.com /2020/09/12/business/why-massachusetts-has-highest-unemployment-rate-country/.

Litt, Edgar. 1965. *The Political Cultures of Massachusetts*. Cambridge, MA: MIT Press.

Manegold, C. C. 2010. "New England's Scarlet 'S' for Slavery." *Boston.com*, January 18, 2010. http://archive.boston.com/bostonglobe/editorial_opinion/oped/articles/2010/01/18 /new_englands_scarlet_s_for_slavery/.

Melnik, Mark, Gail Waterhouse, and Luc Schuster. 2019. "Overview and Regional Analysis." In *Changing Faces in Greater Boston*. Boston: Boston Indicators, the Boston Foundation, UMABoston, and the UMass Donahue Institute. https://www.tbf.org /news-and-insights/press-releases/2019/may/changing-faces-report.

Ndugga, Nambi, Olivia Pham, Latoya Hill, Samantha Artiga, and Noah Parker. 2021. "Latest Data on COVID-19 Vaccinations by Race/Ethnicity." Kaiser Family

Foundation, Hune 23, 2021. https://www.kff.org/coronavirus-covid-19/issue-brief
/latest-data-on-covid-19-vaccinations-race-ethnicity/.

New York Times. 2008. "A Way with Words." *New York Times,* May 13, 2008. https://www
.nytimes.com/2008/05/13/washington/13barneybox.html.

Pappu, Sridhar. 2005. "The Holy Cow! Candidate." *Atlantic,* September 1, 2005. https://www
.theatlantic.com/magazine/archive/2005/09/the-holy-cow-candidate/304196/.

Schuster, Luc, and Pater Ciurczak. 2018a. "Boston's Booming . . . but for Whom?" Boston
Indictors, October 2018. https://www.bostonindicators.org/-/media/indicators/boston
-indicators-reports/report-files/bostons-booming-2018.pdf?la=en&hash=94DE67
E74983CB7DF3EBCB4EFA80F02346719C8B.

———. 2018b. "Boston's More Diverse than You Realize." Boston Indicators, September 28,
2018. https://www.bostonindicators.org/article-pages/2018/september/boston-diversity.

Sommeiller, Estelle, and Mark Price. 2018. "The New Gilded Age: Income Inequality in the
U.S. by State, Metropolitan Area, and County." Economic Policy Institute, July 19,
2018. https://www.epi.org/publication/the-new-gilded-age-income-inequality-in-the
-u-s-by-state-metropolitan-area-and-county/.

U.S. Census Bureau. 2020. "Table H-8: Median Household Income by State." In *Current
Population Survey: Annual Social and Economic Supplements.* https://www.census.gov
/data/tables/time-series/demo/income-poverty/historical-income-households.html.

Walker, Adrian, Andrew Ryan, Todd Wallack, Nicole Dungca, Akilah Johnson, and Liz Kowalczyk. 2017. "For Blacks in Boston, a Power Outage." *Boston Globe,* December 15,
2017. https://www.boston.com/news/local-news/2017/12/14/for-blacks-in-boston
-a-power-outage/.

Weisberg, Stuart. 2009. *Barney Frank: The Story of America's Only Left-Handed, Gay, Jewish
Congressman.* Amherst: University of Massachusetts Press.

World Population Review. 2020. "Cost of Living Index by State 2020." https://worldpopula
tionreview.com/state-rankings/cost-of-living-index-by-state.

Zeigler, Brett. 2020. "Higher Education Rankings." *U.S. News & World Report.* https://www
.usnews.com/news/best-states/rankings/education/higher-education.

CHAPTER 2

LOCAL GOVERNMENT
AND REGIONAL POLITICS

Shannon Jenkins

In Massachusetts, unlike most other states in the United States, all land within the state is part of some municipality; there are no unincorporated areas in the state. As such, county governments, where they still exist, play a limited role in local governance; municipalities, including towns and cities, are the primary form of local government in the commonwealth. Technically, under the U.S. Constitution, local governments in Massachusetts and in the United States are "creatures" of state governments and thus entirely dependent on them. Under Dillon's Rule, based on an 1868 court ruling in Iowa by Justice John Dillon, local governments may exercise only those powers granted to them by state governments. In the wake of this ruling, most states, including Massachusetts in the 1960s, amended their state constitutions to adopt some version of home rule, which grants to local governments the power to self-govern. While some state governments give broad home-rule authority to local governments, the grant of home rule in Massachusetts is fairly weak. One local official from Gloucester noted that local governments have the authority to act on "pooper-scooper" laws, but another town official from Sherborn complained that local governments' ability to act even on dog complaints is heavily constrained by state government authority (Barron, Frug, and Su 2004).

Thus, despite the fact that some of the very first local governments in the country sprang to life in Massachusetts, contemporary local governments find themselves very much constrained by the limited grant of local authority given to them by the state government. This is true of all municipalities in the commonwealth, although the city of Boston, the dominant metropolitan area, finds itself in a somewhat unique position. On one hand, the state capitol is located in Boston, which means state politicians frequently meddle in city affairs. However, much of the state's population is in the Greater Boston area, so a large portion of the state legislative delegation represents the metro area. As a result, state policies tend to benefit Greater Boston, to the consternation of other regions of the state. Often, localities outside of Route 128, especially in western Mass, are treated differently by state government than are eastern Mass cities and towns.

THE HISTORY AND TYPES OF LOCAL GOVERNMENT IN MASSACHUSETTS

The tradition of local governance in the commonwealth predates both the Massachusetts and the U.S. Constitutions. From the founding of the colony, "the basic political unit was the town" (Syrett 1964). The primary structure of government in colonial times was the town meeting. Town meeting is a form of direct democracy, whereby all eligible voters can directly participate in town policy making. Of course, when the town meeting was first established, suffrage and participation were not universal. An early law in effect until 1647 required all voters to be church members, although it is not clear whether this law was enforced; laws limiting participation to white male property owners were in effect in the 1600s and were enforced (Lockridge 1985; Smith and Schudrich 2010).

While Dorchester, now part of Boston, claims it established the first town-meeting form of government in 1633 and the National League of Cities (n.d.a) says the town meeting was established in Marblehead, the New England Historical Society (n.d.) argues the first town meeting in Massachusetts was run by Governor William Bradford at the Plimouth Plantation in 1622. In 1635 the General Court, the name for the Massachusetts legislature, enacted the New Town Ordinance, authorizing each town to dispose of common property, order its civil affairs, and choose its own particular officers in town meetings (NEHS n.d.). In many communities, meetings were initially held weekly and attendance was mandatory, but shortly after, many communities settled into monthly and then ultimately annual town meetings. Early town meetings tended to get raucous, so in 1715 the Massachusetts General Court passed another law requiring the town meeting to elect a moderator (NEHS n.d.); the key responsibility of the town moderator is to preside over town meetings to ensure smooth operations.

To this day, this is the most common form of local government in Massachusetts: an open town meeting with a moderator; as of 2019, 259 communities (or more than 70 percent of all municipalities in Massachusetts) have open town meetings (MMA 2019). This form of government is relatively rare outside of the commonwealth and New England; nationwide, just 5 percent of municipalities have a town-meeting form of government (NLC n.d.b). In contemporary times, each town has had slightly different ways of running its town meetings (SOC n.d.a). Nonetheless, most town meetings have certain common elements. The key responsibilities of town meetings are to set salaries for public officials, vote on appropriations, and vote on the town bylaws, or statutes (SOC n.d.a). Towns that still use the town meeting must hold an annual town meeting, although some communities meet more frequently; additional meetings, known as special town meetings, may be called when necessary. While town meetings tend to be seen as the epitome of participatory democracy, research looking at other forms of participatory local democracy suggests older, long-term male residents are more likely to participate, leading to differences in policy outcomes (Einstein, Palmer, and Glick 2019). Massachusetts politics has not been particularly welcoming to women or minority voters nor women or minority politicians, and the town meeting is another example of where their voices are less likely to have influence. As the *Boston Globe* editors (2021) argued recently, the state can and should do more to increase participation in local government; one of their recommendations was to extend the ability of local governments to hold public meetings virtually.

Nearly contemporaneously to the emergence of the town meeting, the select board, a small group of individuals who meet to oversee town affairs on a more frequent basis, emerged as a counterpoint to the power of the town meeting. In 1634 Watertown chose three men to oversee the civil affairs of the town between meetings, while in 1639 Dedham selected seven men to perform similar duties (Lockridge and Kreider 1966). As other towns moved to adopt these boards, the General Court recognized these select boards, delegating to them numerous duties, including the power to lay out highways, supervise education, and more (Lockridge and Kreider 1966, 551). While the balance of power shifted back and forth between town meetings and select boards, both are features of town-meeting government today.

Select boards generally function as the main legislative bodies in between town meetings in these towns, although they cannot exercise the powers given to town meetings, such as initiating appropriations. Nonetheless, select boards have considerable power, as they appoint board and committee members, set the town-meeting agenda, and grant licenses and permits (MSBA n.d.). Additionally, select boards appoint and oversee the town manager or administrator, who typically functions as the professional manager of town operations. Currently, 147 towns in Massachusetts have a three-member select board, while 144 have a five-member select board; the town of Wakefield has a seven-member town council, which functions legally as a select board (MMA 2019).

Historically, the people appointed to these boards were men; as such, many members of select boards are still called selectmen, even though both men and women serve on these boards in the present. In recent years, about 90 communities have officially made the change from board of selectmen to select board (Thompson 2020). Even though women now serve on select boards, these boards are still not representative of the population at large; out of the approximately twelve hundred board members statewide, just over three hundred are women (Colarusso 2019). As of 2019, there were 85 communities in the state with no women on the select board. Despite the low levels of representation, these numbers represent an increase from 20.6 percent in 2008 (Colarusso 2019). Thus, as described in more detail in chapter 11, women's representation in official local government roles lags in Massachusetts.

Initially, the Massachusetts Constitution did not have provisions for amending the constitution. However, when Maine (which was originally part of the state of Massachusetts) was granted statehood in 1820, conservative political leaders in the state called for a constitutional convention, as certain provisions of the constitution were no longer relevant given Maine's statehood (Sheidley 1991). In 1821, as part of this call to change the constitution, the constitutional convention also adopted an amendment to authorize the state legislature to charter cities for towns with more than twelve thousand residents (Burns and Gamm 1997). Currently, there are 59 municipalities in Massachusetts with a city form of government (MMA 2019). Oddly, there are 14 communities that have a city form of government but are legally known as the "the Town of"; for example, Braintree has a city form of government, but it is legally known as the Town of Braintree (SOC n.d.c).

Municipalities that select a city form of government have the option of selecting a mayor-council or council-manager form of government. Overall, 47 have a mayor-council government, with 3 of these cities (Cambridge, Lowell, and Worcester) have a manager in addition to a mayor and council; just 12 cities have a council-manager government (MMA 2019). In a council-manager government, the council is tasked both with making policy and with overseeing the implementation of that policy; they hire the manager, known as the administrator in some communities, to carry out the day-to-day operations of government (NLC n.d.b). Thus, the administrator is only indirectly (through the council) accountable to the voters. While this form of government is rare in Massachusetts, it is the most common form of municipal government nationwide, with more than 55 percent of municipalities having this form of government as of 2006 (NLC n.d.b).

A mayor-council form of government functions more like the state or national government. Here the council serves as the legislative branch, and the mayor serves as the head of the executive branch, and both are directly accountable to the voters. This is the second most common form of government in the United States, with 34 percent of cities having this form of government (NLC n.d.b). Mayors in mayor-council systems can be strong or weak; the primary differences between strong or weak mayors are whether they possess veto powers and how they are selected. Strong mayors possess veto powers and are directly elected by the people; weak mayors do not have veto powers and are selected from among city councillors.

The method of selection for city councils varies in Massachusetts. Some cities elect all members via at-large elections, meaning all councillors are elected by all voters in the city. Other cities have ward-based representation, where each councillor represents a specific section of the city; finally, some councils have a mix of at-large and ward-based representation. The way a council is elected matters; studies have shown that all at-large seats reduce minority representation on councils (Davidson and Korbel 1981) and that the composition of the council affects policy decisions made by these bodies (Langbein, Crewson, and Brasher 1996). Because of this, how councillors are elected has become a focus of political dispute in some cities, including Lowell, which voted for a hybrid representation system in 2019 (Locke 2019); Haverhill, which is considering a hybrid system (Jonas 2020); and Springfield, which moved from an at-large to ward system in 2009 (Goonan 2009).

As with select boards, city governments in Massachusetts are not particularly diverse. Across the state, just 176 of 603 city council seats were held by women in 2019, and just 10 of 47 mayors are women (Colarusso 2019). Data on the racial and ethnic composition of city councils is harder to come by, but there is some evidence that these councils are slowly becoming more diverse. Boston's first Black woman councillor was Ayanna Pressley, now a representative in the U.S. House, who was in elected in 2010. In 2020 Boston inaugurated the most diverse city council ever, with more people of color and the first majority of women (Valencia 2020). One of those women, Julia Mejia, an Afro-Latina and immigrant, won her at-large seat on the council by just one vote. Additionally, when Boston mayor Marty

Walsh resigned to become the secretary of labor for President Biden, Kim Janey became the first woman and the first Black person to serve as mayor of Boston.[1] In the election to find a permanent replacement for Walsh in 2021, all of the major candidates identify as people of color (Irons 2021). The winner, Michelle Wu, is the first Asian American and first woman elected mayor of Boston. Similar change can be seen in Everett, one of the most diverse cities in Massachusetts. Prior to 2020, all 11 members of the council were white, and 10 of them were men; 72 percent were over the age of sixty. After the 2020 elections, 45 percent of the council are under forty-five, 27 percent are women, and 18 percent are immigrants (Plummer 2020). This is not to overstate the levels of diversity on city councils. Massachusetts as a state is overwhelmingly white, described in more detail in chapter 10, and local governments generally reflect this. Nonetheless, there is some indication that the "original good old boys' club" (Colarusso 2019) is starting to wane.

Under state law, communities with fewer than six thousand residents are required to have an open town meeting; communities with more than twelve thousand residents may opt to become cities. But communities with more than six thousand residents have one more option; they may choose to move from an open town meeting to a representative town meeting (SOC n.d.a). Representative town meetings are also known as limited town meetings. In a representative town meeting, voters elect town-meeting members; these town-meeting members are the ones who conduct town business at town meetings. While town meetings are open for all to join and speak, only elected town-meeting members may vote on town business in a representative town meeting. Other than this, the representative town meeting functions in a similar manner to the open town meeting. Town-meeting members are elected to represent precincts in town; the number of representatives ranges from 45 to 240 (SOS n.d.b). Elections to the representative town meeting are nonpartisan, and terms are for three years. The representative town meeting was first established in Brookline. In 1915 the state legislature passed "An Act to Provide for Precinct Voting, Limited Town Meetings, Town Meeting Members, a Referendum, and

---

1   Under existing law, Walsh's resignation date would have triggered a special election in early 2021 if it had occurred prior to the beginning of March. The mayor elected would hold office for just a brief period, as the regular primary was scheduled for September 2021, followed by the regular general election in November. The city wanted to waive the special election but was unable to do so on its own, so it had to petition the state legislature for permission to skip the special election. Ultimately, Walsh's confirmation date by the U.S. Senate was delayed so that a special election was no longer required. But the fact that Boston could not determine on its own when its elections would be held is an example of the power the state holds over local governments.

an Annual Moderator in the Town of Brookline," and voters from the town of Brookline accepted this act shortly thereafter. In 2019, 33 communities in the commonwealth had a representative town-meeting form of government (MMA 2019); fewer than 1 percent of all municipalities nationwide have a representative town-meeting form of government (NLC n.d.b).

These are the main forms of local governments that persist today in Massachusetts: mayor-council, council-manager, town meeting, and representative town meeting. However, these are not the only local governments, as there are other forms of local government in the commonwealth. Overall, there are 351 general-purpose municipal governments in the state, but there are 861 local governments in total (U.S. Census 2007).[2] One of the most common of these special-purpose local governments is the school district; school districts are responsible for managing education within a defined geographical boundary. There are several kinds of school districts in Massachusetts (MassGIS 2020). Municipal elementary and municipal K–12 districts have boundaries that are contiguous with municipal boundaries; there are 250 of these dependent school districts. They are called dependent school districts as they depend on appropriations from municipal governments, although the amount they receive is highly prescribed by state statute. Multiple municipalities can come together to form a regional school district, offering elementary, secondary, or K–12 education to children from all member towns. Vocational and technical schools in Massachusetts are also regional districts. In total, there are 82 of these different forms of regional school districts. The form of school governance utilized in Massachusetts is correlated with region. Municipal school districts are the dominant form of school governance in the Boston metro area, whereas regional school districts are more common in western Massachusetts, due to the fact that it is much less densely populated. Indeed, 4 towns in western Massachusetts have no schools; instead, they have agreements with neighboring towns where they pay money to have their residents attend neighboring schools (MassGIS 2020).

While some school committees are appointed, most school committee members in Massachusetts are elected in nonpartisan elections.[3] School committees are one form of local government where women are not underrepresented, as they make up about 50 percent of membership on

---

2 All data on the number of local governments comes from the Census. Dependent school districts are not counted as separate governments in Census data; adding the 250 dependent school districts would bring the total number of local governments to 1,111.

3 Personal correspondence with Glenn Koocher, executive director of the Massachusetts Association of School Committees, November 16, 2020.

these boards (Colarusso 2019). This is not uncommon, as nationally women make up approximately 45 percent of school committee members (Strachan et al., 2019). Often women "see school board as less a political stepping stone and more as a way to advocate for their family and the children in their community" (Colarusso 2019). The COVID-19 pandemic of 2020–21 and accompanying school closures increased attention to local schools, such that some districts in Massachusetts are seeing a surge in the number of women running for school committees (Trufant 2021).

Massachusetts law authorizes the creation of a variety of other forms of special district governments; there are 423 of these special districts in the commonwealth. Responsibilities of these special districts range from economic development to fire and water, conservation, housing, transportation, and more (MassGIS 2020).

Finally, county governments do not play a strong role in state government in Massachusetts. Part of this is due to the fact that there is no unincorporated land in the state, as described above. In other states, counties are often vital to providing local government services to residents living in areas that do not belong to any general-purpose municipal government. But because these areas do not exist in Massachusetts, counties are largely redundant. Indeed, between 1997 and 2000, the state abolished eight county governments (SOC n.d.b). Bristol, Dukes, Norfolk, and Plymouth Counties still operate as county governments. The town and county of Nantucket are contiguous, and town select-board members serve as county commissioners, so they are not independent governments. The city of Boston has largely merged city and county government functions under the city umbrella, even though Suffolk County covers more than just Boston. The move to eliminate these governments came on the heels of decades of reduced revenue from the state for these governments, which eroded county governments' abilities to provide services; lax oversight of county finances helped transform county government in Massachusetts "at its worst into an outpost of petty graft and corruption, and at its best into a lazy and ineffective bureaucracy" (Babson 1997). Thus, while county governments serve important roles in many states, they do not in Massachusetts. Functions like registering deeds, probate, and state roads are handled by the state government. As an example, while the registrar of deeds is elected by county voters in abolished counties, the budget for these offices is administered by the secretary of the commonwealth's office (SOC n.d.b).

Ultimately then, county governments in Massachusetts are much like local governments in the state; even during their peak in the 1970s, they "existed at the whim of a benevolent master on Beacon Hill" (Babson 1997), and now because the state has decided to reduce their power, they play a small role in Massachusetts politics. The one exception to this may be sheriffs; elected by the voters, country sheriffs in Massachusetts have no day-to-day supervision, aside from elections held once every six years that hold them accountable to voters (Fanto 2010). While they are independently elected, they must submit their budgets to state government and function as state employees (Fanto 2010). This sets up the potential for clashes between these sheriffs and the state government. For instance, the state legislature has launched investigations of Bristol County sheriff Thomas Hodgson for issues such as pandemic visitation policies, immigration enforcement policies, and suicide rates in the Bristol County Jail. The most recent investigation into Sheriff Hodgson by the state attorney general found that he violated the civil rights of immigration detainees during a violent altercation about pandemic conditions in the jail (Dooling 2020); since then, the sheriff's contract with Immigration and Customs Enforcement was terminated by the Biden administration.

Home Rule in Massachusetts

Even though local government has deep traditional and historic roots in the state of Massachusetts, comparatively speaking, local governments in the state are relatively weak, vis-à-vis state government. One study finds that twenty-nine states grant more autonomy to their local governments than Massachusetts does (Wolman et al., 2010); even this may overstate the degree of local autonomy in Massachusetts, as the rankings rest primarily on the reading of statutes. As described below, statutory grants of authority in the commonwealth appear broad, but in reality the state keeps local governments under tight control.

Historically and comparatively, it was not uncommon for local governments to be relatively powerless. Local governments were assumed to have some powers, but local governments are not mentioned in the national constitution, and many state constitutions were not clear about local government powers. In the late 1800s, the powers of municipal governments were challenged by corporations, primarily railroad companies seeking to establish lines (Massachusetts Division of Local Services n.d.b); a series of court rulings by Iowa Supreme Court justice John Dillon established that while municipalities had some inherent powers, they were dependent on state governments. In other words, they were "creatures" of state government (*Merriam v. Moody's Executors* 1868); this became known as Dillon's Rule.

As a result of this ruling, many states moved to amend state constitutions and statutes in the late 1800s and early 1900s to grant local governments constitutional rights to self-government, also known as home rule. Home rule creates local autonomy and limits the degree of state interference in local governance, although the powers of local governments and limits on state governments are determined by each state. Massachusetts missed the initial wave of home-rule amendments; the state did not take up this issue until the 1960s. Because local governments had to petition the state government for the authority to act, the state legislature found itself dealing with many requests from local governments for special acts, for such things as allowing towns to purchase rain clothing and boots for municipal employees and authorizing the town of Weymouth to discharge a "moral obligation" to pay the retired town assessor a sum of money (Lemega 1967; Timmins n.d.).

Given the volume of legislation related to local governments, the legislature started working on home-rule amendments to the state constitution. The Home Rule Amendment was passed by the legislature in two consecutive constitutional conventions in 1963 and 1965 per constitutional amendment procedures. It was approved by the voters in 1966 and became effective in 1967. The Home Rule Amendment, which is Article 89 of the state constitution, states that it is the intention of the article to affirm the traditional liberties of the people with respect to local government and to "grant and confirm to the people of every city and town the right to self-government in local matters." The Home Rule Procedures Act was passed immediately after the approval of the amendment because it was clear that the general procedures outlined in the amendment would not be sufficient to guide implementation; as such, the act sets forth in greater detail how the powers in the amendment would be enacted (Lemega 1967).

Under these two key acts, there are three main grants of local authority: home-rule charter authority, general home-rule authority, and home-rule petition authority; the term *home rule* in Massachusetts refers both to the general concept of local authority and to these specific grants of authority (Barron, Frug, and Su 2004). The Home Rule Charter Authority authorizes local governments to establish charters, under parameters set by state government. A municipality's charter establishes its framework for government. While the Charter Authority authorized local governments to adopt their own (known as home-rule) charters, many local governments continue to rely on non-home-rule charters, such as those authorized under special legislation from the legislature that predate the home-rule amendments, while others have no charter at all (Barron, Frug, and Su 2004).

The second grant of local authority is the General Grant of Home Rule Authority. Under section six of the Home Rule Amendment, local governments "may, by the adoption, amendment, or repeal of local ordinances or by-laws, exercise any power or function which the general court has power to confer upon it, which is not inconsistent with the constitution or laws enacted by the general court in conformity with powers reserved to the general court by [Section 8 of the Home Rule Amendment, discussed below], and which is not denied, either expressly or by clear implication, to the city or town by its charter." While this appears to give local governments broad authority, Barron, Frug, and Su argue this conclusion is "wrong" (2004, 7). First, immediately following Section 6 is a section that outlines the limits on this authority. The exceptions to this general grant of authority include the powers to regulate elections; levy, assess, and collect taxes; borrow money or pledge the credit of the city or town; dispose of parkland; enact private or civil law governing civil relationships; and define or provide for punishment of a felony or to impose imprisonment. Furthermore, Section 6 states that local governments can act in manners not inconsistent with state law; thus, state government can preempt local power on any matter at any time (Barron, Frug, and Su 2004, 8). When the laws of two governments conflict, the doctrine of preemption holds that the higher-level government will prevail. Every state in the nation allows states to preempt local government to some degree, but many states limit preemption more than Massachusetts (Wolman et al., 2010). For instance, in Massachusetts a local statute can be found to be inconsistent with state law and thus preempted even without a specific statute overriding it; it is enough that the state has been found to act on the general subject matter to deny local governments the power to act (Barron, Frug, and Su 2004).

The final grant of home-rule authority is Home Rule Petition Authority. This is the process by which individual localities can petition the legislature for special legislation. While the legislature is generally not allowed to pass laws that deal with just one local government, local governments can file a home-rule petition asking for special legislation. Barron, Frug, and Su (2004) argue this is the "essence" of home rule in Massachusetts. The authors surveyed local government officials in the Boston area and found that the possibility of preemption induced great uncertainty about the extent of home-rule powers, such that municipal officials were afraid to act independently and were more likely to petition state government for permission. Ironically, this is just the sort of local authority that predates the passage of home rule in Massachusetts. Furthermore, the Home Rule Amendment gives the legislature the right to pass special acts without the consent of a municipality by a two-thirds vote with the consent of the governor, which allows the state to infringe upon home rule (Lemega 1967, 277).

Home rule in Massachusetts was adopted under the premises both that local governments needed and deserved more autonomy and that the state legislature was burdened by the volume of local bills they were handling. But there is little evidence that the passage of home rule in the commonwealth changed these patterns or reduced the volume of local legislation the legislature deals with. Lemega (1967) looked at special bills in 1950, 1956, 1959, and 1960; of 15,809 bills introduced, nearly 20 percent (3202) were related to affairs of cities and towns. Barron, Frug, and Su (2004, 13) argue that special legislation consistently made up more than 50 percent of all laws passed by the state each year in the early 2000s. In the 191st legislative session (2019–20), there were 345 local bills affecting 174 communities, that is, 50.4 percent of all municipal governments in the commonwealth. The state legislature even has a specific page devoted to detailing local bills; it notes that "not all legislation affecting a city or town is filed under Article LXXXIX of the amendments to the Constitution" (Massachusetts Legislature 2020). In other words, this count likely underestimates the number of local bills filed. Indeed, a search of all bills for the words *local government* produces 1,335 results in the 191st legislative session. While some of these presumably deal with significant matters, a reading of the subjects of these bills reveals that the state still imposes a good deal of control over local governments in the commonwealth around issues that would normally seem to be a local government responsibility. For instance, the town of Arlington petitioned the state for the right to establish a means-tested property-tax exemption for senior citizens; the city of Attleboro had to petition the state to make all gender references in the city charter gender neutral.

Of the 345 bills identified on the legislature's list of local bills for the 191st session, just over 10 percent of them (35) dealt with the granting of liquor licenses in local communities. Indeed, the granting of liquor licenses has been a major source of contention between the state and local governments for decades. In the 1930s, state legislators were distrustful of the predominantly Irish Boston City Council; fearful that the council might be too lax in granting liquor licenses, the state took over authorizing these licenses in local communities (Hoover 2016). The state allocated Boston 980 licenses under that act in 1933; by 2016 they had increased the number of licenses in Boston by just 130 to 1,110. While the city was able to argue successfully for the expansion of liquor licenses in the city to neighborhoods with few licenses like Dorchester, Roxbury and Mattapan (which also happen to be neighborhoods with some of the highest concentrations of minority residents), the city was able to do so only with the permission of the state legislature (Hatic 2017).

Thus, even a quick glance at the state legislative docket suggests that the volume of special bills has not declined, despite the passage of home rule in Massachusetts. Overall, then, while the grant of home-rule authority in Massachusetts appears on the surface to be moderately robust, the reality is that municipal governments in Massachusetts are severely constrained in their power to exercise independent powers. Barron, Frug, and Su's survey of local officials found more than 80 percent of the officials they surveyed felt home-rule power was not important; they argue that local officials believe home-rule authority over local matters is "nonexistent" (2004, 9).

Finally, it is worth noting that it is not just the state legislature and other branches of government that constrain the power of local governments in Massachusetts. Citizens themselves, via the ballot initiative and referendum process described in chapter 9, can and have passed legislation that has a profound impact on the power and independence of local governments. The most important of these ballot initiatives, from the perspective of local governments, might be Proposition 2½. In 1980 voters approved a ballot proposition that capped the local tax levy at 2.5 percent of property tax values and limited increases in the local taxation level to 2.5 percent more than the previous year's levy; increases beyond this limit needed to be approved by half of the voters in a town election (Roscoe 2014).[4] While proponents celebrate the success of the initiative in constraining property-tax increases in the state (Citizens for Limited Taxation n.d.), opponents argue the law has made local governments heavily dependent on state aid, exacerbated disparities in local services between wealthy and less affluent communities, and resulted in cuts

---

4   The actual history of the law is more complicated than explained here. Initially, two-thirds of voters were required to approve overrides; that was changed to a simple majority by the legislature. There are some exceptions to the 2.5 percent increase limit; for instance, towns can increase the levy by more than this amount if new growth occurs in the tax base. See Roscoe (2014) for a more detailed history and the Massachusetts Division of Local Service's (n.d.a) primer on Proposition 2½ for more information on how the law currently operates.

to local services (Oliff and Lav 2010). Regardless of where one stands on the success or failure of this proposition, it is clear that it severely limited the ability of local governments to exercise independent power.

Thus, local governments in Massachusetts have diminished capacity to exercise power; one ranking of local government autonomy across the states ranks Massachusetts thirtieth (Wolman et al. 2010). Granting more autonomy and discretion to local government would surely enhance the power and status of local governments in Massachusetts. For instance, it's not unreasonable to believe that local governments are better situated to make decisions about liquor licenses than the state. In addition, the state could act to give more fiscal discretion to local governments; one of the key reasons local governments rank so low in the aforementioned study is their lack of fiscal discretion. Proposition 2½ limits property-tax increases to that number, which is somewhat arbitrary as it has no relationship to the growth in the costs of services or goods (Oliff and Lav 2010). Local government costs have been increasing at a rate higher than 2.5 percent, driven by increases in things like health care (13 percent between 2001 and 2006), leaving local governments strapped for cash. This has also led local governments to be more dependent on state aid (Oliff and Lav 2010), exacerbating existing problems in the relationship between state and local governments.

At the same time, empowering local governments seemingly stands in contrast to the need for more regional thinking about problems that exist in the state. Problems don't end at town lines, and regional approaches to issues like land use and transportation are needed. Regional approaches to policy problems in the commonwealth have been distressingly rare. For instance, as Barron, Frug, and Su (2004) note, state law allows local governments to create regional school districts; creating these districts would certainly save towns money, as they could consolidate many administrative functions (fiscal management, maintenance, technology, and so forth). Yet there are few regional school districts in the state. But here, too, one of the major barriers to more regional cooperation is state regulations that restrict the kinds of agreements that localities are empowered to pursue under their current grant of authority from the state (Barron, Frug, and Su 2004). Empowering local governments to act more independently and incentivizing them to pursue regional approaches might enhance local governance in the state. However, this would require the state legislature to surrender power to local governments, which seems unlikely.

Regional Politics

In looking at how the state relates to local governments, the relationship between the state and its largest city, Boston, is an exemplar of the dominance of the state in these relationships. The Massachusetts-Boston relationship is frequently cited by social scientists as a leading example of a state interfering in a city's affairs (Burns and Gamm 1997, 90). The recent clash between the state and city over liquor licenses, extending over much of the 2010s, illustrates the way the state micromanages municipalities in general and the city of Boston in particular.

But that does not mean that Boston always finds itself at a disadvantage in state politics. The state's population is heavily skewed toward Boston; more than 10 percent of the state's population lives in Boston itself, and more than 50 percent live in the Boston metropolitan region (U.S. Census 2007).[5] Because of this, many of the state's legislative delegation have connections to the Boston metropolitan area, so many state policies benefit the region.

Furthermore, while the Massachusetts economy was booming for much of the 2010s, this growth and economic development have largely been concentrated within the Route 128 ring. Other areas of the state, including central, southern, and western Massachusetts, feel left behind and left out. For instance, income and education levels in other regions of the state, like western and southeastern Massachusetts, lag behind those in the Boston metro area. The median household income in Berkshire ($49,956) and Franklin ($55,221) Counties in western Massachusetts is much lower than in Greater Boston counties like Middlesex ($85,118) and Norfolk ($88,262) (Hinds and Hodge 2017). While poverty is certainly a problem in Boston, two-thirds of Massachusetts residents living in areas of concentrated poverty are in cities located outside of the Boston area (Forman and Mallach 2019). Indeed, Governor Baker launched an Economic Development Planning Council in 2019 to create a plan to engage all regions of the state in recognition of these disparities in economic development and growth (Polito and Kennealy 2019).

---

5   The Greater Boston metropolitan statistical area contains more than 4.8 million people, which is a significant portion of the state's approximately 6.8 million people. However, the Greater Boston MSA also includes Providence and parts of New Hampshire, so the number of people in that MSA is not an accurate estimate of the percent of the *state* population in the region.

As a result, there is a strong regional element to Massachusetts politics, even though regional governments in the state are not particularly robust. For example, State Senator Adam Hinds, who represents the rural towns in the westernmost part of the state, notes that "parts of Western Massachusetts feel neglected from the economy and politics of the state capital" (2017). Hinds argues this is not surprising since TV stations in the region often carry newscasts from Albany, New York, as well as New York Jets football games instead of Boston newscasts and New England Patriots games. Residents of the western, southeastern, and central regions of the state feel that the state's policies benefit the Greater Boston metro area and leave them out; this regional divide is both evident in and exacerbated by transportation policy. As Sullivan argues, "Complaints from the west have centered on spending priorities, especially when the state backs the Big Dig and other massive transportation projects that benefit Boston and its suburbs but do little for the Pioneer Valley and the Berkshires" (2005).

While Boston's public transportation systems are notoriously unreliable and facing major backlogs for repairs, at least the Boston metro area has access to public transportation. There are no other public rail systems, such that all other regions rely on buses for public transportation. As Chen says, "If you live outside of greater Boston and depend on public transportation, it's likely that commuting has become a daily challenge" (2019). The state's Big Dig project, where nearly $15 billion was spent to replace Boston's six-lane elevated central artery with an underground tunnel, has transformed downtown Boston, yet in 2013 the state resumed collecting tolls from Stockbridge to Springfield, in western Massachusetts, to pay for roadway improvements along the western part of I-90 (Johnson 2013). Commuter rail systems provide transportation for workers in the Boston metro area to ride to work into the city, but other regions of the state do not have access to rail linking them to job opportunities in other metro areas, like Springfield or Worcester.

The state has promised investments in projects such as South Coast Rail, which would link the southern part of the state to Boston, and has started to study rail projects to connect the western region of the state to Boston via high-speed rail. But even as the state moves to expand transportation to other regions of the state, it is clear that the Boston-focused nature of state policy remains, given that both of these projects look to connect other regions of the state to Boston. Furthermore, these projects tend to divide regions in the state rather than unite them. While the western and southern regions both have reason to be upset at Boston-centric transportation spending, the high costs of the Big Dig (the state continues to pay debt related to this project) means there are fewer resources for other major transportation projects, creating competition between regions over proposed projects rather than cooperation. It is clear that Massachusetts needs increased rail connectivity to disperse future growth more evenly across the state, yet the state still adopts a project-based approach as opposed to a more regional or statewide approach (Corley 2020).

This regional element to state politics is not new. The state capital has always been in Boston, and before the advent of modern transportation, this was problematic for representatives in the western part of the state, who had difficulty getting to the capitol and therefore higher levels of absenteeism in the legislature (Sullivan 2005). Thus, the "great east vs. west battle" (Sullivan 2005) in state politics continues to flare up, and local governments and different regions of the state, rather than organizing together, are often pitted against each other in competition for state resources.

Conclusion

It is somewhat ironic that Massachusetts is seen by many as the advent of local government, yet local governments in the state have little independent power. The story of the Pilgrims landing at Plymouth Rock and establishing local self-government is taught around the country, yet, comparatively, Massachusetts' local governments have little ability to exercise the powers granted to them under home rule. The state keeps local governments on short leashes, even when it comes to local leash laws (Baron, Frug, and Su 2004).

In recent years, some progress has been made in granting local governments the freedom to act independently of the state, as is evidenced by a 2016 law making "helpful changes to update obsolete statutes and practices that have been imposed on cities and towns for years," according to the Massachusetts Municipal Association's executive director, Geoff Beckwith (Schoenberg 2016). Changes like these are needed to empower local governments and to have more locally controlled local governments. The state also needs to do more to promote regional approaches to issues like land use, transportation, and climate change; incentivizing local governments to work collaboratively should go hand in hand with increases in autonomy. However, the state government, and particularly the state legislature, will not easily let go of its grasp on power over municipalities; for example, in the final version of the

2016 reform bill, the legislature removed proposals by Governor Baker to allow local governments, not the state legislature, to determine the number of liquor licenses each local community may approve. As another example, the historical process of redistricting in Massachusetts has been for local governments to draw their precincts and wards first, with the state then drawing districts using these as building blocks for the district, but in the latest round of redistricting based on 2020 Census results, the house has moved to flip this process, with the legislature drawing first. While this brings Massachusetts more in line with the practices in other states, local officials don't quite see it that way, calling the move a power grab that will sow disarray (Stout and Platoff 2021).

Despite the granting of a bit of freedom to local governments, power in Massachusetts is still concentrated in the Boston area. Politically, the concentration of population and the legislative delegation in the Boston metro area ensures that power and policy benefit the Greater Boston metro area, to the detriment of other regions of the state. This doesn't mean, though, that Boston is allowed to do as it pleases, because institutionally, the state government and in particular state legislators are loathe to give up their own power in a highly transactional political culture, as described in more detail throughout this book. As a result, the granting of home-rule authority in the state constitution and statutes appears robust but is, in reality, quite weak. Thus, local governments still play an important, but subservient, role in politics and policy making in Massachusetts.

WORKS CITED

Babson, Jennifer. 1997. "County Governments." *CommonWealth Magazine*. https://common wealthmagazine.org/politics/county-government/.

Barron, David, Gerald Frug, and Rick Su. 2004. "Dispelling the Myth of Home Rule: Local Power in Greater Boston." Rappaport Institute for Greater Boston. https://www.hks .harvard.edu/sites/default/files/centers/rappaport/files/home_rule.pdf.

Boston Globe Editorial Board. 2021. "The Pandemic Has Taught Us a Better Way to Do Public Meetings." *Boston Globe*, May 27, 2021. https://www.bostonglobe.com/2021/05/27 /opinion/pandemic-taught-us-better-way-do-public-business/.

Burns, Nancy, and Gerald Gamm. 1997. "Creatures of the State: State Politics and Local Government, 1871–1921." *Urban Affairs Review* 33, no. 1: 59–96.

Chen, Mia Ping-Chieh. 2019. "You Can't Get There from Here: Massachusetts Transportation Problems Extend beyond Boston." *Daily Hampshire Gazette*, October 31, 2019. https:// www.gazettenet.com/Transportation-29901954.

Citizens for Limited Taxation. n.d. "CLT's Proposition 2½." http://cltg.org/#proposition.

Colarusso, Laura. 2019. "'Original Old Boys' Club.'" WGBH, March 24, 2019. https://www
.wgbh.org/news/original-old-boys-club.

Corley, Tracy. 2020. "Transpo Answer: Regional Ballot Initiatives." *CommonWealth Magazine*, March 3, 2020. https://commonwealthmagazine.org/opinion/transpo-answer
-regional-ballot-initiatives/.

Davidson, Chandler, and George Korbel. 1981. "At-Large Elections and Minority-Group Representation: A Re-examination of Historical and Contemporary Evidence." *Journal of Politics* 43, no. 4: 982–1005.

Dooling, Shannon. 2020. "AG Report: Bristol County Sheriff Violated Civil Rights of Immigrant Detainees; Calls for Transfer of Those in Custody." WBUR, December 15, 2020. https://www.wbur.org/news/2020/12/15/healey-hodgson-bristol-immigration-detainees
-report

Einstein, Katherine Levine, Maxwell Palmer, and David M. Glick. 2019. "Who Participates in Local Government Meetings? Evidence from Meeting Minutes." *Perspectives on Politics* 17, no. 1: 28–46.

Fanto, Clarence. 2010. "There's No Question Massachusetts Sheriffs Have Power. But Is It Too Much?" *Berkshire Eagle*, August 8, 2010. https://www.berkshireeagle.com/stories/theres
-no-question-that-massachusetts-sheriffs-have-power-but-is-it-too-much,117399.

Forman, Ben, and Alan Mallach. 2019. "Building Communities of Promise and Possibility: State and Local Blueprints for Comprehensive Neighborhood Stabilization." *Mass Inc.*, January 2019. https://2gaiae1lifzt2tsfgr2vil6c-wpengine.netdna-ssl.com/wp-content
/uploads/2019/01/Building-Communities-of-Promise-and-Possibility.pdf.

Goonan, Peter. 2009. "Ward Representation Brings a Change to Voting in Springfield Municipal Election." *MassLive*, August 2009. https://www.masslive.com/news/2009/08
/ward_voting_brings_change_to_s.html.

Hatic, Dana. 2017. "City of Boston Proposal Would Add 152 Liquor Licenses over Three Years." *Eater Boston*, March 7, 2017. https://boston.eater.com/2017/3/7/14841000
/boston-proposal-adds-liquor-licenses.

Hinds, Adam. 2019. "A Massachusetts Model for Reaching Neglected America." *CommonWealth Magazine*, March 5, 2019. https://commonwealthmagazine.org/opinion
/a-massachusetts-model-for-reaching-neglected-america/.

Hinds, Adam, and Dan Hodge. 2017. "Western Mass. Needs Regional Economic Development Plan." *CommonWealth Magazine*, May 30, 2017. https://commonwealthmagazine
.org/economy/western-mass-needs-regional-economic-development-plan/.

Hoover, Amanda. 2016. "Why Boston Needs Liquor License Reform." *Boston Magazine*, December 18, 2016. https://www.bostonmagazine.com/restaurants/2016/12/18/reform
-liquor-licenses-boston/.

Irons, Meghan E. 2021. "Boston Fields Historically Diverse Crop of Mayoral Candidates; All Candidates Identify as People of Color." *Boston Globe*, May 11, 2021. https://www
.bostonglobe.com/2021/05/11/metro/boston-fields-historically-diverse-crop-mayoral
-candidates-all-top-candidates-identify-people-color/.

Johnson, Patrick. 2013. "After a 17-Year Free Ride, MassPike Tolls Return in Western Massachusetts." *MassLive*, October 15, 2013. https://www.masslive.com/news/2013/10/
after_a_17-year_free_ride_mass.html.

Jonas, Michael. 2020. "Haverhill May Scrap All At-Large City Council." *CommonWealth Magazine*, January 12, 2020. https://commonwealthmagazine.org/government/haverhill
-may-scrap-all-at-large-city-council/.

Langbein, Laura I., Philip Crewson, and Charles Neil Brasher. 1996. "Rethinking Ward and At-Large Elections in Cities: Total Spending, the Number of Locations of Selected City Services, and Policy Types." *Public Choice* 88, nos. 3–4: 275–93.

Lemega, John W. 1967. "Chapter 16. State and Municipal Government: Home Rule." *Annual Survey of Massachusetts Law.* https://lawdigitalcommons.bc.edu/cgi/viewcontent .cgi?article=1401&context=asml.

Locke, Kaitlyn. 2019. "Lowell City Council Votes for 'Hybrid' At-Large, District Councilor Election System." WGBH, November 20, 2019. https://www.wgbh.org/news/local -news/2019/11/20/lowell-city-council-votes-for-hybrid-at-large-district-councilor -election-system.

Lockridge, Kenneth A. 1985. *A New England Town.* New York: W. W. Norton.

Lockridge, Kenneth A., and Alan Kreider. 1966. "The Evolution of Massachusetts Town Government, 1640 to 1740." *William and Mary Quarterly* 23, no. 4: 549–74. https:// doi.org/10.2307/1919125.

Massachusetts Division of Local Services. n.d.a. "Proposition 2½ and Tax Rate Process." https:// www.mass.gov/service-details/proposition-2-12-and-tax-rate-process.

———. n.d.b. "What Is Home Rule?" https://www.mass.gov/files/documents/2017/09/09 /homerule.pdf.

Massachusetts Legislature. 2020. "Browse by City/Town." https://malegislature.gov/Bills /CityTown.

Massachusetts Municipal Association (MMA). 2019. "Forms of Municipal Government." *Massachusetts Municipal Directory.* https://41g41s33vxdd2vco5w415s1e-wpengine.netdna-ssl .com/wp-content/uploads/2017/12/FormsofGov2019-2020MassMuniDirectory.pdf.

Massachusetts Select Board Association (MSBA). n.d. "Massachusetts Select Board Association." https://www.mma.org/members/msa/.

MassGIS. 2020. "MassGIS Data: Public Schools Districts." https://www.mass.gov/info-details /massgis-data-massachusetts-schools-pre-k-through-high-school.

Merriam v. Moody's Executors, 25 Iowa 163 (1868).

National League of Cities (NLC). n.d.a. "Cities 101—Delegation of Power." https://www.nlc .org/resource/cities-101-delegation-of-power.

———. n.d.b. "Forms of Municipal Government." https://www.nlc.org/forms-of-municipal -government.

New England Historical Society (NEHS). n.d. https://www.newenglandhistoricalsociety.com /oldest-town-meeting-6-states/.

Oliff, Phil, and Iris J. Lav. 2010. "Hidden Consequences: Lessons from Massachusetts for States Considering a Property Tax Cap." Center for Budget and Policy Priorities, May 25, 2010. https://www.cbpp.org/research/hidden-consequences-lessons-from-massachusetts -for-states-considering-a-property-tax-cap.

Plummer, Laura. 2020. "The New City Council Reflects Everett's Diversity." *Everett Independent,* January 16, 2020. https://everettindependent.com/2020/01/16/the-new -city-council-reflects-everetts-diversity/.

Polito, Karyn, and Mike Kennealy. 2019. "Engaging Regionally to Advance Massachusetts' Economic Development Plan (Viewpoint)." *MassLive,* May 15, 2019. https://www .masslive.com/opinion/2019/05/engaging-regionally-to-advance-massachusetts -economic-development-plan-viewpoint.html.

Roscoe, Douglas D. 2014. "Yes, Raise My Taxes: Property Tax Cap Override Elections." *Social Science Quarterly* 95, no. 1: 145–64.

Schoenberg, Shira. 2016. "Massachusetts Legislature Okays Bill Updating Municipal Laws, without Liquor License Reforms." *MassLive*, July 31, 2016. https://www.masslive.com /politics/2016/07/massachusetts_legislature_pass_2.html.

Secretary of Commonwealth (SOC). n.d.a. "CIS: Citizen's Guide to Town Meeting." https:// www.sec.state.ma.us/cis/cistwn/twnidx.htm.

———. n.d.b. "County Governments." https://www.sec.state.ma.us/cis/cislevelsofgov /ciscounty.htm.

———. n.d.c. "Massachusetts City and Town Incorporation and Settlement Dates." https:// www.sec.state.ma.us/cis/cisctlist/ctlistalph.htm.

Sheidley, Harlow Walker. 1991. "Preserving the 'Old Fabrick': The Massachusetts Conservative Elite and the Constitutional Convention of 1820–1821." *Proceedings of the Massachusetts Historical Society* 103, no. 3: 114–37. https://jstor.org/stable/25081035.

Smith, Michael A., and Arianna Z. A. Schudrich. 2010. "A Study on Structural Changes in Local Government in the Commonwealth of Massachusetts." Massachusetts Municipal Management Association, May 7, 2010. https://www.mma.org/resource/a-study -on-structural-changes-in-local-government-in-the-commonwealth-of-massachusetts/.

Stout, Matt, and Emma Platoff. 2021. "A Fight Is Breaking Out over How to Redraw Massachusetts' Political Boundaries—and Democrats Are on Both Sides." *Boston Globe*, June 10, 2021. https://www.bostonglobe.com/2021/06/10/metro/fight-is-breaking -out-over-how-redraw-massachusettss-political-boundaries-democrats-are-both-sides/.

Strachan, J. Cheri, Lori M. Poloni-Staudinger, Shannon Jenkins, and Candice D. Ortbals. 2019. *Why Don't Women Rule the World? Understanding Women's Civic and Political Choices*. New York: CQ/Sage.

Sullivan, Robert David. 2005. "A Toast to the General Court." *CommonWealth Magazine*, April 10, 2005. https://commonwealthmagazine.org/politics/a-toast-to-the-general-court/.

Syrett, David. 1964. "Town-Meeting Politics in Massachusetts, 1776–1786." *William and Mary Quarterly* 21, no. 3: 352–66.

Thompson, Elaine. 2020. "Goodbye, Selectmen; Hello, Select Boards." *Worcester Telegram & Gazette*, January 20, 2020. https://www.telegram.com/news/20200120/goodbye -selectmen-hello-select-boards.

Timmins, James S. n.d. "Home Rule in Massachusetts: Who Is Really in Charge?" Massachusetts Municipal Lawyers Association. https://www.mma.org/resource/home -rule-in-massachusetts-who-is-really-in-charge/.

Trufant, Jessica. 2021. "Pandemic Pushes Mothers to Run for School Committee Seats." *Patriot Ledger*, April 12, 2021. https://www.patriotledger.com/story/news/2021/04/12 /growing-number-moms-run-school-committee-wake-covid/4823602001/.

U.S. Census. 2007. "Massachusetts." https://www2.census.gov/programs-surveys/gus /publications/ma.pdf.

Valencia, Milton J. 2020. "Boston Ushers in Historic Diversity with New City Council, Leadership." *Boston Globe*, January 6, 2020. https://www.bostonglobe.com/metro /2020/01/06/boston-ushers-historic-diversity-with-new-city-council-leadership/aqiFX usPSmHDnAmNXyJf8N/story.html.

Wolman, Hal, Robert McMammon, Michael E. Bell, and David Brunori. 2010. "Comparing Local Government Autonomy across States." In *Property Tax and Local Autonomy*, edited by Michael E. Bell, David Brunori, and Joan Youngman, 69–114. Cambridge, MA: Lincoln Institute of Land Policy.

CHAPTER 3

MASSACHUSETTS
ON THE NATIONAL STAGE

Peter Ubertaccio

It was a night unlike any in memory for Massachusetts politicos: a New Hampshire presidential primary featuring a candidate from Massachusetts who would walk away empty-handed.

In fact, the February 2020 primary featured three candidates from the Bay State: Senator Elizabeth Warren, former governor Deval Patrick in the Democratic primary, and former governor Bill Weld in the Republican primary. Warren came in a distant fourth at 9.2 percent of the vote, with Patrick an even more distant ninth at 0.4 percent. Weld barely dented the incumbent president, registering just 9.1 percent to Donald Trump's 85.6 percent. None of them won any delegates.

It got worse for Massachusetts fans. Patrick and Weld would soon drop out of the race, joining Representative Seth Moulton in withdrawing from the presidential sweepstakes. Warren's campaign would come to an ignominious end almost a month later when she lost Massachusetts to Joe Biden and Bernie Sanders, placing third with only 21.43 percent of the vote.

It was a first and not in a good way, like having Tom Brady bring your team down the field to allow Adam Vinatieri to kick a field goal in the final seconds of Super Bowl XXVI. No, this was more of a Bill Buckner botched ground ball from Game Six of the 1986 World Series. From John and Ted Kennedy to Michael Dukakis, Paul Tsongas, John Kerry, and Mitt Romney, presidential contenders from Massachusetts were typically a force to be reckoned with in primary elections. All these Democrats won the important New Hampshire primary. Romney lost it to John McCain in 2008 by five points but came back to win in 2012. All went on to win their own state and, with the exception of Ted Kennedy running against an incumbent president and Paul Tsongas running against Bill Clinton, four of them secured the presidential nomination, with Romney becoming the first Republican presidential nominee from Massachusetts since Calvin Coolidge in 1924.

But in 2020, not just one but four candidates from Massachusetts came up short in a drive toward the nomination. Before Kennedy's loss to Carter in

1980, one would have to go back to 1964 to find a more dispiriting presidential season for the commonwealth. Then, former senator and UN ambassador Henry Cabot Lodge lost the Republican nomination to Barry Goldwater, but even Lodge won New Hampshire.

The results of 2020 were a stunning downfall for a state that had grown accustomed to national leadership. Warren was an early favorite among Democratic voters, and the trailblazing Patrick had provided a campaign model for Barack Obama's presidential run in 2008. Even Seth Moulton had achieved a degree of national recognition with his dramatic, come-from-behind victory in a Democratic primary against incumbent US representative John Tierney in 2014.

It all begged a question about whether Massachusetts might lose its prominence as a producer of presidents and presidential nominees and what this change in political fortunes might mean for the commonwealth's leading role in American politics and public policy. Four American presidents came from the Massachusetts political environment (John and John Quincy Adams, Coolidge, and Kennedy), and statewide and congressional leaders from the state are, by dint of custom and tradition, frequently introduced to national audiences. Congresswoman and "squad" member Ayanna Pressley illustrated this in just her first term in office.

This chapter focuses on the historical development of political leadership from the commonwealth and the exceptional nature on the state's political dominance in national affairs.

Massachusetts has been one of the leading exporters of national political talent from the founding era through the twenty-first century. Consider that from 1939 through 2012, a politician from Massachusetts served in one of the following offices: chair of a House or Senate committee, House minority whip, House minority leader, House majority leader, Senate minority whip, or Speaker of the House. Of the four Massachusetts figures to occupy the White House, three—John Adams, Calvin Coolidge, and John F. Kennedy—served a portion of their term with a Speaker of the House from their home state—Theodore Sedgwick, Frederick Gillett, and John McCormack. Another Speaker, Thomas P. "Tip" O'Neill, became the public face of opposition to the policies of the Reagan administration from 1981 to 1987. O'Neill would also become the first Speaker to achieve national recognition as the leader of his party, his visage used successfully to raise funds for Republicans.

The state has produced some of the country's great political dynasties: Adams, Lodge, Kennedy. Writing in 1976, Neal Peirce noted, "The names of some Massachusetts politicians, especially those named Kennedy, have been household words in America for more than a decade now" (1976, 91). He mentioned Brooke, Richardson, Volpe, O'Neill, and others. In 2020 names such as Warren, Baker (routinely one of the nation's most popular governors), Pressley, Markey, Kennedy, and Patrick continued to resonate across the country, if not easily translated into votes in presidential primaries.

Senator Ted Kennedy's death in 2009 seemed to rupture this important historical axis. Kennedy was the longest-serving senator from the commonwealth, the keeper of his family's historical memory, and a prodigious policy maker. His early terms coincided with the final House terms of John McCormack and Joe Martin, who were, incidentally, the only members of the delegation to serve under two Massachusetts presidents, Kennedy and Coolidge. Kennedy also served with Leverett Saltonstall, the last Senate Republican from the state to hold a leadership position in that body. Saltonstall's namesake, his great-grandfather, served in the House with former president John Quincy Adams. Together with senior members of the House such as Tip O'Neill, Joe Moakley, Ed Boland, and Silvio Conte, Ted Kennedy ensured that "Massachusetts has enjoyed such clout in Congress" to keep the state in a leadership position on budgets and other important public policies (Hogarty 2002, 14). Ted Kennedy had multiple chapters in American political history overcoming personal tragedies, personal scandals, and a rare scare with possible political defeat in 1994. From the 1990s onward, he was one of the rare elder statespersons in the country, a bipartisan leader in the Senate while also a stalwart defender of the progressive wing of the Democratic Party, boosting the campaigns of both John Kerry in 2004 and Barack Obama in 2008.

The 2010 special election to fill Kennedy's Senate seat was won by a little-known Republican state legislator, Scott Brown, who instantly became a national figure as a result of winning a seat held by JFK and Teddy. In 2012 Brown would lose to Elizabeth Warren, whose own star would then rise considerably, rivaling Kennedy as the leader of the progressive side of the Democratic Party and ensuring a line of continuity in terms of national recognition, and policy influence, of the senator from Massachusetts.

Is there something in that "dirty water" down by the River Charles that moves Massachusetts to the forefront of American political life? Yes, and though the Standells (1965) are not a hometown band, their song about an experience along the Charles River that separates Boston from Cambridge has been adopted by locals as an authentic anthem. Massachusetts political culture encourages national participation. That culture derives from a variety of unique factors: history and tradition, success that begets itself, geography that is replete with media, and a higher-education landscape that rewards outsize influence in American political life. Massachusetts' impact is significant, though its reputation across the United States is more complicated. "Massachusetts liberal," for some, is an insult and, for others, aspirational. Massachusetts, and Boston in particular, still conjures forth realities of racism and racial strife for many while espousing a "do as I say but not as I do" racial liberalism. Outsize historical and contemporary national influence remains.

Of Plymouth and the Pilgrims

Political scientist Richard Hogarty noted, in his study of Massachusetts politics and governance, that the state "can legitimately lay claim to many social and political innovations. It was the first state to have a written constitution with a separate Bill of Rights included; the first newspaper, the first public library, the first college, and the first public high school were all founded here" (2002, 3).

One might suggest it was preordained that the state would loom large in American politics given its foundational role in American history. Though not the first colonists on American soil, the Pilgrim landing in Plymouth looms large in the American imagination. "The ship *Arbella* was one of seventeen vessels that sailed to Massachusetts in the year 1630," wrote David Hackett Fischer. "She led a great migration which for size and wealth and organization was without precedent in England's colonization of North America" (1989, 14–16). These Pilgrims brought with them habits, mores, and customs that would establish what Fischer refers to as "folkways" that would largely govern much of New England. Their conservatism—frugality, devotion to God, and promotion of "ordered liberty"—defined much of Massachusetts' political trajectory and the early colonial history of America. The "thriving religious community" they—the early Pilgrims of Plymouth and the later Puritans—created "profoundly shaped American ideas of liberty of conscience, the nature of individual spiritual experience and the notion of Americans as a chosen people" (PBS n.d.).

The Puritan contribution to American history is easily symbolized by one of the most often-repeated refrains in political speechmaking, the city on the hill. "It would be a city on a hill," John Winthrop wrote of the

Massachusetts Bay Colony his Puritans were building, an example to the entire world. Winthrop was calling his fellow travelers to obey the commands of God, lest their experiment fail. On the *Arbella*, Winthrop addressed his shipmates in the sermon "A Model of Christian Charity," noting that, "as a city upon a hill, the eyes of all people are upon us" (1630). According to Francis Bremer, "Winthrop was expressing his belief that it was the task of all, individuals and communities alike, to live exemplary lives and witness to religious truth. New England was not to be the only arrow in the quiver of reform, but it was to be one such weapon in the war against Antichristian forces" (Bremer and Winthrop 2005, 181). Despite the religious and moral calling of the Puritans, Winthrop's turn of phrase has been used by all manner of American politicians, often with the added word *shining* and just as often neglecting the note of judgment and caution implicit in Winthrop's speech. It became mythologized as the "keynote of American history" and has been appropriated by leaders from John Kennedy to Ronald Reagan to Barack Obama (Boorstin 1958).

The new life of the speech began in 1962 when it was used as a guide by John F. Kennedy to outline his understanding of the role of Massachusetts in American history and politics. Kennedy, with a rhetorical flourish that became a hallmark for him, told those gathered in the statehouse on January 9, 1962, "For what Pericles said to the Athenians has long been true of this commonwealth: 'We do not imitate—for we are a model to others.'" He'd go on to compare 1960s America to the voyage of Winthrop and the Pilgrims, quoting Winthrop and then proclaiming that he was "guided by the standard John Winthrop set before his shipmates on the flagship Arbella three hundred and thirty-one years ago, as they, too, faced the task of building a new government on a perilous frontier" (Kennedy 1961).

Kennedy articulated a theme that would dominate the state's political culture and view of itself, summed up by Michael Barone: "Massachusetts . . . has always assumed it has a lot to teach others" (Barone and Cohen 2007, 783). Ronald Reagan used Winthrop's phrase as bookends to his presidency, both in an address the night before the 1980 election and during his farewell address in 1989. Politicians of both parties have appropriated the phrase, and it became the title of a Showtime network TV show in 2019 set in mid-1990s Boston.

Much like Winthrop's turn of phrase, Plymouth looms large in American history. To begin with, one can still visit the Rock—not the actual Plymouth Rock but a perfectly acceptable representation. Though it does not continue to penetrate public discourse in the way it did through the early twentieth century, Plymouth and the Rock were "from the start a political icon, and though an ensuing century of conflict would further embue it with ecclesiastical associations, it would endure to the end as a statist symbol" (Seeyle 1998, 1).

Jamestown may have been first, but the Pilgrims, Puritans, and Plymouth combined to put Massachusetts as the central character in the development of early colonial history. Combined with the Boston Tea Party, the Battles of Lexington and Concord, and then Bunker Hill, among the most significant of the early American Revolution against the British, Massachusetts cemented its history as foundational to American politics. The comparison with Virginia is particularly apt, as both states claim a primary role in the founding of the United States. Judged from the early-nineteenth-century perspective, Virginia clearly outpaced Massachusetts in national leadership. Four out of the five first presidents were from Virginia, all reelected, whereas Massachusetts' John Adams suffered the first presidential reelection defeat. But post–Civil War America soured on national leadership from the home of the Confederacy. The only Virginian to win the presidency since was Woodrow Wilson, who had to establish a political career in a northern state (New Jersey) as a means of achieving national leadership. No Speakers of the House emerged from Virginia since John Winston Jones, who served from 1843 to 1845.

Further, as an industrial state victorious in the Civil War, and with a competitive party system in the twentieth century, Massachusetts was poised to build on its history as a state foundational to the American experience.

The Adams Family

Once the foundation was laid, early American political leadership was largely turned over to Virginians, with two notable exceptions: John Adams and his son John Quincy Adams. Both were not exactly poster children for national leadership by Bay State citizens as they shared an ignominious attribute: they were the first two American presidents to be defeated in their attempt at a second term of office.

Adams did not exactly shine as the nation's first vice president, though it is not clear anyone could have done so. Among the precedents established by George Washington was to treat the vice presidency as a member of the legislative branch and an outsider to executive councils. This precedent would last until the latter part of the twentieth century. But as president of the Senate, Vice President Adams had little power over that institution, as senators construed the office as simply a presiding officer, empowered by the Constitution only to cast a tie-breaking vote. This Adams did frequently, twenty-nine times in total, the second most of any vice president. He also stirred anger among his colleagues, often due to his gruff and pompous manner.

The Adams presidency was marked by four years of partisan discord. First, he had the unenviable task of succeeding Washington, the one figure of continental stature in the new republic. Second, Adams was constantly hobbled by his own party, especially the faction known as the Arch-Federalists who tried to push the new president into war with France. Adams tried to rise above it all with little success and was sent home to Quincy, Massachusetts, after one term, not even pausing to attend his successor's inauguration.

John Quincy Adams became president in the most inauspicious way. As party factions grew in power and strength, Quincy Adams was an antiparty man and the only president of the century not to be nominated by some sort of party organization. He attempted to reinstate a founding ideal of presidential selection where candidates would be assessed by merit and value, not partisan affiliation. In his inaugural address, Adams asked the American people to join him in "discarding every remnant of rancor against each other and yielding to talent and virtue alone that confidence which in times of contention for principles was bestowed only upon those who bore the badge of party communion" (1825). But he was ultimately no match for the spirit of the times and only came to power in what was later referred to as "the corrupt bargain," an election thrown into the House of Representatives, where the Speaker, Henry Clay, threw his support to Quincy Adams over the hero from the battle of New Orleans, Andrew Jackson. Quincy Adams then appointed Clay as secretary of state, the position from which four presidents had sprung. The whole affair tainted his administration.

Their difficult presidencies obscured their many other accomplishments. Both would find their historical reputation enhanced much later with the production of the 1997 film *Amistad* and the publication of *John Adams*, the Pulitzer Prize–winning biography from David McCullough in 2001. In *Amistad* Anthony Hopkins portrays John Quincy Adams, who, as a seventy-three-year-old former president, now represents the twelfth congressional district in Massachusetts. An ardent antislavery figure, Adams is recruited to represent enslaved captives on the ship *La Amistad* in their battle for freedom before the Supreme Court. The publication of *John Adams* set off many years of historical reckoning of Adams' life and presidency. McCullough also joined an effort to erect a monument to Adams in Washington, DC, where only a building of the Library of Congress bears his name (Cunningham 2016).

John Adams was the primary author of the Massachusetts Constitution, as we see in chapter 6. In the beginning of their analysis of the document, Lawrence Friedman, author in this volume, and Lynnea Thody note, "In many respects, the constitutional history of Massachusetts is the constitutional history of the United States" (2011, 1). Bicameralism and independent executive and judicial bodies were all part of Adams' design to ensure protections against "democratic excesses," and his thoughts and suggestions on the structure of government became the blueprint for other states and the federal system (Friedman and Thody 2011, 10).

Adams' defense of the British soldiers who fired on a mob in Boston (the Boston Massacre) has also secured his position as the preeminent defender of the rule of law in American history.

Quincy Adams, having served as a senator, ambassador, and secretary of state before assuming the presidency, returned to Massachusetts and won election to the U.S. House in 1830, where he served until his death in 1848. He became the only former president to win a subsequent election to Congress. Descendants of the two Presidents Adams would go on to their own distinguished careers in politics, law, and the academy, but none would achieve the heights of John or John Quincy.

The second cousin of John Adams also helped establish the reputation of the commonwealth as a leader in national politics. Samuel Adams was, according to his biographer, "arguably both America's first professional politician and its first modern politician" (Alexander and Adams 2002, ix). Sam Adams also had a complicated relationship with historians and the public memory, depicted both as a radical revolutionary and as a strict and pious Calvinist. Thomas Jefferson believed him to be "truly the Man of the Revolution" (Maier 1980, 5). Much like his cousins, Samuel Adams would get a new introduction to new generations of Americans via a form of popular culture, in his case the eponymous beer referred to as "your cousin from Boston."

After John Quincy Adams left the presidency, it would take ninety-four years before another Massachusetts figure served in the White House and only so because of the death of incumbent president Warren Harding. Calvin Coolidge would go on to win election on his own in 1924 and become a symbol of the conservative Yankee stock that governed much of New England at the time. Coolidge, originally from Vermont, had more in common with the congressional leaders from Massachusetts than later national leaders such as the Kennedys: he worked up and through local and regional politics. Before, during, and beyond Coolidge's time, throughout the nineteenth and twentieth centuries, national leadership from Massachusetts tended to emerge from the halls of Congress.

Senate Leadership and Speakers of the House

No figure from Massachusetts has ever served as majority or minority leader of the U.S. Senate, though Henry Cabot Lodge Sr., senator from 1883 to 1924, fulfilled this role in an unofficial capacity and Leverett Saltonstall did chair the Republican conference and serve as Republican whip. The Senate has more often seen figures from Massachusetts chairing important committees. Daniel Webster chaired the Senate Finance Committee. Charles Sumner, Lodge, and Kerry ruled the Foreign Relations Committee. Sumner did so after enduring a caning on the Senate floor for his antislavery crusade. Lodge helped torpedo Woodrow Wilson's League of Nations. David Walsh chaired Education and Labor, and Ted Kennedy chaired the Senate Health, Education, Labor, and Pensions Committee. George Frisbie Hoar and Kennedy chaired the Judiciary Committee.

Of the fifty-four individuals who have served as Speaker of the U.S. House, eight have been from Massachusetts, the most of any state. Theodore Sedgwick served as the fourth Speaker, and first from Massachusetts, though only from December 1799 through March 1801. Joseph Bradley Varnum (1807–11), Robert Winthrop (1847–49), and Nathaniel Banks (1858–61) all served before the creation of the modern, and much more powerful, Speakership of the late nineteenth and early twentieth centuries. Banks was known as a conciliator and as acceptable to all factions in the House, even though it took *133 ballots* and months of deliberation for him to become Speaker.

Frederick Gillett (1919–25) was known mostly as a compromise candidate who secured the Speakership over the then Republican minority leader. Gillett was the chair of the Judiciary Committee at the time, a moment when the power of the office was in steep decline after the autocratic Joseph Cannon was dethroned in 1910. He was the last Speaker, until Dennis Hastert in 1999, to assume the Speakership without having been elected to a party leadership post first (Davidson, Oleszek, and Lee 2008). As a feud between factions within the Republican Party mounted in the mid-1920s, it took 9 ballots to renominate Gillett. When a substantial number of Republicans voted against him for Speaker in 1923, "he scampered off to the Senate the following year" (Nelson 2014, 1). In so doing, he became the longest-serving member of the House to win election to the U.S. Senate, succeeded in that feat only in 2013 by Massachusetts representative Ed Markey, who served in Congress for thirty-seven years before winning a Senate seat.

Joseph Martin was the first Republican to hold the Speakership since 1931, and he represented the last power play by a Massachusetts leader against the rising acceptance of a more liberal Democratic Party. Martin himself would serve in the House under the conservative Calvin Coolidge and liberal John F. Kennedy and watch the Massachusetts political environment shift gears as well. Martin was an ardent anti–New Dealer but also a committed institutionalist. Under Martin, some party control returned to the Speaker's office. He once noted that "in the few years that I served as Speaker . . . no Republican went on an important committee without my approval" (Davidson and Oleszek 1990, 163). He brought newfound energy to party councils. Martin served as the leader of House Republicans for two decades and stayed in Congress for another eight years, until he was defeated in a primary by Margaret Heckler in 1966. During his career, he helped to reestablish the Republican Party as an opposition force to Roosevelt and Truman. His biographer James Kenneally notes that "several observers believed Martin was the strongest leader in years," in part through the creation of an "elaborate 'whip' organization which provided Martin with an accurate count of voting strength and a means of rapidly getting his forces to floor votes" (2003, 49). Martin himself would be discussed as a possible presidential candidate during his time in office and was, before Eisenhower's election in 1952, the most prominent Republican in the country.

If Martin and successor Tip O'Neill were public figures and recognized spokespersons for their parties, John McCormack was the antithesis. Serving during the Kennedy, Johnson, and pre-Watergate Nixon presidencies, McCormack was among the last of the machine politicians to emerge from Boston and rule over Democratic Party politics in the state while maintaining a national profile. Machine politics, particularly in Democratic Party councils in Massachusetts, would give way to greater candidate-centered organizations, providing leaders with less resources than they had in the days of McCormack. But the political culture of patronage predated McCormack and outlived him in various forms. Those, like McCormack, who are skilled in understanding the needs of members are rewarded in Massachusetts with relatively secure leadership positions.

A committed institutionalist like Martin and O'Neill, McCormack "enjoyed and took pains to preserve his relative public obscurity" (Nelson 1999, 8). What distinguishes McCormack, according to Garrison Nelson, is "not his oft-told rags-to-riches Horatio Algerish rise from the Boston Irish tenements to the Speaker's chair on Capitol Hill but the fact that McCormack was in the room for so many major political events that altered the course of American life" (1999, 9). Those events ran from the New Deal to the New Frontier, the Great Society, and the Vietnam War. McCormack was also the first Catholic Speaker of the House.

Thomas P. "Tip" O'Neill is the truly transformative Speaker from Massachusetts. "O'Neill was an old-style politician who realized that the post-reform House called for a new style of leadership" (Smith 1987, 29). His immediate predecessor, the quiet Carl Albert of Oklahoma, was the last Speaker to be able to avoid the national spotlight.

Tip was working-class Cambridge at a time when the party in Massachusetts was moving toward Hyannis Port and the Kennedys. "O'Neill is a big (six-foot-two, 260 pound), bluff Irishman," noted Neal Peirce, comparing him to the fictional, strong-willed machine politician Frank Skeffington in the 1956 novel *The Last Hurrah*, and "an issue-oriented Congressman who surprised everyone by breaking with the Johnson Vietnam policies in 1967 to become an avowed, persistent dove" (1976, 92). Unlike McCormack, the liberal O'Neill had to contend with outsider presidents—the moderate Democrat Jimmy Carter and the conservative Republican Ronald Reagan.

Though he was as drawn to machine politics as his mentor McCormack, O'Neill was thrust into the political limelight by virtue of changing technology and the nationalization of political issues. Republicans found in O'Neill a perfect foil, or so they thought. After putting together a conservative coalition of Republicans and Democrats in 1981 to advance Reagan's domestic agenda, House Democrats gained twenty-seven seats in the 1982 midterm election, solidifying O'Neill as the personification of opposition to the Reagan agenda. Upon retiring from the Speakership in 1987, O'Neill would go on to newfound fame as a commercial personality for brands such as Comfort Inn, American Express, Miller Lite, and even the Trump Shuttle between Boston, New York, and Washington, DC.

O'Neill was also the last of the Speakers from Massachusetts who formed the Austin-Boston connection within the Democratic Party, a symbolic unity in congressional leadership between the party's more conservative southern members and its northern liberals. From the New Deal through the Reagan era, party leadership alternated between these two poles, favoring savvy political leadership from both areas. O'Neill's chief deputy was the congressman from Fort Worth, Texas, Jim Wright, the final Speaker who formed this connection.

After the 2020 elections concluded, Congresswoman Katherine Clark won a contested race to serve as assistant Speaker, the fourth-highest leadership position in the majority party in the House. Clark's ascent through the House leadership since her election to Congress in 2013 has fueled speculation she could one day emerge as the first Speaker of the House from Massachusetts since O'Neill left Congress and the ninth person from the commonwealth to lead the institution. Like O'Neill, McCormack, Martin, and Gillett, Clark served in the Massachusetts legislature before her election to Congress. The Great and General Court, as the legislature is formally known, provides an important backdrop and education to would-be Speakers of the U.S. House. A leadership-dominant institution in a state with a high tolerance for party machines and party patronage, the legislature rewards those who appreciate and understand the electoral and political needs of its members. As an institution that traces its lineage back to 1629, it also rewards those with the interest and skill to learn parliamentary procedure. Clark moved from the local politics of a school committee in Melrose, Massachusetts, to the statehouse and then to Congress and now to leadership, fertile training ground for the kind of listening and patience typically rewarded by securing the votes of colleagues for a leadership position. "Katherine Clark is a new face, doing it in an old-fashioned way," notes Erin O'Brien. "She's working the leadership. She's raising a lot of money, and she's spreading the money out. She's making friends. . . . Like Pelosi she knows what every member needs" (Bidgood 2020).

From the Lodges to the Kennedys

When Congressman John F. Kennedy defeated incumbent U.S. senator Henry Cabot Lodge in the 1952 election, it signaled a fundamental shift in political power. "For more than 200 years," wrote Neal Peirce, "a homogenous Yankee Protestant population had held sway on the shores of Massachusetts Bay" (1976, 64).

Symbolically, Lodge represented the conservative Yankee hold on the state's politics, while Kennedy's ascent was viewed as a turn toward the Catholic Democratic power that had been building for years. Lodge's grandfather and incumbent senator Henry Cabot Lodge Sr. successfully turned back a challenge to his seat in 1916 by JFK's grandfather and former Boston mayor John F. "Honey Fitz" Fitzgerald. When the younger Kennedy defeated the younger Lodge, it was the last time a Lodge held statewide office in Massachusetts. Interestingly, the Lodge-Kennedy election of 1952 was not the greatest clash of dynasties in the state's history.

The 1962 special election to fill JFK's Senate seat featured a Republican primary won by Lodge's son George. Ted Kennedy won the Democratic primary against Eddie McCormack, the nephew of Speaker of the House John McCormack. Kennedy would go on to defeat Lodge that fall, one of the few elections in Massachusetts' political history pitting multiple family legacies against one another. The general election also featured an independent candidate, Stuart Hughes, the grandson of the former governor of New York, Supreme Court chief justice, and 1916 Republican nominee for president, Charles Evans Hughes Sr.

The Kennedys did not create this type of intergenerational transfer of power and political prominence in Massachusetts, but they both accommodated and furthered it. The Lodges would give way to the Kennedys as the state's preeminent political family but not before JFK himself would seek out Lodge for a prominent position in his administration. After losing to Kennedy-Johnson as the Republican Party's 1960 vice presidential candidate, Lodge agreed to serve as ambassador to South Vietnam for JFK, an important symbolic nod to the importance of power families.

As important is the fact that the Kennedys would both serve with Massachusetts Republicans of the Lodge disposition: Leverett Saltonstall and Ed Brooke, moderate Republicans who worked well with their Democratic colleagues. Brooke, the first African American elected to the U.S. Senate post-Reconstruction, was an early proponent of Richard Nixon's resignation and would lose his second reelection battle to Paul Tsongas of Lowell in 1978.

Both JFK and Ted served with Saltonstall ("Salty"). The former patrician governor of old Yankee stock took a liking to them both. When JFK was recovering from a recurrence of his back pain, Salty conferred with Kennedy aide Ted Sorensen and "handled many bills concerning Massachusetts in which [he] knew [Kennedy] would be interested." Salty continued, "One time I left Kennedy's name off a piece of legislation because I thought it would be an unpopular position for him to take. But Sorensen got mad at me because I hadn't consulted him first, as I usually did. When Kennedy came back to the Senate, I told him about the incident and he smiled and said, 'Oh, you mean you were doing business with Senator Sorensen?'" (1976, 185). Both Kennedys could count on the support, rapport, and guidance of their senior Republican colleague without political repercussion, helping them establish power within the state and within the Senate.

JFK would go on to become the symbol of national leadership by a Massachusetts figure. He served less time in Congress than Henry Cabot Lodge Sr. and less time as president than Calvin Coolidge, but his tenure in the White House and the tragic and public nature of his death remain deeply seared in the country's collective memory. It was a time of ascendancy for the postwar generation and the Irish Catholics in Boston. JFK would go on serve as the symbol of Camelot, a mythologized version of his time in office that seemed a mark of demarcation, a time before the Vietnam War, before Watergate, before special counsels investigating executive malfeasance, and it secured both President Kennedy and Massachusetts in the public imagination. This hold remains, less tight than before, but present nonetheless. When Senator Ed Markey was fending off a challenge from JFK's grandnephew, Representative Joseph Kennedy III, Markey funded an ad that featured him saying, "With all due respect it's time to start asking what your country can do for you." In response, Speaker Nancy Pelosi made a rare entry into intraparty politics by endorsing Kennedy, her House colleague. Capitol Hill whisperers indicated that Pelosi was troubled by Markey's thinly veiled attacks on the Kennedy legacy.

That the younger Kennedy's attempt to topple Markey failed is an indication of the limits of the family name in contemporary American politics. The Kennedy name made it possible for a relatively junior congressman to challenge a popular, if uncharismatic, sitting senator in his own party with whom he largely shared a policy outlook. However, in the political moment of 2020 when privilege was suspect in progressive quarters of the Democratic Party, the Kennedy name proved a double-edged sword.

Still, it was Ted who established the greatest legacy for the family in the Bay State. The Kennedys are often synonymous with Democratic Party politics in the state and nationally, but they have always existed outside normal party politics. Garrison Nelson recounts, in his study of John McCormack, with whom the Kennedys were often feuding, that the "Kennedy organization operated outside the Massachusetts Democratic Party and wished not to be tainted by it" (Nelson and McCormack 2017, 484). Ted benefited from the organization that his family had created and cultivated over the course of two decades, and he became the longest-serving senator from Massachusetts in history and the fourth-longest-serving senator in American history. He established a public policy legacy that touched on nearly all major issues in modern American politics—exceptional policy influence originating from the Bay State.

It wasn't clear by the early 1980s, however, that the legacy would last. Longtime *Boston Herald* columnist Peter Lucas seemed to capture the end in early 1981 as Democrat Jimmy Carter was about to move into the White House. Lucas noted, "Kennedy is operating in a different atmosphere these days. Gone are the Secret Service agents, and the vast staff of the Judiciary Committee and the presidential campaign. It was time to go and watch the inaugural of the 40th President of the United States. And it wasn't him" (Lucas 1983, 91).

According to Peter Cannellos, Ted's position by the 1990s had hardened. Respected on the Left, he remained the symbol on the Right of a spent ideology, the perfect embodiment of political and personal self-indulgence. Even in his own party, his liberalism had seemed, at times, outmoded as the "'third way' of the Clintons gained ascendance in the Washington of the 1990s" (2009, 349). The Clinton years, at first, called into question the viability of the liberalism of Ted but also the ability of Democrats to govern. For the first time since the Eisenhower years, Democrats lost control of both houses of Congress in 1994. It was not the first time Ted was in the minority. Republicans ran the Senate from 1981 to 1987, but it was the first time he had to fight for his electoral life. Even the Chappaquiddick scandal of 1969 didn't hurt Ted's electoral chances, and he took 62 percent of the vote in the 1970 general election.

Kennedy's win in 1994 was what Steve Kornacki called one of the "errant scraps of good news" during a terrible cycle for Democrats (2018, 280–81). Even still, the fact that Kennedy was down in polls behind Mitt Romney in September of that year demonstrated the degree to which the Kennedy name was no longer considered the gold standard in the commonwealth's electoral calculations. Still, the senator who "has done much to set national policy on any number of issues" pulled out a victory with 58 percent of the vote (Barone and Cohen 2007, 791). After the 1994 election and with his own presidential aspirations over, Kennedy coasted to future reelections and set himself on a trajectory to become the "liberal lion of the Senate" for which he'd be remembered.

The Kennedy era in Massachusetts would come to an end when another U.S. senator, Ed Markey, took up the charge to promote and defend the progressive wing of the Democratic Party against, of all people, a Kennedy. When Ted died, there was no Kennedy left in Congress from this state. His nephew Joseph P. Kennedy II had left Congress after the 1998 elections. Ted's son Patrick, a member from Rhode Island, left Congress after the 2010 election, the same year his cousin, and Ted's grandnephew, Joseph P. Kennedy III won a congressional seat from Massachusetts.

As noted, the younger Kennedy ran against incumbent senator Ed Markey for the Democratic nomination in 2020 and lost. It was the first time a

Kennedy lost a race in Massachusetts in modern history, and it was largely done because Markey picked up the causes of Ted: he ran as an unabashed progressive and painted his opponent as a conservative. Not only did Kennedy lose by eleven points, but Markey also demonstrated appeal by attacking the Kennedy family explicitly and implicitly. His charge to "ask what your country can do for you" turned JFK's most important phrase on its head. Markey also went after Kennedy's father, who was funneling his campaign money into political action committees to benefit his son in 2020. Markey's repeated phrase during the debates to "tell your father" to stop his secret funding, where he stressed his Boston accent by pronouncing *father* as *fatha*, became a national meme.

The 2020 election in Massachusetts seems to have ended the pattern of family legacies in Massachusetts politics but did not lessen Massachusetts' exceptional influence in DC. The new era presages continued influence in American congressional politics. Congressman Richard Neal remains chair of the powerful Ways and Means Committee, Senators Ed Markey and Elizabeth Warren returned to Congress secure as leaders of the progressive wing in that body, Assistant Speaker Katherine Clark continues her upward ascent, and Ayanna Pressley is, for some, the face of the Democratic Party as one of the four "squad members." But also, for the first time since the nineteenth century, no member of the congressional delegation is the descendant or spouse of a former member. No Kennedy, Lodge, Saltonstall, or other political family is in the mix of today's delegation.

Those GOP Governors

The commonwealth's national politics are firmly Democratic. A Republican has not won a House seat since 1994. While Scott Brown managed a win for a U.S. Senate seat, it was only under the unusual circumstances of a January special election with low turnout in a bad year for Democrats. Once he secured the seat, he became one of the Senate's most endangered incumbents, losing his reelection attempt to Elizabeth Warren. Since the 1928 presidential election, only Dwight Eisenhower and Ronald Reagan have won the state and its electoral votes (twice each), and few Republican candidates for president make any play here.

Still, the party has been quite competitive at the gubernatorial level, producing a string of victories and popular leadership from 1990 through the reelection of Charlie Baker in 2018. Only Deval Patrick managed to break the streak, and he was only narrowly reelected in 2010. This prominence has not translated into national power, with Mitt Romney as the lone exception, but it has given Massachusetts Republicans a visible role as leaders of the small band of moderate Republicans and as a counter to the conservatives of the southern and western variety.

Those GOP governors have made their own successful national profiles. Bill Weld was a favorite of the national GOP in the early 1990s for taking back the state just two years after Dukakis lost his presidential bid. Weld would demonstrate the limits of Republican influence in the state. Safely confined to working with, and perhaps checking the influence of, the Democratic legislature, Massachusetts voters remain reluctant to send Republicans to DC. In 1996 Weld would give incumbent Democratic senator John Kerry the challenge of his electoral life. Just two years earlier, Weld won reelection by the largest electoral margin of any gubernatorial candidate in the state's history, and Kerry never achieved the political popularity of Ted Kennedy. Still, Weld could not translate his success as governor to a successful elevation to federal office. Kerry would win reelection, setting him on his own path toward a presidential nomination.

Ultimately, Weld tired of his gubernatorial duties and accepted an offer by Bill Clinton to serve as ambassador to Mexico. He resigned his office before his confirmation hearings that never took place—due to his earlier public battles with the GOP chair of the Senate Foreign Relations Committee, Jesse Helms of North Carolina. Weld's lieutenant governor and successor, Argeo Paul Cellucci, was a favorite of the Bush family and, after securing his own election as governor in 1998, went on to serve as ambassador to Canada during the administration of George W. Bush.

Mitt Romney came back from his failure in 1994 to unseat Ted Kennedy to secure the governorship in 2002 after a successful stint managing the 2002 Salt Lake City Winter Olympics. Romney, itching to secure the presidential nomination of his party that was denied his father many decades earlier, moved to the right and twice ran for president, winning the nomination in 2012. Romney would go on to become a U.S. senator from Utah and only the second person, after Sam Houston, to serve as governor of one state and senator from another (Ostermeier 2017).

Charlie Baker, a former cabinet secretary to Weld and Cellucci, attempted to align himself with the emerging Tea Party movement in Massachusetts and challenged incumbent governor Deval Patrick in 2010, only to come up short. Baker ran again as a moderate manager in 2014 and won. Since then he has routinely polled as one of the most popular governors in the nation. Like his Republican forebears going back to John Volpe in the 1960s (Volpe would resign the office to become Richard Nixon's secretary of transportation), Baker has been unable to translate his popularity into success for his party at the legislative level or other statewide offices. Despite his popularity, he has also failed to dominate party organizations in the state. Rather, the governor has used a political action committee to support both Republican and Democratic candidates in the state. Working around the party label has helped to ensure Republicans like Baker remain popular political figures here but, unlike Democrats who can translate their statewide popularity to national prominence, it keeps GOP governors limited in their ability to influence party politics beyond the state's border. This is symbolized by the fact that Baker was mentioned as a possible cabinet secretary not for Donald Trump but for Joe Biden. Though Trump didn't often direct his ire at Baker he did use his social media to call the governor a RINO (Republican in name only).

Republicans have been caught in the inexorable decline in demographics. The party in Massachusetts was built on Yankee stock that has been in permanent decline. Nationally, they have tried to hold back the moral and populist conservatism of a party moving its base southward and westward. Republican attorney general and future senator Ed Brooke tried to sound the alarm after the Goldwater defeat in 1964. Writing one year later, he bemoaned that his party had not "been able to adjust [their] thinking to that of the majority of the American people" (1966, 104).

Brooke's lament highlights the limits of national leadership. While Republicans can compete at the gubernatorial level in Massachusetts, they've largely been unable to translate their personal popularity into national office or leadership. Weld would eventually leave the GOP, though not until after running for governor of New York, to join the Libertarian Party. He'd return to challenge Donald Trump, but his political fortunes have largely been quixotic. Romney abandoned his centrism to chase the Republican nomination for president, eventually landing in the more hospitable climate of Utah. Baker remains popular but limited by the state's political culture and more often than not at odds with his own state party committee while maintaining warm relations with Democratic legislative leaders.

Policy Leadership: Welfare Reform, Proposition 2½, and Health Care

Postwar Massachusetts might have been viewed as an unlikely candidate for innovative public policies and a string of national leaders. "The incidence of corruption in Massachusetts public life during the 1950s, the continuous round of investigations, grand-jury proceedings, indictments, convictions, and exposés of flagrant conflict of interest have so affected public opinion that the stereotype of the politician as a crook has become common in the Bay State" (Levin 1962, 130). Largely due to efforts by good-government groups and pragmatic reformers such as State Representative Michael Dukakis as well as landmark cases from the Supreme Judicial Court, the commonwealth largely traded in its reputation as a bastion for corruption to become a leader as a laboratory of democracy.

Public policies from the Bay State have caught the attention of leaders elsewhere and in Washington, from both the Right and the Left. In 1980 Proposition 2½ empowered local government entities by reducing the power of public unions while at the same time limiting overall property-tax increases to 2.5 percent per year. Municipalities seeking an increase greater than 2.5 percent have to present voters with a plan for a Proposition 2½ override vote. Jerome Mileur and Jeffrey Sedgwick noted that the reform passed handily in 1980, with voters viewing the measure as a means to "cut property taxes and reduce government spending, though many also saw its passage as a way to force tax reform" (1983, 94).

In their study of the immediate impact of Prop 2½, authors Lawrence Susskind and Cynthia Horan begin by quoting a column by conservatives Rowland Evans and Robert Novak that "Massachusetts now rivals California as a laboratory for supply-side economic theory" (1983, 158). Quite an unusual juxtaposition for a liberal state.

Welfare reform was another signature Massachusetts-inspired policy. Michael Dukakis, defeated in the Democratic primary of 1978 by the conservative Ed King, spent time at the Harvard Kennedy School of Government preparing for his future. One of the key efforts of his second term—after coming back to defeat King in the 1982 Democratic primary—was welfare reform. King had attempted a version of a traditional work training program that had very little success. Dukakis developed a program called Employment and Training Choices (ET) "that would get welfare recipients permanently off public assistance and into entry-level private sector jobs that would launch them on productive careers" (Kenney and Turner 1988, 189). The success of ET gave Dukakis the pragmatic policy he needed that aided in his attempt at the presidential nomination in 1988: "With ET, the governor finally had the ladder that he had been seeking for many years. But he did not find peace with his historic adversaries on the political left despite the rave reviews he received for switching gears and backing a program as innovative and as progressive as ET" (Gaines and Segal 1987, 224). The Dukakis ET program became the model for the 1988 federal Family Support Act, a version of welfare reform.

Health-care reform was, perhaps, the commonwealth's greatest contribution to public policy models in contemporary American politics. In their study of state politics and government, Thomas Dye and Susan McManus note, "Massachusetts led the way with mandated health insurance" (2012, 574). The creation of universal health care in the state brought together previous opponents: "In 2006, Republican Governor Mitt Romney and the Democratic-controlled state legislature, together with an unlikely alliance of business leaders and consumer advocates, agreed on this 'bold, positive, and necessary' program" (574–75). Ted Kennedy also became an avid supporter of the initiative spurred by his former rival Romney.

As he signed the health-care reform bill that created the Massachusetts Health Connector, Romney said, "Every uninsured citizen in Massachusetts will soon have affordable health insurance and the costs of health care will be reduced" (Yelowitz and Cannon 2010, 1). Yet as he ran for president against Barack Obama in 2012, Romney turned against his own signature achievement, perhaps the first leader from the commonwealth to run away from the product of his leadership. It wasn't the only policy innovation from Massachusetts that Romney disavowed.

As a candidate against Senator Ted Kennedy in 1994, Romney projected an openness to fairness and equality for gay and lesbian Americans but quickly turned against gay marriage after becoming governor in 2002. The Supreme Judicial Court, in the landmark 2003 cases *Goodrich v. Department of Public Health*, ruled that it was unconstitutional to deny marriage rights to same-sex couples. The state became the first in the country to recognize same-sex marriages.

Policy innovation from the commonwealth has spanned the political spectrum from welfare reform and tax reform to same-sex marriage, complicating popular impressions of the state as a bastion of liberalism alone. Evan Horowitz of the *Boston Globe* noted in 2018 that the commonwealth has been an innovative policy leader in a variety of areas that spread to other states: "For the better part of two centuries we were among the most prolific states, incubating policies in a variety of areas. Here are just a few of the laws that took shape in Massachusetts before spreading to at least 30 other states: a felony ban on animal cruelty (1804), the first freedom of information act (1851), a system of probation to help people right their lives without prison (1878), a retirement system for state employees (1911), and mandatory car insurance (1945)" (2018). Horowitz worried that the commonwealth might be losing its status as a policy innovator. Since 1990 the commonwealth could boast of only twelve policy innovations—those policies adopted first by one state that then spread to others. California had thirty-seven. Theories range from a more activist federal government in areas traditionally left to states, particularly in education under both Democratic and Republican presidents, to more states practicing greater innovation.

Media and Higher Education: A Competitive and High-Profile Landscape

The history and tradition of Massachusetts' political leadership on a national level is furthered by two additional factors: the competitive media environment in the region and the presence of some of the most well-known higher-education and research institutions in the world.

The Boston metropolitan area extends from the capital city through Worcester and Providence and includes southern New Hampshire. With about 4.8 million people, it's the eleventh largest in the United States. But, according to the Pew Research Center, 2 percent of all newsroom employees work in the area, outpacing the far larger areas of Dallas, Philadelphia, and Houston (Grieco 2019). Boston is within the top-ten media markets in the country and retains a healthy media environment. While traditional print media has changed dramatically, with the number of locally owned daily newspapers on the decline, the state enjoys a competitive ecosystem that includes multiple daily newspapers and television affiliates in two main markets (Boston and Springfield), NPR stations, talk radio, and news and political magazines and journals.

Proximity to New Hampshire, a purple state, also impacts the exposure of both Massachusetts political leaders to other national media outlets and Massachusetts media to political leaders from around the country. Voter-rich southern New Hampshire is an important part of the Boston media market.

Massachusetts also remains a state where a leading print and digital news source, the *Boston Globe*, retains a DC bureau. The *Globe*'s editor, Brian McGrory, told *Politico*, "Our readership drinks in politics at the national level. . . . We know it from our readership numbers, that we need to cover national politics in an in-depth and enterprising way" (Calderone 2018).

The relative health of the media environment is also due, in part, to educational attainment in the commonwealth. Forty-two percent of Massachusetts citizens hold bachelor's degrees, while 18.7 percent hold advanced degrees, the highest among all the states. In addition, the state is a magnet for those seeking higher education. "Massachusetts has education resources rivaled only by California's," wrote Neal Peirce in the mid-1970s. "It has 117 institutions of higher learning, including fifteen which grant Ph.D. or equivalent degrees. Massachusetts attracts more students from out of state . . . than any other state" (1976, 101). The numbers have shifted over the years, but the state still has 114 institutions of higher education, and the state is the eighth most popular for the nation's college-bound students (Pohle 2015).

Massachusetts politicians in Washington have a built-in advantage shared by only a few other states: they have a national media outlet covering their work in DC. That coverage is fed nationally with *Globe* bureau reporters appearing on national networks such as CNN to offer analysis. But it is also fed locally back to the Boston media market that crucially overlaps with the first-in-the-nation primary state, New Hampshire.

In addition, Massachusetts has an oversized influence on the education of national political leadership. According to *Harvard Magazine*, crimson is a popular color on Capitol Hill, with fifty-three members of the 116th Congress holding Harvard degrees. It's by far the most popular school in national politics, which stands to reason as it's the most prominent. *Politico* research has Massachusetts and California at the top of the list for alma maters for members of Congress at the undergraduate level. "Massachusetts was the most popular out-of-state college choice—34 members who attended college in Massachusetts came from other states" (Thomas 2019). College proves formative in political socialization (Alwin, Cohen, and Newcomb 1991), and Harvard, embedded in Massachusetts political culture, has reach among politicians exceeding all other states.

Harvard figures (alumni, faculty) have served as secretaries in every cabinet position, from Thomas Pickering as secretary of state in 1795 (one of eleven from Harvard) through each of the fifteen traditional agencies with the exception of Veterans Affairs. Forty percent of the individuals to serve as cabinet secretaries to Barack Obama had Massachusetts connections either as political figures there or via their education or both. Of the thirteen who had Massachusetts connections, just under 70 percent were Harvard connections, the exceptions being Wellesley College (Hillary Clinton), Boston University School of Law (Gary Locke), and Boston College and the Massachusetts Institute of Technology (Ernest Moniz as an undergraduate and faculty member). Among recent presidents, George H. W. Bush was born in Massachusetts and went to high school at the exclusive Phillips Academy in Andover, Massachusetts. His son and forty-third president of the United States, George W. Bush, also a Phillips alum, received his MBA from Harvard, the same locale where Obama earned his law degree.

Conclusion

Politics in Massachusetts is like its professional sports teams, historical and serious. Given that the state is one of just over a dozen to host all four major sports leagues, it's an important metaphor. Boston sports teams are second only to New York in the number of overall league championships, and, since 2000, Boston teams combined have won more often (twelve times) than those of any other city, and it is the only city that has won in each league at least once. In the six presidential elections held during the same time, two have featured candidates from Massachusetts (Kerry and Romney) and five more who were educated, in part, in Massachusetts (Al Gore, Bush, Obama, Hillary Clinton, and Tim Kaine).

Massachusetts has been the stomping grounds for prospective national leaders since the founding, and it is as elementary to the state's political culture as the divisions between "workers" and "managers" discussed throughout this volume. National political aspirations do not harm candidates for office here. Ted Kennedy never took less than 55 percent of the popular vote, and that was during his first general election campaign in 1962 when his brother was in the White House. The seemingly sole critique that was often repeated by the Republican opposition to Elizabeth Warren's reelection campaign in 2018 was that she intended on running for president in 2020. She largely dodged the issue and still took home 60 percent of the vote. Seth Moulton unsuccessfully ran for the Democratic presidential nomination in 2019 and won reelection to his Massachusetts congressional seat in 2020 with 64.8 percent of the vote. Citizens here expect their leaders to have national aspirations, and the political subcultures that compete for influence in Massachusetts reinforce upward trajectories.

Among the nation's political class, Massachusetts' educational institutions loom large, and the state has a robust media culture with national exposure due, in part but not exclusively, to its proximity to New Hampshire. What then might explain why Massachusetts pols came up short in the 2020 Democratic primary? Many factors exist: a crowded Democratic field, a poorly run campaign by Moulton, a far too late entry by Patrick, Warren peaking too early, and the quixotic nature of Bill Weld postgovernorship. But it is also far too early to conclude that Massachusetts political figures are spent on the national level. The next class of national leadership—Clark, Warren, Markey, Pressley, and others—suggests the 2020 elections were an anomaly and Massachusetts will continue to be an exceptional state for its contributions to national political leadership.

WORKS CITED

Adams, John Quincy. 1825. "Inaugural Address." https://avalon.law.yale.edu/19th_century/qadams.asp.

Alexander, John K., and Samuel Adams. 2002. *America's Revolutionary Politician.* New York: Rowman & Littlefield.

Alwin, Duane F., Ronald L. Cohen, and Theodore M. Newcomb. 1991. In *Political Attitudes over the Life Span.* Madison: University of Wisconsin Press.

Barone, Michael, and Richard E. Cohen. 2007. *The Almanac of American Politics, 2008.* Washington, DC: National Journal Group.

Bidgood, Jess. 2020. "Katherine Clark Rises to Fourth-Ranking House Democrat." *Boston Globe,* November 18, 2020. https://www.bostonglobe.com/2020/11/18/nation/katherine-clark-rises-fourth-ranking-house-democrat-after-winning-leadership-election/.

Boorstin, Daniel. 1958. *The Americans: The Colonial Experience.* New York: Random House.

Bremer, Francis J., and John Winthrop. 2005. *America's Forgotten Founding Father.* New York: Oxford University Press.

Brooke, Edward W. 1966. *The Challenge of Change: Crisis in Our Two-Party System.* Boston: Little, Brown.

Calderone, Michael. 2018. "Morning Media." *Politico,* December 4, 2018. https://www.politico.com/media/newsletters/morning-media/2018/12/04/boston-globe-dc-plans-democrats-fox-news-candidate-zucker-001673/.

Cannellos, Peter, ed. 2009. *Last Lion: The Fall and Rise of Ted Kennedy.* New York: Simon & Schuster.

Cunningham, Lillian. 2016. "The Case of the Missing John Adams Monument." *Washington Post,* January 17, 2016. https://www.washingtonpost.com/news/on-leadership/wp/2016/01/17/the-case-of-the-missing-john-adams-monument/.

Davidson, Roger H., and Walter J. Oleszek. 1990. *Congress and Its Members.* 3rd ed. Washington, DC: Congressional Quarterly.

Davidson, Roger H., Walter J. Oleszek, and Frances E. Lee. 2008. *Congress and Its Members.* 11th ed. Washington, DC: CQ Press.

Dye, Thomas R., and Susan A. McManus. 2012. *Politics in States and Communities.* 14th ed. Boston: Pearson.

Fischer, David Hackett. 1989. *Albion's Seed: Four British Folkways in America*. New York: Oxford University Press.

Friedman, Lawrence, and Lynnea Thody. 2011. *The Massachusetts State Constitution*. New York: Oxford University Press.

Gaines, Richard, and Michael Segal. 1987. *Dukakis and the Reform Impulse*. Boston: Quinlan Press.

Grieco, Elizabeth. 2019. "One-in-Five U.S. Newsroom Employees Live in New York, Los Angeles or DC." *FactTank: News in the Numbers*, October 24, 2019. https://www.pewsresearch.org/fact-tank/2019/10/24/one-in-five-u-s-newsroom-employees-live-in-new-york-los-angeles-or-d-c/.

Hogarty, Richard A. 2002. *Massachusetts Politics and Public Policy: Studies in Power and Leadership*. Amherst: University of Massachusetts Press.

Horowitz, Evan. 2018. "Massachusetts Was a Policy Trailblazer. Not Anymore." *Boston Globe*, June 3, 2018. https://www.bostonglobe.com/metro/massachusetts/2018/06/03/massachusetts-was-policy-trailblazer-not-anymore/d5yJUA4ANbyCq8gvsvWajK/story.html.

Kenneally, James Joseph. 2003. *A Compassionate Conservative: A Political Biography of Joseph W. Martin, Jr.: Speaker of the US House of Representatives*. Lanham, MD: Lexington Books.

Kennedy, John F. 1961. "Address of President-Elect John F. Kennedy to a Joint Convention of the General Court of the Commonwealth of Massachusetts." JFK Library, January 19, 1961. https://www.jfklibrary.org/archives/other-resources/john-f-kennedy-speeches/massachusetts-general-court-19610109.

Kenney, Charles, and Robert L. Turner. 1988. *Dukakis: An American Odyssey*. Boston: Houghton Mifflin.

Kornacki, Steve. 2018. *The Red and the Blue: The 1990s and the Birth of Political Tribalism*. New York: HarperCollins.

Levin, Murray. 1962. *The Compleat Politician: Political Strategy in Massachusetts*. New York: Bobbs-Merrill.

Lucas, Peter. 1983. *Pols & Politics: Collected Columns of the "Boston Herald"'s Peter Lucas*. Boston: Boston Herald.

Maier, Pauline. 1980. *The Old Revolutionaries: Political Lives in the Age of Samuel Adams*. New York: Alfred A. Knopf.

Mileur, Jerome M., and Jeffrey L. Sedgwick. 1983. "Fiscal Policy in Massachusetts under Proposition 2 1/2." *Publius* 12:93–102.

Nelson, Garrison. 1999. "Irish Identity Politics: The Reinvention of Speaker John W. McCormack of Boston." *New England Journal of Public Policy* 15, no. 1: 7–34.

———. 2014. "John Boehner's Uneasy Crown." *Political Sciences and Public Affairs* 2, no. 2: 1–2.

Nelson, Garrison, and John William McCormack. 2017. *A Political Biography*. London: Bloomsbury.

Ostermeier, Eric. 2017. "Mitt Romney Prepares for Unusual Senate Bid." *Smart Politics*, September 14, 2017. https://smartpolitics.lib.umn.edu/2017/09/14/mitt-romney-prepares-for-unusual-us-senate-bid/.

Peirce, Neal R. 1976. *The New England States: People, Politics, and Power in the Six New England States*. New York: W. W. Norton.

Pohle, Alison. 2015. "Massachusetts Is the 8th Most Popular Destination for College Students." *Boston.com*, September 1, 2015. https://www.boston.com/news/education/2015/09/01/massachusetts-is-the-8th-most-popular-destination-for-college-students.

Public Broadcasting Services (PBS). n.d. "People and Ideas: Early American Groups." *The American Experience*. https://www.pbs.org/wgbh/americanexperience/features/godinamerica -early-american-groups/.

Saltonstall, Leverett. 1976. *Salty: Recollections of a Yankee in Politics*. Boston: Boston Globe.

Seeyle, John. 1998. *Memory's Nation: The Place of Plymouth Rock*. Chapel Hill: University of North Carolina Press.

Smith, Steven S. 1987. "O'Neill's Legacy for the House." *Brookings Review* 5, no. 1: 28–36.

Standells. 1965. *Dirty Water*. Tower Records, 1965, vinyl.

Susskind, Lawrence, and Cynthia Horan. 1983. "Proposition 2 1/2: The Response to Tax Restrictions in Massachusetts." *Proceedings of the Academy of Political Science* 35, no. 1: 158–71.

Thomas, Taylor Miller. 2019. "Alma Maters of the 116th Congress." *PolitcoPro Datapoint on Education*, March 6, 2019. https://www.accesslex.org/sites/default/files/2019-03 /POLITICO%20Data%20Point%20-%20116%20Congress%20Education.pdf.

Winthrop, John. 1630. "A Model of Christian Charity (1630)." Collections of the MA Historical Society, Boston, 1838, 3rd ser, 7:31–48. http://history.hanover.edu/texts/winthmod.html.

Yelowitz, Aaron, and Michael F. Cannon. 2010. "The Massachusetts Health Plan: Much Pain, Little Gain." *Policy Analysis* 657:1–16.

PART II

Institutions

CHAPTER 4

THE MASSACHUSETTS GENERAL COURT
Exceptionally Old-School

Shannon Jenkins

The epicenter of political power in Massachusetts is the General Court, the official name of the state legislature. For decades, the Democrats have held veto-proof majorities in the legislature; as such, the important divisions in Massachusetts currently are those within the Democratic Party, rather than those that separate Democrats and Republicans. Because of the tradition of one-party dominance in the state legislature, two of the most powerful figures in Massachusetts politics are the Speaker of the house and the president of the senate, and the fault lines between these two bodies has become increasingly prominent in recent years. Interestingly, Massachusetts' legislative leaders rank fairly low (thirty-six out of fifty) on measures of formal leadership power (Clucas 2001) but rank at or near the top in rankings of perceived leadership power (first in 1981 and third in 1995) based on surveys of state legislators (Clucas 2007). Thus, power is exceptionally concentrated in the General Court, and to understand political power and politics in Massachusetts, one needs to understand how parties and legislative leaders wield power in the legislature.

Contrary to the vision of Massachusetts as a bastion of progressive, liberal politics, leadership in the legislature has tended to be fairly conservative, reluctant to loosen the reins and distribute power broadly throughout the chamber. Rather, leaders in Massachusetts, particularly in the house, tend to rule with an iron fist, distributing perks and benefits to friends and allies and keeping rank-and-file legislators in check. This system has also been marked with corruption, with three recent house Speakers indicted and a recent senate president being forced to resign under a cloud of suspicion and allegations. This exceptional concentration of power in legislative leaders' hands, particularly in the house, along with a willingness to disregard the rules, means that power in the legislature is wielded in a top-down fashion rather than coming from the bottom in a progressive flourishing of ideas. Furthermore, all roads for policy change must meet approval of the singularly most powerful person in the state: the Speaker of the house. For better and for worse, then, the story of contemporary Massachusetts politics centers on the General Court. While both the Massachusetts and the U.S. Constitutions were designed with legislative supremacy in mind, only the Massachusetts variety has endured. As the balance of power in Washington shifted, and indeed continues to shift, to the chief executive, Massachusetts legislative leaders remain firmly in control on Beacon Hill. In Washington divided control of the political branches has produced gridlock and open partisan combat. At the Massachusetts State House, governors of both parties carefully avoid antagonizing the legislature.

The Institution of the General Court

HISTORY

The structure, function, and powers of the General Court have deep historical roots, dating back to the 1600s. Indeed, the name of the state legislature in Massachusetts, the General Court, reflects the fact that the legislature possessed both legislative and judicial powers during parts of its colonial history (Massachusetts Legislature 2002). Under the original charters granted to Massachusetts, the Crown tried to vest much authority in the colonial governor and his assistants, who were known originally as the Court of Assistants. Colonists fought back against this by establishing representative assemblies, and it is in these early assemblies that one can find the origins of the Massachusetts state legislature.

The first General Court was established in 1634; the charter initially stipulated that the General Court needed the concurrence of the governor and the Court of Assistants to meet, but after pressure from the colonists, the right of the General Court to meet independently and separately from the Court of Assistants was established. The right to meet independently and the requirement that bills must be accepted by both bodies were established after a dispute between the two bodies over the ownership of a pig, perhaps the first and only example of porcine-induced institutional change (Moran 1895). Because of this, some mark the establishment of a bicameral legislature in 1644 (Squire and Hamm 2005).

Massachusetts was given a new charter in 1691, and for others this new charter marked the establishment of a bicameral legislature, creating a lower chamber and upper chamber appointed independently of the Crown (LWV 1970). Thus, while the development of a bicameral legislature sprang out of "peculiar circumstances" (Moran 1895), these unique circumstances became an exemplar for the nation. Under the new charter, the house was elected by "freemen"; the house then selected the councillors who functioned as the upper chamber. The governor, selected by the Crown, also sat with the councillors (Schuck 1961). The newly created legislature was adept at wielding two important financial powers granted to it: setting the governor's and judges' salaries and appropriating money. There were frequent struggles between the legislature and the governor over the payment of his salary, and the general fund was somewhat frequently empty due to disputes between the legislature and the governor about the appropriation and expenditure of money (LWV 1970). Schuck says this was known as the period of "perpetual discordance" (1961, 18). Thus, from the start, the struggle between legislative and executive power was at the heart of Massachusetts politics; given that executive power was associated with the Crown and legislative power was associated with the fledgling colony, it is no surprise that the original constitution, as drafted, struck a balance in favor of the legislature. Schuck states, "The Massachusetts Constitution writers had clearly established the General Court as the paramount institution in state government in 1780" (1961, 25).

After the adoption of the constitution, described in chapter 6, government in Massachusetts remained limited. "The citizens of Massachusetts had reserved to themselves all powers not specifically assigned to the state or nation, and they were zealous in delegating only such powers as were necessary to establish a framework of law and order under which individuals could develop freely. In the period from 1790 to 1820, the inhabitants of the growing Commonwealth needed little assistance or regulation from their newly established government" (LWV 1970, 22–23). But as the economy transformed with the Industrial Revolution, demands on state government increased with calls for universal education, regulation of working conditions, and more. While most of the growth of state government in this period occurred in the executive branch, the state legislature also increased in capacity and remained dominant by retaining some degree of control over the agencies, departments, and commissions created in the executive branch. Importantly, during the late 1800s and early 1900s, as other states moved to strengthen the governorship, Massachusetts remained largely insulated from these developments, as Schuck argues: "Almost no legislative power was clipped; no new gubernatorial powers were added" (1961, 34).

With the advent of the Progressive Era, there was intense debate over the appropriate role and powers of the governor, culminating in the 1917–19 Constitutional Convention. Voters approved a variety of amendments from this convention that both increased the power of the governor, including the line-item veto, and decreased the power of the legislature, with the adoption of the referendum and initiative. The period following these changes may be the only time when there was somewhat of a balance of power between the legislature and the governor. Writing in 1961 at the conclusion of a Tufts University Symposium on Massachusetts State Government and Responsibility, Robbins wrote that the people of Massachusetts "look first and foremost to the governorship, whoever may be the holder of that high office, for strength of initiative, creative and responsible leadership, and popular guidance in assessing the problems which confront the state government and developing acceptable public responses and ultimate solutions" (5). During this period of transition from Republican to Democratic Party dominance in the legislature, the governor rose in prominence in Massachusetts politics, as compared to the legislature. Yet even during this period of supposed gubernatorial dominance, Robbins questioned, "Why is it that the Governor, assigned under our Constitution to be our 'supreme executive Magistrate,' in reality is far from being supreme in his legitimate sphere, so often falls short of our expectations or fails utterly in performing the key role in which he is cast?" (6).

Ultimately, then, while there has been debate about the appropriate balance of power between the legislature and the governor, this debate has nearly always been decided in favor of the legislature. As Schuck argues, the Massachusetts governor is little more, but a good deal less, than his colonial prototype and rarely more, but often less, than his contemporaries in the other forty-nine states (1961, 11). Even when the "most popular governor in the U.S." (Cillizza 2017) holds the office, the legislature is the dominant institution in state politics, and the legislature still does mostly what the legislature wants. In this way, the Massachusetts General Court stands out from other state legislatures; the combination of legislative prominence in the constitution and single-party dominance in the legislature gives the legislature a much more prominent role than in other states.

LEGISLATIVE STRUCTURE, ORGANIZATION, AND PROCESS

Anyone familiar with the structure of the national government in the United States will be familiar with the structure of the Massachusetts legislature as established in the constitution, in large part because the Massachusetts Constitution served as an inspiration for the U.S. Constitution. The Massachusetts Constitution establishes a bicameral legislature, continuing the form of government established during the colonial period. The upper chamber is the senate; it consists of 40 members. Members were originally selected from districts that were proportionate to the amount paid in taxes, but they are now elected from districts based on population. The house is the lower chamber, and, like Congress, it was designed to be closer to the people and more equal. Initially, house districts were based around towns, with variation in representation based on town population; as with the senate, districts are now based on population. Originally, the house had 200 members, but in 1978 that number was reduced to 160.

Like the U.S. Congress, there are two important differences in the authority of these chambers in Massachusetts. First, money bills must originate in the house, and, second, the house has the power to impeach, while the senate holds the power to convict. Unlike Congress and most other state legislatures, the Massachusetts Senate does not have the power to confirm executive appointments; instead, that power rests with the Governor's Council, described in more detail in chapter 5. Since its inception, the General Court has met annually; initially, sessions spanned just one year, but now, like in the U.S. Congress, sessions span two years. In 2021, the General Court convened its 192nd session.

Generally speaking, the Massachusetts Constitution vests extensive authority in the General Court. The first part of the constitution is a declaration of rights (unlike in the U.S. Constitution where these rights come at the end as the first ten amendments in the Bill of Rights), but the first chapter of the second part of the Massachusetts Constitution focuses on the legislature. Other branches of government come after; while this distinction might seem trivial, it is not. The framers of the Massachusetts Constitution consciously put individual rights first to signal their importance, and the placement of the legislature before other bodies is a purposeful statement about the arrangement of the formal institutions of government. In addition to the broad delegation of authority in the constitution, amendments such as the power to charter cities, provide zoning for towns and cities, and take land have expanded the power of the legislature. Provisions for home rule, described in chapter 2, have empowered local governments at the expense of the legislature somewhat, but generally speaking the General Court still exerts considerable control over local governments in the commonwealth, much to their chagrin. The other amendment that has weakened the power of the legislature somewhat was the addition of the initiative and referendum, the focus of chapter 9.

As with the structure of the legislature, the internal organization of the General Court should seem familiar to those familiar with the organization of the U.S. Congress. Indeed, in some respects, the General Court resembles the U.S. Congress more than it does other state legislatures. Both chambers have nearly complete control over their own organization; they are the final judges of qualifications for office, choose their own officers, and determine their own rules of procedure (LWV 1970). The leader of the house is the Speaker, while the leader of the senate is the senate president. The Massachusetts legislature is fairly well resourced as well. Political scientists often talk about the capacity of legislatures using a measure known as legislative professionalism; this concept focuses on the resources available to legislators, including the time they have to do their jobs, the benefits (including things like salary, per diems, and other perks) they receive while performing their job, and the staff afforded to them to help them do their jobs. Based on these measures, the Massachusetts General Court is largely recognized as one of the most professional legislatures in the nation, ranking as the second most professional state legislature in one study, bested by only California (Squire 2017). In this sense, then, Massachusetts seems to have more in common with the U.S. Congress than it does our neighbor to the north, New Hampshire, which ranks as the least professional state legislature. Massachusetts legislators are paid well, have annual sessions that meet most of the year, and have staffers at their disposal. For instance, in 2019 Massachusetts legislators received a 5.9 percent raise, bringing their base salary to more than $66,000 (with opportunities to earn more, as described below); they are eligible for pensions after meeting certain requirements and receive generous health benefits (Murphy 2018a; CSG 2018). As one Massachusetts legislator noted, "We're here to get things done" (NCSL n.d.).

In terms of legislative process, the legislative process in the General Court is fairly unremarkable on paper. Bills are introduced in each chamber, heard by committees, and then voted on by the floor. If the chambers disagree (and the chambers nearly always disagree in recent years), then a conference committee is needed. Conference committees play an important role in Massachusetts. One senator noted, "Everything ends up going to conference"; furthermore, the conference committees do not meet in public, and their reports cannot be amended on the floor (NCSL n.d.). Once both chambers agree, the bill is sent to the governor. If the governor vetoes the bill or uses his line-item veto, the legislature may override that veto with a two-thirds majority vote. Given large Democratic majorities in the chamber and the tight party control over members (see below), legislators can override the governor's vetoes easily, so the governor wields this veto only occasionally, preferring to work to incorporate suggestions into the bill during the process. Indeed, Governor Baker, who has been dubbed the most popular governor in America by some, issued no line-item vetoes to the fiscal year 2020 state budget, perhaps due to the fact that during previous years in his tenure, the legislature regularly overrode those vetoes (Mohl 2019b).

But there are some relatively unique features of the General Court that are worth highlighting here, and it is also worth examining how well the legislative process is functioning. One unique feature of the Massachusetts legislative process is the "right of free petition." Dating back to 1641, the people's right to introduce legislation was preserved in the 1780 constitution; under this provision, all Massachusetts citizens can introduce or refile a bill in the legislature (Davis 2017). In most other states, only legislators can file legislation. Often, Massachusetts legislators will file these bills "by request," indicating they do not necessarily support this citizen request. While these bills do not generally advance very far in the legislative process absent support of a state legislator, they can attract a good deal of attention, particularly when the legislator introducing the bill forgets to indicate it is a citizen petition. Such was the case in 2019, when Boston representative Daniel Hunt introduced a bill to make it illegal to call someone a bitch; Hunt was introducing the bill on behalf of a constituent but forgot to check the box indicating this. There was a good deal of outcry about the bill; Hunt was reported to have received nasty emails "by the hundreds" (Hawkins 2019). But as Hunt noted on Twitter, "One of the responsibilities of all Representatives is to serve as a conduit for direct petitions from our constituents" (Brown 2019). By one estimate, there were 192 citizen petitions out of more than 6,000 total bills filed as of October 2019; "almost all of them—if not *all* of them—will ultimately die a quiet death" (Brown 2019).

Perhaps the most notable difference in organization and process, and one that makes Massachusetts fairly unique, is the committee system. While little is known about the early development of committee systems in state legislatures, the evidence suggests that committees and a committee system developed early in Massachusetts, sometime in the late 1700s (Squire and Hamm 2005, 106). Currently, Massachusetts has a joint committee system, whereby bills are heard in committees consisting of members of both the house and the senate. Joint committees typically have six senators and eleven representatives, with the leaders of each chamber appointing a cochair for each committee. Just two other state legislatures, Connecticut and Maine, have a similar system (NCSL 2018). Squire calls these joint committee systems "evolutionary deviations" in the development of committee systems; their origins are not entirely clear but are almost certainly due to the long history of these legislatures in New England states (2012, 281). Indeed, given that Maine was originally part of Massachusetts, this deviation presumably originates almost entirely from the Bay State.

While these joint committees must hold a hearing on all bills submitted to the committee, this doesn't mean a full or timely hearing or vote on each measure. Committees can vote to issue a "study order"; while this technically authorizes the committee to meet to "study" the measure during a recess, committees almost never meet or study these bills during a recess. As such, in the General Court, a study order is the standard way for committees to kill bills. While some argue for joint committee systems on the basis of efficiency, claiming that having just one set of committees, hearings, and such will expedite the legislative process (Squire and Moncrief 2015, 119), research suggests that members of chambers with joint committee systems, particularly members of the senate, were more likely to identify procedural inefficiencies with these committees than members of chambers without joint committees (Francis and Riddlesperger 1982). Senators' displeasure with these systems largely stems from the fact that the joint committee system clearly favors the house. While house members claim that senators have a higher proportion of committee seats (35 percent) as compared to their overall membership in the General Court (20 percent), the fact is that the house has clear majorities on each committee, and they often use this to their advantage by holding bills they do not want to consider in the committees (Jonas and Mohl 2016). In 2016 then senate president Stanley Rosenberg threatened to "go nuclear" and change the joint rules to split committees between the chambers at the outset of the 2015 session. For instance, Rosenberg said in 2016 that three of the four major bills passed in the previous legislative session came to the senate from the house and the committees with very little time for review; he argued, "That's not fair to the Senate. It's not fair to the public. It's not fair to the process" (Jonas and Mohl 2016). Indeed, the joint committee system remains a major bone of contention between the two chambers, described in more detail below.

Overall, then, the organization, structure, and processes in the Massachusetts legislature resemble those of Congress and indeed many other state legislatures in the United States. This is due at least in part to the fact that the Massachusetts Constitution and bicameral legislature served as an inspiration for the U.S. Constitution (Herwick 2016). The General Court is also widely recognized as a highly professional and well-functioning institution. However, it does have some unique characteristics, such as the joint committee system, that sets it apart from other state legislatures. It is also more prominent in state politics, as compared to legislatures in other states. This, in conjunction with a history of one-party dominance in the legislature, has allowed chamber leaders to consolidate power and further extend the outsize role of the legislature in state politics, particularly in recent years. As a result, it's worth examining the role of parties and party leadership in the house and the senate before turning to the role of the General Court in Massachusetts politics more generally.

THE ROLE OF PARTIES AND PARTY LEADERS IN THE GENERAL COURT

The Massachusetts state legislature is characterized by a strong degree of leader control over the legislature. "The party organizations sit astride the channels through which all legislation must flow" (Lockard 1959, 161). This is attributable, in part, to the lack of party competition in the state; since 1978 Democratic majorities in the state legislature have never dropped below 75 percent. Mileur argues that Massachusetts politics has been organized by a "succession of one-party regimes that, once in place, have remained in place for an extended period of time" (1997, 78). For example, in the 2018 election, nearly two-thirds of all state legislators ran unopposed in the general election (Brown 2018). From the 1920s to the late 1950s, there was a brief period of two-party competition in the state and in the state legislature, during a transition from Republican Party dominance to Democratic Party dominance. Writing during this period, Lockard described a "Republican party organization [that] is manifestly more unified and powerful than the Democratic state organization" (1959, 157). This is in stark contrast to current times; in late 2018, a Republican state committee person wrote an email to fellow committee members calling the state Republican Party "all but irrelevant" (Murphy 2018b), and polling data from the same period indicates that just 31 percent of state voters viewed the party favorably (MassInc Polling 2018).

Thus, once a legislator wins a position in the state legislature, that job is generally theirs for as long as they want it. Life in this position can be made more or less attractive by the perks and benefits bestowed by party leaders, such that these party leaders tend to dominate in the legislature. For instance, writing in the 1950s, Lockard (1959) identifies patronage as a critical weapon used by both the governor and the state legislature to entice party loyalty. Legislators were given jobs for relatives, friends, supporters, and constituents in return for supporting the positions of both private interests and the party. While patronage is technically now illegal in Massachusetts, that does not mean that patronage as a mechanism for ensuring party loyalty has completely abated, as described below. These days, the more common mechanism for ensuring party loyalty is the dispensing of perks, which include plum assignments in the party leadership and on committees that command significant supplemental salaries. Additionally, one former lobbyist notes, "Those who opposed the Speaker (or who simply annoy him) will get terrible committee assignments, one staffer, and cramped, dank offices hidden away in the State House basement. These committees do little, have few bills, and have no authority. Meanwhile, powerful committee chairs get additional staff, nice offices, and the opportunity to hobnob with leadership members" (Sego 2018).

For a good period of time, then, the Massachusetts legislature has been characterized by a fairly high level of party unity in roll-call voting (Jewell 1955). Lockard argues that in the Massachusetts legislature, "loyalty to the party and to its general ideological orientation, if not a sine qua non of longevity, seems nevertheless to accompany it. Legislators adapt to the surroundings, and the role of party is such in Massachusetts that adaptation to it is nearly mandatory" (1959, 151). He ranks Massachusetts among the top half-dozen states in terms of party influence over legislators and policy making.

A key reason that parties are so strong in the Massachusetts legislature is due to the leaders who wield their power and enforce party discipline in the legislature. As noted in the introduction, while party leaders in the General Court rank low as compared to other states on measures of formal power, they rank near the top on measures of informal power. In surveys of legislators in the state, more than 90 percent of legislators ranked the party leaders as having the strongest influence over policy outcomes, as compared to other political actors in the state (Battista 2011). Phillip Sego (2018), a former lobbyist in the Massachusetts legislature for the Sierra Club, published a scathing indictment of the operations of the General Court, stating, "Don't confuse what goes on in this building with democracy." Over the past forty years, Sego argues, leaders have become increasingly controlling, with a leadership style that is "more dictatorial and less democratic" than their predecessors. Two former lawmakers characterized this as a "culture of utter deference," arguing that the house had become "the personal fiefdom of the individual in the speaker's office" (Hecht and Provost 2020). The top leaders of the majority party, which over the past forty years has been the Democratic Party, tightly control all aspects of legislative life in the General Court. George Bachrach, a former state senator argues, "The big problem on Beacon Hill is the concentration of power in the hands of the Speaker and Senate President, who appoint all leaders in their respective branches, determine how much they get paid through the dispensation of leadership stipends, and have total control over the flow of legislation" (Mohl 2019c). To start, they award party leadership positions and plum committee assignments to their closest allies. For instance, Robert DeLeo easily won reelection as the house Speaker in 2019; one legislator, Russell Holmes (D–Mattapan), who has opposed DeLeo and proposed some rules changes in the house for the new term, noted that several legislators had wanted to vote for his rules changes but told him they couldn't "for fear they would lose their leadership positions and the $15,000 to $30,000 stipends that accompany them" (Mohl 2019a). DeLeo stepped down in 2020, and he was replaced by a longtime ally, Representative Ron Mariano, a seventy-year-old representative who has been a member of the house for three decades; progressives were disappointed, bemoaning the continuation of an all-white leadership team that is con-servative in nature (Difazio 2020). As discussed in greater detail in chapter 11, women and women of color have generally been locked out of power in the state legislature; indeed, there has never been a woman Speaker of the house in Massachusetts.

As another example, former state representative Jay Kaufman (D–Lexing-ton) claims that former Speaker DeLeo told him that if he voted against a bill to raise the state's gas tax, Kaufman would lose his position as chair of the Revenue Committee; DeLeo disputed Kaufman's claims, calling him a "liar" (Metzger 2019). Holmes has used the terms *dictatorship* and *kingdom* to describe the former house Speaker (Smith 2019).

The leader works with an inner circle, and this inner circle makes key decisions—which bills advance, which projects get funded, when hearings and votes happen, and more. As Sego argues, "Nothing gets voted on without the speaker and his inner circle approving it" (2018). A National Conference of State Legislatures (NCSL) (n.d.) survey of state legislators confirms this picture. Summarizing operations in the house, they argue that DeLeo ran a tight ship, relying on his chief of staff, the majority leader, and the Ways and Means Committee to guide decisions. Committees do not move bills forward unless the Speaker supports them and delays votes on legislators' important bills in order to ensure party loyalty, which led critics to say DeLeo dictated priorities to his members and stifled meaningful debate (NCSL n.d.). All indications are that business will continue as usual under newly elected Speaker Mariano; Mariano has been described as a "back-room deal maker" (Schoenberg 2020). Two outgoing members of the house called Mariano's election a "cynical power grab" and the "culmination of insider politics" (Hecht and Provost 2020).

Previously, the senate and house leadership functioned in similar ways; Senate President William Bulger, who served in that role from 1978 to 1996, ruled the senate with the same iron-fist approach as the house leaders. Senator Bulger was the brother of Whitey Bulger, former mobster and one of the Federal Bureau of Investigation's most wanted criminals; one article compared the two, noting that "at the peak of their powers, they controlled their respective constituencies the same way—with fear and intimidation" (Seeyle 2013). But in the past few decades, the senate's mode of operation has diverged from that in the house. While leadership in the house has become increasingly concentrated in the hands of the few, the senate has seen the opposite trend. For instance, former senate president Stanley Rosenberg sought to create a more inclusive style in the senate; he told the NCSL, "We're trying to undo the centralized power of the president's office; it's hard and it has to be gradual. It's a cultural shift that requires senators to realize that with additional authority comes responsibility" (n.d.). The NCSL offers the example of Rosenberg bringing a charter-school bill to the floor of the senate with only twelve of the twenty-one votes that were needed to pass; during the debate over this bill, Rosenberg met with each senator to find out what they wanted in the bill, adding amendments until they got to the twenty-one votes needed to pass the bill. Rosenberg's successor as senate president, Karen Spilka, has followed in this path; in 2019 she described her plans to "delegate many decisions" (Smith 2019). Perhaps this sort of leadership style is more possible in the smaller 40-member senate as opposed to the 160-member house. Some criticized Rosenberg's democratization of power, arguing the senate has become less effective vis-à-vis the house because of this. Ultimately, the NCSL argued that what legislators want is a better balance between leadership control and members' freedom of action.

The difference in leadership styles is not the only source of friction between the two chambers. While the senate has traditionally been the more conservative body, in recent years the senate has become the more liberal body. Mileur (1997) argues that the election of leadership in 1996 changed the ideological tenor of the chambers. Incoming senate president Thomas Birmingham was more liberal than outgoing senate president William Bulger and incoming house Speaker Thomas Finneran more conservative than outgoing house Speaker Charles Flaherty, which affected relations between the two bodies (Mileur 1997). It is perhaps this divergence in ideological positions that has driven the difference in leadership, culture, and process. As Murphy (2016) notes, the key divides between the house and senate these days are basically ideology and process. Thus, the senate accuses the house leadership of using its tight party discipline and control over the legislative process to bottle up the more liberal proposals of the senate. The Speaker's outsize role in policy making extends beyond the legislature, too. Not only does the house Speaker use his power to control the General Court, but he can also use it to influence other political leaders in the state. For instance, former governor Deval Patrick testified that then house Speaker Salvatore DiMasi pressured him into approving two state contracts that were important to the Speaker (LeBlanc 2011).

Why was the former governor testifying about this? These contracts, federal prosecutors successfully argued, were part of a kickback scheme that earned DiMasi $65,000 from the companies who secured those contracts; the former Speaker was ultimately convicted by a federal jury on charges of conspiracy, extortion, and theft of honest services by fraud in 2011 (LeBlanc 2011). In fact, three recent Speakers of the house, Salvatore DiMasi, Thomas Finneran, and Charles Flaherty, were all convicted of felonies committed while they were in office. DiMasi's predecessor, Finneran, was convicted of obstruction of justice for giving false testimony about his role in the redistricting process in 2000; Finneran lied about the extent of his role in this process, claiming he played little part, while the records showed he played a considerable role in developing plans that diluted the power of minority voters in order to protect the interests of incumbent legislators, including himself (Jenkins and Pettey 2013). Finneran's predecessor, Flaherty, was forced from office after pleading guilty to federal income tax evasion. This has led to some concerns about the concentration of power in the hands of this office; as LeBlanc asks, is "the power of the office just too great a temptation for mischief—or worse?" (2011). Previously, house rules had limited the number of years a Speaker could serve to eight (rules DeLeo pushed for when he assumed the role), but DeLeo pushed through rules changes in 2015 that allowed him to continue in this position beyond eight years. DeLeo was the longest continuously serving Speaker in Massachusetts history (Stout 2019), before he stepped down in 2020.

Moreover, a culture of corruption is not a new development in the history of the General Court. Writing about the early to mid-1900s, Lockard says that in "Massachusetts the open employment of patronage promises seems to play a significant role in the recruitment of extra legislative votes. . . . More frequently [than perks for legislators themselves] involved are jobs for supporters and constituents with which a member can mend a legislative fence" (1959, 160). While patronage is now technically illegal in Massachusetts, it was the focus of another recent government scandal; in 2016 the *Boston Globe* revealed that the probation commissioner, John O'Brien, hired hundreds of politically connected but not otherwise qualified people in his department, including friends and family members of Speaker DeLeo and his deputies (Allan and Farragher 2010). In 1981 a special state commission to investigate government corruption concluded, "Bribery, extortion, tax evasion, illegal campaign contributions, and the laundering of money to disguise its origins were commonplace and there is a tacit understanding between public servants and private professionals that this is how business is done in Massachusetts" (Knight 1981). Corruption and controversy have not been limited to the legislative leaders of the house. In 2018 Senate President Stanley Rosenberg was forced to resign after an ethics report found he had "abrogated his leadership responsibilities" by allowing his husband, Bryon Hefner, who had pleaded guilty to racially and sexually harassing multiple men while bragging to them about his influence over the senate, "unfettered access to the Senate" (Miller and Stout 2018). In 2017 former senate assistant majority leader Brian Joyce was arrested for more than a hundred counts of using his senate office for personal gain, taking bribes and kickbacks; Senator Joyce died before his case could come to trial. In 2008 Senator Dianne Wilkerson was taped stuffing cash bribes into her bra by an FBI agent. There is not sufficient space here to detail all of the allegations and cases against leaders and legislators in the General Court over the past several decades, but suffice it to say that it appears that this culture of corruption has not yet been eliminated.

Ultimately, though, the tight grip that party leaders hold over members of their chambers reinforces constitutional provisions towards legislative dominance. Little happens without the approval of the leaders, such that the governor is forced to work with leaders rather than appealing to members outside of this channel of power. And even then, the governor cannot be sure that he will get what he wants. For example, the state legislature recently overrode Governor Baker's proposed amendment to split spending authority over nearly $5 billion in federal funding between the legislature and the governor; instead, the legislature voted to put nearly all of that money under the control of the legislature (Deehan 2021). Generally speaking, this tight grip over power has advantaged the more moderate wing of the Democratic Party. As noted in chapter 11, the legislature is not a particularly diverse place. Furthermore, progressives tend to be locked out of power, such that they have had little success in making the legislature more transparent and open to a variety of ideas.

THE PLACE OF THE GENERAL COURT IN MASSACHUSETTS POLITICS

Given the not infrequent incidents of corruption and scandal in the General Court, one has to wonder why the Democratic Party continues to dominate in the legislature and why the General Court continues to dominate state politics. For the latter, shifting the balance of power away from the General Court would require constitutional change, and constitutional change is hard. Given the myriad other pressing issues facing the commonwealth today, this one is low on the priority list. But Massachusetts has not always been dominated by the Democratic Party; while one-party rule has been the norm for quite some time now in Massachusetts, the party that controls the legislature can and does change. So how do Democrats manage to maintain their hold? First, state legislators in Massachusetts have a very high degree of job security, so they have little incentive to rock the boat. As discussed previously, the Republican Party in Massachusetts is in disarray presently. While the party is competitive for the top positions in state government (governor and lieutenant governor), Republicans rarely compete for other state-level offices and have just a small minority in the state legislature. As of this writing, Republicans have just 29 members in the House (less than 20 percent) and 3 members in the Senate (7.5 percent). As such, most legislators are rarely challenged about their behavior in office, as few state legislators face competition in the general election.

Additionally, few state legislators face competition in the primary either; in 2018 only 16 of 130 Democratic state representatives had primary challenges (Jonas 2018). Occasionally, it happens; for instance, in 2018 two political newcomers defeated longtime, well-connected state legislators in Democratic primaries. House Ways and Means Committee chair Jeffrey Sánchez lost to Nika Elugardo, who painted Sánchez as a defender of the status quo and argued constituents wanted to shake up how business is done in the house (Dowling 2018). Representative Byron Rushing, another member of DeLeo's inner circle, also lost. Some see this as a harbinger of change, calling these losses "stunning" (Murphy 2018c) or the tip of a "tsunami of change" (Jonas 2018). But as Speaker DeLeo noted, only 3 sitting Democratic state legislators lost their seats in 2018 (just about 2 percent), in an election year that nationally was marked by dramatic change. Whether these defeats are just aberrations or mark the start of a real challenge to the way the house does business remains to be seen. The election of Mariano to become Speaker suggests that even though there are a few more progressives in the chamber than there were previously, this doesn't seem to have made an impact on the way the legislature does business.

The other key reason Democratic Party dominance in the General Court persists is because the system works for those with power, particularly for incumbents and business interests. As noted above, redistricting efforts have generally focused on protecting sitting incumbents, particularly the 2000 redistricting process, which was called an "incumbent protection plan" by some and brought down then house Speaker Thomas Finneran (Jenkins and Pettey 2013). Most observers agreed that the 2010 redistricting process, led by Senator Stanley Rosenberg before he became senate president, was more open and less focused on incumbent interests, yet competition for incumbents still hasn't increased in the wake of these changes. And while the state legislature passed sweeping changes to the state public records law in 2016, the committee convened to determine whether the state legislature would be bound by these laws disbanded in early 2019 without issuing a report; as such, Massachusetts is the only state in the nation where the legislature, judiciary, and governor's office all claim to be exempt from public records laws (Wallack 2019). The party caucuses in the legislature convene in secret, barring public access to decisions made in them (Johnson 2015), and decisions about important state legislation, like the budget, are made in back rooms. Thus, the legislature conducts its business in ways that make it hard for the public to determine what is going on.

Furthermore, these incumbents, working with lobbyists on Beacon Hill, have developed close relationships with special interests, leading some to argue that Speaker DeLeo and the house leadership were in the pockets of business interest groups (Murphy 2016). For instance, Representative Sarah Peake of Provincetown told *CommonWealth Magazine* that the house should be proud of its relationship with the business community; she said, "I don't think that's a bad thing. I'm cozy with my business community. I go to chamber of commerce events. I support local businesses. I buy locally. Until we closed shop this year, I was a small business owner with a bed and breakfast. To paint all business with a broad brush of being somehow the evil empire is unfair and a gross mischaracterization. Business gives people jobs" (Murphy 2016).

Additionally, for the most part, the general public doesn't seem to have a problem with the current arrangements on Beacon Hill. The current governor, Baker, enjoys high levels of popularity and a generally good working relationship with the legislature. Though tensions over the state's response to COVID-19 and issues including police reform in the state did produce an unusual amount of public disagreement between the governor and legislature in 2020 and 2021, Duquette argues in this volume that Democrats in the legislature prefer to work with Republican governors, as these governors are not likely to pressure them to adopt policies that are outside the comfort zone of the more moderate members of the party. Thus, for most people, the system isn't broken, so why mess with it?

The cozy relationship between the governor, the state legislature, and powerful interests coupled with the job security of sitting legislators and the tightly controlled legislative process has led some to claim that Massachusetts is no longer a policy leader in the United States. Former state senator Ben Downing, a one-time candidate for governor in 2022 (exited race in December 2021), argues that the process "benefits one group and one group only entrenched special interests. Without time for public debate and input, special interests defending the status quo have an outsized voice. They are able to kill or water down some of the very proposals which could help tackle the major issues Massachusetts is facing, simply because the legislature waited till it was too late. Instead of having to defend their position multiple times under the harsh light of public scrutiny they are able to do so once or twice, if at all, in hushed conversations in the State House halls" (2018). Former senate president Rosenberg agrees, arguing the final days of the session have become "'swap meets' where items in bills are traded, not serious forums that try to arrive at the best policy outcome" (Jonas and Mohl 2016). Furthermore, the tight control over the process and the punishment that comes from bucking the system make it difficult for those who are part of the system to challenge it. Sego argues, "It's difficult—taboo, actually—for anyone who's part of the process to engage in this type of criticism. Any lobbyist who criticizes the State House's power structure would instantly become ineffective, shunned by both Democrats and Republicans. Reporters who expose the system's corruption would lose access to their sources. Even State House staff, as we've recently learned, were forced to sign nondisclosure agreements upon their departure.

The system thus protects itself from scrutiny" (2018). This argument is buttressed by the fact that two of the three representatives who did not vote in support of Speaker Mariano were leaving the chamber (Schoenberg 2020).

Though Massachusetts has long been exceptional in terms of policy leadership, from implementing the first public schools to health-care reform under Governor Mitt Romney, the state appears to be losing its edge in this regard. There are few policy innovations that have come out of the state in recent years. Indeed, research suggests that other states are taking the lead from Massachusetts as policy innovators (Boehmke et al. 2018). As UMass Lowell historian Robert Forrant says, "The legislature and Governor have mastered the fine art of appearing very, very busy while standing very, very still" (Horowitz 2018). The house and senate have been moving in opposite directions in their approaches to leadership, culture, and process in recent years, producing critical fault lines within the Democratic Party between these two bodies. One of the more interesting questions for the future of Massachusetts politics, then, is whether the progressive, more liberal approach of the senate or the conservative, centralized approach of the house will prevail. The exceptional concentration of power in the Massachusetts legislature and in the hands of the Speaker of the house makes this *the* political battle to watch in the years to come.

WORKS CITED

Allan, Scott, and Thomas Farragher. 2010. "Evidence of Insider Job Deals at Agency." *Boston Globe*, July 25, 2010. https://www.bostonglobe.com/metro/2010/07/25/evidence -insider-job-deals-agency/72JtrEKsGXKAo8V8OhSqNJ/story.html.

Battista, James Coleman. 2011. "Formal and Perceived Power in U.S. State Legislatures." *State Politics & Policy Quarterly* 11:102–18.

Boehmke, Fred, Desmond Wallace, Mark Brockway, Bruce A. Desmarais, Jeffrey J. Harden, Scott LaCombe, Fridolin Linder, and Hanna Wallach. 2018. "The Influence of Ideological Compatibility and Clarity on Policy Innovation and Innovators." Paper presented at the 2018 annual meeting of the American Political Science Association, Boston.

Brown, Steve. 2018. "Two-Thirds of State Legislators Are Unopposed in General Election." *WBUR*, November 1, 2018. https://www.wbur.org/news/2018/11/01/massachusetts -state-house-election-preview.

———. 2019. "About That Bill to Ban the 'B Word': You and Anyone Else Can File Legislation in Mass." *CommonWealth Magazine*, October 24, 2019. https://www.wbur.org /news/2019/10/24/bitch-bill-massachusetts-legislature.

Cillizza, Chris. 2017. "The Most Popular Governor in the Country Is a Republican from Massachusetts. Yes, Really." *CNN*, July 22, 2017. https://www.cnn.com/2017/07/22 /politics/charlie-baker-q-and-a/index.html.

Clucas, Richard. 2001. "Principal-Agent Theory and the Power of State House Speakers." *State Politics and Policy Quarterly* 2:319–38.

———. 2007. "Legislative Professionalism and the Power of State House Leaders." *State Politics and Policy Quarterly* 7:1–19.

Council of State Governments (CSG). 2018. *The Book of the States*. Lexington, KY: Council of State Governments.

Davis, Jon. 2017. "Who Can Introduce Bills? Legislators, Mostly . . ." http://knowledgecenter .csg.org/kc/content/who-can-introduce-bills-legislators-mostly.

Deehan, Mike. 2021. "Beacon Hill Democrats Strip Baker of New Federal Spending Authority." WGBH, June 22, 2021. https://www.wgbh.org/news/politics/2021/06/22/beacon -hill-democrats-strip-baker-of-new-federal-aid-spending-authority.

Difazio, Joe. 2020. "Longtime Quincy Rep. Ron Mariano Becomes Massachusetts House Speaker." *Patriot Ledger*, December 30, 2020. https://www.patriotledger.com/story/news/2020/12/30 /its-official-quincys-ron-mariano-becomes-ma-house-speaker/4085332001/.

Dowling, Brian. 2018. "High-Profile Beacon Hill Ousters Seen as 'Teachable Moment.'" *Boston Herald*, September 6, 2018. https://www.bostonherald.com/2018/09/06/high -profile-beacon-hill-ousters-seen-as-teachable-moment/.

Downing, Ben. 2018. "Ben Downing: End of Season." WAMC, July 31, 2018. https://www .wamc.org/commentary-opinion/2018-07-31/ben-downing-end-of-session.

Francis, Wayne L., and James W. Riddlesperger. 1982. "U.S. State Legislative Committees: Structure, Procedural Efficiency, and Party Control." *Legislative Studies Quarterly* 4:453–71.

Hawkins, Derek. 2019. "Why a Lawmaker Floated a Bill to Penalize the Use of a Profane Word (That Rhymes with Witch)." *Washington Post*, October 23, 2019. https://www .washingtonpost.com/nation/2019/10/23/why-lawmaker-floated-bill-penalize-use -profane-word-that-rhymes-with-witch/.

Hecht, Jonathan, and Denise Provost. 2020. "House Progressives Need to Cry Foul: A Mariano Speakership Would Be Culmination of Insider Politics." *CommonWealth Magazine*, December 20, 2020. https://commonwealthmagazine.org/opinion/house-progressives -need-to-cry-foul/.

Herwick, Edgar B., III. 2016. "4 Things Worth Knowing about the Massachusetts Constitution, Which Is 236 Years Old." WGBH, June 21, 2016. https://www.wgbh.org/news /2016/06/21/local-news/4-things-worth-knowing-about-massachusetts-constitution -which-236-years-old.

Horowitz, Evan. 2018. "Massachusetts Was a Policy Trailblazer. Not Anymore." *Boston Globe*, June 3, 2018. https://www.bostonglobe.com/metro/massachusetts/2018/06/03/massachusetts -was-policy-trailblazer-not-anymore/d5yJUA4ANbyCq8gvsvWajK/story.html.

Jenkins, Shannon, and Samantha Pettey. 2013. "Down and Up, In and Out: Redistricting in Massachusetts." In *The Political Battle over Congressional Redistricting at the State Level*, edited by Will Miller and Jeremy Walling, 165–85. Lanham, MD: Lexington Books.

Jewell, Malcolm. 1955. "Party Voting in American State Legislatures." *American Political Science Review* 49:773–91.

Johnson, Akilah. 2015. "In Mass., Caucuses Are Secret. Elsewhere It's a Different Story." *Boston Globe*, February 6, 2015. https://www.bostonglobe.com/metro/2015/02/06/mass -caucuses-are-secret-elsewhere-different-story/bAstsD3dg1cXaYwVIOs93H/story.html.

Jonas, Michael. 2018. "DeLeo Spins a Positive Role." *CommonWealth Magazine*, September 6, 2018. https://commonwealthmagazine.org/politics/deleo-spins-a-positive-tale-2/.

Jonas, Michael, and Bruce Mohl. 2016. "The Codcast: Rosenberg Laments Broken System." *CommonWealth Magazine*, August 4, 2016. https://commonwealthmagazine.org /politics/the-codcast-rosenberg-laments-broken-system/.

Knight, Michael. 1981. "Massachusetts Told of Wide Corruption." *New York Times*, January 1, 1981. https://www.nytimes.com/1981/01/01/us/massachusetts-told-of-wide-corruption.html.

League of Women Voters (LWV). 1970. *Massachusetts State Government*. Cambridge, MA: Harvard University Press.

LeBlanc, Steve. 2011. "A Tale of 3 Speakers—Salvatore DiMasi, Thomas Finneran and Charles Flaherty: Is Lure of Power Too Tempting?" *MassLive*, July 4, 2011. https://www.masslive.com/news/2011/07/a_tale_of_3_speakers_--_salvat.html.

Lockard, Duane. 1959. "Lawmaking in Massachusetts: Traditional Pomp and Political Circumstance." In *New England State Politics*. Princeton, NJ: Princeton University Press.

Massachusetts Legislature. 2002. "Massachusetts Legislative History." http://www.mass.gov/legis/legishistory.htm.

MassInc Polling. 2018. "The MassGOP Struggles for Relevance." https://www.massincpolling.com/the-topline/2018/11/16/the-massgop-struggles-for-relevance.

Metzger, Andy. 2019. "Ex-Rep: DeLeo Told Me, Vote for Transportation Bill or Lose Chairmanship." *CommonWealth Magazine*, October 28, 2019. https://commonwealthmagazine.org/politics/ex-rep-deleo-told-me-vote-for-transpo-bill-or-lose-chairmanship-2/.

Mileur, Jerome M. 1997. "Party Politics in the Bay State: The Dominion of Democracy." In *Parties & Politics in the New England States*, edited by Jerome M. Mileur, 7–94. Amherst, MA: Polity.

Miller, Joshua, and Matt Stout. 2018. "Bowing to Pressure, Rosenberg Resigns after 31 Years." *Boston Globe*, May 3, 2018. https://www.bostonglobe.com/metro/2018/05/03/stan-rosenberg-resign-senate-seat/UU267HiMCCrS1lV2spUZpL/story.html.

Mohl, Bruce. 2019a. "Beacon Hill Notes: DeLeo Cruises to Speaker Reelection." *CommonWealth Magazine*, January 2, 2019. https://commonwealthmagazine.org/politics/beacon-hill-notes-deleo-cruises-to-speaker-reelection/.

———. 2019b. "A First: Baker Signs Budget with No Spending Vetoes." *CommonWealth Magazine*, July 31, 2019. https://commonwealthmagazine.org/state-government/a-first-baker-signs-budget-with-no-spending-vetoes/.

———. 2019c. "Rules Reform in the House Is Not Over." *CommonWealth Magazine*, January 7, 2019. https://commonwealthmagazine.org/politics/rules-reform-battle-in-house-not-over/.

Moran, Thomas Francis. 1895. "The Rise and the Development of the Bicameral System in America." In *Historical and Political Science*, edited by Herbert B. Adams. Baltimore: Johns Hopkins Press. http://webapp1.dlib.indiana.edu/inauthors/view?docId=VAC1305&doc.view=print.

Murphy, Matt. 2016. "House, Senate Lawmakers Trade Fire." *CommonWealth Magazine*, August 4, 2016. https://commonwealthmagazine.org/politics/house-senate-lawmakers-trade-fire/.

———. 2018a. "Lawmaker Salaries Going up 5.9%." *CommonWealth Magazine*, December 27, 2018. https://commonwealthmagazine.org/state-government/lawmaker-salaries-going-up-5--9/.

———. 2018b. "State GOP Committee Member Calls Party 'All But Irrelevant' in Mass." *Boston Globe*, December 28, 2018. https://www.bostonglobe.com/metro/2018/12/28/gop-committee-member-calls-party-all-but-irrelevant/K7kUTCWBOCodNLJ6FZjJ2l/story.html?event=event25&fbclid=IwAR1rn7AyHqRnxAKTgcVgocw7p1-pEoqEqhJpim-Fp6nskWlekV_jnYp56eA.

———. 2018c. "Voters Oust High-Ranking Mass. Reps. Sanchez and Rushing." WBUR, September 4, 2018. https://www.wbur.org/news/2018/09/04/reps-sanchez-rushing-ousted.

National Conference of State Legislatures (NCSL). n.d. "State Legislative Policymaking in an Age of Partisan Polarization." http://www.ncsl.org/Portals/1/HTML_LargeReports/Partisanship_1.htm.

————. 2018. "Learning the Game." http://www.ncsl.org/research/about-state-legislatures
/learning-the-game.aspx.

Robbins, Robert R. 1961. Introduction to vol. 3 of *State Government and Public Responsibility,
1961: The Role of the Governor in Massachusetts*, edited by Robert R. Robbins, 3–10.
Papers of the 1961 Tufts Assembly on Massachusetts Government. Lincoln Filene
Center for Citizenship and Public Affairs, Tufts University, Medford, MA.

Schoenberg, Shira. 2020. "Ronald Mariano Elected Speaker of the Massachusetts House."
CommonWealth Magazine, December 30, 2020. https://commonwealthmagazine
.org/politics/ronald-mariano-elected-speaker-of-the-massachusetts-house/.

Schuck, Victoria. 1961. "The Massachusetts Governorship: Hamstrung by History?" In vol. 3
of *State Government and Public Responsibility, 1961: The Role of the Governor in Massachusetts*, edited by Robert R. Robbins, 11–76. Papers of the 1961 Tufts Assembly on
Massachusetts Government. Lincoln Filene Center for Citizenship and Public Affairs,
Tufts University, Medford, MA.

Seeyle, Katharine. 2013. "Sticking by a Murderous Brother, and Paying for It Dearly." *New
York Times*, November 24, 2013. https://www.nytimes.com/2013/11/25/us/sticking
-by-a-murderous-brother-and-paying-for-it-dearly.html.

Sego, Philip. 2018. "Ex-Lobbyist Reveals How the House Really Works." *CommonWealth Magazine*, December 19, 2018. https://commonwealthmagazine.org/opinion/ex-lobbyist
-reveals-how-the-house-really-works/.

Smith, Jennifer. 2019. "Holmes Laments Life in DeLeo's 'Kingdom.'" *Dorchester Reporter*, January 16, 2019. https://www.dotnews.com/2019/holmes-laments-life-deleo-s-kingdom-0.

Squire, Peverill. 2012. *The Evolution of American Legislatures: Colonies, Territories, and States,
1619–2009.* Ann Arbor: University of Michigan Press.

————. 2017. "A Squire Index Update." *State Politics & Policy Quarterly* 17:361–71.

Squire, Peverill, and Keith E. Hamm. 2005. *101 Chambers: Congress, State Legislatures, and the
Future of Legislative Studies.* Columbus: Ohio State University Press.

Squire, Peverill, and Gary Moncrief. 2015. *State Legislatures Today: Politics under the Domes.*
New York: Rowman & Littlefield.

Stout, Matt. 2019. "DeLeo, the Longest Continuously Serving Speaker, Says He'll Seek Another
Term in the Top Post." *Boston Globe*, October 28, 2019. https://www.bostonglobe
.com/metro/2019/10/28/speaker-deleo-hopes-remain-post-until-least/ELdwh4WiI1KIg
JChyOgSMN/story.html.

Wallack, Todd. 2019. "State Lawmakers Fail to Reach Consensus on Whether to Expand
Public Records Law." *Boston Globe*, January 10, 2019. https://www.bostonglobe.com
/metro/2019/01/10/state-lawmakers-fail-reach-consensus-whether-expand-public-record
-law/XvwfD0402TtQ4HWqmxioBO/story.html.

CHAPTER 5

THE GOVERNOR
OF THE COMMONWEALTH
A "Not So" Supreme Executive Magistrate

Jerold Duquette

Massachusetts' reputation for exceptionalism owes quite a bit to the fact that the state's founders, the designers of its form of government, were also at the epicenter of America's founding and the design of America's exceptional form of government. Much of what the framers of the U.S. Constitution understood about executive power in a democratic society came from experimentation with the colonial governors of Massachusetts between 1630 and 1780.

The concept of American exceptionalism itself can be traced to a phrase written in 1630 by the governor of the Massachusetts Bay Colony, John Winthrop, whose sermon "A Model of Christian Charity" included the phrase "a city on a hill." Winthrop saw himself and his fellows as divinely ordained to establish a new society designed to be a noble example for all the world to see. The first governor of the Commonwealth of Massachusetts, elected in 1780, was John Hancock. His résumé for the job included the presidency of the Second Continental Congress, a post to which he was elected a month before his Massachusetts neighbors fired the first shots of the American Revolution and in which he presided over the drafting, debating, and signing of the Declaration of Independence. The U.S. Constitution was modeled on the Massachusetts Constitution of 1780, the primary author of which, John Adams, became the first vice president and second president of the United States. The controversial practice of manipulating the boundaries between representative districts known as "gerrymandering," an issue getting more than its share of attention at present, takes its name from the ninth governor of the commonwealth, Elbridge Gerry, who went on to serve as vice president to James Madison.

Just as the architects of the U.S. Constitution brought their Massachusetts knowledge and experience to the job, so too did the architects of the modern institutional presidency and administrative state that emerged in the 1930s. The institutional arrangements of the modern presidency and administrative state can be traced to the work of the President's Committee on Administrative

Management, commonly known as the Brownlow Committee, and the enact-ment of their handiwork in the Reorganization Act of 1939, which greatly increased the president's administrative capacity and control over executive branch management and budgeting. The substance of this pivotal national reform bore a striking resemblance to the modernization of the Massachusetts executive branch enacted in the Massachusetts Reorganization Act of 1919. This was, of course, no coincidence. One of the three principal authors of the Brownlow Report, Luther Gulick, had published an exhaustive study of the administrative capacity and powers of the Massachusetts state government in 1920 (Gulick 1920).

In the aftermath of President Johnson's prosecution of the Vietnam War and President Nixon's abuse of office, political scientists trying to figure out how the modern presidency had devolved into an "imperial presidency" looked to the experiences of state governors, including Massachusetts', for clues (Lockard et al. 1976). Nearly five decades later, as the nation struggles to understand the causes and consequences of the dysfunctional polarizing partisanship that has gripped our national politics and severely distorted our expectations and under-standing of presidential power and authority, the example of Massachusetts governors might, once again, help scholars and practitioners find the way forward. Unlike American presidents and many fellow governors, the Bay State's twenty-first-century governors, irrespective of party, have found ways to advance their political and policy agendas without resorting to the kind of divisive partisanship poisoning politics in America today.

Massachusetts has been a proving ground for the principles, practices, institutions, and arguments at play in American government and politics since 1620. In this chapter, we will survey and examine the development of the state's chief executive office through what historians call the state's colonial, provincial, and commonwealth periods with an eye toward under-standing the place of "His Excellency, the Governor" in twenty-first-century Massachusetts government and politics. Democratically accountable executive power has always been and remains among the most precarious elements of America's democratic experiment. Massachusetts governors have grappled with the ultimately unresolvable tension between democratic accountability and effective governance for longer, and under more diverse circumstances, than any other institutional actors in American history.

In many respects, the contemporary Massachusetts governorship reflects the intentions and hopes of the men who designed the U.S. presidency better than does the twenty-first-century presidency itself. The modern presidency has long since betrayed the framers' hopes for legislative supremacy and the avoidance of the "mischiefs of faction." In Massachusetts, however, the governor's place largely adheres to John Adams' 1780 vision of separation of powers and checks and balances—which is to say the governor operates in the shadow of the Great and General Court on Beacon Hill and as a beacon of bipartisan, cooperative leadership.

As Washington, DC, and other state capitals across the country have devolved into polarized partisan combat, politics at the Massachusetts State House remains remarkably calm and stable by comparison. Despite the fact that all but one of the state's governors in the past thirty years have been Republicans facing veto-proof Democratic majorities in the state legislature, Massachusetts politics has not been dominated by the pathological partisanship that accompanies divided party control of government elsewhere (Duquette 2019). In contemporary Massachusetts, the primary political divide is not partisan in an ideological sense; it is, rather, a contest between insiders and outsiders. The insiders are willing to accept the influence of established interests and actors and to participate in an interest-based political bargaining approach to policy making at the statehouse. The outsiders are good-government and social justice activists on the left and antitax and antigovernment activists as well as conservative culture warriors on the right who try, largely in vain, to confront and challenge the individualistic and transactional political status quo on Beacon Hill.

Why does what has come to be known as the "corner office" at the Massachusetts State House operate so differently than the Oval Office, which was in many ways literally modeled on the Massachusetts governorship? The answer lies in the resilience of the state's political institutions, norms, and culture, cultivated and fortified over four centuries, that have essentially allowed the state to escape the ugliest and most dramatic impacts of the increasingly aggressive and polarized two-party competition in Washington and in many other state capitals over the past fifty years. In modern times, this escape has undoubtedly been eased by the fact that Democrats have controlled both chambers of the General Court since 1958 and have done so with the benefit of veto-proof majorities since 1992. Democrats have also dominated the other statewide elected constitutional offices, the attorney general, secretary of the commonwealth, state treasurer and receiver-general, and state auditor. With the brief exception of Republican Joe Malone's tenure as treasurer from 1991 to 1999, Democrats have controlled all four of these posts for more than a half century. This seemingly impenetrable Democratic control has greatly reduced the partisan stakes of gubernatorial elections for Beacon Hill Democrats. In fact, modern Democratic legislative leaders have all but openly preferred Republican gubernatorial incumbents to their Democratic challengers several times in the past thirty years, revealing their preference for collegial, cooperative, and transactional interbranch relations, irrespective of party, over broad programmatic and ideological combat or conformity (Duquette 2013). As we saw in chapter 1's treatment of Massachusetts political culture, these "insiders" do not seek to rock the boat—they prefer, reinforce, and play a game known for decades.

The Governor of Massachusetts Bay Colony, 1630–1691

Unlike the Puritan separatists who arrived at Plymouth Rock on the *Mayflower* ten years earlier in 1620, Governor John Winthrop and company were in possession of a royal charter that signaled their continuing loyalty to and dependence on the Crown. While Winthrop and company saw themselves as servants of God, to the king of England they were agents of the Crown serving the economic interests of the British Empire.[1] Four centuries later, Winthrop's twenty-first-century successors would see themselves as servants/representatives of "the people" and as agents of the state's economic interests. Balancing the often conflicting obligations to God and king has evolved into balancing the timeless dictates of democratic politics and the rapidly changing methods of effective governance.

The colony's charter government, installed in 1630, consisted of a governor, a deputy governor, and eighteen assistants, elected by the freemen of the company, who met monthly to conduct the colony's affairs (Brown 1954).[2] Starting in 1634, representatives were elected by townspeople to the General Court. In 1644 the governor and assistants became the upper chamber of the General Court, while elected representatives called deputies served as the lower chamber (Schuck 1961). Because the governor and assistants were elected separately from deputies, they gradually began seeing themselves as separate from and not accountable to the deputies. "Thus began the separation of the

---

1   The Massachusetts Bay Company was founded in 1628 and was governed by officials who remained in England. While Winthrop was the first governor of the royally chartered colony, there had been two previous governors of the Massachusetts Bay Company, Matthew Cradock and John Endecott.
2   The term *freemen* simply meant those qualified, in terms of religion and property ownership, for full citizenship in the colony.

executive and legislative branches," a century and a half before separation of powers and checks and balances were conceived by the constitutional framers of the state and the nation (*Manual for the Constitutional Convention* 1917, 8).

Though Winthrop and most of his successors during this period would have considerable personal influence on the colony's governance and be reelected repeatedly (Winthrop was elected twelve times), the colony's day-to-day governance was increasingly controlled by the Court of Assistants. The precursor to what is today the Massachusetts Senate and Governor's Council, assistants had executive, legislative, and judicial power. They served as the upper chamber of the legislature, whose consent was required for every act, and acted as local magistrates (that is, judges) as well. The first chief executives of what would become the Commonwealth of Massachusetts flourished and succeeded by accepting their place among many, rather than by asserting dominance, an approach that continues to help the state's governors achieve their goals four centuries later.

The Massachusetts Bay Colony enjoyed considerable independence from the British Crown for more than a half century, despite occasional efforts to bring the colony under greater royal control (Spencer 1905). Frustrated with the inability to control the colony, King Charles II annulled the Massachusetts Bay Colony Charter in 1684. In 1686 the colony was folded into the Dominion of New England. "The Dominion was ruled by a President or Governor and Council appointed by the King, all elections and representative institutions [except] the town meeting [were] abolished. When news arrived of the Revolution of 1688 in England, the people of Boston, on April 18, 1689, rose up against [the royally appointed] Governor Andros and imprisoned him in the fort on Castle Island [in today's South Boston]. The Assistants elected in 1686 then took charge, and summoned a convention of Deputies from the towns, with whose permission (and subsequently the royal approval) they declared the old charter government provisionally restored" (*Manual for the Constitutional Convention* 1917, 9).

The Royal Governor of the Province of Massachusetts Bay (1691–1775)

In 1691, after what historians call the "intercharter period," Massachusetts was granted a new royal charter. In what would become a familiar refrain among those seeking to reform Massachusetts government, the charter of 1691 granted by William and Mary sought to increase the power of the governor and council and thereby increase the efficiency of the colony's government, which to the British monarchy was still an agent of the empire's interests. While members of the lower house of the General Court would continue to be popularly elected as they had been under the first charter, the provincial charter created a royally appointed governor, lieutenant governor, and secretary, all serving at the king's pleasure. The governor was given formal control of the militia and an absolute veto over decisions of the General Court, including appointments to the Provincial Council. The governor was also granted the power to appoint (with the advice of the council) provincial judges. Unlike its more powerful predecessor, the Court of Assistants, the twenty-eight-member Provincial Council created by the charter did not have judicial authority (Spencer 1905). Though William and Mary hoped the charter of 1691 would elevate the governor, and in so doing the influence of the Crown over the governance of the colony, governors between 1691 and 1775 were just one of several influential officials ruling the colony collaboratively and, like their predecessors, increasingly more in the interests of the colonists than the king.

While the provincial charter increased the executive power of the governor, it also included the means by which royal governors would become subservient to the legislature. The charter of 1691 expressly granted the power of the purse to the popularly elected legislature. It was this authority that gave force to growing popular opposition to the rule of royal governors, which would ultimately doom British monarchs' efforts to tame the American colonies. Historian Charles H. J. Douglas linked the increasingly adversarial relations between Massachusetts colonists and royal governors between 1691 and 1780 with the development of what would become a familiar antigovernment sentiment in America. While the charter of the Massachusetts Bay Company may have introduced the separation of the executive and legislative branches, the 1691 charter added the necessary ingredients for the development of an adversarial relationship between the branches of government, a rivalry that naturally pitted the people's representatives against the king's representatives (Douglas 1892).

Royal governors battled with popularly elected legislators over all manner of things during the provincial period. In 1725 the royal governor was so frustrated with the legislature that he urged the Crown to issue a clarification of the charter that clearly distinguished the power balance between the royally appointed executive and the popularly elected legislators of the province. Among the clarifications was a declaration that the choice of a

Speaker of the Massachusetts House of Representatives must be formally approved by the governor (Schuck 1961). By the mid-twentieth century the house Speaker's informal approval of the choice of governors had become the far more influential endorsement.

The origins of what would become the U.S. and Massachusetts constitutional framers' preference for legislative supremacy are evident in the acrimonious and adversarial relations between the royal governors of provincial Massachusetts and the popularly elected members of the legislature under the charter of 1691. Luther Gulick, in his *Evolution of the Budget in Massachusetts* (1920), concisely summarized the resulting principles and practices of executive-legislative relations developed by the experience of governing under the charter of 1691 as follows:

1. wide separation of the executive and legislative departments
2. absolute control of the people's representatives over the levy of taxes and appropriation of funds
3. gradual assumption of executive power by the legislature through the agency of its financial control
4. establishment of the principle that financial measures must originate with the "people's representatives"—the lower house
5. evolution of a "legislative budget" as a means of restricting the executive and keeping taxes down.

Gulick's colorful descriptions of what he dubs "incidents in the struggle" include vengeful legislators refusing to appropriate the funds to pay the governor's salary, as well as incidents that look a lot like the debt-limit standoffs between President Obama and congressional Republicans in 2011 and 2013. This suggests Americans started writing the modern playbook for executive-legislative relations more than three hundred years ago in provincial Massachusetts.

Ultimately, royal governors between 1691 and 1775 occupied an increasingly precarious place in Massachusetts government and politics. As the king's representatives, they bore the brunt of popular dissatisfaction with attempts by the Crown to exploit the colonies. Armed with the formal power of the purse and the informal power of popular electoral mandates, Massachusetts legislators got the best of royal governors more often than not. The story of Massachusetts governors during this period is about the limits of formal executive authority and of chief executives uninterested and unskilled in the management of public opinion.

It is important to note that the charter of 1691, despite its grant of consid-erable formal power to royal governors, was nonetheless very well regarded by the people of Massachusetts. Residents saw the charter as a solemn con-tract—a written contract—between the people of the province and the king of England himself, not merely the king's representative in the governor's chair (Spencer 1905). Spencer writes, "Massachusetts took up arms in 1775, not to win new powers, but to resist the encroachment of parliament upon what the province had come to regard as her constitution, and the system to which she resorted in the interregnum of war, the constitution which she set up in revolution to fight for and defend was the system set forth in the Charter of 1691" (1905, 20–21).

The last civilian royal governor of Massachusetts, Thomas Hutchinson, was replaced by the king in the spring of 1774. General Thomas Gage became the military governor of the colony, whose mission was to regain control in the wake of colonial resistance to the recently passed Coercive Acts, dubbed the "Intolerable Acts" by colonists. This resistance most famously included the Boston Tea Party. One of the acts was an amendment to the provincial charter changing the method of appointment for the twenty-eight-member Provincial Council, which served both as the upper house of the legislature and as advisers to the governor, from election by the General Court to direct appointment by the king (*Manual for the Constitutional Convention* 1917). The decision to strengthen the king's hand by removing the legislature's leverage over the Provincial Council was an acknowledgment of sorts that royal governors were outmatched by the popularly elected members of the lower house of the General Court.

While Governor Gage of Massachusetts Bay was trying to restore law and order, American colonial leaders were attempting to govern Massachusetts in hastily organized provincial congresses. John Hancock presided over the first two of them. On May 5, 1775, the Third Provincial Congress "declared General Gage no longer the lawful Governor, and on June 20th it ordered the election of a regular General Court under the Province charter" (*Manual for the Constitutional Convention* 1917, 12). On July 21, 1775, the newly elected members of the lower house of the General Court elected a new Provincial Council. Because, according to the Americans, the king's appointed executives had ceased to perform their proper duties, the elected council became the de facto executive branch that governed Massachusetts until the ratification of the Massachusetts Constitution of 1780. The experience of being governed by the twenty-eight-member Provincial Council provided compelling evidence that too many chefs could indeed spoil the stew. Not only was the elected council horribly inefficient, but its members were not shy about partaking in the personal benefits of patronage politics. Despite his preference for legislative supremacy, the unsatisfactory experience of executive government by committee during this period would not be forgotten by John Adams in his design of the state's constitution (*Manual for the Constitutional Convention* 1917).

"His Excellency, the Governor" under the Massachusetts Constitution, 1780–Present

Though it included familiar elements, such as residency, property, and religious qualifications, as well as annual gubernatorial election, the Massachusetts Constitution of 1780 also included less familiar arrangements.[3] The impotence of royal governors owing to dependence on colonial legislators was not lost on John Adams' frame of government, which required governors be paid a fixed salary established by statute. Unlike the first constitutions of the other twelve of the original thirteen states, the first (and still only) Massachusetts Constitution gave quite a bit of independence and authority to the governor, including a clear separation of powers that expressly carved out an independent sphere of influence for "His Excellency, the Governor."

While Adams' constitution was more generous to the chief executive, it was no blueprint for executive supremacy. Requirements for the "advice and consent" of the Governor's Council, a body to be made up of state senators from different regions of the state elected by the legislature, were designed to provide meaningful constraints on the governor's power. The requirements for council cooperation on gubernatorial appointments, requests for advisory opinions from the state's Supreme Judicial Court, the removal of judges, the granting of pardons, and even the expenditure of funds from the treasury all reflected Adams' effort to balance executive energy with democratic accountability (Schuck 1961). The actual operation of the council, however, did not live up to the design. Though sitting state senators were supposed to make up the nine-member body, by 1805 no senators elected to the council by fellow legislators were willing to serve. A change from election by the legislature of sitting state senators to the council to election by the legislature from the people at large was passed by the Massachusetts Constitutional Convention of 1820 but rejected by the voters at the ballot box in 1821. This change to

---

3   The property and religious oath requirements were eliminated in 1821. The governor's term of office was increased to two years in 1919 and four years in 1966.

the council's membership was not affected until being passed by voters in 1841 (Schuck 1961). The governor's councilors would not become popularly elected officials until 1855.

The constitution contained more direct legislative checks on the governor as well. Despite strong support for an absolute legislative veto from the document's primary author, the final draft allowed the legislature to override a gubernatorial veto by a two-thirds majority (*Manual for the Constitutional Convention* 1917). More important, the power to raise taxes and appropriate funds was squarely consigned to the state legislature.

The method of election for governor, which was elaborately and precisely described in the constitution of 1780, signaled the office's dependence on both state legislators and local elected officials. Local officials ("selectmen") were required to collect, count, and publicly announce the gubernatorial votes in an open town meeting. The county sheriff was then required to "transmit" the results to the secretary of the commonwealth, who would "lay the same before the senate and the house of representatives" (MA Constitution, chap. 2, sec. 1, art. 3). If one candidate won a statewide majority, he would be declared the winner, but if no candidate won a majority, the Massachusetts House of Representatives would choose two candidates from the top four vote getters and then send those names to the senate, who would choose the governor from one of the two candidates sent from the house. The potential for mischief of this method was made clear to all in the state election of 1850 when the Democrats in the legislature brazenly exploited the constitution's majority-vote requirement for election to the governor's office. By forming an alliance with members of the Free-Soil Party, Democrats were able to prevent the Whig candidate from earning the needed majority. Having also won control of the General Court, they were able to install Democrat George Boutwell in the governor's office (*Manual for the Constitutional Convention* 1917).

This episode did not sit well in Massachusetts, which like the rest of the country was swept up in the popular democratic spirit of mid-nineteenth-century American politics. As a result, the majority-vote requirement for electing governors was replaced with a required plurality in 1855, effectively nullifying the elaborate procedures by which the legislature had been able to choose the governor five years earlier. The creation of the commonwealth's "long ballot" was another manifestation of democratic populism in 1855. The secretary of state, treasurer, auditor, and attorney general all became independent and popularly elected constitutional officers. At the same time, governors were also stripped of their authority to appoint sheriffs, registrars of probate, court clerks, and district attorneys.[4] It was not until the early twentieth century with the ascendance of progressive reformers, confident that accountable but powerful political executives were necessary for effective governance in the modern world, that the office of governor would once again be vested with meaningful additional power and authority.

THE IMPACT OF EARLY-TWENTIETH-CENTURY PROGRESSIVISM ON THE MASSACHUSETTS GOVERNOR

In his exhaustive study of the evolution of the budget process in Massachusetts, Luther Gulick chronicles the stages of a gradual shift during the early twentieth century from governors as often unsuccessful competitors for political power to what late-twentieth- and early-twenty-first-century scholars would call "leader-managers" who see themselves as the principal vessels of the public's interest in the efficient and effective administration of government. Gulick finds the seeds of this shift in the personal leadership qualities of late-nineteenth-century governors who used their public platforms to position themselves between the public and the politicians in the legislature in ways reminiscent of the popular legislatures during the provincial period who had likewise positioned themselves between the colonists and the king's representative in the governor's office (Gulick 1920). Provincial governors were easily pushed around by the General Court. The most influential governors of the late nineteenth and early twentieth centuries, however, endeavored to flip the script by positioning themselves as the people's defenders against the corruption and profligacy of the partisan politicians on Beacon Hill. By the twenty-first century, this would become a consistent, if only softly spoken, posture for Massachusetts governors, regardless of party.

The Walker Act of 1910 was among the first significant efforts to empower the state's governors to become guardians of the treasury. It made Massachusetts the first state to give the governor the opportunity to formulate an executive budget (Gulick 1920). A decade later, in the Budget and Accounting Act of 1921, U.S. presidents were given similar influence over the federal budget process. The requirement that the governor organize, supervise, and submit

---

4 The governor's control of the state's military and pardon power was eventually reduced as well. The governor's authority as "commander-in-chief of the army and navy" was downgraded by the transfer to the General Court of the authority to recruit, equip, organize, train, and discipline the state's "military and naval forces," in 1918. The governor's constitutional power to pardon all but those convicted upon impeachment by the Massachusetts House of Representatives was reduced in 1944 by granting to the General Court the power to "prescribe the terms and conditions upon which a pardon may be granted" when the offense is a felony.

annually to the legislature a recommended budget for the entire executive branch was designed to improve the efficiency of government by consolidating and rationalizing this important governmental process under the leadership of the governor. The power to frame the budget for the legislature and the public annually would become a key resource for modern Massachusetts governors trying to overcome the legislative supremacy written into the state constitution and deeply embedded in the state's political history and culture.

The governor's formal authority would be strengthened further less than a decade later in 1918 by constitutional amendments doubling his term of office from one to two years and empowering him to declare emergencies and to return legislation unsigned to the legislature with recommended amendments (Schuck 1961, 57–58).[5] The governor's role and influence in the budget process was further increased by granting him several new prerogatives. These included the right to recommend to the legislature "the term for which any loan shall be contracted," the power to "require any board, commission, officer, or department to furnish him with any information which he may deem necessary" for the purpose of preparing his annual budget recommendations, as well as what has come to be called "line-item veto" authority, which allows the governor to return items in appropriations bills to the legislature for reconsideration without having to veto entire appropriations bills (MA Constitution, art. 62, sec. 3; art. 63, sec. 2). Each item returned to the legislature by the governor must be reconsidered as a single bill. The support of two-thirds of each legislative chamber is needed to override a vetoed item (Schuck 1961, 57–58).

Another significant change involving the governor emerging from the state's 1917–19 constitutional convention was a limit placed on the number of departments in the executive branch under the governor and council. Legislation consolidating a sprawling and haphazard array of administrative units had to be enacted by January 1, 1921. The resulting Reorganization Act of 1919 consolidated more than a hundred departments, boards, and commissions into twenty-one departments, including the governor and council (Gulick 1920).

While this reorganization could be said to have begun the journey of the state's executive branch into the modern bureaucratic age, it was definitely not a wholesale transfer of administrative authority to the governor. Even though it gave the governor the power to appoint the heads of the fifteen

---

5   The governor was required to exercise his power to recommend amendments within five days of receiving a bill from the legislature, increased to ten days in 1968.

new departments not under the purview of the other elected constitutional officers, it also fixed the terms of office of those department heads, many of which would be longer than the governor's two-year term. The fixed terms of office for the new department heads ranged from two to seven years, making many virtually unaccountable to the governor (Gulick 1920). This streamlining of government was a quantitative reduction of nominal departments, but not the creation of the top-down management and accountability structure envisioned by progressive reformers. The departments were still headed by various forms of leadership, including commissions, single commissioners, and single heads with advisory commissions.

According to Mount Holyoke College professor Victoria Schuck, "Individual and group pressures explain many of the characteristics of the [reorganization] statute" (1961, 60). In other words, legislative compromises aimed at satisfying influential constituencies, rather than a modernization of government reflecting the latest management science, are what the Reorganization Act of 1919 was about. Professor Schuck's assessment was made four decades later, which was the next time that reformers pushed hard to improve the efficiency and effectiveness of state government in Massachusetts by strengthening the governor. Of the forty years between the reorganization and her 1961 assessment, Schuck wrote, "This has been a period constitutionally when the state has sought to hedge both the Governor and the General Court with more restrictions on power. After all the maneuvering [however], it was the Governor's Office that suffered a net loss in authority" (60). Schuck continued, "Central management continues under a plural head whose members, except for one, serve longer terms than the Governor. The constitutional requirement of twenty departments has been only a slight deterrent to the General Court in creating new agencies to administer new functions—in the nineteenth-century manner" (65).

Professor Schuck argued that Massachusetts governors were "hamstrung by history," a point she substantiated with a lengthy list of gubernatorial limitations imposed on the governor between 1780 and 1944.[6] She concluded, "At mid-century, the General Court still maintains a preferential position.

---

6   Schuck's list includes: "The 1780 Constitution giving him the Council; The 1855 Amendment taking away the possibility of his appointing the major administrative officials; The 1917 Convention authorizing a two-year term instead of a four-year term; The 1919 reorganization act carrying on the organizational traditions of the nineties; The 1917 Convention and the 1919 act in not empowering him to make removals; The 1922 act creating a plural executive agency to handle the function of central management; The 1915 and 1948 constitutional Amendments limiting the character of the income tax and earmarking highway funds; and [t]he 1944 Amendment restricting his power to pardon" (1961, 57–58).

The Governor is [expected] to supply political leadership and to formulate policy on anything from what to do about hurricane damage, transit strikes, taxes, and education to reorganization and law enforcement. If he requires the freedom to cope with the problems of a modern urban society, he needs the time and formal power to gain their solution" (66–67). Despite meaningful increases in the formal power of Massachusetts governors since this assessment, twenty-first-century occupants of the corner office remain at least somewhat "hamstrung," but not by insufficient formal authority. Rather, it is the state's particular brand of politics, transactional in nature and patronage based in practice, that continues to give legislative leaders on Beacon Hill considerable leverage in their dealings with the occupants of the corner office.

A FOUR-YEAR TERM, A RUNNING MATE, AND A CABINET GOVERNMENT

Progressive reformers' efforts to match state government capacities with its rapidly increasing responsibilities helped fuel changes that enhanced the governor's ability to exert stronger and more lasting leadership over the direction of state government. In 1964 voters approved three constitutional amendments designed to enhance the leadership capacity of governors. One created four-year terms for all statewide constitutional officers, which gave governors more time to accomplish their goals before facing the voters again. Another empowered governors to seek advisory opinions from the justices of the state's supreme court, the Supreme Judicial Court, on questions of law. The third measure eliminated the statutory authority of the Governor's Council, leading to the elimination of the requirement that governors obtain council approval for nonjudicial appointments (Lockard et al. 1976). In 1966 voters eliminated separate elections for governor and lieutenant governor, requiring them to run together as a "ticket," which eliminated the possibility of governors having lieutenant governors from the opposition party, a situation that had occurred multiple times in the recent past. These changes, as well as reorganization authority (discussed below), were designed to empower the governor and were consistent with those being given to governors across America at the time and since. Confidence in popular and powerful executives in American statehouses and the White House was high in the 1960s, and unlike presidential power, this confidence in governors was not dimmed by the Vietnam War and the Watergate scandal. What makes Massachusetts exceptional here is the degree to which gubernatorial empowerment has not produced executive supremacy in Massachusetts government and politics as much as it has in both Washington, DC, and other state capitals (Seifter 2017).

In 1966 Massachusetts voters approved a process for governors to reorganize executive agencies by statute. With reorganization authority, modern Massachusetts governors have been able to increase their influence over the state's bureaucracy. The governor's reorganization authority allows him to submit reorganization plans to the legislature, where such plans must be voted up or down without amendment within sixty days. The first modern Massachusetts governor-initiated reorganization act, passed under the authority created in 1966, was signed by Republican governor Frank Sargent in 1969. While it did give the governor more influence over the executive branch, it did not and has not fundamentally changed the balance of political power on Beacon Hill, where legislative leaders remain in the driver's seat.

The only structural change emerging from the governor's initial statutory reorganization authority enacted in 1966 was the creation of ten cabinet departments, each one headed by a gubernatorially appointed secretary.[7] More than three hundred executive agencies scattered among the twenty existing executive departments were placed into the ten cabinet departments. Nobody was fired or transferred. The cabinet secretaries were merely installed above. It was the newly appointed secretaries themselves who would be tasked with doing the dirty work. The statute gave them two years to recommend the more difficult reorganizational changes that would have to occur within each cabinet department. In his analysis of the reorganization bill, the former director of the Modernization Systems Unit for the state, Robert Casselman, explained that "the postponement of any bureaucratic bloodshed aided enormously in getting the bill enacted" (1973, 131). It also signaled the state legislature's intention and ability to limit the degree to which reorganization authority would interfere with their political and policy agendas.

Executive branch reorganization in Massachusetts during the 1970s clearly illustrated the wisdom of the aphorism "The devil is in the details." The battle over the nuts and bolts of subcabinet executive reorganization quickly devolved into a bitter fight between the leaders of the Democratic-controlled legislature and Republican governor Frank Sargent. Though Sargent had a good working relationship with Democrats on Beacon Hill, and a long list of bipartisan policy-making achievements, the details of executive branch reorganization were not as easily compromised because the threat to Democrats on Beacon Hill was professional, not partisan.

---

7   The first cabinet departments were as follows: Communities and Development, Consumer Affairs, Education, Elder Affairs, Environment, Human Services, Manpower, Public Safety, Transportation and Construction, and Administration and Finance.

The modernization of executive branch organization and management threatened the livelihoods of professional politicians on Beacon Hill. The fact that the staffs of the ten new cabinet secretaries would be exempt from civil-service protection meant that the cabinet secretaries serving at the governor's pleasure would have staffs serving at their pleasure. One of the ways legislators monitor and exploit the operations of the executive branch is by cultivating relationships with career administrators in key executive branch positions. If the governor is able to install political loyalists two levels deep in a reorganized and more streamlined executive branch, the value to legislators of their administrative contacts would surely decrease (Hogarty 2002). In other words, reorganization plans based on transforming government into a more efficient and businesslike enterprise by centralizing administrative authority threatened to disrupt "politics as usual" on Beacon Hill. An important part of "politics as usual" is the ability of legislative leaders to cultivate close and mutually beneficial working relationships with career administrators and interest groups. These relationships between legislators in committee, interest groups, and the bureaucracy form what political scientists call "iron triangles" because they operate like policy gatekeepers vetting policy proposals for consistency with the interests of major political and economic stakeholders.[8]

Efforts to modernize the organization and administration of state government in the 1970s laid bare the central and enduring dynamic of Massachusetts government and politics, which, unlike politics in Washington and most state capitals, has very little to do with particularly partisan or ideological agendas. The failure of Governor Sargent to oversee meaningful progress in the modernization of state government had nothing to do with the fact that he was a Republican facing a legislature controlled by Democrats. The tenure of Sargent's successor, Democrat Michael Dukakis, revealed that the central cleavage in Massachusetts politics was (and is) fueled by the tension between the individualistic, professionalized, and transactional approach to politics that predominates in the state legislature and the more managerial approach that tends to better suit governors and presidents. This tension, combined with the complete absence of two-party competition in the legislature, protects the exceptionally nonideological insider-versus-outsider dynamic of contemporary Massachusetts state politics.

---

8   With the increased transparency of government and politics ushered in by both procedural reforms and advancements in inter- and mass communications, the number of actors with influence over policy making has expanded, transforming closed iron triangles into more open and complex "issue networks."

MIKE DUKAKIS WAS RIGHT

Before Michael Dukakis became the sixty-fifth governor of Massachusetts in 1975, he had spent eight years in the Massachusetts House of Representatives where he was a leader of the Democratic Party's progressive ideological faction, a group of young legislators determined to move the party away from patronage politics toward a more progressive and programmatic focus. As he has indicated in dozens of interviews and speeches about his service in the Massachusetts House of Representatives, Dukakis was a thorn in the side of house Democratic Party leaders. He was an impatient, ideological reformer who, nonetheless, had serious personal political ambitions. Before his successful run for governor in 1974, Dukakis had run unsuccessfully for state attorney general in 1966 and had been the Democratic Party's unsuccessful lieutenant governor nominee in 1970.

Dukakis' first term in the "corner office" revealed for all to see, including Dukakis himself, the real balance of the forces at play in Massachusetts politics, a balance still at play nearly a half century later. A creature of a then ascendant progressivism focused on reducing government corruption by opening up and democratizing the policy-making process as well as depoliticizing policy implementation, Governor Dukakis got a rude awakening when the Democrats on Beacon Hill did not go along with the program during his first term. The man who would become the longest-serving governor in Massachusetts history came to realize that "right doesn't make might" in the Massachusetts State House. During the four years between losing his own party's nomination for governor in 1978 and winning another term as governor in 1982, Dukakis learned that "political skills" are essential for governors (Cundy 1999). Having been such an aggressive critic of patronage politics in his first campaign for (and first term as) governor, Dukakis failed to cultivate and maintain the political relationships necessary to bring disparate individuals and groups together behind his agenda (White 1982).[9] His first-term efforts to avoid even the appearance of political cronyism led him to alienate key friends, supporters, and legislators. His use of the term *political skills* became Dukakis' acknowledgment that not all political horse-trading amounts to corruption. Dukakis learned that governors have to obtain buy-in from influential stakeholders, in the legislature and elsewhere, on their own

---

9   Political scientist John White emphasized the role, in Dukakis' 1978 defeat by Ed King, of cultural hot-button issues exploited by King (who later became a Republican) that look a lot like the culture war partisanship of contemporary Republicans.

terms, even if those terms are based on pure political or economic self-interest or both (Michael Dukakis, interview, July 9, 2020).

During his second and third terms as governor from 1982 to 1990, Dukakis set the terms for what has become the modus operandi of the twenty-first-century Massachusetts governorship. He integrated political coalition building into his management philosophy and presented himself as a sort of reformed reformer. Though still committed to better government through attention to professionalism, in terms of both management processes and leadership style with an explicit focus on integrity as a central prerequisite for effectiveness, Dukakis made peace with the deeply embedded transactional, patronage politics of Beacon Hill. He came to believe that "politics as usual" was not always incompatible with progress and that in order to be successful and effective leaders, governors have to be both skillful political bargainers and effective managers. He would come to believe that state legislators are effectively the governor's "board of directors" whose perspective and preferences have to be considered and respected on their own terms (Michael Dukakis, interview, July 9, 2020). One real casualty of Dukakis' tenure as governor was the harsh antipolitics progressivism of the Far Left that was ascendant in the Democratic Party during the late 1960s and 1970s. Once a passionate ideological progressive, Dukakis set the stage for what would become known as a "third way," the fiscally minded center-left approach that helped Bill Clinton win the Democratic nomination and the presidency in 1992.

While transactional and moralistic politics driven by ideology were colliding in Washington and state capitals across the country, they were being accommodated in Massachusetts. The contrast between the political fates of Michael Dukakis' and Jimmy Carter's approach to state governance is instructive. Both served as governors during the 1970s, and both held strong progressive values as well as the belief that a better and more efficiently managed government would be the surest way, politically and administratively, to translate those progressive values into public policy. While both ultimately fell short in their national political aspirations, in no small part because their approaches were incompatible with the emerging hyperpartisanship of national governance and politics at the time, the governors offices they left behind hint at the unique compatibility between their progressive yet managerial inclinations and the Massachusetts governorship. All of Dukakis' successors of both parties have followed his lead, which is to say that none have employed partisanship as their primary instrument in legislative relations, while the Georgia governor's office has, since the 1970s, descended into the same partisan madness that has overwhelmed twenty-first-century American national politics.

Historian Lily Geismer argues that Governor Dukakis' approach to the Massachusetts governorship heralded nothing less than the transformation of the modern American Democratic Party. She writes that Dukakis' "agenda of private sector business growth, low taxes, and market-oriented solutions explicitly recast the Democratic Party's longstanding approach to economic development, welfare, and organized labor . . . [offering] an alternative middle ground between the urban ethnic old guard of the Democratic Party and progressive constituencies" (2015, 252). While the national Democratic Party and national politics in general continues to be hobbled by internecine warfare between moralistic ideologues and individualistic establishment interests and players, the same cannot be said of Massachusetts Democrats or politics. Every Massachusetts governor since Dukakis has remained squarely on this "middle ground," choosing to leverage their public popularity to pursue their governing agendas without running afoul of the political or policy interests of Democratic leaders on Beacon Hill. Dukakis' successors of both parties, by embracing his approach to accommodating policy goals and political interests, have been able to achieve many objectives without forcefully attacking the legitimacy of patronage politics or the integrity of patronage politicians on Beacon Hill.

The approach to leadership that earned Dukakis his second and third terms as governor, as well as the Democratic Party's presidential nomination in 1988, was spelled out in a book he wrote decades later with fellow Northeastern University political science professor John Portz. In *Leader-Managers in the Public Sector: Managing for Results*, Dukakis and Portz distilled what Dukakis learned in (and out of) the governor's office and what they learned in extensive interviews with public managers into the following "six common practices that constitute the foundation for an effective leader-manager":

1. Picking & motivating your people
2. Walking around . . . listening . . . learning
3. Fostering collaboration & support
4. Building effective organizations
5. Communicating with the public
6. Demonstrating character & integrity (2010, 7–8)

Each one involves "political skills," which is to say the willingness to bring interested and contending individuals and groups into decision-making processes on their own terms and to consciously strive to achieve sufficient buy-in from key stakeholders in order to move forward without unnecessarily burning political bridges (Dukakis and Portz 2010). This amounts to an explicit acknowledgment that individualistic, transactional politics is an inescapable part of politics that cannot be shamed or reformed into submission. Dukakis' leadership model gave his successors a road map to guide them around the increasingly harsh and confrontational partisan routes being taken in Washington and in state capitals across the country ever since.

Mike Dukakis' first term as governor was a lot like Jimmy Carter's only term as president in terms of leadership style and rocky executive-legislative relations, despite single-party control of both the executive and the legislative branches. His second and third terms, on the other hand, stabilized the clash between moralistic, antipolitics, ideological activism and individualistic, transactional, patronage politics on Beacon Hill. As of this writing, five Republicans and one Democrat have served as governor since Dukakis left office in 1990. Every one of them has understood and accepted the accommodations established by Dukakis between the "old-school" transactional politics of Beacon Hill and the "leader-manager" role of the modern governor. Furthermore, every governor since Dukakis who has chosen to run for reelection, regardless of party affiliation, has been reelected, a fact that signals the bipartisan acceptance of this accommodation, as well as the primacy of an insider-outsider (as opposed to a left-right) cleavage in Massachusetts government and politics.

The day after Governor Charlie Baker's first election in 2014, Michael Jonas' *CommonWealth Magazine* article about Baker's emphasis on competence over ideology reinforced the significance of Dukakis' approach to the job. The title of the article was "Mike Dukakis Was Right" (Jonas 2014).

FROM GOVERNOR DUKAKIS TO GOVERNOR "FIX-IT"

Since Dukakis left office in 1990, five men and one woman have occupied the corner office at the statehouse; all but one was Republican. Republican William Weld (1991–97) resigned during his second term to pursue an ultimately failed effort to become a U.S. ambassador. His lieutenant governor, Paul Cellucci, took over in 1997 before being elected in his own right in 1998. Unlike Weld's, Cellucci's efforts to become a U.S. ambassador were successful. He resigned the governorship in 2001 to become U.S. ambassador to Canada and his lieutenant governor, Jane Swift, served out the remainder of Cellucci's term and then retired from elective politics, making way for the GOP to nominate Mitt Romney in 2002. Romney defeated State Treasurer

Shannon O'Brien to win his single term in the governor's chair (2003–7). He won, in part, because O'Brien's hard-fought Democratic primary victory over then state senate president Tom Birmingham and former U.S. labor secretary Robert Reich created divisions among Democratic leaders, organizers, and constituencies that couldn't be entirely resolved by Election Day in November.

Governor Romney's higher political ambitions were no secret during his governorship and may well have accounted for his occasional willingness to be confrontational in his relations with Beacon Hill Democrats. However, he ultimately balked at full-scale partisan combat with Democrats because he knew it would be fruitless and because he wanted to achieve a policy victory that he hoped would improve his chances for a political promotion. The landmark health-insurance reform law he signed in 2006, a product of complex and difficult negotiations with Democratic legislative leaders, seemed to Romney at the time just what the doctor ordered. However, Romney's assumption that his ability to broker a market-friendly health-insurance reform law in bright-blue Massachusetts would enhance his presidential prospects was ultimately frustrated by a crucial difference between Massachusetts partisanship and national partisanship. Washington Republicans were willing to attack Obama's version of Romneycare as government-run health care and socialized medicine, despite having been strong proponents of its basic elements in their own health-care policy proposals during the Clinton administration. This illustrates the stark contrast between the win-at-all-costs partisanship of national politics and the virtually nonpartisan deal making at the Massachusetts State House. It also made Romney's greatest public policy accomplishment considerably less useful or valuable on the 2012 presidential campaign trail.

The governorships of the two men who followed Governor Romney, one Democrat and one Republican, both of whom served two full terms, best reflect the exceptionally nonideological and nonpartisan ways of state governance in Massachusetts. Democrat Deval Patrick, elected in 2006 and reelected in 2010, brought a combination of progressive and managerial values very much like those of the last Democrat to win a gubernatorial election in the state twenty years earlier. The first Black governor of Massachusetts, elected in his first run for public office, began his tenure with considerable support and enthusiasm from the state's progressive activists and constituencies. Patrick's soaring rhetoric and innovative Internet-based campaign technologies and techniques turned out to be test runs for a friend running for president in 2008. His campaign manager, David Axelrod, used his experience running

Patrick's 2006 gubernatorial campaign to guide Barack Obama's victorious run for the White House two years later.

Patrick's twenty-point margin of victory over Mitt Romney's lieutenant governor, Kerry Healey, in 2006, as well as his ability to characterize his predecessor's tenure as divisive, was made easier by the fact that Romney's intention to move on to greener pastures after one term had become quite clear during his last two years in office. Patrick's brief 2020 presidential campaign characterized him as having been a governor who created lasting reforms by being able to bring together competing factions, a characterization that might seem surprising for a Democratic governor in a state where Democrats had complete control of both chambers of the state legislature (Andersen 2019). This 2020 boast is not just campaign spin. Patrick was swept into office with a great deal of progressive energy and momentum, yet his governorship was hardly the lurch to the left you might expect after sixteen years of Republican governors. Patrick's accomplishments as governor included pension reform, legalization of casino gambling, an overhaul of the state's parole board, increased investments in the state's transportation infrastructure, and an education reform law that increased the number of charter schools in the state (Andersen 2019). Solid accomplishments to be sure, but it was hardly the progressive record many had anticipated. The exceptionally unconventional partisanship of Beacon Hill Democrats even escaped prominent scholar of American governorships Thad Beyle. His annual national gubernatorial power rankings named Governor Patrick as the most powerful governor in America in 2007 precisely because he assumed that total Democratic Party control on Beacon Hill after sixteen years would translate into unrivaled partisan accomplishment for Patrick (Prah 2007).

Patrick's successor, and current governor at the time of this writing, was Republican Charlie Baker. Baker, who had been a high-level appointee in Governor Weld's administration, ran on an explicitly nonideological and even nonpartisan appeal. In his successful 2014 campaign for governor against Democratic attorney general Martha Coakley, Baker's campaign took great pains to frame the race in candidate-centric terms by casting himself in the role of a successful administrator and manager with impressive experience in the public and private sectors against a "career politician." The temptation to attack Democrats on Beacon Hill was heightened by an unfolding patronage scandal in the summer of 2014 that revealed decades of corrupt hiring practices in the state's Probation Department that implicated a number of longtime Democratic legislators. Despite a great deal of pressure to feature

Democratic corruption at the Probation Department, Baker very wisely stopped short of an all-out attack on the legitimacy of Beacon Hill patronage politics. He understood that such a direct attack wouldn't necessarily help him win because it would risk framing the contest in partisan terms, rather than candidate-centric terms, which is never a good idea for a Republican candidate in Massachusetts. Second, Baker understood that such a partisan approach would poison his ability to work with Democratic legislative leaders after the election. Without such a relationship, no Massachusetts governor, regardless of party, can hope to succeed in office.

Governor Baker, dubbed "Governor Fix-It" for his decidedly nonideological approach to the job, was very easily reelected in 2018, in part because of his positive working relationship with the Democratic legislature. Beacon Hill Democratic leaders all but openly supported the Republican governor over their own party's nominee in 2018, something they had also done for sitting Republican governors in the past. Baker beat former Patrick administration official Jay Gonzalez on Election Day 2018 by more than a two-to-one margin.

Charlie Baker has spent his entire tenure to date at or near the top of national gubernatorial popularity rankings. Baker was the most popular governor in America for more than three years, according to the Morning Consult poll, until dropping to third most popular in January 2020 (DeCosta-Klipa 2020). Governor Baker's posture toward Donald Trump played a role in his popularity. He was a frequent and vocal critic of President Trump, a stance that alienated the Republican governor from his own party leaders and voters in the state. In fact, during Trump's White House tenure, Baker had consistently higher approval ratings among Democrats in the state than among Republicans (Koczela 2020; Pindell 2018). Trump's 2020 defeat did not dim Massachusetts Republicans' disapproval of Governor Baker. Bay State Republicans strenuously objected to Baker's use of emergency powers to unilaterally impose far-reaching measures to address the COVID-19 pandemic. While Baker's schools and business closures drew harsh criticism and an unsuccessful court challenge from his right, the governor's slow and poorly communicated rollout of the state's vaccination effort drew harsh criticism from the left. Through it all, however, Baker's popularity dipped only briefly during the early stages of the state's vaccine rollout. Baker's poll numbers eventually went back up and until his December 1, 2021, announcement that he wouldn't, he was widely expected to run for an unprecedented third consecutive four-year term.

Conclusion

The increases in formal powers described in this chapter have placed the state's twenty-first-century governors at or near the top of national gubernatorial formal power rankings, but they have not translated into executive supremacy at the statehouse. Massachusetts governors have four-year terms and no term limits. Their veto powers, budgetary authority, and power to issue executive orders all equal or surpass those of their fellow governors across the country. Their legal authority to reorganize executive branch agencies is no less impressive than that of other governors. At the same time, Massachusetts governors have never found themselves shut out of the national political arena. As was discussed in chapter 3, Bay State governors have always enjoyed an outsize share of national political attention and influence. Modern Massachusetts governors have made excellent use of the same communications technology breakthroughs that have advanced the policies, profiles, and political leverage of American governors and presidents for decades. Despite all this, Bay State governors, regardless of party, continue to carefully avoid open or prolonged confrontation with a state legislature that brazenly operates according to rules and norms openly disdained by most Americans, even many of the Americans living in Massachusetts, preferring instead to accommodate rather than substantively attack "politics as usual" on Beacon Hill.

Governor Dukakis' "leader-manager" approach to the governorship created an essentially nonpartisan template for his successors designed to adapt the office to ever-increasing political and policy demands and pressures. Accommodation over confrontation with the state legislature remains the surest route to success and progress for twenty-first-century Massachusetts governors. Finding common purpose between progressive values and managerial thinking, as well as common ground with the "old-school" transactional politicians running the state legislature, Dukakis' approach insulated the corner office, and all of its occupants since, from dependence on narrowly partisan or ideological interests and helped to protect the office from the bitter, destructive partisanship of contemporary national politics.

A lot of ink has been spilled trying to figure out why Massachusetts voters have so often over the past thirty years split their tickets between Republican gubernatorial candidates and Democratic candidates for everything else. Governor Dukakis' transformative approach provides many, if not most, of the pieces to this puzzle. Also, the eminently secure veto-proof Democratic majorities in both chambers of the legislature significantly reduce the partisan stakes of gubernatorial elections, allowing legislative leaders to avoid expending partisan political capital in gubernatorial elections and to focus instead on gaining the cooperation of sitting governors regardless of party. Indeed, Republican governors provide Beacon Hill Democrats with useful political cover from the pressure and policy demands of progressive activists and special interests in the state. In this way, the top-down control of the state legislature by old-school, transactional, professional Democratic politicians may actually give Republican candidates for governor an advantage on Election Day.

Meaningful, important, and bipartisan achievements can and have been accomplished by modern Massachusetts governors. This is thanks in large part to innovative and accommodating adaptations of the office to a legislatively dominated style and manner of governing that has withstood the targeting of critics, commentators, and reformers left, right, and center for more than a century in American politics. This endurance of what amounts to "old-school," patronage-based, transactional politics, to which Massachusetts governors have always deferred, if not embraced, reflects the impact and endurance of a political culture older than any other in America. Massachusetts governors have been negotiating the social, political, and cultural tensions between moralistic/ideological and individualistic politics and government since 1630.

The governorship framed in John Adams' 1780 state constitution harnessed the wisdom of more than 150 years of Massachusetts experience. The key lesson learned then was not principally different from the lesson learned and implemented by Michael Dukakis two centuries later, a lesson no less useful to every governor since Dukakis. Personal ambition and power politics will always find their way around the antiestablishment rhetoric and moralistic zeal of political insurgents and reformers. The same lesson underwrote the U.S. Constitution as well, though two and a half centuries later John Adams' handiwork has held up much better than James Madison's. The contrast can, in part, be traced to political party development. In American national politics, where the stakes have often been higher and the two-party competition much more vigorous and vicious, the competitive allure of morally infused antiestablishment rhetoric has too often been irresistible. So often weaponized by both sides in national politics, condemnation of "politics as usual" finds its way into virtually every contemporary political candidate's rhetoric, gradually degrading and even delegitimizing the individualistic political assumptions embedded in the work of the framers. In Massachusetts politics, on the other hand, one-party domination has been the rule, and this condition has limited the competitive advantage of moralistic, antiestablishment appeals and insulated the state's politics from the escalating partisanship that now finds national partisans abusing their institutional prerogatives with increasing regularity. The ability of Massachusetts governors to honor the framers' constitutional preference for legislative supremacy and to nonetheless provide the state with energetic and meaningful policy and political leadership stands in stark contrast to the experience of modern American presidents as well as many fellow governors across the country.

For nearly four centuries, kings, colonists, activists, scholars, and reformers measuring the political clout and constitutional capacities of the Massachusetts governorship have judged the office lacking. The seemingly permanent and often indecipherable dominance of the state legislature on Beacon Hill has no doubt fostered this perspective and in the late twentieth century even helped win governors the constitutional and statutory powers and prerogatives that now place the office at or near the top of national gubernatorial formal power rankings. Ultimately, like the commonwealth's politics in general, the exceptionalism of the office of governor lies in its seniority, the oldest political executive office in America, and in its long testimony to the wisdom of preserving space for energetic executive leadership without slaying—or surrendering to—individualistic, interest-based, political bargaining in democratic governance.

WORKS CITED

Andersen, Travis. 2019. "The Highs and Lows of Deval Patrick's Tenure as Governor." *Boston Globe*, November 12, 2019. https://www.bostonglobe.com/metro/2019/11/12/the-highs-and-lows-deval-patrick-tenure-governor/ZGpCt2jGCT153BrJzoLosM/story.html.

Brown, Katherine. 1954. "Freemanship in Puritan Massachusetts." *American Historical Review* 59, no. 4: 865–83.

Casselman, Robert. 1973. "Massachusetts Revisited: Chronology of a Failure." *Public Administration Review* 33, no. 2: 129–35.

Cundy, James. 1999. "Images of the Executive: Michael Dukakis and the Progressive Legacy." PhD diss., University of Massachusetts, Amherst. https://scholarworks.umass.edu/dissertations/AAI9950147.

DeCosta-Klipa, Nik. 2020. "Charlie Baker's Long Reign as America's Most Popular Governor Is Over." *Boston.com*, January 17, 2020. https://www.boston.com/news/politics/2020/01/17/charlie-baker-not-so-popular-but-still-pretty-popular.

Douglas, Charles H. J. 1892. *The Financial History of Massachusetts: From the Organization of the Massachusetts Bay Colony to the American Revolution*. New York: Columbia University.

Dukakis, Michael S., and John H. Portz. 2010. *Leader-Managers in the Public Sector: Managing for Results*. New York: M. E. Sharpe.

Duquette, Jerold. 2013. "Bay State Politics in the Post–Scott Brown Era." *New England Journal of Political Science* 7, no. 2.

———. 2019. "Mass Politics after the 2018 Elections: Still 'Safe Harbor for Old School Pols & Politics.'" *MassPoliticsProfs* (blog), May 14, 2019. https://www.masspoliticsprofs.org/2019/05/14/mass-politics-after-the-2018-elections-still-safe-harbor-for-old-school-pols-politics/.

Geismer, Lily. 2015. *Don't Blame Us: Suburban Liberals and the Transformation of the Democratic Party*. Princeton, NJ: Princeton University Press.

Gulick, Luther H. 1920. *Evolution of the Budget in Massachusetts*. New York: Macmillan.

Hogarty, Richard. 2002. *Massachusetts Politics and Public Policy: Studies in Power and Leadership*. Amherst: University of Massachusetts Press.

Jonas, Michael. 2014. "Mike Dukakis Was Right." *CommonWealth Magazine*, November 5, 2014. https://commonwealthmagazine.org/politics/024/.

Koczela, Steve. 2020. "Mass. GOP Voters Like Trump More than Their Republican Governors." WBUR, March 2, 2020. https://www.wbur.org/news/2020/03/02/charlie-baker-trump-republicans-poll.

Lockard, Duane, Victoria Schuck, Eugene J. Gleason, and Joseph Zimmerman. 1976. "A Mini-Symposium: The Strong Governorship: Status and Problems." *Public Administration Review* 36, no. 1: 90–98.

A Manual for the Constitutional Convention, 1917. Boston: Wright and Potter.

Pindell, James. 2018. "Our Republican Governor Is More Popular with Democrats. Wait, What?" *Boston Globe*, September 25, 2018. https://www.bostonglobe.com/metro/2018/09/25/more-democrats-give-high-marks-charlie-baker-than-republicans-survey-finds/xmOKfMhxPoBCJwRk5XIDZO/story.html.

Prah, Pamela. 2007. "Massachusetts Gov Rated Most Powerful." *Pew Charitable Trusts: Stateline*, March 9, 2007. http://www.pewtrusts.org/en/research-and-analysis/blogs/stateline/2007/03/09/massachusetts-gov-rated-most-powerful.

Schuck, Victoria. 1961. "The Massachusetts Governorship: Hamstrung by History?" In vol. 2 of *State Government and Public Responsibility, 1961: The Role of the Governor in Massachusetts*, edited by Robert R. Robbins. Papers of the 1961 Tufts Assembly on Massachusetts Government. Lincoln Filene Center for Citizenship and Public Affairs, Tufts University, Medford, MA.

Seifter, Miriam. 2017. "Gubernatorial Administration." *Harvard Law Review* 131, no. 2: 484–542. https://harvardlawreview.org/wp-content/uploads/2017/12/483–542_Online.pdf.

Spencer, Henry Russell. 1905. *Constitutional Conflict in Provincial Massachusetts*. Columbus, OH: Press of Fred J. Heer.

White, John K. 1982. "All in the Family: The 1978 Massachusetts Democratic Gubernatorial Primary." *Polity* 14, no. 4: 641–56.

CHAPTER 6

THE COURTS AND THE CONSTITUTION
Exceptionally Enduring

Lawrence Friedman

It is no idle boast to claim as exceptional both the Massachusetts Supreme Judicial Court and the constitution it is chiefly responsible for interpreting. The SJC remains "the oldest court in continuous service in the hemisphere, operating under the oldest still functioning written constitution anywhere" (Kaplan 1990, 6). And while the Massachusetts Constitution of 1780 was not the first postrevolutionary charter, few state constitutions have proved to be as influential: "No constitution was ever more thoroughly studied," the sociologist George C. Homans observed, "or more democratically accepted by the people who were to abide by it" (1981, 287).

Today the SJC remains a leader among state courts dedicated to developing their state's constitutional law. To the extent this effort requires the SJC to steer the court system through the treacherous shoals of Massachusetts politics, it often relies not just on its historical pedigree but also on a sense of its institutional limits. Sometimes, a prominent role for the court in the commonwealth's political life appears unavoidable. For instance, while the framers of the Massachusetts Constitution embedded the protection of various individual rights and liberties in the text itself, it has been through judicial interpretation of these provisions that the framers' vision continues to be realized today, in circumstances they could not have imagined in 1780. If nothing else, what remains exceptional about the SJC is its commitment to carefully interpreting the Massachusetts Constitution to ensure that it remains vital. This commitment is matched by an exceptional respect for both the court and the constitution that is shared by judges, lawyers, and citizens. Such respect suggests a reason that, unlike in nearly every other state in the Union, the citizens of the commonwealth have over more than two centuries formally tinkered with their constitution relatively rarely, and generally at the margins.[1]

---

[1] For example, the Alabama Constitution has been amended 909 times since its adoption in 1901, while the Massachusetts Constitution has been amended just 119 times since its adoption in 1780. See https://ballotpedia.org/Number_of_state_constitutional_amendments_in_each_state.

This chapter examines the SJC and the Massachusetts Constitution, beginning with a brief discussion of the constitution's provenance, framework, and historical importance. The chapter next addresses the SJC and its role in government throughout the commonwealth's history, with particular attention to the court's relationships with the General Court and the governor. These relationships are illustrated by three cases that attracted a great deal of attention at the time each was decided: *Bates v. Director of the Office of Campaign and Political Finance*, which addressed the Massachusetts Clean Elections Law; *Goodridge v. Department of Public Health*, which addressed the statutory prohibition on same-sex marriage; and *Desrosiers v. Governor*, which addressed the governor's use of emergency powers during the coronavirus pandemic. These cases highlight the tensions between the court and the political branches and the ways in which the court has sought to mediate those tensions. Finally, the chapter turns to the endurance of the SJC and the state constitution, the quality that continues to define both as exceptional.

A Brief History of the Massachusetts Constitution and Its Historical Importance

The people of Massachusetts, having renounced British rule following the Battles of Lexington and Concord, in the late spring of 1775 blessed the creation of a new legislative body: the General Court (which is discussed in chapter 4). Within a little more than a year's time, of course, the colonies would formally declare their independence from the Crown and the new states would begin to design systems of government to replace the architecture of colonial rule they had abandoned. The people of Massachusetts expressed their desire for a governing charter through their town governments, and the General Court responded by resolving itself into a constitutional convention and, in early 1778, producing a draft for the citizenry's consideration.

The reaction to the draft constitution was decidedly negative. After its rejection at the polls, some towns filed returns containing extensive criticisms and suggestions. One such response, "The Essex Result"—from the towns of Essex County, and essentially the work of the young lawyer Theophilus Parsons (who would later become chief justice of the SJC)—took the draft apart in no small detail. Among other suggestions, the "Result" advocated for a constitution that would contain mechanisms sufficient to deter and prevent the rise of the tyranny from which the colonies had sought escape—a charter that would protect individual rights and liberties and, at the same time, effectively limit the potential for governmental overreaching (Friedman and Thody 2011, 9).

This guidance echoed the counsel earlier advocated by Massachusetts lawyer John Adams. Adams had famously defended the British soldiers accused of murder during the Boston Massacre; he would later serve as a delegate to the Continental Congress and, eventually, the second president of the United States. In his "Thoughts on Government," published in the spring of 1776, Adams argued that constitutions ought to separate and divide the respective powers of the different departments of state government—the legislative, executive, and judicial branches—to the end of ensuring that a state would be, as he put it, "an empire of laws and not of men" (1776, 87). Such a scheme of governance would, he believed, deter the threat posed by a concentration of all these powers in one department, through which government officials "would make arbitrary laws for their own interest, execute all laws arbitrarily for their own interest, and adjudge all controversies in their own favour" (1776, 88). Perhaps no thinker of the time had devoted more attention to constitution making than Adams—and none would play a more pivotal role in the development of postrevolutionary Massachusetts government.

The first attempt to draft a constitution for the commonwealth having failed, the next would be led not by the General Court but by a convention of delegates who were elected by all resident freemen—that is, by men twenty-years of age or older and not enslaved. The delegates to the convention were dedicated solely to the work of crafting a new charter for the commonwealth. The convention met on September 1, 1779, in Cambridge and elected a committee of thirty of its members to draft the new constitution; when that committee convened thereafter in Boston, it assigned its task to a subcommittee composed of John Adams, his cousin Samuel Adams, and James Bowdoin, the convention's president. The subcommittee in turn delegated the bulk of the drafting to John Adams, and, when the convention again assembled at the end of October, it was essentially his draft that the delegates discussed, debated, and refined (Friedman and Thody 2011, 10).

On March 2, 1780, the convention released its draft for consideration by the commonwealth's resident freemen. The convention had requested that towns separately record votes, comments, and suggestions in respect to each article of the constitution—which made it difficult, when the convention met again in June, to tabulate the results and to determine whether the charter had been approved. In the end, the convention concluded that nearly all the articles appeared to be supported by the necessary two-thirds majority, and on June 15 it declared that a new constitution for the commonwealth had been adopted (Morrison 1917).

For the most part, the Massachusetts Constitution of 1780 represented Adams' vision, notwithstanding that "the convention," as one modern commentator remarked, "debated freely, patiently, and at length to bend [Adams'] draft to its wishes" (Taylor 1980, 344). The constitution's preamble announces the central aim: "to secure the existence of the body politic, to protect it, and to furnish the individuals who compose it with the power of enjoying in safety and tranquility their natural rights" (MA Constitution 1780). The preamble further defines the body politic and establishes that the government of Massachusetts should reflect the will of the people, a novel affirmation of popular sovereignty that would inspire constitution makers elsewhere. Respect for the legislature as the agents of the people, moreover, would over time come to inform the SJC's deference to the legislature when construing its enactments, a deference that the court continues to show today.

Unlike the first draft constitution, which had been roundly rejected, the new constitution contained express commitments to the protection of an array of individual rights and liberties. These commitments comprise the first thirty provisions of the constitution, known as "the Declaration of Rights." Some of the declaration's guarantees may be traced to the Magna Carta, such as the protection of what we today call due process, which Chief Justice Lemuel Shaw aptly described as "the ancient established law and course of proceedings, by an adherence to which our ancestors in England, before the settlement of this country, and the emigrants themselves and their descendants, had found safety for their personal rights" (*Jones v. Robbins* 1857, 343). Other protections represented innovations for the time, including commitments to, among other things, equal treatment by the government, participation in elections, privacy, and freedom from cruel or unusual punishment. Throughout the Declaration of Rights, Adams and the framers placed reminders of the need for government to be ever subservient to the desires of the people themselves. As Article V states, all power resides "originally in the people," with the officers of government understood to be "their substitutes and agents, and . . . at all times accountable to them." One commentator noted that "the duty of the Commonwealth to protect and promote the welfare of its citizens jumps out as a pervasive theme" (Soifer 1992, 208).

In detailing the structural framework of Massachusetts' government, the constitution echoes many of the themes Adams explored in "Thoughts on

Government," particularly the necessity of separating the different powers of government. The Massachusetts Constitution accordingly divides the General Court's legislative power between a house of representatives and a senate—a legacy of the bicameral nature of the colonial legislature. With each house serving a different constituency, the citizenry may be more thoroughly represented, and each house can act as a check upon the other. Further, the constitution establishes the office of a chief executive, the governor, who is directly accountable to the people. The governor, in turn, may check the General Court through the veto and controls the functioning of state government through the authority to make appointments, including members of the judicial branch, with the advice and consent of a separately elected Governor's Council. And, not least, the constitution provides for an independent judiciary, with judges beholden to no other governmental department or officer for their positions, so that they might administer justice with special favor toward no one.

If Adams and the framers had not made sufficiently plain the ultimate end of preserving freedom by dividing governmental powers between and among legislative, executive, and judicial departments, Article 30 of the Declaration of Rights leaves little doubt about their intent. The article mirrors Adams' belief that, in the end, individual liberty will be secure only to the extent that the great powers of government remain separate, so as to prevent one department from exercising another's authority—a situation, as he observed in "Thoughts," in which "a people cannot be long free, nor ever happy" (1776, 88). Thus, Adams embedded in Article 30 a promise to the citizenry: that they would be able to enjoy living in Massachusetts under a government not "of men" but "of laws."

Beyond its importance to the people of the commonwealth, of course, the Massachusetts Constitution of 1780 served as a model for constitution makers elsewhere in the United States. It has been called "the most important" constitution of the postrevolutionary period (Lutz 1980, 129). It served as a model in at least two ways. First, the method of adoption was uniquely democratic for its time. In addition to its place among the first constitutions produced by a convention specifically devoted to the task of drafting and debating a new charter, the Massachusetts Constitution was democratic in another respect: its ratification was sanctioned not by an existing governmental body or ruling elite but by the citizens themselves, voting through their local governments. The adoption of a constitution by popular vote inspired democratic constitution-making efforts throughout the young nation.

Second, the Massachusetts Constitution benchmarked for other constitution makers the principal features of a republican governmental scheme, prescribing a government that would not be separate from the citizenry but representative of and accountable to it, the ally of individual liberty and not its enemy. In the structure and features of the Massachusetts Constitution lay the foundation for many of the American constitutions that followed—including, of course, the U.S. Constitution, which the people of the United States would ratify less than a decade later. Today, all American constitutions, including the U.S. Constitution, retain the core tripartite departmental design of the Massachusetts Constitution, as well as its express commitment to the protection of particular individual rights and liberties.[2] That these structural features and protections are so common in American constitutionalism suggests that succeeding generations of constitution makers have viewed them as essential.

Of course, the framers of the Massachusetts Constitution could not envision every problem that one day might require a constitutional solution. By 1850 citizens of small towns sought a constitutional convention to address the issue of representation in the General Court, for by this time they were losing legislative power relative to the more populous regions of the commonwealth (Friedman and Thody 2011, 20). When the convention eventually met, in 1853, party divisions plagued the proceedings. That fall, none of the proposals for constitutional change that emerged would win acceptance by a majority of voters, as all of the amendments were weighed down by a central proposal for a new constitution that would have changed standards for, among other things, voter eligibility and representation in the house.

By the early 1900s, calls for another constitutional convention could not be ignored. The people voted to hold a convention in November 1916. The delegates would begin meeting in 1917 and continue into 1918 as they debated a variety of amendments, but most important a proposal that would permit the people to prevent laws they disfavored from being executed (the referendum) and to enact laws the legislature would not (the initiative) (Friedman and Thody 2011, 22). Some delegates feared creating a mechanism by which the constitution could be changed whenever a temporary majority of voters so desired. A compromise emerged, pursuant to which certain kinds of amendments would be excluded from consideration via the initiative, including those related to the judiciary, religious institutions, and many of

---

2   While Nebraska's constitution creates three governmental departments, it is the only American state constitution that does not feature a bicameral legislature.

the individual interests protected under the Declaration of Rights (Friedman and Thody 2011, 23). Ultimately, the convention adopted, and the voters approved, what is now known as Article 48 of the constitution, creating, as one commentator remarked, one of "the most complicated [amending processes] in any state constitution" (Goldings 1968, 380).

The Role of the Supreme Judicial Court

The SJC's ancestry can be traced to the late seventeenth century, when the legislature of the Province of Massachusetts Bay, pursuant to the Province Charter of 1691, created a simple court system with the Superior Court of Judicature at its apex (Osgood 1992). Less than a century later, the Massachusetts Constitution of 1780 would establish a purely independent judicial department headed by the SJC. Adams sought to protect the independence of the SJC and Massachusetts courts through Article XXIX of the Declaration of Rights, which provides that judges must be "as free, impartial and independent as the lot of humanity will admit," and Part II, Chapter II, Article I, which provides that "all judicial officers, duly appointed, commissioned and sworn, shall hold their offices during good behavior" (MA Constitution 1780). These commitments reflect Adams' vision of a judiciary "distinct from both the legislative and executive, and independent of both, that so it may be a check upon both" (1776, 91).

Following the adoption of the new constitution—from approximately the time of its ratification through the second half of the nineteenth century—the court "came to be seen, in a way not repeated in many other American jurisdictions, as a major feature of government" (Osgood 1992, 18). Some part of this understanding may be traced to the passage of time: the longer an institution operates, the more likely its simple competence might be viewed as something more. On the other hand, it is true that, while the SJC did not flaunt its independence following the adoption of the constitution, it did establish in its earliest days a commitment to taking seriously its responsibility to interpret and apply the constitution—a through line that extends into the twenty-first century. In 1783, for example, with the SJC sitting as a trial court, Chief Justice William Cushing, while charging the jury, famously questioned the implications for slavery of the recognition of Article I that "all men are born free and equal" ("*Commonwealth v. Jennison*" 1783).

Further, from early on the SJC unceremoniously embraced what we now call judicial review—"the province and duty" of the court, as U.S. Supreme Court chief justice John Marshall famously explained, to say "what the law is" (*Marbury v. Madison* 1803, 177). In its 1799 decision in *Derby v. Blake*, for example, the SJC concluded that an act of Georgia's legislature was inconsistent with the U.S. Constitution, because it was a "flagrant, outrageous violation of the first and fundamental principles of social compacts."[3] Just a few years later, in the 1805 case *Mountfort v. Hall*, the SJC entertained an argument from defense counsel that assumed the court had the power to declare an act of the General Court unconstitutional—an assumption about which the justices registered no objection (though the defense did not in the end prevail on the merits of the case). And in *Holden v. James*, the court held a legislative effort to suspend a statute of limitations as to a particular individual contrary to "the first principles of civil liberty and natural justice," as well as "the spirit of our constitution and laws" (1814, 405).

The work of the SJC in the middle decades of the nineteenth century served to enhance its reputation. During this time, the court, led by "America's greatest magistrate," the aforementioned Lemuel Shaw (as famous today, perhaps, for having been Herman Melville's father-in-law), played a pivotal role in shaping the direction of the common law in response to profound economic and technological changes (Levy 2000, 217). As well, Shaw promoted judicial deference in cases challenging the validity of legislative regulation, favoring an approach that emphasized "great caution," so that a court might examine a law "in every possible aspect," to the end of finding an enactment invalid only when its "nullity and invalidity" were "beyond reasonable doubt" (*In re Wellington* 1834, 96–97). Such judicial restraint was not inevitably democracy enhancing: in *Roberts v. City of Boston*, the SJC upheld the city's segregated school system under a theory of "separate but equal," the doctrine upon which the U.S. Supreme Court would later rely in sanctioning state laws mandating racial segregation in numerous areas of American life (1849).

The court would not remain untouched by other contemporary currents in American law. At the end of the nineteenth century and into the twentieth, the SJC, like many other state courts, took to overturning regulations that the justices saw as infringing what they viewed as constitutionally protected economic interests, like the right to pursue a particular trade. Ungrounded in the text or history of the Massachusetts Constitution, these decisions provided little consistent guidance to lawmakers and others that indicated which regulations were likely to survive judicial review and which were not. In 1909, for example, the court held unconstitutional a law requiring all

---

3   The U.S. Supreme Court would reach the same conclusion a decade later in *Fletcher v. Peck*, 10 U.S. 87 (1810).

undertakers to be licensed embalmers, because, the court reasoned, the rule violated the right to engage in a calling of one's choosing. On the same day, it upheld a law governing the assignment of wages by an employee because the legislature believed the regulation would provide some advantage to the community (Friedman 2006, 415). Both laws involved the regulation of economic interests—interests related to the various sectors of the Massachusetts economy that the General Court sought to manage in order to promote and protect the health, safety, and welfare of the entire citizenry. But the SJC treated each case differently—and, in the case of the undertakers, with little of the deference to the legislature that the court in an earlier time, under Chief Justice Shaw's leadership, had favored.

This approach to economic legislation changed in the New Deal era. At that time, the U.S. Supreme Court stopped crediting economic interests as worthy of special constitutional protection. The end of judicial protection of such interests could have been a response to the dire situation many Americans faced in the wake of the Great Depression, or an acknowledgement that the court's decision making in cases involving economic legislation had been essentially unprincipled. Regardless, the SJC soon followed suit, returning, in most instances, to the deferential judicial review of economic legislation that had prevailed when Shaw had led the court. The SJC, however, would not entirely abandon these precedents. In a 1965 case, for example, the court overturned a regulation aimed at protecting the dairy industry by prohibiting the sale of nondairy coffee creamers. The court stated in *Coffee-Rich, Inc. v. Commissioner of Public Health* that "what is permissible under the Federal Constitution in matters of State economic regulation is not necessarily permissible under State law," as the Massachusetts Constitution "may guard more jealously against the exercise of the State's power" to protect the health, safety, and welfare of citizens (1965, 421). Since *Coffee-Rich*, the SJC has held fast to the view that there may be particular instances in which other constitutional considerations should compel the courts to review economic legislation more intensely.

The 1970s brought fundamental systemic change to the SJC and the Massachusetts court system. The General Court authorized the creation of a midlevel appeals court, which reduced the workload of the SJC and allowed the justices to focus on cases of first impression, as well as cases that arose in areas in which the law remained unsettled. The court also issued rules governing civil, criminal, and appellate procedure and adopted a code of professional conduct for attorneys (Kaplan 1990). Not least, the people of Massachusetts adopted an amendment to the constitution providing that judges must retire at age seventy.

This decade, moreover, ushered in what would later be called "the new judicial federalism." In the 1960s, the U.S. Supreme Court had expanded many individual rights under the U.S. Constitution. The 1970s marked a shift in the locus of individual constitutional rights development away from the federal courts as the U.S. Supreme Court began to retreat from its earlier rights expansion. Supreme Court justice William Brennan promoted this shift in a widely read *Harvard Law Review* essay in which he encouraged lawyers to rediscover state constitutions as sources of individual rights protection (Brennan 1977). State courts, after all, have the unreviewable authority to interpret their state's constitution, "the binding supreme law of the state" (Williams 2009, 136). The SJC was ready to embrace this "new judicial federalism," and advocates sought to build upon the approach the SJC had adopted in *Coffee-Rich, Inc.*—that in appropriate cases the Declaration of Rights "guard[s] more jealously against the exercise of the State's power" than the U.S. Constitution (1965, 421). There followed, intermittently at first and then regularly, decisions in which the SJC held that the Massachusetts Constitution's protection of a particular individual right or liberty—especially in the context of criminal procedure—extended more broadly than the parallel federal protection.

The SJC's commitment to developing a body of state constitutional law independent of federal law continues to the present day. For example, in 2014, the court in *Commonwealth v. Augustine* recognized that Part I, Article XIV, of the Declaration of Rights protects an individual's reasonable expectation of privacy in their cellular telephone call location data, even when such information is available to third parties. At the time the SJC decided *Augustine*, it was just one of a small number of state courts to conclude that state constitutional protections against unreasonable searches and seizures should be extended to encompass this digital information, presaging the U.S. Supreme Court's similar holding under the U.S. Constitution two years later.

More recently, the SJC in *Commonwealth v. Mora* addressed whether law enforcement surveillance of a home using video cameras hidden on public telephone and electrical poles over an extended period of time violates Article XIV. Contrary to the conclusion of the federal courts that had considered the issue, the SJC ruled that long-term and continuous surveillance of the defendants' homes raised concerns under the Massachusetts Constitution. The court grounded its holding in the framers' intent "to preserve the people's security to forge the private connections and freely exchange the ideas that form the bedrock of civil society" (2020, 20). As the court put it, "If the home is a 'castle,' a home that is subject to continuous, targeted surveillance is a castle under siege" (21).

Perhaps unsurprisingly, the SJC's expansive interpretation of state constitutional commitments to criminal procedure protections, including Article XIV's protection against unreasonable searches and seizures, as well as to such commitments as due process, free expression, and religious liberty, has not been without controversy. Indeed, in some instances these decisions have tested the ability of the independent judiciary Adams so prized to hold its own against a powerful state legislature, upon which it remains dependent for funding and resources, and a determined governor, who not only chooses the commonwealth's judges but can also claim to represent the will of the people. These tensions are captured by three cases: *Bates v. Director of the Office of Campaign and Political Finance* (2002), in which the court addressed the legislature's refusal to fund a voter-initiated law compelling public election financing; *Goodridge v. Department of Public Health* (2003), in which the SJC resolved a state constitutional challenge to the law prohibiting same-sex marriage; and *Desrosiers v. Governor* (2020), in which the court reviewed the breadth of the governor's emergency authority.

The Clean Elections, Same-Sex Marriage, and Pandemic Cases: The SJC Navigates the Separation of Powers

Pursuant to the initiative provision of Article 48, Massachusetts voters in 1998 approved the Clean Elections Law. The law was designed to provide public campaign financing to candidates for certain public offices, so long as the candidates agreed to abide by limits on the amount and sources of private campaign contributions. In its 2002 decision in *Bates v. Director of the Office of Campaign and Political Finance*, the SJC confirmed that, under Article 48, the legislature must act either to repeal or to fund such a law after the voters approve it. The court held that "the clean elections initiative was validly enacted into law by the people of Massachusetts," and "nothing in that law relieve[d] the Legislature of its constitutional duties under art. 48" (148). The court noted, moreover, that it lacked the power to order the director of campaign finance to distribute funds that the office did not have and could not reach—but the court notably presumed that the commonwealth would honor the obligations the constitution plainly imposed.

Following its decision, the SJC assigned a single justice to retain jurisdiction for the purpose of ensuring that the qualified candidates received the funding to which they were entitled under the Clean Elections Law. Months passed and the General Court took no substantive steps toward repealing or funding the initiative. When it eventually became clear that the legislature would not be appropriating the funds, qualified candidates requested that the court order the seizure and sale of commonwealth property so that they might be able to obtain funding in advance of the next election. The court agreed, reasoning that nothing other than actual disbursement of public campaign funds pursuant to the law would satisfy the judgment in *Bates*. Only then, when the court began the process of selling off property owned by the commonwealth, did the General Court move to repeal the Clean Elections Law, as required under Article 48 of the state constitution.

The *Bates* case shows that, notwithstanding the respect accorded both the court and the constitution, the legislature remains the center of Massachusetts government. The length of time it took for the legislature to fulfill its constitutional responsibility—and then only after the court sought to secure the funding to which qualified clean-elections candidates were owed through alternative means—suggests the extent to which lawmakers believed they would not have to follow a constitutional command. Notably, the court did not act with haste but out of deference for the legislature's appropriations authority and the belief that each department would honor its constitutional commitments; indeed, the court did not approve the process of selling commonwealth property to fund the clean-elections campaigns until it became clear the General Court would not act.

The SJC would clash with the General Court again just one year later, in another high-profile case. In its 2003 decision in *Goodridge v. Department of Public Health*, the SJC overturned a statutory prohibition on the issuance of civil marriage licenses to same-sex couples, holding that the marriage ban ran afoul of the state constitution's commitments to equality and due process. The court reasoned that, because the law excluding same-sex couples from civil marriage implicated the significant personal interest in marrying a person of one's own choosing, the commonwealth had to not just articulate a legitimate regulatory end—the traditional, deferential test applied to most state legislation—but also show that keeping same-sex couples from civil marriage would actually serve that end.

For its part, the commonwealth argued the exclusion of same-sex couples from civil marriage promoted three legitimate goals: providing a favorable setting for procreation, ensuring an optimal environment for child rearing, and preserving scarce financial resources. Accepting these ends as legitimate, the SJC nonetheless concluded that the commonwealth had failed adequately to support the existence of a connection between each and the discrimination against same-sex couples. First, the exclusion did not promote a favorable setting for procreation, because the law did not prohibit infertile opposite-sex couples, or opposite-sex couples with no intention of having children, from marrying—the commonwealth had never imposed as a condition of marriage that a couple have the ability and desire to bear children. Second, limiting civil marriage to opposite-sex couples did not advance the cause of creating optimal environments in which to raise children—the commonwealth acknowledged that same-sex couples could be "excellent" parents (*Goodridge* 2003, 334). Finally, an absolute prohibition "on same-sex marriage [bore] no rational relationship to the goal of economy" (336), as the commonwealth made assistance "available to married couples regardless of whether they mingle their finances or actually depend on each other for support" (337).

Without a remedy for the violation of a protected right, that right may be meaningless. When a court—any court—seeks to define both the scope of a constitutional right and the remedies for that right's violation, it risks becoming a target of government officials and others who see a decision in which a democratically enacted rule is struck down as judicial overreaching. As Chief Justice Shaw emphasized in the nineteenth century, courts ought to defer to legislative enactments because elected lawmakers are accountable to the people for their policy decisions in ways that unelected judges are not. But *Goodridge* represents that rare instance in which the court, agreeing with the plaintiffs that the law was inconsistent with the constitutional commitment to equality, acted counter to the will of the people's representatives. Recognizing the potential impact of its decision regarding same-sex marriage, the SJC did not immediately seek to impose a remedy for the constitutional violation. Instead, the court remanded the matter to the trial court and stayed the entry of judgment for the plaintiffs for six months, so that the General Court could "take such action as it [might] deem appropriate" in light of the court's decision (344).

The delay created by the six-month stay created an opportunity for the legislature to convene and consider the implications of a change in the legal understanding of who, under Massachusetts law, would be eligible for a civil marriage license. The court could have ordered the issuance of marriage licenses to same-sex couples, but doing so might have pressed the limits of its ability to define the boundaries of governmental power through the resolution of constitutional disputes (Friedman 2008, 405). Indeed, simply ordering the issuance of marriage licenses would have carried with it the risk that the commonwealth's political departments might ignore any such decree—not a remote possibility, given the recent experience in *Bates* with the Clean Elections Law. In fact, then governor Mitt Romney "tried to do everything within his limited powers to block implementation" of *Goodridge* (Miller 2006, 304). At a minimum, the failure of the legislature or the governor to respect an order immediately allowing civil marriage licenses to be issued to same-sex couples would have undermined the court's authority. Coupled with the legislature's recalcitrance following the court's decision in *Bates*, such disrespect by the political branches might have persuaded the justices to pause in a future case before fully addressing "the substance, scope, and reach of an individual rights provision" (Friedman 2008, 405).

As it happened, the General Court did take action in response to *Goodridge*. The legislature proposed a law allowing same-sex couples to participate in civil unions, with all the benefits and privileges of marriage, but not the name. In Massachusetts, unlike in the federal system, the constitution authorizes the General Court and the governor to seek advisory opinions from the SJC. These requests seek to identify any constitutional issues with proposed legislation, before it becomes law. Here, the legislature sought an advisory opinion on the civil-unions proposal. Upon review, the SJC held that the creation of a separate-but-equal status for same-sex couples would violate the constitution (*Opinion of the Justices* 2004). While the court in *Goodridge* had provided the legislature no particular instructions, in the advisory opinion it indicated that it had expected at least an effort to "conform the existing statutes to the provisions of [*Goodridge*]" (*Opinion of the Justices* 2004, 1204). By the end of the grace period, the General Court had failed either to codify the common law understanding of the couples eligible for marriage or to propose some constitutionally acceptable alternative plan. Only then did the SJC allow the entry of judgment for the *Goodridge* plaintiffs.

By postponing a judicially imposed remedy, the *Goodridge* court sought to create a temporal space in which the people's elected representatives could debate and discuss the implications of the court's conclusion that same-sex couples should have equal access to civil marriage. The SJC, in other words, carved out an opportunity for democratic deliberation in the General Court. This approach is in keeping with the tradition of judicial deference toward the legislature and its lawmaking authority. It represents a recognition by the court that representatives and senators were entitled to a deliberative space in which they could engage the processes of lawmaking to consider how best to respond to and effectuate the *Goodridge* ruling. As well, the six-month stay created an opportunity for discourse in the public square about these same issues.

The SJC's delay in imposing the remedy sought by the *Goodridge* plaintiffs also served to blunt the decision's impact: as one commentator noted, while relations between the legislative and judicial branches may have suffered following the decisions in *Bates* and *Goodridge*, the legislature did not launch any "serious and substantial attacks on the [Massachusetts] courts as an institution" (Miller 2006, 406). Indeed, the court's imposition of a stay in *Goodridge*, like the delay in taking action when the legislature failed to fund the Clean Elections Law after the decision in *Bates*, effectively acknowledged the reality of the court's place in the Massachusetts governmental scheme—an essential check in the scheme of separation of powers John Adams designed, but with a more limited role to play in governance than the governor or, especially, the General Court.

If nothing else, the six-month stay in *Goodridge* suggested a certain self-awareness on the court's part—that, notwithstanding the security John Adams sought to provide for an independent judiciary in Massachusetts, the justices should not seek to resolve constitutional disputes at an unreachable remove from lawmakers or the citizens they represent (Friedman 2008). Most recently, the court would embrace the spirit of this approach in the midst of the coronavirus pandemic when, in *Desrosiers v. Governor*, it considered a challenge to an array of emergency orders issued by Governor Charlie Baker. Though the orders sought to curb the spread of the deadly coronavirus, the plaintiffs maintained that the governor had "usurped" the General Court's role, violating both the separation of powers and the plaintiffs' constitutional rights to due process and free assembly. In its 2020 decision, the court rejected these arguments, concluding both that the Civil Defense Act of 1950 authorized the governor's actions and that his actions violated neither the separation of powers nor the plaintiffs' individual rights.

More than anything else, the justices in *Desrosiers* recognized that unelected judges ought not second-guess the decisions of the governor and other officials whose competence and expertise exceeded their own. In this way, the court again acknowledged the institutional limits of the judiciary: though the courts, pursuant to Adams' design, serve to enforce individual constitutional rights, like due process and free assembly, still there are times in which deference is necessary—as when the commonwealth faces a life-threatening public emergency. Contrary to the plaintiffs' belief, such deference recalls the constitutional role for the courts emphasized by Shaw—one defined, in the main, by humility. *Desrosiers* serves as a reminder from the SJC about where citizens should direct complaints when they are unhappy with the governor's actions or the General Court's oversight of the commonwealth's chief executive.

The Endurance of the SJC and the Massachusetts Constitution

As noted at the start of this chapter, endurance may be the quality that most continues to define the SJC and the Massachusetts Constitution as exceptional. While the citizens of numerous states have amended, revised, or replaced their constitutions with great frequency, Massachusetts consistently has resisted efforts at wholesale change. Massachusetts is not alone in this respect, of course; the New Hampshire Constitution has also endured in much its original form (Friedman 2014). But, given that the framers of the Granite State's constitution regarded the Massachusetts Constitution of 1780 as a model, literally and figuratively, the New Hampshire example may simply emphasize the Massachusetts charter's unique hold on the popular imagination.

In *The Endurance of National Constitutions* (2009), Elkins, Ginsburg, and Melton track the elements that they believe forecast a national constitution's tendency to endure. They suggest that a constitution's long-term survival turns on the extent to which its framers designed it to accommodate change, with endurance a function of three discrete features: inclusion, flexibility, and specificity. *Inclusion* refers to the participation of societal groups in the development, formulation, and maintenance of the constitution, as well as its continued enforcement. *Flexibility* refers to a constitution's capacity to adapt to the emergence of new social and political developments, through amendment or judicial interpretation. Finally, *specificity* refers to a constitution's level of detail and the scope of the topics it covers. In *Endurance*, Elkins, Ginsburg, and Melton suggest that these design features may come together in a way that gives a particular constitution what they call the "Goldilocks quality"—namely, the right mix of inclusion, flexibility, and specificity to guarantee the constitution's survival in moments of crisis (2009, 19).

For Elkins, Ginsburg, and Melton, the constitutions that possess the "Goldilocks quality" are the ones that appear more "statutory" in form and substance. "Statutory" constitutional provisions may be distinguished from those that are essential to the very functioning of the government the constitution sets out; they often represent specific bargains with interest groups and have constitutional status merely because they exist in the text. The Massachusetts Constitution has its share of these provisions—for example, Amendment LXXVIII in the Articles of Amendment, which concerns the "use of revenue from operation of motor vehicles." For the most part, though, the provisions of the Massachusetts Constitution reflect the higher-order considerations Adams and the framers saw as necessary to the creation of a durable and appropriately accountable government. Indeed, the Massachusetts Constitution speaks, for the most part, to general principles of moral agreement concerning the protections of liberty, equality, and other rights enjoyed by citizens, as well as the general obligations of government toward the governed.

Consider two of the provisions discussed earlier in this chapter. Part I, Article XIV, of the Declaration of Rights protects individuals against unreasonable searches and seizures to the end of safeguarding the interest in privacy as against the government, but nowhere defines the scope of this interest. Part I, Article XXX, embraces separated and divided legislative, executive, and judicial powers, but nowhere accounts for the many instances in which rigid distinctions between departments would impede the very functioning of government. Rather than being dominated by detailed statutory prescriptions, in other words, the Massachusetts Constitution is replete with calls to high principle, particularly when compared to younger state constitutions, which feature many provisions that are more statutory in nature. The Michigan Constitution, for instance, contains more than two dozen provisions relating to local government, addressing such topics as the size of counties, the compensation of county officers, and the grant of public utility franchises; the Massachusetts Constitution, on the other hand, devotes just a handful of provisions to the workings of local government.

Given that the Massachusetts Constitution is not particularly statutory, it would appear to fall outside the category of charters that Elkins, Ginsburg, and Melton describe as possessed of the "Goldilocks quality." Yet it has endured. Part of the explanation may lie in the longevity of the SJC itself, for a constitution composed of abstract principles will engender frequent disputes over meaning—disputes that require resolution by a court of last resort. Though the Massachusetts Constitution contains provisions allowing for its amendment, as with the U.S. Constitution the judiciary is primarily responsible for determining and announcing the meaning of its textual commitments. It may be, then, that, despite the fact that it is not particularly statutory, the Massachusetts charter endures because judicial review is readily available, providing what Elkins, Ginsburg, and Melton call "the connective tissue," that link between an eighteenth-century document and the modern world (2009, 108). The constitution's endurance, in other words, may be a reflection of "the particular ability, readiness, and willingness" of the commonwealth's courts in appropriate cases "to implement the constitution's many higher-order . . . principles" (Friedman 2014, 216–17).

To the extent that regard for the SJC has contributed to its ability to serve as "the connective tissue" between the text and its application, the moderating influence of gubernatorial nominations to the high court should be noted. Consider the appointments made by the Republican governor Charlie Baker, who by the end of 2020 had selected each of the SJC's members—including Kimberly Budd, the first Black woman to lead the court as chief justice. Yet the court betrayed no discernible ideological bent, true to Baker's 2016 promise that he would not subject nominees to an "ideological litmus test" (Schoenberg 2020). Such moderation will tend to enhance respect for the court, which in turn enhances its ability to play the role Adams intended for it—and to associate the institution in the minds of citizens with the respect they hold for the constitution itself.

Conclusion

John Adams knew that the Massachusetts Constitution and the independent judiciary it authorized would not endure without the support of the citizenry over successive generations. One of the ways in which he sought to encourage due regard for the constitution and its commitments to individual rights and liberties, as well as for separated and divided governmental powers, was through the cultivation of an active and enlightened electorate. Indeed, Adams is said to have counted as his favorite provision Chapter V, Article II (McCullough 2004), which created in the General Court a duty to "cherish the interests of literature and the sciences" and spread "the opportunities and advantages of education in the various parts of the country, and among the different orders of the people," to the end of securing "wisdom, and knowledge, as well as virtue, diffused generally among the body of the people, being necessary for the preservation of their rights and liberties."

It may be, though, that Adams and his fellow framers were not quite so sanguine about the salutary effect of an educated populace. While they endeavored to design a governmental scheme in which the people would be able, as the preamble puts it, to enjoy "in safety and tranquility their natural rights, and the blessings of life," at the same time they hedged, urging the people, as the preamble continues, "whenever these great objects are not obtained," to "alter the government, and to take measures necessary for their safety, prosperity and happiness." And, as noted, such measures have been taken, as evidenced by the amendments to the constitution since its adoption in 1780. Yet in the more than two hundred years since, a majority of the people has not been moved to alter fundamentally the government that Adams envisioned, to ignore the commands of the charter that frames it, or to disregard reliance upon the courts of the commonwealth to say what it means. That in itself may be regarded as an exceptional achievement.

WORKS CITED

Adams, John. 1776. "Thoughts on Government." In *The Papers of John Adams*, edited by Robert J. Taylor, 65–93. Cambridge, MA: Harvard University Press, 1980.

Bates v. Director of the Office of Campaign and Political Finance, 436 Mass. 134 (2002).

Brennan, William. 1977. "State Constitutions and the Protection of Individual Rights." *Harvard Law Review* 90:489–504.

Coffee-Rich, Inc. v. Commissioner of Public Health, 348 Mass. 414 (1965).

Commonwealth v. Augustine, 467 Mass. 230 (2014).

"*Commonwealth v. Jennison*." *Proceedings of the Massachusetts Historical Society (1873–1875)* 13:292–99.

Commonwealth v. Mora, 2020 WL 4516093 (Mass. 2020).

Derby v. Blake (1799) (reported in 226 Mass. 618 [1917]).

Desrosiers v. Governor, 486 Mass. 369 (2020).

Elkins, Zachary, Tom Ginsburg, and James Melton. 2009. *The Endurance of National Constitutions*. Cambridge: Cambridge University Press.

Friedman, Lawrence. 2006. "Ordinary and Enhanced Rational Basis Review in the Massachusetts Supreme Judicial Court: A Preliminary Investigation." *Albany Law Review* 69:415–48.

———. 2008. "Justice Martha B. Sosman and the Jurisprudence of Rights and Remedies." *New England Law Review* 42:397–406.

———. 2014. "The Endurance of State Constitutions: Preliminary Thoughts and Notes on the New Hampshire Constitution." *Wayne Law Review* 60:203–18.

Friedman, Lawrence, and Lynnea Thody. 2011. *The Massachusetts State Constitution*. New York: Oxford University Press.

Goldings, Morris M. 1968. "Massachusetts Amends: A Decade of State Constitutional Revision." *Harvard Journal on Legislation* 5:373–93.

Goodridge v. Department of Public Health, 440 Mass. 309 (2003).

Holden v. James, 11 Mass. 396 (1814).

Homans, George C. 1981. "John Adams and the Constitution of Massachusetts." *Proceedings of the American Philosophical Society* 125:286–91.

Jones v. Robbins, 8 Gray 329 (Mass. 1857).

Kaplan, Benjamin. 1992. "Introduction: An Address." In *The History of the Law in Massachusetts: The Supreme Judicial Court, 1682–1992*, edited by Russell Osgood, 1–8. Boston: Supreme Judicial Court Historical Society.

Levy, Leonard W. 2000. *Ranters Run Amok, and Other Adventures in the History of Law.* Chicago: Ivan R. Dee.

Lutz, Donald. 1980. *Popular Consent and Popular Control: Whig Political Theory in the Early State Constitutions.* Baton Rouge: Louisiana State University Press.

Marbury v. Madison, 5 U.S. 137 (1803).

Massachusetts Constitution. https://malegislature.gov/laws/constitution.

McCullough, David. 2004. *John Adams and the Good Life of the Mind.* Boston: Boston Athenæum.

Miller, Mark C. 2006. "Conflicts between the Massachusetts Supreme Judicial Court and the Legislature: Campaign Finance Reform and Same-Sex Marriage." *Pierce Law Review* 4:279–316.

Morrison, Samuel Eliot. 1917. "The Struggle over the Adoption of the Massachusetts Constitution, 1780." *Proceedings of the Massachusetts Historical Society* 50:356–411.

Mountfort v. Hall, 1 Mass. 443 (1805).

Opinion of the Justices (Civil Unions), 440 Mass. 1201 (2004).

Osgood, Russell. 1992. "The Supreme Judicial Court, 1692–1992: An Overview." In *The History of the Law in Massachusetts: The Supreme Judicial Court, 1682–1992*, edited by Russell Osgood, 9–42. Boston: Supreme Judicial Court Historical Society.

Roberts v. City of Boston, 59 Mass. 198 (1849).

Schoenberg, Shira. 2020. "For SJC, Baker Tends to Favor Smart, Moderate Judges." *CommonWealth Magazine*, September 16, 2020. https://commonwealthmagazine.org/courts/for-sjc-baker-tends-to-favor-smart-moderate-judges/.

Soifer, Aviam. 1992. "The Supreme Judicial Court of Massachusetts and the 1780 Constitution." In *The History of the Law in Massachusetts: The Supreme Judicial Court, 1682–1992*, edited by Russell Osgood, 207–40. Boston: Supreme Judicial Court Historical Society.

Taylor, Robert J. 1980. "Construction of the Massachusetts Constitution." *Proceedings of the American Antiquarian Society* 90:317–46.

In re Wellington, 16 Pick. 87 (Mass. 1834).

Williams, Robert F. 2009. *The Law of American State Constitutions.* New York: Oxford University Press.

PART III

Organizations
and Paths to Influence

CHAPTER 7

POLITICAL PARTIES AND ELECTIONS

Maurice T. Cunningham and Peter Ubertaccio

Massachusetts is unusual in its party structure in that its elected institutions are dominated by one party—but, depending on the office, not the same party. So Democratic is the commonwealth that a local television pundit crabbily deemed it the Bluest State, which it is in the legislature, most state-wide offices, and federal elections (Keller 2017). Since 1990 the Republicans have held the governorship for all but eight years. Since the state moved to four-year terms for governors in 1966, Republicans have won eight of thirteen gubernatorial elections. The GOP will have held the office for twenty-four of the past thirty-two years when GOP governor Charlie Baker ends his second term in 2022. Though one might assume a Republican governor to be under constant siege in the Bluest State, Baker is almost never assailed by legislative leaders and has been praised as the most popular governor in America. When he finally "slipped" to third most popular governor in 2020, it was big local news (Murphy 2020).

Party History in Massachusetts

The recent split between the governorship and other offices is unique. For much of Massachusetts history one party has claimed dominance. For twenty-first-century observers it might seem that party would always be the Democrats. But for most of the state's history, the real power lay with the party of the high born—Federalists, Whigs, and Republicans. It was rising tides of immigration from the Irish, Italians, Polish, Jews, French Canadians, and others through the mid-eighteenth and early nineteenth centuries that made the Democrats competitive and, finally, the overriding power. One important milestone in this transformation was 1928 when the Democratic Party nominated Al Smith of New York for president. Smith was the first Catholic nominated by either party for the nation's highest office, and Catholic turnout in Massachusetts soared, giving the Democratic Party candidate a majority of the state's voters in a presidential election for the first

The authors thank Anya G. Cunningham for research assistance.

time.[1] The Republican Party held all the statewide constitutional offices as well as both houses of the legislature, but 1928 signaled a brief few decades of close party competition. From 1930 through 1960, the Democrats became competitive in presidential and statewide contests, winning each presidential contest except for the two Eisenhower runs in the fifties. They began regularly winning senate elections and gubernatorial contests, effectively splitting with the Republicans, and winning down-ballot statewide offices. Still, with the help of gerrymandering, the GOP held the legislature (Mileur 1997).

Democrats feared that 1948 would be a bad year for the party given the unpopularity of President Harry Truman, who succeeded Franklin Delano Roosevelt in 1945 and was running for a term of his own. But four ballot questions aided the Democrats, three of them restricting labor rights and a fourth from Planned Parenthood that would have liberalized birth-control laws in the state. Union families and Catholics both felt threatened by these measures. Labor went all out to defeat the proposals aimed at curtailing workers' rights. The Catholic Church, under Archbishop Richard Cushing, mobilized its institutional structure with parishes, sports leagues, schools, charities, and fraternal organizations in virtually every locale in the state to defeat the birth-control measure. A former mayor of Boston formed a committee in opposition that adopted the campaign slogan "Birth control is *still* against God's law" (O'Toole 1985, 52–53). With turnout spurred by the presidential election and the ballot questions, Democrats turned out in droves. The party took control of the Massachusetts House of Representatives, elevating Thomas P. "Tip" O'Neill of Cambridge to the Speakership. The Democrats lost the house in 1952, regained it in 1954, and have held it ever since. Four years later, in 1958, the Democrats seized control of the state senate and have never relinquished command. The presidential election of 1960 saw Massachusetts' own John F. Kennedy elected as the nation's first Catholic president. The rise of the Kennedy family in post–World War II politics also signified in Massachusetts a new framework among Irish Catholic Democratic politicians toward the cool professionalism of the Kennedys and away from the roguish politicians of yore such as James Michael Curley and JFK's own grandfather and former Boston mayor John F. "Honey Fitz" Fitzgerald. Yet even Kennedy's elevation to the presidency did not secure the state for the Democrats. Republican John Volpe won the governorship that year.

---

1   Democrat Woodrow Wilson took Massachusetts in 1912 with about 35 percent of the vote against Theodore Roosevelt and William Howard Taft.

The Democratic Party that fought to surpass the Republicans in the postwar period, and the party that has maintained its strength from the seventies to the present, is constituted in different fashions. The rising Democrats of midcentury were what the historian of Massachusetts political culture Edgar Litt described as workers. They were largely unionized and urban residents, descendants of Irish, Italian, French Canadian, and Polish immigrants (Litt 1965). Their party reflected their priorities: "liberal on issues of economic security and social welfare, but, like the Catholic Church, traditional and conservative on issues of culture and morality" (Mileur 1997, 80).

By the 1960s, though, Litt could already see that the group he called the managers would surpass the workers. The managers were well educated, often second- or third-generation descendants of white ethnic workers, or highly skilled individuals who came to the state for higher education and stayed to enjoy the opportunities available in university labs and the emerging high-tech industry (Litt 1965). They populated the suburbs more than the state's aging urban cores. If one figure captures the ascendancy of managers over workers, it would be Michael Dukakis, the cool, analytical, and progressive politician who ushered in the era of managerial dominance of the governor's office. In her recent work on the suburbanization of politics, Lily Geismer (2014) sees the high-tech sector as central to the policies of Dukakis and the Democrats in the eighties. Managers' faith is in technology. This may be captured in a 2014 Democratic debate for governor, where all five candidates expressed their belief that the state's management problems would require more technology. As one candidate expressed it, "The answer is technology."

The Democrats have maintained their dominance even as their coalition has transformed. Diversity in the ranks and among officeholders has helped the party to stay in charge. Maura Healey became the nation's first openly gay state attorney general. Ayanna Pressley became the state's first African American congresswoman. Elizabeth Warren is the first woman U.S. senator from Massachusetts. Rachael Rollins is the first African American woman to be elected district attorney of Suffolk County. But note the repetition of the word *first*—something Professor O'Brien delves into in chapter 11 where she documents the state's relatively poor record of electing women and women of color. In 2021 the six candidates heading into the primary election for mayor of Boston were all people of color, including four women.

Litt's scheme of political culture includes two other groups that tend to be Republican: the patricians and the yeomen. The patricians were the high-born elite descendants of the state's Puritan ancestry, who led not only the state but its major legal, medical, philanthropic, and cultural organizations as well. Names like Cabot, Saltonstall, Lodge, and even Weld evoke this heritage. The patricians became the exemplar of the moralistic reformer in politics against the self-interested, contract-dispensing, patronage-addicted individualist worker representatives personified by Irish Democrats. Litt wrote of the yeomen, "The prevailing ethos is that of nineteenth-century America with its emphasis on individual initiative, its distrust of bigness in government, corporations, labor unions, and international organizations." Litt mentioned "the predominance of the John Birch Society in several state senatorial districts" (1965, 7–11, 12, 14). During the Obama administration, and in aid of Scott Brown in 2010, the yeomen had a brief resurgence as the Tea Party. They remain in some form to support Jim Lyons as GOP party chair in 2020 and to bedevil the Republican governor, Charlie Baker. Geoff Diehl, Massachusetts' cochair of former president Trump's failed 2020 campaign, and Republican candidate for governor in 2022, also embodies this tradition. Unfortunately for the GOP, the patricians and yeomen have shrunk in numbers over the years and sharply diverged in their political leanings. Better, the attributes of patricians are a neat fit with the traits of managers that have made Mitt Romney and Charlie Baker so successful.

Yeomen do have one notable area of strength in the commonwealth. Governance in Massachusetts remains a local affair. Most municipalities use a town-meeting form of government. The town meeting is a municipality's legislative branch with boards of selectmen serving as the executive branch. Day-to-day administrative duties are handled by town managers. Local elections in the state are nonpartisan (candidates do not have a *D* or *R* next to their name), and low turnout is the norm. Even the largest cities see relatively few voters on Election Day for purely local races. As Angela Yang reported in the *Daily Free Press* on November 6, 2019, Boston's 2019 city council race saw a 17 percent voter turnout, for example. With relatively few citizens engaging at the local level, the most conservative elements of the Republican Party retain strength in certain areas of the state, particularly Barnstable, Bristol, Essex, Plymouth, and Worcester Counties. These voters, the active base of the state's Republican Party, use the national Democratic Party's success here to their own advantage, much in the same way national Republicans have used the image of a Massachusetts liberal to advance their causes.

Geismer (2014) argues that Massachusetts suburban liberals came to believe in the exceptional nature of their identity, but Dukakis' defeat to George H. W. Bush in the presidential contest of 1988 burst that belief. Bush had campaigned specifically against the frame of the Massachusetts liberal:

The identity of Massachusetts, particularly the residents of the Route 128 suburbs, had long rested on the ways in which the state's liberal credentials made it distinctive and different from the rest of the country. The commitment to this ideal relied on a consistent denial of the structures and political trends that actually made the state and its suburban residents representative and in line with the rest of the nation. Thus, when Dukakis aimed to show that he and the state represented larger economic, political, and social processes and forces, it proved difficult to transcend the boundaries and power of the exceptionalist ideology of the Massachusetts liberal label promoted by liberal residents and their critics. (Geismer 2014, 272)

In spite of trying to distance themselves from the 1988 defeat, party leaders like those who founded the Democratic Leadership Council adopted many of the traits Dukakis brought to national politics. His four immediate Republican gubernatorial successors in Massachusetts did so too. Geismer argues that national politics reflects that the nation has gone the way of Massachusetts: a shift away from workers and toward the managers of "suburban knowledge professionals and high-tech corporations" (2014, 279). Philip Davies and John Kenneth White (1985) called them "New Class Democrats." And for whatever value the suburban liberals' notion of Massachusetts leading the way might have, Massachusetts managers and high-tech devotees like Romney, Kerry, Paul Tsongas, and the wonkish scholar Elizabeth Warren have been unable to achieve the presidency, while decidedly more shallow politicians like George W. Bush and Donald J. Trump have won the office.

Party in the Electorate

The Kennedys were but one signal of a change in state politics in the post–World War II period. Many returning servicemen took advantage of the GI bill, went to college, and moved into middle-class and upper-middle-class positions (Mettler 2005). Parochial Catholics who might never have strayed from their Boston neighborhoods found themselves overseas with Americans of all backgrounds. When they came back, they discovered a changing environment in which they might gain entry into elite law firms, medical establishments, and corporate boardrooms. Manufacturing jobs left the state, but high-tech, defense, and university research began to employ well-educated engineers and allied professionals who found jobs along Route 128 and settled in a suburban ring around Boston where new roads eased their commutes and good schools supported their children (Brown and Tager 2000; Geismer 2014).

Voter registration statistics available at the secretary of state's website tell an interesting story. In 1948 there was an even split between the parties—632,543 Democrats and 628,624 Republicans, with 1,223,771 Unenrolled (the Massachusetts term for independents). By 1960 the Democrats had forged ahead of the Republicans, 808,319 to 657,774 with just over 1.2 million Unenrolled. By 1964 the gap between the parties continued to grow, and Democrats pulled ahead of the Unenrolled by just shy of 90,000 voters. It wasn't until 1990 that the Unenrolled exceeded Democratic registrants again, and the Republicans continued fading down to just 441,942 registrants (while winning the governorship for the first time since 1970). By 2002 there were more than 500,000 more who were Unenrolleds than Democrats and just over 530,000 Republicans. The Unenrolleds continue as the largest group of registered voters as of October 2020 with just over 2.7 million to the Democrats' 1.5 million and the Republicans' 476,480. While partisan attachment has loosened over the years, the Democrats' hold on the statehouse hasn't—mostly.

Voter turnout, unfortunately, has decreased. In the critical presidential election year of 1948, turnout was at 86.74 percent, and four years later 94.89 percent went to the polls. The statewide election of 1950 saw 78.66 percent vote. In 1960 almost 91.73 percent turnout helped propel local son John F. Kennedy to the presidency. But the presidential race of 2016 attracted only 74.51 percent to the polls and the gubernatorial election year of 2018 just 60.17 percent. The much more competitive gubernatorial election year of 2014 saw only 50.84 percent of voters turn out to vote, the lowest statewide turnout in the period since 1948.

Elections in Massachusetts for governor are usually hard fought and to a striking degree go to the Republican Party. The blue in Massachusetts is most evident in the other constitutional offices and in the legislature where the Republicans are hard-pressed to put up a fight against Democratic hegemony.

Party Organization

Political party organizations in Massachusetts have been critiqued for being too weak to provide much help to their candidates, and that is not an unfounded charge. Look below the surface, though, to party composition, platforms, and conventions, and we can gain fascinating insights into the

worldview and workings of the activists who make up the party organization. Documents available at the Democratic and Republican Parties' state
websites illustrate different membership structures and policy priorities. The
Democratic Party has a much larger and more diverse membership than the
Republican Party, as it does nationally. State law covering both parties provides
for one man and one woman to be elected at the time of the presidential
primary from each of the forty senate districts. The Democratic Party adds
another man and woman from each senate district, to be chosen by representatives from the ward and town committees. A number of elected officials
and members of the Democratic National Committee are automatically
members of the Democratic State Committee. The State Democratic Party
requires representation for young persons including College Democrats and
Massachusetts Young Democrats. There are Affirmative Action members
not to exceed 10 percent of total membership. Representation is secured
for two veterans and ten representatives of organized labor. Members of the
LGBTQ+ community are ensured representation. The party requires six
disabled members, two French speaking, two Portuguese speaking, and two
senior citizens. Twenty-year members become life members. Former chairs
are members. At all times the party seeks gender balance. The Democratic
State Committee is big and unwieldy, and it has numerous subcommittees
to do its work. The Republican State Committee, on the other hand, has
no Affirmative Action or outreach and far fewer members: the male and
female members of the Republican National Committee and one man and
one woman from each senatorial district, elected at the presidential primary.

The Democrats' party platforms reflect the diversity of interests among
the members, encompassing a range of issues, many of them focused on the
core value of equality. They take positions on economic justice and growth,
education, the environment, ethics, gender and racial equality, health care and
human services, housing, immigration, civil rights and civil liberties, labor
and workforce, public safety and crime prevention, revenue and expenditures,
transportation and infrastructure, veterans, and voting and democracy. For
each issue, they list what Democrats will fight for. Do elected officials feel
bound by all these positions? No. But they do set out a road map for the
party, and they allow for change to percolate up from the membership.

Where the Democrats emphasize equality, the Republicans stress private
property and individual responsibility. Their list of priorities includes, first, the
economy, and in particular they decry heavy-handed regulations that impair
entrepreneurs. They call for accountability, stronger ethics in government,

and more transparency—an area where the Democratic legislature has been notably passive. The party seeks compassionate governance with an emphasis on "self-sufficiency and independence." The platform points proudly to the Americans with Disability Act and Individuals with Disability Education Act, both signed into law by Republican president George H. W. Bush. The party highlights education and the environment (with a strong emphasis on the primacy of property rights). It praises the state's health-care system and seeks independence from Obamacare. On taxes and spending, the party supports "lowering all taxes," "streamlining" government, and the "outright elimination" of some programs. Under justice there is again an emphasis on private property as well as opposition to "granting them ["illegal immigrants"] the same rights, benefits and privileges as citizens and legal residents." Finally, the State Republican Party's values reinforce a prolife position and "the institution of traditional marriage" (Massachusetts Republican Party State Committee 2018).[2]

The processes for nomination of statewide candidates of party organizations in the commonwealth are unique. Nominees are chosen in a yearlong sequence of local caucuses, state conventions, and primary elections. Political parties in the state have town, city, and ward committees. Local activists caucus early in a statewide election year for the purpose of sending delegates to the party conventions. At both conventions, prospective nominees vie for the endorsement of the party and placement on the primary ballot. It takes 15 percent of the total delegate vote for a candidate to earn a spot on the September primary ballot. It requires a majority vote of delegates to earn the party's endorsement.

It's rare that the parties deny spots to candidates on the primary ballot, though it does happen. Democrats denied two gubernatorial candidates, Juliette Kayyem and Joe Avellone, a spot on the ballot in 2014. The structure of party nominations is a by-product of the 1982 rematch between Michael Dukakis and Ed King. Dukakis, a master practitioner of grassroots politics, worked to ensure changes to Democratic Party rules requiring a 15 percent vote at the convention. This tactic helped the former governor ensure a two-person race against his unpopular successor. Though modifications have been made over the years, the 15 percent rule and the fundamental structure of nomination in the parties remain largely unchanged.

---

2   The Massachusetts Supreme Judicial Court found a right to same-sex marriage under the Massachusetts Constitution in 2003. The U.S. Supreme Court upheld the right of same-sex couples to marry in 2015.

The Democrats hold a party convention each year, endorsing conventions for statewide elections including the U.S. Senate in even-numbered years and issue conventions in odd-numbered years. The Republicans hold an endorsing convention for statewide offices in gubernatorial election years. Though the battles for 15 percent and the party endorsement can be heated, the wider electorate does not necessarily heed the wishes of the party. In 2014 State Treasurer Steve Grossman handily won the endorsement of the party's convention but lost the gubernatorial primary to Attorney General Martha Coakley. This is not uncommon. In 1990 John Silber was leading in the polls but did not seem to have enough delegates to leave the convention with a ballot position. He squeaked by with just over 15 percent and went on to thrash the convention's choice, former attorney general Frank Bellotti, in the primary. In 2006 Attorney General Tom Reilly was the Democrats' most prominent constitutional officer and went after the gubernatorial nomination. But the virtually unknown Deval Patrick outorganized him at party caucuses and then bested him and another candidate at the convention and primary, going on to be elected governor. In 2014 liberal former state senator and lieutenant governor candidate Warren Tolman was the most well-known Democrat seeking the office of attorney general (and he had the backing of the AFL-CIO, led by his brother). Tolman narrowly edged out former assistant attorney general Maura Healey at the convention, but primary voters dismissed the party's endorsement, choosing Healey as their nominee in the primary. The party's blessing is a mixed one.

On the Republican side in 2014, it appeared that Charlie Baker would glide to victory and keep Tea Party candidate Mark Fisher from gaining a spot on the primary ballot. At least that was the hope of the party establishment and of Baker. But as delegation counts were announced to the convention, a number of observers and media members had Fisher getting the 15 percent needed to move on. The party leaders retreated to a back room and emerged hours later to announce to a few stragglers that Fisher had not met the threshold. Legal wrangling ensued for several weeks, with the party finally acquiescing. Fisher made the ballot and was trounced by Baker.

This brings us to the contentious power struggles that have animated the Massachusetts Republican Party over the years. In 1997 Jerome Mileur wrote of the party, "As the enrollment of GOP voters continued to drop, the struggle within the party seemed to grow in intensity" (82). Acrimonious intraparty disputes have only accelerated, as Governor Baker has lost control of his party's state committee to supporters of President Trump.

It is commonplace that when the party is holding the corner office, the governor chooses the party chairperson, and if the party is not in power a commanding candidate like Charlie Baker in 2014 should get his nominee. It's not always that easy. In 2013 establishment chair candidate Kirsten Hughes won the post, but narrowly, over right-wing opponent Rick Green.[3] Hughes was unopposed in 2015. As governor, Baker then campaigned in 2016 to elect a state committee more amenable to his moderate political and governing ways, and this required ousting some more conservative members. He succeeded. Then in 2017 Hughes was challenged from the right again, prevailing in that race too. Meanwhile, Baker was gearing up for what seemed to be an easy reelection run in 2018. As the only possible statewide hope for the party and a widely popular politician, Baker might have expected a free ride in the 2018 Republican primary, but that's not the Massachusetts Republican Party way. This time he was challenged by Scott Lively, a person so extreme that in 2020, the website of the Southern Poverty Law Center described him as "actively propagandizing against LGBT people since the early 1990s, but he's perhaps best-known for co-writing the thoroughly discredited, Holocaust revisionist book The Pink Swastika: Homosexuality in the Nazi Party." In the Republican Party of 2018, Lively took 36 percent of the vote.

Then in 2019, Hughes left her position, setting up a contest for party chairperson. Governor Baker backed the party treasurer, Brent Andersen. Notable conservative Geoff Diehl, who had just run and lost against Senator Elizabeth Warren, announced his candidacy only to back out and throw his support behind the establishment candidate Andersen after the entry of Jim Lyons into the race. Lyons, recently defeated for reelection to his house seat and known as the most conservative politician in the statehouse, won an easy victory, nonetheless.

Baker and Lyons had enjoyed at least a polite relationship before, but Lyons moved to distance the party apparatus from Baker. Most important, a dispute erupted over fund-raising. After his 2014 victory, Baker's fund-raising team engineered a complicated but lucrative fund-raising arrangement between the state party and the Republican National Committee it dubbed the Massachusetts Victory Committee. As the *Boston Globe* explained in an August 2019 article, under Lyons the arrangement was allowed to wither and die, leaving millions of dollars behind (Stout 2019). Lyons also proved

---

3   Green was the head of a dark money operation called the Massachusetts Fiscal Alliance. In 2018 he was defeated as a Republican candidate for the third congressional district.

himself an ardent advocate for President Donald Trump and brought the party over to the president's corner. Meanwhile, Baker was considering a run for a third term and being careful to keep a proper distance from Trump, the most unpopular political figure in the state. Lyons went on to preside over several losing efforts in special legislative elections in 2020, including for seats long held by Republicans, as well as a further erosion of already tiny Republican minorities in the state house and senate in the 2020 general election. In 2020, not only did Baker make an endorsement in a Democratic congressional primary (choosing incumbent Richard Neal over progressive insurgent challenger Alex Morse), but a political action committee aligned with the governor backed thirteen Democrats in legislative primaries in 2020 versus only four Republicans.

A political party as weak as the Massachusetts Republicans maintaining open war with its only statewide elected official because he openly backed Democrats may seem bizarre by most lights. In Massachusetts it is almost commonplace.

Party in Government

One might suppose that with the Democrats having unshakable control of large legislative majorities and the Republicans usually holding the governor's seat that Massachusetts' government would regularly feature heated policy and political battles. That hasn't been the case. Republican governors and Democratic legislators usually work well together—often better than Democratic governors and Democratic legislators. This may dismay some partisans, but as Republican governor Frank Sargent once explained, "I pissed off some Republicans, but there was no other way to get anything done" (Hogarty 2002).

Since Volpe won the governorship in 1960, Republican gubernatorial candidates have done exceedingly well, even as the rest of the party on the federal, statewide, and legislative levels has fallen apart. Volpe lost to a Democrat in 1962 but came back to win in 1964 and in 1966 was the first Massachusetts governor elected to a four-year term. When he left to become secretary of transportation in Richard M. Nixon's cabinet in 1969, he was succeeded by his lieutenant governor, Frank Sargent, who went on to win a term of his own in 1970. Then Sargent was defeated for reelection in 1974 by Democrat Michael Dukakis from the bordering Boston suburb of Brookline. Dukakis had startled the Democratic Party's insiders by defeating establishment figure

Speaker Robert Quinn for the party's nomination. John Kennedy demonstrated the success of running outside the regular party apparatus. A candidate-centered family, the Kennedys were not party builders, but neither did they directly attack the traditional party organizations and allegiances. Dukakis' victory over Quinn was quite different: it heralded the ascendancy of the manager type over the worker type in Massachusetts partisan politics (Litt 1965). Every governor since except one has fit the manager profile. But that exception threw the Democrats into turmoil in 1978 when the conservative worker Irish Catholic Ed King challenged Dukakis in the primary. King's strategy, according to an aide, was to put "all the hate groups in one pot and let it boil" (King 1978). He was successful. But Dukakis roared back in "the rematch" in 1982 and went on to win back the governorship and reelection in 1986. King was so conservative as to earn the description Ronald Reagan's favorite Democrat, but, still, the Democrats held the governorship for sixteen consecutive years. King would later join the Republican Party. From 1960 through 1990, the split was Democrats eighteen years in office, Republicans a healthy twelve.

Since 1990, though, Republicans have only once ceded the corner office, to Democrat Deval Patrick for two terms. In 1990 the state was in the throes of a severe economic crisis, Dukakis had grown unpopular and was retiring, and after a brutal primary Democratic voters chose conservative Boston University president John Silber as their nominee, the last nominee of either party with primary appeal to the workers. The Republicans put up former U.S. attorney William Weld, who had come from behind to defeat more established candidates in the GOP primary. Weld prevailed against the badly fractured Democrats. He showed successive Republican candidates how to win: offer a platform that combines fiscal prudence and a tough-on-crime approach mixed with social-issue liberalism. (Both Weld and Silber were fiscal conservatives, but the libertarian Weld was far more progressive on social issues, including abortion, than was Silber.) Weld also played on the permanence of the Democrats in the legislature to make the case that the state can't leave the Democrats, who have known their share of corruption cases and could be accused of wild spending, solely in charge of government. Social liberalism, fiscal conservatism, and a tough-on-crime approach helped secure Republican gubernatorial dominance in the 1990s. Weld and Cellucci both took a hard line on crime, with the latter working to take voting rights away from felons and attempting to reintroduce the death penalty. Perhaps the greatest cause of all Republican governors was their plea to the electorate to allow them to serve as a check on the overwhelmingly Democratic legislature.

Deval Patrick, the state's first African American governor, won the first of two terms in 2006 succeeding Mitt Romney. When he ran for reelection in 2010 he faced off against Charlie Baker, a former Weld cabinet official known as "the smartest man in state government." Patrick won, but Baker returned in 2014 to narrowly defeat Attorney General Martha Coakley. Baker proved so popular that the strongest Democrats avoided him entirely in 2018, and he easily won reelection against a second-tier candidate. When Baker finishes his second term, the Democrats will have held the governorship for only eight of thirty-two years since 1990 and the Republicans for twenty-four years. Not a bad performance in the Bluest State.

In a progression of manager governors since Dukakis, Baker may adhere most tightly to the managerial traits. He is data driven and a former chief executive officer of a health-care company, as well as having served as secretary of administration and finance under Weld. In his 2014 campaign he did not attack the edifice the Democrats had built, instead promising to make it work much more reliably and efficiently.

The additional elected statewide constitutional offices in Massachusetts are the lieutenant governor, attorney general, treasurer, secretary of state, and auditor. By constitutional amendment in 1966, governor and lieutenant governor candidates have to run as a ticket. Since 1990 that has provided the Republicans at least two constitutional offices, except for the Patrick years. Lieutenant Governors Paul Cellucci (under Governor William Weld) and Jane Swift (under Cellucci) both served as acting governor when Weld and Cellucci left midterm, and Cellucci won a term of his own. With one exception, Republicans have not been competitive for the other constitutional offices for decades. The exception was in 1990 when Republican Joe Malone won an open seat for treasurer in a disastrous statewide climate for Democrats. Malone proved popular, winning reelection in 1994 but then losing to Cellucci in the 1998 Republican primary for governor. Malone's successor, Democrat Shannon O'Brien, did emerge from her one term as treasurer to gain her party's nomination for governor in 2002, but she was defeated by Mitt Romney. Treasurer, auditor, and secretary of state are offices that usually do not attract much press attention, but the attorney general has a higher profile with real policy power, and Massachusetts attorneys general have used those powers in progressive ways. The office increased in professionalization under Frank Bellotti from 1975 to 1987. Scott Harshbarger from

1991 to 1999 set a standard for pro–consumer activism, joining several other state attorneys general in a winning lawsuit against Big Tobacco. In 2014 Maura Healey won the office, becoming the first openly gay attorney general in the nation. She has championed causes such as gun control and abortion rights, and been a thorn in the side of the Trump administration, and as of this writing is widely expected to be a formidable candidate for governor soon. Democrats have used the office of attorney general as a launching pad for gubernatorial ambitions, with uniformly poor results. One of the downsides of taking the tough stands required of attorneys general is that these positions do not always play well in gubernatorial elections.

At the county level, Republicans enjoy moderate success, currently holding two out of fourteen sheriff offices and five out of eleven district attorney offices. Though county government hasn't been significant for decades, county-level elected offices have always been, and remain, important vehicles for party patronage and voter mobilization in the state. For example, recently retired Hampden County sheriff Democrat Mike Ashe served the western Mass county for forty-two years and was considered the dean of western Mass politics. His support and organizational assistance in western Mass was instrumental to every statewide Democratic candidate for four decades. Sheriff Ashe's annual "clambake" was a required stop for every local and statewide candidate on the late-summer campaign trail for thirty-nine years (Johnson 2016).

As for legislative seats, the Democrats have been virtually unassailable, routinely holding between 32 and 36 seats in the 40-member senate. In 1990, the calamitous year for Democrats, Republicans took 16 state senate seats. In 1992 they lost 7 of them in a rout that produced veto-proof majorities in both chambers of the state legislature. The house has proved equally uncompetitive. In 2004 Governor Mitt Romney announced a "Romney Reform Team" of 131 Republican candidates. Other than the incumbents, they all lost (Cunningham 2008). As data from the secretary of state's website shows, in 2008 Republicans won just 16 house contests to the 160-member lower chamber, including special elections. In 2010 they rebounded to win 32, dropping back to 31 in 2020. The civic organization MassInc found that the Democrats hold 80 percent of seats in the legislature, but only about half of voters are registered or lean Democratic. Though 27 percent of the state's voters are Republican or lean Republican, the GOP holds only 20 percent of the seats in the legislature. Massachusetts also resides at the bottom of state measures for competitive elections, in both general and primary contests. This is a long-standing problem (Levin, Forman, and Bliss 2019). Legislative power in Massachusetts is concentrated at the top, with the house speaker and senate president. There have been scant power-sharing exceptions—Speaker George Keverian from 1985 to 1991, Senate President Stanley Rosenberg from 2015 to 2017—but academic studies going back to 1985 routinely judge the Massachusetts legislative leadership as among the most powerful in the nation (Clucas 2007). Yet, as Jerold Duquette explains in chapter 5, the Democratic legislative leadership is often quite pleased to have a Republican as chief executive. For one thing, as Frank Sargent recognized, Massachusetts politics is more transactional than partisan. Democratic leaders understand that they have a supermajority in the legislature, and so if they really care about an issue, they can have their way. Sometimes they like having a Republican governor to kick around (Mitt Romney comes to mind). Yet when the leadership is happy with a Republican governor, they do little to undermine the chief executive, and that includes not bashing the governor or giving aid and comfort to the Democratic challenger for the state's highest office. Also, when a Democrat is in the corner office, legislators might be expected to respond to a progressive agenda that is not entirely comfortable to them (Duquette 2013). This happened in 2013 when Governor Deval Patrick announced in his State of the Commonwealth speech a proposal to restructure the tax system to pay for additional services in education and transportation. Notably, he also proposed to make the system more progressive by doubling personal exemptions, cutting the sales tax, and increasing the income tax. The overall package would raise $1.9 billion. The legislative leadership met the proposal with reserve, and it was never passed (Phillips 2013).

The Patrick tax proposal raised the specter of endangering Democratic seats in the legislature; some Republican operatives were chortling, and even the *Boston Globe* was raising the possibility of destabilizing the drowsy regularity of the Democrats' Beacon Hill majority. But one key to the success of the Democratic leadership is to prevent their members from having to take risky votes. For instance, in 1998 the voters passed a clean-elections measure that would provide for public financing of political campaigns, as a ballot initiative. This was entirely unwelcome to legislators, who prefer to go through life unchallenged. But the fact that the measure was passed by the people seemed to put them in a politically precarious place. Speaker Thomas Finneran protected his members by refusing to fund the measure and eventually killing it off, without even a recorded vote (Duquette 2003, 2002).

In another case Democratic legislators discovered they were against casino gambling before they were in favor of it. Following his 2010 reelection, Governor Patrick announced that he had decided to revive a proposal to bring casino and slot-parlor gambling to the commonwealth. The governor's original casino legislation had been killed in the house in 2008. Support seemed to exist in the senate under President Therese Murray, but in the house Speaker Sal DiMasi was an implacable foe of gambling and at his urging house members killed the legislation by a 106–48 vote—a sharp rebuke to the governor from a Speaker who seemed to enjoy such moments. Subsequently, however, DiMasi resigned amid rumors of a scandal that eventually resulted in his indictment and conviction in federal court on charges that he had defrauded the taxpayers of his honest services by steering two contracts worth $17.5 million to software company Cognos in exchange for kickbacks. Robert DeLeo of Winthrop ascended to the Speakership, and DeLeo favored casinos. Lo and behold, in 2010 the house voted 120–37 in favor of casino legislation. DeLeo "flipped 64 members who voted against Patrick's bill and won the support of 13 of the 17 new members since the 2008 vote" (Sullivan 2010). Although most of the switching members said they had come to regard jobs as more important than risks like gambling addiction and crime, one unusually candid veteran indicated that she had changed her vote because of fear of the political consequences to anyone bucking the Speaker (Sullivan 2010).

However, even the emergence of a Speaker who could deliver the votes was not sufficient for gambling legislation to pass in 2010. Instead, the Speaker and the governor engaged in a standoff on the issue of awarding slots to existing racetracks, two of which existed in Speaker DeLeo's district. The measure died again. Nonetheless, in one of those other curious features of the legislative process in Massachusetts, Governor Patrick, Speaker DeLeo, and Senate President Murray—the "Big Three"—got together in 2011 and hammered out an agreement to authorize three full-scale casinos and one slot parlor to be sited in different regions of the state. The key feature here was that the three leaders settled their differences behind closed doors before filing the legislation; no messy hearings or further public comment was needed. The predictable outcry arose from casino opponents and even a few state legislators opposed to the legislation; however, when the Big Three agree on major legislation, voting is almost a formality (Levenson and Bierman 2011).

The "Big Three" formula works just as handily with a Republican governor. It was under Governor Mitt Romney, who in a later presidential campaign boasted of being "severely conservative," that the state passed universal health-care legislation. In 2004 there was mounting interest in the state to tackle the problem of the uninsured, and Romney filed his own bill to address the problem. He worked with the legislative leadership, even dropping in on the homes of the Speaker and senate president when the effort seemed to founder. He gained the approval of Senator Edward M. Kennedy. Eventually, the legislature passed its own version, including a provision that businesses with more than eleven employees that did not provide health care would have to pay the state a $295 assessment to help support the state's free care pool. Romney vetoed that provision and several others, and in another feature of the relationship between the Democrats and a Republican governor, the legislature overrode those vetoes—as Romney knew they would. Nonetheless, the governor deserved a great deal of credit. Romneycare became Obamacare nationally, which caused the governor grief among Republicans in his 2012 effort to unseat President Barack Obama (Mooney 2011).

Sometimes there are partisan fights, of course. The legislature refused to pass an income tax cut desired by Governor Cellucci, so in 2000 the governor went over their heads and passed the tax cut as a ballot initiative. Even at that, the legislature slowed down the cut so significantly that it was not fully implemented until 2020.

An unsavory feature of legislative dominance by the Democrats has been recurring charges of corruption. At one point, three consecutive Speakers of the house faced federal charges involving corruption. Two pleaded guilty, and a third went to trial and was convicted. Then the next Speaker was named by federal prosecutors as an unindicted coconspirator in a patronage scheme involving the state Probation Department. The case led to the conviction of three department employees. Those convictions were later overturned by a U.S. court of appeals. That did nothing to flatter the government's characterization of the Speaker as an unindicted coconspirator. Two of the previous prosecutions were arguably prosecutorial overreach as well. None of that changes the fact of the convictions or the lingering perception of a one-party Democratic legislature riven by bad and sometimes criminal behavior.

Most Republican governors have followed Frank Sargent's advice. Weld campaigned against the legislature in 1990 and had some early pitched battles but came to enjoy cordial relations with the legislature, especially Senate President William M. Bulger. Bulger, the symbol of Beacon Hill power brokers, noted that their relationship was "symbiotic" early in Weld's term, and "it became more trusting and relaxed as we came to know each other better" (Bulger 1996, 270). It was Weld who suggested regular meetings of the governor, Speaker, and senate president, much to the consternation of party activists on both sides.

Paul Cellucci was a well-regarded former state senator, as was Jane Swift. The exception was Romney, whom legislators regarded as standoffish. But no one questioned his competency or command of data, and when it came to getting health care done, policy won out over politics. No chief executive of either party has been able to work as harmoniously with the Democrats as Governor Charlie Baker. He is both a data-driven policy wonk and a savvy politician. He rarely, if ever, takes a cheap shot at the legislature (an easy punching bag) or does things that would undermine the relationship. At the same time, he fights for his priorities and wields the veto pen when he deems it necessary. In turn the Democrats in the legislature enjoy working with Baker and also eschew political attacks on him. The Massachusetts Democratic Party chair takes an occasional shot, but the party organization isn't powerful and no one seems to mind the party chair doing the job of a party chair. In a blog post at *MassPoliticsProfs*, political scientist Jeffrey Berry christened the state under the Democrats and Baker as "Niceachusetts."

Skeptics who argue that parties don't matter can't overlook the consequences when Governor Baker lost control of the Republican state committee in 2019. His favored candidate for chairperson was defeated by the Trump loving Jim Lyons. Lyons' victory was attributable to a sea change in the elected membership of the state committee, a transformation Baker tried and failed to forestall. Lyons and allies from the dark money operation Massachusetts Fiscal Alliance set out to purge moderates from the party. They succeeded. In December 2021, both Baker and Lieutenant Governor Karyn Polito announced that neither of them would seek the corner office in 2022. Massachusetts has long prided itself as the summit of rock ribbed Yankee Republican moderation. That claim to exceptionalism is washing away in the Trump tide.

Parties and Federal Office

Massachusetts' Democratic nature has been overwhelmingly evident in elections to federal office, whether it be for president, senator, or the U.S. House of Representatives. The state has gone Democratic in every presidential year since 1928 except for 1952 and 1956, when the state voted for Dwight D. Eisenhower, and in 1980 and 1984, for Ronald Reagan. Reagan won a plurality in a three-way contest in 1980 and with just over 51 percent of the vote in his 1984 national landslide. In the House, the GOP enjoyed a brief resurgence in 1992 when its candidates Peter Blute and Peter Torkildsen ousted two Democrats caught up in scandals. Both of them lost in 1996, and the Republicans have been unable to fill a House seat since.

In a special election in 2010 to replace the late senator Edward M. Kennedy, Republican Scott Brown shocked the state and nation by winning the seat. He thus became the first GOP U.S. senator from Massachusetts since Edward Brooke was defeated by Paul Tsongas in 1978. Brown campaigned as an everyman, driving a pickup truck and clad in a barn jacket. His opponent, Attorney General Martha Coakley, ran a listless campaign. Recovery from the Great Recession had yet to make an appearance in Massachusetts, and many voters blamed President Obama. Turnout dropped in Democratic strongholds, and the energetic Tea Party provided organizational support for Brown. He was so popular that there was even speculation about him someday running for president. As 2012 loomed, Brown faced the task of winning a full term in a general election, though. The demoralized Democrats were unable to attract a top-tier candidate. Then Elizabeth Warren jumped into the race, clearing a weak field. Brown de-emphasized partisanship as much as possible, arguing that his record showed him to be the most bipartisan member of the Senate. Brown hoped Massachusetts' political history might repeat itself. Voters here "turned to George McGovern by nine points in 1972 while reelecting Republican Senator Ed Brooke by nearly 30 points. Ronald Reagan won Massachusetts by just under 3 percent in 1984 the year voters sent the liberal John Kerry to the Senate for the first time, defeating his opponent by 10 points" (Ubertaccio 2012). But those days of split-ticket voting at the national level have long since passed. On Election Day 2012, polls still showed Brown as the most popular politician in Massachusetts. And he lost by just under eight points, an outcome predicted ten months earlier on the *MassPoliticsProfs* blog by Professor Duquette, whose analysis made clear that Scott Brown's special-election victory had been an anomaly.

The most interesting recent event concerning the Massachusetts congressional delegation involves the 2018 victory of Ayanna Pressley, a Black woman, over Michael Capuano, a white man, in the Democratic primary for the Seventh Congressional District. Capuano was a well-regarded and progressive veteran House member and a former mayor of Somerville first elected to the House in 1998. There was no scandal and no apparent unhappiness with Capuano in the district. But the congressional district had been redrawn to take in a healthy percentage of minority communities in the redistricting of 2012. Pressley was a savvy politician herself, having served on the staffs of former congressman Joseph P. Kennedy and Senator John Kerry and on the Boston City Council. By 2018 the district had become more diverse and more progressive. There was little difference between the candidates on issues dear to Democrats, but Pressley's argument that "the people closest to the pain should be closest to the power" resonated throughout the district, and she defeated Capuano by seventeen points. Pressley became the first woman of color to serve in the Massachusetts congressional delegation (Levenson 2018). Pressley quickly showed that she would be no ordinary freshman, speaking out on women's issues and racial justice, becoming a leader of "the squad," and attracting the ire of President Donald Trump. Perhaps thus inspired, progressive Democratic challengers announced against two other incumbent Democrats for Congress in 2020. Both, however, lost.

Conclusion

Could the election of Pressley be a signal of incipient change in Massachusetts? Further down the ballot, two progressive newcomers knocked off long-serving incumbent Democrats for state house of representative seats in 2018. Twenty-eight-year house member Byron Rushing lost to Jon Santiago, an emergency room physician. Jeffrey Sánchez, powerful chairman of the House Ways and Means Committee, lost to Nika Elugardo. Suffolk County, which includes Boston, elected its first woman of color as district attorney, Rachael Rollins. As WBUR reported in January 2020, when Pressley assumed her seat on the Boston City Council in 2010, she was the first woman of color to ever sit on that body. In 2020 the thirteen-member body included seven people of color and eight women, including Julia Mejia, the first Latina to serve on the council (she won her seat by just one vote). This is encouraging, but in Massachusetts people of color are not represented in the legislature or in municipal government in proportion to their populations (Levin, Forman, and Bliss 2019). For those seeing 2018 as the start of a surge in the progressive wing of the party, 2020 was a disappointment. A report analyzing the result noted that for the past three decades, "Republicans and conservative Democrats" have had their way on Beacon Hill and that an establishment coalition, not progressive Democrats, prevailed on primary day (Hillman and Rivera 2020).

Yankee patricians did not easily cede power to Irish and other "new ethnic" workers, and the workers did not graciously stand aside for suburban managers. Liberal as they may be, the suburban liberals' policy priorities have not easily meshed with those of other Democratic constituencies, including working people and people of color. Geismer argues that the suburbs have prioritized "low taxes, high property values, quality education, and the security and safety of children" (2014, 11) How will this mesh with a politics that aims to bring power "closest to the pain"? If the 2020 Massachusetts Democratic primaries are a barometer, the answer is that power will once again be given up grudgingly, if at all.

It would be difficult to make a much easier path for the Democrats in Massachusetts than they already have, but a Trumpified Republican Party seems determined to do just that. When Governor Charlie Baker moves on, statewide victories will be harder to come by. The Democrats will remain in power, but the key will be what kind of Democratic Party evolves.

WORKS CITED

Brown, Richard, and Jack Tager. 2000. *Massachusetts: A Concise History.* Amherst: University of Massachusetts Press.

Bulger, William M. 1996. *While the Music Lasts: My Life in Politics.* New York: Houghton Mifflin.

Clucas, Richard. 2007. "Legislative Professionalism and the Power of State House Leaders." *State Politics and Policy Quarterly* 7, no. 1: 1–19.

Cunningham, Maurice. 2008. "Massachusetts Republicans: The 2004 Challenge to Democratic Legislative Hegemony." *New England Journal of Political Science* 3, no. 1: 30–48.

Davies, Philip, and John Kenneth White. 1985. "The New Class in Massachusetts: Politics in a Technocratic Society." *Journal of American Studies* 19, no. 2: 225–38.

Duquette, Jerold. 2002. "Campaign Finance Reform in the Bay State: Is Cleanliness Next to Godliness?" In *Money, Politics, and Campaign Finance Reform Laws in the States*, edited by David Schultz. Durham, NC: Carolina Academic Press.

———. 2003. "Massachusetts Politics in the Twenty-First Century: Recognizing the Impact of Clashing Political Cultures," *New England Journal of Political Science* 1, no. 1: 1–19.

———. 2013. "Bay State Politics in the Post–Scott Brown Era." *New England Journal of Political Science* 7, no. 2.

Geismer, Lily. 2014. *Don't Blame Us: Suburban Liberals and the Transformation of the Democratic Party.* Princeton, NJ: Princeton University Press.

Hillman, Jon, and Wilnelia Rivera. 2020. "September 1st Massachusetts Primary and Deep Democracy 2.0 Analysis." Memorandum to Maria Jobin-Leeds, Partnership for Democracy and Education.

Hogarty, Richard. 2002. *Massachusetts Politics and Public Policy: Studies in Power and Leadership.* Amherst: University of Massachusetts Press.

Johnson, Patrick. 2016. "Hampden County Sheriff Michael Ashe, Corrections Innovator, Stepping Down after 42 Years." *MassLive*, December 30, 2016. https://www.masslive.com/news/2016/12/hampden_county_sheriff_michael_10.html.

Keller, John. 2017. *The Bluest State: How Democrats Created the Massachusetts Blueprint for American Political Disaster.* New York: St. Martin's Press.

King, Nick. 1978. "King—Simple Issues." *Boston Globe*, September 20, 1978.

Levenson, Michael. 2018. "'Are You Ready to Bring Change to Washington?' Pressley Stuns Capuano on Historic Night." *Boston Globe*, September 14, 2018. https://www.bostonglobe.com/news/politics/2018/09/04/capuano-pressley-count-experience-support-win-primary/BexLGYivjWMnwv4jaYTC1N/story.html.

Levenson, Michael, and Noah Bierman. 2011. "State Leaders Agree on Casino Bill: Proposal Would Allow 4 Gambling Facilities: Private Talks Criticized." *Boston Globe*, August 24, 2011.

Levin, Peter, Benjamin Forman, and Laurel Bliss. 2019. "MassForward: Advancing Democratic Innovation and Electoral Reform in Massachusetts." *MassInc*, November 23, 2019. https://massinc.org/2019/11/23/massforward-advancing-democratic-innovation-and-electoral-reform-in-massachusetts/.

Litt, Edgar. 1965. *The Political Cultures of Massachusetts*. Cambridge, MA: MIT Press.

Massachusetts Republican Party State Committee. 2018. "Massachusetts Republican Party Platform." Adopted April 5, 2018. https://d3n8a8pro7vhmx.cloudfront.net/massgop/pages/1756/attachments/original/1523035066/2018_MRSC_Platform.pdf?1523035066.

Mettler, Suzanne. 2005. *Soldiers to Citizens: The G.I. Bill and the Making of the Greatest Generation*. New York: Oxford University Press.

Mileur, Jerome M. 1997. "Party Politics in the Bay State: The Dominion of Democracy." In *Parties and Politics in the New England States*, edited by Jerome M. Mileur. Amherst, MA: Polity Press.

Mohl, Bruce, and Michael Jonas. 2020. "Baker-Linked PAC Backs 13 Dems, 4 Republicans in Primary Battles." *CommonWealth Magazine*, August 24, 2020.

Mooney, Brian. 2011. "Romney and Health Care: In the Thick of History." *Boston Globe*, May 30, 2011. http://archive.boston.com/lifestyle/health/articles/2011/05/30/romney_and_health_care_in_the_thick_of_history/.

Murphy, Matt. 2020. "Gov. Charlie Baker No Longer Most Popular Governor in the Nation." WGBH, January 20, 2020. https://www.wgbh.org/news/local-news/2020/01/20/gov-charlie-baker-no-longer-most-popular-governor-in-the-nation.

O'Toole, James M. 1985. "Prelates and Politicos: Catholics and Politics in Massachusetts, 1900–1970." In *Catholic Boston: Studies in Religion and Community, 1870–1970*, edited by Robert E. Sullivan and James M. O'Toole. Boston: Archdiocese of Boston.

Phillips, Frank. 2013. "Patrick's Tax Plan Has Risk, Reward: Legacy, Stability of Democratic Hold on Hill on the Line." *Boston Globe*, January 20, 2013. https://www.boston.com/news/politics/2013/01/19/patricks-plan-carries-risk-the-chance-of-legacy-building/amp.

Southern Poverty Law Center. n.d. "Scott Lively." https://www.splcenter.org/fighting-hate/extremist-files/individual/scott-lively.

Stout, Matt. 2019. "A Fund Raising Effort Collapses. Rift between Baker and Mass. GOP Grows." *Boston Globe*, August 26, 2019. https://www.bostonglobe.com/metro/2019/08/26/chasm-between-baker-state-gop-grows-lucrative-fund-raising-operation-dismantled/QeF9kYWfcVL6bQxUMsaDTO/story.html.

Sullivan, Jack. 2010. "DeLeo Flips 64 Votes: Gambling Vote Shows Dramatic Turnaround in House from Just Two Years Ago." *CommonWealth Magazine*, April 15, 2010. https://commonwealthmagazine.org/politics/deleo-flips-64-votes/.

Ubertaccio, Peter. 2012. "Scott Brown Must Rely on His Personal Appeal to Win in November." *HuffPost*, June 13, 2012. https://www.huffpost.com/entry/scott-brown-massachusetts_b_1595202.

Yang, Angela. 2019. "Why the City Council Elections See Lower Voter Turnout." *Daily Free Press*, November 6, 2019. https://dailyfreepress.com/2019/11/06/why-the-city-council-elections-see-lower-voter-turnout/.

CHAPTER 8

VOTER ACCESS in MASSACHUSETTS
From Laggard to Leader

Erin O'Brien

Back of the pack is not a place Massachusetts likes to be. As recently as 2010, that is exactly where Massachusetts was in terms of effectiveness in running national elections. The "Election Performance Index," now housed at the Massachusetts Institute of Technology, provides a "nonpartisan objective measure of how well each state is faring in managing national elections" based on seventeen indicators, including problems with registration of absentee balloting, accuracy of voting technologies, rejected or returned ballots, and whether online registration was available (EPI 2018).[1] Massachusetts placed a dismal thirty-second in 2008 and fared similarly in 2010, ranking thirty-first. Starting in 2012, however, Massachusetts saw gains—twenty-second in 2012, twenty-fifth in 2014, all the way to ninth in 2016, and a slight regression to eleventh in 2018.[2]

This chapter examines this shift and what it has meant for voter registration, turnout, and racial gaps on both measures. Readers will learn that Massachusetts has actually underperformed compared to the other fifty states once we take into account the relatively high socioeconomic status of the state's residents. However, the past is not prologue. While the commonwealth scored poorly on voter access, the state has made exceptional gains in expanding the ability of residents to vote via changes including online voter registration, automatic voter registration (AVR), and some early voting. It responded nimbly to COVID-19 with universally accessible mail-in voting for the pandemic period. Notably, these policies were adopted in

---

The author thanks Jane JaKyung Han for truly *exceptional* research assistance—often under very challenging circumstances. Jane, please look in the mirror in awe of what you've negotiated the last eighteen months.

1   The full seventeen indicators consist of the following: data completeness, disability- or illness-related voting problems, mail ballots rejected, mail ballots unreturned, military and overseas ballots rejected, military and overseas ballots unreturned, online registration available, postelection audit required, provisional ballots cast, provisional ballots rejected, registration or absentee ballot problems, registrations rejected, residual vote rate, turnout, voter registration rate, voting information lookup tools, and voting wait time (EPI 2018).

2   This was the last year available at the time of writing.

the context of efforts in states like Wisconsin, Texas, and North Carolina to make it harder to vote—most saliently via photo identification requirements (Horwitz 2016). A fair reading of Massachusetts when it comes to voter turnout and access then is that the commonwealth is improving—with more work to do. While Massachusetts is on the path to exceptionalism in voter access, getting there will require political mobilization and tough legislative work.

Massachusetts Partisanship

First things first, if we want to understand the Massachusetts electorate, we need to understand partisanship. Ask nearly any American not residing in Massachusetts what Massachusetts voters are like, and you will get themes on one answer—a bunch of liberals. An accurate description is more nuanced—Democrats certainly but with some twists.

Table 8.1 provides the party breakdown of enrolled Massachusetts voters by decade. Democrats outpace Republicans. This trend skyrockets following party realignment in the 1960s. Since 1970 the gap has always been at least twenty points between Democrats and Republicans. The Republican share of the electorate has steadily declined so that as of 2021, less than one in ten registered voters in Massachusetts identifies as Republican.

TABLE 8.1. Percentage of Massachusetts Voter Enrollment by Political Party, 1950–2021

	DEMOCRAT	REPUBLICAN	UNENROLLED
1950	26.7	26.0	47.2
1960	29.7	24.1	46.1
1970	43.2	20.8	36.0
1980a	45.9	14.2	40.0
1990a	44.2	13.5	42.2
2000a	36.3	12.9	50.3
2010b	36.9	11.3	51.6
2021a	31.6	9.7	57.4

Data from Massachusetts Secretary of the Commonwealth, https://www.sec.state.ma.us/ele/eleenr/enridx.htm.

Note: Massachusetts consistently allowed for third-party registration in 1992. Hence, percentages do not always total 100 percent.

a February data for 1980, 1990, 2000, 2021.
b August 2010 due to data omission in original.

The third column in table 8.1 is likely surprising to many, though. Unenrolled voters are essentially "independents," as Massachusetts does not allow for the independent designation. These are voters who choose not to enroll in either major party and, therefore, can vote in either party's primaries. Beginning in 2000, and foreshadowed in 1990, the percentage of unenrolled voters in the state climbed sharply. Since 2000 the majority of the commonwealth's voters *do not declare allegiance to either major party.* This helps explain the taste for Republican governors, as seen in chapter 5, despite such a deep-blue electoral record for other offices.

The stereotype of Massachusetts voters as Democrats is borne out then but woefully incomplete, as the majority of voters, regardless of the pattern of votes they actually cast, prefer not to identify with either major party. This provides policy makers and elected leaders with more wiggle room than many outsiders expect—the demand for Far Left policy is simply not there to the degree typified. Bay State political culture tilts left but does not careen so, as we see in several chapters in this volume.

Voter Registration and Turnout

MASSACHUSETTS VOTER REGISTRATION AND VOTING
IN THE NATIONAL CONTEXT

Table 8.2 provides state voter registration levels in the 2020 presidential race overall and by race and ethnicity.[3] The first column provides the overall registration rates for each state. Here Massachusetts falls just short of the U.S. average by 0.3 percentage points and ranks twenty-eighth among the fifty states and District of Columbia. Interestingly, Massachusetts ranked sixteenth for voter registration in the 2016 presidential election. While the absolute percentage of citizens who are registered voters in Massachusetts changed little from 2016 to 2020—73.7 versus 72.4 percent—the nationwide registration and mobilization efforts in advance of the 2020 election largely skipped the electorally certain Bay State.

What about turnout? The Massachusetts Secretary of the Commonwealth's Office reported that 279,204 more state residents voted in 2016 compared to 2020 (Galvin 2020d; DeCosta-Klipa 2020b). For context, table 8.3 provides state voting rates among eligible citizens in the 2020 election. Overall rates tell a similar story about voting as on registration. The former is always

---

3   Data from the U.S. Census Bureau, "Current Population Survey." Margins of error for the race and ethnicity breakdowns are sometimes large and should be viewed as instructive for how a state performs but somewhat fluid when it comes to exact state ranking.

lower than the latter in the United States. Massachusetts fell 0.5 percentage points below national turnout rates, placing it twenty-seventh among the fifty states and DC. As was the case with registration, the comparison to 2016 is instructive. In the 2016 presidential contest, just over 66 percent of eligible residents voted in Massachusetts. In 2020 it was a near mirror image—66.3 percent. But because of the highly polarizing and deeply contested Trump versus Biden contest, turning out at just 2016 levels in 2020 dropped Massachusetts to just the middle of the pack for voting. It bears repeating that because Massachusetts is no mystery come election night, neither Biden or Trump nor the national Democratic and Republican Parties invested significant resources in the state to increase turnout.

TABLE 8.2. State Citizen Voter Registration Rates by Race and Ethnicity, November 2020

	OVERALL	ASIAN	BLACK	HISPANIC	WHITE
U.S.	72.7	63.8	69.0	61.1	76.5
ALABAMA	68.0	*	60.6	*	71.0
ALASKA	74.2	*	*	*	77.5
ARIZONA	76.4	70.2	79.2	66.8	80.1
ARKANSAS	62.0	*	57.1	36.4	64.1
CALIFORNIA	69.4	62.9	68.1	60.4	78.2
COLORADO	71.3	49.9	56.0	60.5	74.4
CONNECTICUT	73.3	60.5	68.3	67.8	77.3
DELAWARE	75.1	*	69.8	*	77.1
DC	86.9	*	83.2	*	91.5
FLORIDA	67.1	56.4	65.4	58.7	71.2
GEORGIA	70.7	56.9	68.5	47.6	75.1
HAWAII	68.7	66.7	*	*	75.6
IDAHO	69.3	*	*	53.2	71.5
ILLINOIS	74.4	73.3	67.8	52.4	79.4
INDIANA	69.3	66.1	65.5	53.5	70.7
IOWA	76.0	*	63.5	46.8	78.2
KANSAS	70.8	*	71.4	51.5	75.3
KENTUCKY	75.9	*	74.6	*	76.5
LOUISIANA	69.3	*	68.7	64.3	70.5
MAINE	77.4	*	*	*	78.1

MARYLAND	78.6	69.7	79.3	76.7	78.3
MASSACHUSETTS	72.4	57.1	42.2	60.4	77.6
MICHIGAN	73.8	49.6	72.4	58.9	75.2
MINNESOTA	82.9	79.4	70.5	74.7	84.1
MISSISSIPPI	80.4	*	83.1	*	79.2
MISSOURI	75.7	*	73.6	71.3	76.8
MONTANA	77.5	*	*	*	77.8
NEBRASKA	70.9	*	*	*	72.9
NEVADA	66.2	69.7	66.8	52.0	73.1
NEW HAMPSHIRE	78.3	*	*	*	80.5
NEW JERSEY	84.6	84.5	77.5	82.0	86.2
NEW MEXICO	68.6	*	*	59.9	78.0
NEW YORK	70.5	58.2	68.6	61.6	74.0
NORTH CAROLINA	69.8	76.4	68.3	54.3	71.7
NORTH DAKOTA	77.3	*	*	*	79.7
OHIO	77.0	60.6	72.8	75.8	78.4
OKLAHOMA	67.3	*	56.4	42.8	73.5
OREGON	79.9	64.8	62.2	60.8	82.7
PENNSYLVANIA	76.3	51.4	76.5	61.4	77.8
RHODE ISLAND	74.1	*	*	*	75.4
SOUTH CAROLINA	70.0	*	60.5	47.5	75.1
SOUTH DAKOTA	67.4	*	*	*	68.8
TENNESSEE	74.3	*	77.1	47.6	75.2
TEXAS	71.8	63.5	70.3	63.2	78.5
UTAH	67.4	*	*	55.4	69.2
VERMONT	73.0	*	*	*	74.6
VIRGINIA	76.0	66.1	67.7	63.8	80.9
WASHINGTON	74.8	63.9	64.7	61.0	79.7
WEST VIRGINIA	67.3	*	*	*	67.0
WISCONSIN	76.7	*	47.7	61.0	80.1
WYOMING	69.3	*	*	*	69.3

Data from U.S. Census Bureau, "Reported Voting and Registration by Sex, Race, and Hispanic Origin for States: November 2020," table 4b, https://www.census.gov/data/tables/time-series/demo/voting-and-registration/p20–585.html.

* Citizen population base is fewer than 100,000 and therefore too small to show the derived measures.

TABLE 8.3. State Citizen Voting Rates
by Race and Ethnicity, 2020

	OVERALL	ASIAN	BLACK	HISPANIC	WHITE
U.S.	66.8	59.7	62.6	53.7	70.9
ALABAMA	60.5	*	54.8	*	63.0
ALASKA	63.8	*	*	*	71.0
ARIZONA	71.9	67.9	69.1	60.8	77.0
ARKANSAS	54.0	*	44.7	34.6	57.0
CALIFORNIA	65.1	59.9	64.0	54.6	74.6
COLORADO	67.6	43.2	53.1	51.1	71.9
CONNECTICUT	66.6	56.6	65.2	56.4	71.0
DELAWARE	67.7	*	64.7	*	68.4
DC	84.0	*	70.3	*	88.8
FLORIDA	62.1	55.6	58.7	52.7	66.8
GEORGIA	66.1	53.3	64.0	44.2	70.3
HAWAII	64.3	61.4	*	*	72.7
IDAHO	64.9	*	*	46.3	67.5
ILLINOIS	68.4	69.3	63.8	46.8	72.9
INDIANA	61.0	59.9	60.2	44.0	62.0
IOWA	70.5	*	46.2	44.2	73.0
KANSAS	65.7	*	61.0	45.5	70.7
KENTUCKY	68.5	*	62.5	*	69.6
LOUISIANA	64.7	*	57.9	55.1	64.7
MAINE	71.3	*	*	*	71.8
MARYLAND	73.6	64.1	75.3	74.4	72.3
MASSACHUSETTS	66.3	44.9	36.4	50.7	72.4
MICHIGAN	66.9	45.1	63.8	54.7	68.2
MINNESOTA	77.9	64.0	66.1	62.7	79.9
MISSISSIPPI	70.3	*	72.8	*	69.8
MISSOURI	66.8	*	69.2	*	67.9
MONTANA	73.5	*	*	*	74.6
NEBRASKA	65.2	*	*	*	66.6
NEVADA	61.5	68.9	58.5	46.4	69.7
NEW HAMPSHIRE	74.0	*	*	*	76.4
NEW JERSEY	78.3	77.9	71.3	72.1	81.1

NEW MEXICO	62.6	*	*	53.8	62.6
NEW YORK	64.7	51.9	62.7	54.9	69.0
NORTH CAROLINA	64.7	70.9	63.4	48.8	66.6
NORTH DAKOTA	67.1	*	*	*	71.5
OHIO	70.1	57.5	65.1	58.7	71.9
OKLAHOMA	58.3	*	49.5	30.3	65.0
OREGON	74.1	60.6	51.2	51.9	77.7
PENNSYLVANIA	70.2	49.1	70.8	54.3	71.7
RHODE ISLAND	66.3	*	*	*	66.8
SOUTH CAROLINA	63.4	*	53.9	38.3	69.0
SOUTH DAKOTA	58.5	*	*	*	60.3
TENNESSEE	66.4	*	69.4	41.4	72.0
TEXAS	63.9	58.7	60.8	53.1	72.0
UTAH	63.6	*	*	49.6	65.7
VERMONT	68.4	*	*	*	69.9
VIRGINIA	71.5	61.8	63.9	51.3	77.3
WASHINGTON	71.5	62.8	61.9	53.7	77.0
WEST VIRGINIA	56.1	*	*	*	56.1
WISCONSIN	73.6	*	43.5	58.4	77.2
WYOMING	65.5	*	*	*	66.8

Data from U.S. Census Bureau, "Reported Voting and Registration by Sex, Race, and Hispanic Origin for States: November 2020," table4b, https://www.census.gov/data/tables/time-series/demo/voting-and-registration/p20–585.html.

Note: Categories include Asian alone, Black alone, Hispanic any race, and white alone.

* Citizen population base is fewer than 100,000 and therefore too small to show the derived measures.

Other tabulations place Massachusetts a bit higher in turnout. The United States Election Project calculates the voting-eligible population "by adjusting the voting-age population for non-citizens and ineligible felons, depending on state law. National estimates are further adjusted for overseas eligible voters, but no state level adjustments are made since there is no reliable method of apportioning overseas voters to states" (McDonald 2020). By contrast, the Census Bureau figures in the charts are based on samples of eligible citizens, and there is some controversy regarding how they code "no votes" (Jacobson 2013). The Election Project data calculates Massachusetts presidential turnout at 71.6 percent in 2020 (up from 67.2 percent in 2016)—making it fourteenth among the fifty states and DC. Regardless of which measure one prefers, it is clear that turnout in Massachusetts was not among the top quarter of states in 2020.

Why is Massachusetts fairly average in turnout? The single best predictor of whether Americans vote remains socioeconomic status (SES) (Verba and Nie 1972; Leighley and Nagler 2013). Massachusetts has the highest percentage of citizens with a bachelor's degree or higher (42.6 percent versus 31.3 percent for the national average) according to the National Center for Education Statistics (2018). It is fifth for median income (World Population Review 2020). These metrics indicate Massachusetts should be at or near the top among the fifty states for both voter registration and turnout. Neither the Census Bureau nor the United States Election Project indicates this is the case. Some might note that since the winner of the presidential race in Massachusetts is a foregone conclusion, it is unrealistic to expect higher turnout. However, this argument falls short when nonbattleground states like Vermont, New Jersey, and Montana exceed Massachusetts voter turnout despite lower SES.[4] Not being a presidential battleground state cannot then solely explain why Massachusetts falls short of SES expectations.

More cold water appears when we turn to the racial and ethnic gaps in voter registration and turnout. Returning to table 8.2, we see that the last four columns provide registration rates by state for Asians, Blacks, Hispanics, and whites. The margins of error in the Census Bureau's "Current Population Survey" surrounding these figures are sometimes substantial—especially when states have relatively small numbers of a particular racial or ethnic group. Figures reported should therefore be interpreted for trends and not necessarily exact counts. No other state-level longitudinal data exists over time by race and ethnicity, however, so these figures are the best available.[5] Table 8.2 indicates that the gaps between white and Asian (-20.5), Black (-35.4), and Hispanic (-17.2) registration rates are dramatic in Massachusetts. By comparison, Maryland is another Eastern Seaboard state that is solidly blue in presidential contests, with a taste for Republican governors and comparatively high SES among residents. Yet the registration gaps between whites and Asians (-8.6), whites and Blacks (+1.0), and whites and Hispanics (-1.6) in Maryland are markedly different from those of Massachusetts. California (-15.3, -10.1, -17.8) and Illinois (-6.1, -11.6, -27), two fairly affluent blue states, also report far smaller gaps between whites and Asians as well as whites and Blacks compared to Massachusetts. California is similar to Massachusetts in

---

4   This holds for both Census Bureau and U.S. Elections Project data.
5   This issue found its way into oral arguments during the landmark *Shelby* decision during questioning by Chief Justice Roberts (Jacobson 2013).

Latinx gaps, and Illinois exceeds the Massachusetts gap. All four states have work to do, but Massachusetts stands out among them for heavy lifting.

The picture is similar—and with more pressing impact when it comes to gaps in voting rates. After all, elected leaders are responsive to voters, not the state populace at large. In states where the voting gaps are smaller between the more and less affluent, social and economic policy is more equitable (Avery and Peffley 2005; Franko, Kelly, and Witko 2016).

Recall that Massachusetts was twenty-seventh among the fifty states in overall turnout according to the Census Bureau in 2020 and fourteenth according to the U.S. Elections Project. On this metric, the gaps in turnout for Massachusetts are staggering. Table 8.3 shows that in the Bay State, 72.4 percent of eligible whites voted in 2020. Eligible Asian Americans voted at a rate of 44.9 percent, Blacks at 36.4 percent, and Hispanics at 50.7 percent. This makes for respective gaps of negative 27.5, negative 36, and negative 21.7. Sadly, 2020 was not anomalistic. Indeed, it was largely worse than 2016, where the respective gaps were negative 19, negative 8, and negative 23.9. Again, margins of error on race and ethnicity figures are sometimes large at the state level, so the precise numbers should be read with some caution. The trend, however, is clear: there are significant racial and ethnic gaps in turnout in the Bay State.

This too cannot be explained away by Massachusetts not having a competitive presidential race. There is no a priori reason to expect that living in a solidly blue or red state begets substantial racial and ethnic gaps in turnout. Solidly blue Maryland shows narrower gaps between white turnout and that of Asians (-8.2) and inverse gaps for Blacks (+3) and Hispanics (+2.1) than Massachusetts. The same was true in 2016 comparisons between Massachusetts and Maryland. Illinois and California too had substantially smaller gaps between white turnout and that of Asians and Blacks in 2020 (Illinois -3.6, -9.1; California -14.7, -10.6). Gaps for Latinx populations are greater in Illinois (-26.6) and the same in California (-20.0) compared to Massachusetts. A solidly red state like Mississippi reports *higher* turnout among Blacks compared to whites.[6] The takeaway from all this for Massachusetts is that the racial and ethnic gaps in turnout are comparatively dramatic and not explained away by a lack of electoral competition.

---

6   Note that the margins of error in the "Current Population Survey" are substantial when states have relatively small numbers of a particular racial or ethnic group. As noted in the charts, an asterisk represents states where meaningful statistical estimates could not be derived as the *n* was too low. Figures reported should therefore be interpreted for trends and not necessarily exact counts. No other state-level data exists over time by race and ethnicity, however, so these figures are the best available.

These snapshots of registration and turnout across the fifty states make for several key takeaways. For registration, Massachusetts rates are in the middle of the pack. For voting, even using the most generous metric, Massachusetts is not in the top quarter. Given the strong causal relationship between socioeconomic status and voting, and Massachusetts' place at the pinnacle on measures of SES, Massachusetts should exhibit higher rates for both registration and voting. The racial and ethnic gaps in registration and turnout also make clear that Massachusetts is far from exceptional among the fifty states when it comes to equitable voter participation.

MASSACHUSETTS VOTER REGISTRATION AND VOTING OVER TIME

But what happens when we look beyond singular elections? Methodologists know that longitudinal data paints a more complete picture than cross-sectional data. Do the patterns described above hold when we consider elections over time? After all, 2016 featured two historically unpopular candidates, and 2020 saw major upswings in turnout across the nation due to extreme political polarization and the anomaly of carrying out an election during a pandemic.

Table 8.4 contextualizes Massachusetts over time. It provides registration rates overall and by race and ethnicity for 2000–2020. Midterm election years and presidential election years are grouped separately because citizens are motivated to vote at higher rates in presidential cycles, thereby affecting registration rates.

Over the full course of each panel, registration rates have held fairly steady in Massachusetts. In 2000 registration rates in the commonwealth were 70.3 and sat at 72.4 in 2020. In the 2002 midterm races, 64.8 percent of eligible individuals were registered, and by 2018 that increased to 68 percent. There are dips and jumps between cycles, but the trend lines are fairly steady.

The story is more nuanced when we turn to registration rates over time by race and ethnicity. Looking at presidential years, the registration gap between whites and Asian Americans closed considerably (33.7 points) from election 2000 to 2020, as did the registration gap for Hispanics (14.5 points). For Blacks in the commonwealth, the registration gap increased in 2020 from 2000 by 17.2 after having narrowed from 2000 to 2016 by 7 points. Over the course of midterm elections between 2002 and 2018, the gap again narrowed for Asians (22.2 points) and Hispanics (33.3 points).

It grew, however, for Blacks by 3.4 points. Asian and Hispanic citizens of the commonwealth are registering with far more frequency, and the gaps relative to white residents are closing. Black Bay Staters, however, have seen increased registration gaps over the full course of the presidential and midterm cycles of the twenty-first century.

TABLE 8.4. Voter Registration among Massachusetts Citizens, 2000–2020

YEAR	OVERALL	ASIAN	BLACK	HISPANIC	WHITE
2000	70.3	21.5	55.8	41	72.7
2004	72	40.3	50.7	43.5	73.5
2008	72.6	38.4	64.1	53.6	74.8
2012	78.7	55.9	71.2	66.9	80.7
2016	73.7	52.4	65.9	50.1	75.8
2020	72.4	60.1	43.5	60.4	77.6
2002	64.8	25.1	55.5	23.4	67.4
2006	72.4	62.6	58.4	47.1	73.5
2010	68.8	47	46.5	38.8	70.9
2014	67.5	40.1	46	49.7	70.9
2018	68	50.8	55.6	60.2	70.9

Data from U.S. Census Bureau, "Voting and Registration in the Election of November XXXX," table 4 or 4b depending on the year.

Note: Categories include Asian alone or in combination, Black alone or in combination, Hispanic any race, and white alone.

Table 8.5 provides voter turnout rates overall and by race/ethnicity for the same period, 2000–2020. Massachusetts voter turnout rate increased 6.3 points from 2000 to 2020. Again, turnout rates fluctuate a bit cycle to cycle, but voting is up in presidential contests. The same is true of midterm elections, where the increase from 2002 to 2018 is 8 points. As we will see in the next section, these increases are due to policy interventions in the commonwealth.

TABLE 8.5. Voting Rates among Massachusetts Citizens, 2000–2020

YEAR	OVERALL	ASIAN	BLACK	HISPANIC	WHITE
2000	60.1	21.5	50.8	20.4	64.6
2004	63.7	32	43.5	32.9	67
2008	67.1	35.4	64.1	39.9	68.9
2012	70.8	43.3	64.2	62.7	72.9
2016	66.7	49.5	60.3	44.6	68.5
2020	66.3	48.7	37.4	50.7	72.4
2002	47.5	14	43.6	14.7	49.3
2006	55.4	33.9	47.3	56.7	58.6
2010	52.2	32.6	38.2	14	53.8
2014	46.9	19.7	25	17	50.4
2018	55.5	44.1	43.7	42.7	57.7

Data from U.S. Census Bureau, "Voting and Registration in the Election of November XXXX," table 4 or 4b depending on the year.

Note: Categories include Asian alone or in combination, Black alone or in combination, Hispanic any race, and white alone.

Turnout increased across all racial and ethnic categories but for Blacks in presidential (though not midterm) contests. This increase was dramatic— increases of 26.6 points for Asians, 30.3 points for Hispanics, and 7.8 points for whites in presidential contests. Blacks, though, saw an almost 10-point gain between 2000 and 2016 eviscerated in the 2020 contest. Midterm elections are more volatile in terms of turnout, but every category saw some net increase between 2002 to 2018, with Asians and Hispanics seeing the most substantial improvement in voter turnout rates.

In short, Massachusetts has experienced overall increases in voter registration, turnout, and a narrowing of racial gaps between whites and both Asians and Hispanics. The data is less uniform for Blacks, suggesting that "a steady march forward" does not typify the Black experience in Massachusetts. Gains are made but not always kept between presidential cycles.

Changes to Voter Access Policies in Massachusetts

The increases in voter turnout and registration in Massachusetts are directly attributable to policy changes by the state legislature and a sometimes-reluctant secretary of the commonwealth. Activists, left-leaning policy think tanks, and nonpartisan good-government groups like the League of Women Voters Massachusetts, MassVOTE, and Common Cause Massachusetts have long advocated for reforms. It took considerable time, but elected officials in Massachusetts responded. Recall from the opening of this chapter that the Election Performance Index placed Massachusetts thirty-second among the fifty states in 2008 but eleventh in 2020. These changes occurred because Massachusetts made policy moves. Additional policy moves can quicken the narrowing of racial and ethnic gaps and ensure that Black Bay Staters enjoy higher voter registration and turnout across midterm and presidential cycles.

In January 2014, Massachusetts did not have online voter registration or early voting. Automatic voter registration was "pie in the sky." Despite a solidly blue state legislature, Massachusetts voter access policies were notable for how antiquated they were. This was particularly striking given that the Democratic Party views itself as pushing the franchise forward. Elected officials in Massachusetts won their seats under antiquated rules, though, and this provides little incentive to alter the rules of the game. Few elected politicians embrace electoral uncertainty. When one wins the game repeatedly, one rarely calls for changes on the field. As a result, for example, Massachusetts residents lived in one of only fifteen states that had no form of early voting until quite recently (Green and O'Brien 2014).

On May 22, 2014, however, Massachusetts made substantial progress, moving the commonwealth from laggard to, increasingly, a leader on voter access policy. Governor Deval Patrick, a Democrat, signed a bill into law that put online voter registration into place, provided early voting in biennial elections statewide starting eleven business days before Election Day and ending two business days before the election,[7] allowed for preregistering sixteen- and seventeen-year-olds so that they would be registered automatically when they turn eighteen, and directed the secretary of the commonwealth to provide a website whereby state residents could check their registration status and polling place (Schoenberg 2014; Massachusetts Trial Court 2014).[8] These policy shifts explain why Massachusetts moved up so dramatically in EPI rankings after 2014 (the 2016 ranking captures implementation of the 2014 law). That the May 2014 law includes a mix of policies that lower

7 The business-day designation means that early voting does not include the weekends before Election Day. From the perspective of expanding voter access across racial lines, this distinction makes early voting associated with Black churches, "souls to the polls" after service, impossible on Sundays.
8 The senate version included same-day voter registration, but this provision was dropped in reconciliation. Republican efforts to get photo ID requirements included were thwarted by Democratic majorities.

the registration barrier, as well as those referred to as "convenience voting measures," helps to explain both the increase in registration and turnout and the narrowing of many racial gaps. Research reveals convenience voting measures, like early voting, primarily assist those who would already vote to do so. Policies that tackle the registration barrier, like online registration, best address inequality in voter turnout (Rigby and Springer 2011).

One can also reasonably expect that registration and turnout rates will continue to rise and that racial and ethnic gaps will further narrow as a result of these policy choices. This is made even more likely by legislation signed into law by Republican governor Charlie Baker in August 2018. The new law made Massachusetts one of seventeen states plus the District of Columbia with automatic voter registration (NCSL 2020a). As the commonwealth website explains, "The Automatic Voter Registration process will be implemented as part of the Permit, License, or ID transaction for new applications and renewals. Under the requirements of the new state law, the RMV will provide basic information from all license/ID transactions to the Secretary of State's office for voter registration purposes." The Division of Medical Assistance and Health Insurance Connector Authority joins the Registry of Motor Vehicles as agencies that help administer AVR. Massachusetts citizens who do not want to be registered can "opt out." This makes the default option in Massachusetts to register all residents who are eligible to vote. This policy directly confronts the registration barrier and thus can be expected to narrow racial and ethnic gaps in turnout (Rigby and Springer 2011).

Election 2020 too showed Massachusetts' new willingness to adapt and modernize when it comes to voter access. Governor Baker signed a bill into law that allowed for the first time in Massachusetts "early voting before its state primary election on Sept. 1, along with four additional days of early voting ahead of the general election. For both elections, all registered voters [had] the option to mail in their ballot—with no excuse needed" (DeCosta-Klipa 2020a). Applications to vote by mail were sent to all registered voters in July and September (for those who did not apply in July). No postage was necessary to return these ballots. In addition, the secretary of the commonwealth's office designed a "track my ballot" website whereby those who mailed their ballot could verify that it had been received and accepted.

From the perspective of political participation and equity, these policy changes in Massachusetts deserve applause—though the 2020 changes were limited to that election cycle alone. Still, no other state made EPI gains like Massachusetts over the period examined. To use the language of this volume's theme, this is exceptional progress.

Work remains. Same-day voter registration, permanent no-excuse absentee voting, permanent universal mail-in voting options, and early in-person voting on the weekend before the presidential contest ("souls to the polls") are next on most good-government groups' wish lists. Same-day voter registration means that one can register to vote on Election Day and cast a ballot in that same election. It remains necessary, as many potential voters do not interact with the agencies implementing AVR, and research indicates same-day registration is the single best reform for lessoning inequality in turnout along economic lines (Rigby and Springer 2011). And since registration rates are lower for racial and ethnic minorities, there is more of a "pool of eligibles" among these communities for same-day registration to reap turnout benefits. "Souls to the polls" would positively affect Black voters in particular, as they are more apt to use this voting option (Herron, Shino, and Smith 2021).

No-excuse absentee voting is particularly important for elections not covered by the August 2014 law's mandate of early voting or the onetime COVID election changes. The 2014 law covers only biennial statewide elections, meaning the majority of elections do *not* enjoy an early-voting option.[9] But for the 2020 exception, casting an absentee ballot in Massachusetts is possible only if the potential voter will be out of their city or town on Election Day, has a physical disability, or if a religious belief prevents voting on Election Day (Galvin 2020a). They must apply and then, if granted, return the ballot by mail or set up a time with the relevant local official to vote in-person ahead of the election. Far preferable for voting advocates is "no-excuse absentee balloting" whereby the registered voter can request an absentee ballot without an excuse and mail or drop the ballot off at city hall. The popularity and smooth implementation of the universally targeted no-excuse mail-in voting option in the 2020 election suggests it too should become permanent. Assuming the goal is to assist all eligible Massachusetts residents in casting their ballot, it is a no-brainer. Town clerks and other election officials have already shown themselves more than capable of implementing this change. In June 2021, the Massachusetts House agreed, passing a "provision that would permanently allow every registered voter to cast a ballot by mail in state primaries, general elections, and some municipal races, extending what had been embraced as a pandemic-era option" (Stout 2021). A senate option passed in October 2021 would make permanent "early voting options that were temporarily adopted during the height of the coronavirus pandemic,"

---

9   Biennial statewide covers the elections most residents participate in but does not cover the seemingly innumerable number of city and town elections, as well as special elections.

including no-excuse voting by mail, in-person early-voting periods, and even adding same-day voter registration in Massachusetts (LeBlanc 2021). As of October 2021, this senate version was headed to the house.

MASSACHUSETTS IN THE NATIONAL CONTEXT: VOTER ACCESS POLICIES

Seeing how Massachusetts stacks up compared to the other forty-nine states and DC punctuates the fact that a promising policy shift has occurred—while highlighting ways to further expand voter access in the state. It is difficult to reverse course in American politics (Pierson 2000; Peters 1999), but not impossible. The current status is then best viewed as a snapshot that requires political will to maintain, solidify, and improve upon.

Figure 8.1 graphs eight impediments to voting in each of the fifty states and District of Columbia. Because of the stipulation that the 2020 COVID changes were limited to that cycle alone, they are not included in the state comparisons that follow. Policies included are ones that do not have an expiration date. The first three capture the existence of an affirmative impediment in a state: requiring a photo ID, having the registration cutoff sixteen days or more before the election, and requiring an excuse for early voting. States receive one point for each of these policies they have on the books. The next five capture the *absence* of policies that make it easier for eligible individuals to cast a legal ballot in a state. States earned one point if they *do not have* any of the following: early voting, same-day registration, universal vote-by-mail option, online voter registration, or automatic voter registration. Figure 8.1 thus captures both what a state does to impede voter access and what a state does not do to promote it along a uniform scale. The higher the count, the more cumbersome it is to cast a legal ballot in the state.

The rankings made visible in figure 8.1 do not perfectly overlap with the EPI scores. That the two are not mirror images is no surprise. Recall EPI captures policy provisions, like online registration, as well as election efficiency measures, like provisional ballots cast and polling locale wait times. Still, Massachusetts does comparatively well among the fifty states when we look at voter access policies alone, if not as well as the number eleven EPI rank. Thirty-two states fare worse than Massachusetts on the number of policy impediments to voting, and another nine tie with the commonwealth with four impediments among their policies governing voting. Policies absent in Massachusetts include registration-day cutoffs less than two weeks, universal adoption of no-excuse early voting, same-day voter registration, and consistently allowing mail-in ballots for all eligible voters. Massachusetts does as well as it does on the comparisons made visible in figure 8.1 because of the 2014 and 2018 legislation.

FIGURE 8.1 Policy Impediments to Voter Access
by State, 2020

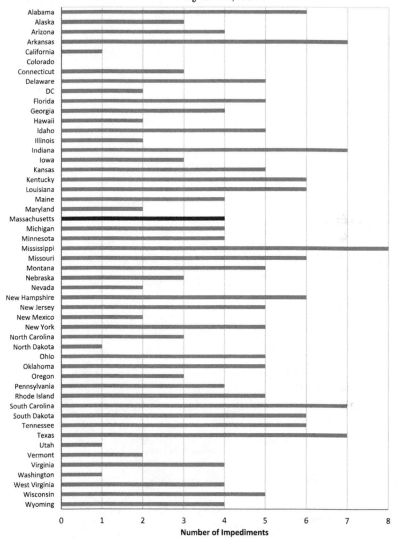

Data from Ballotpedia (https://ballotpedia.org) and the National Conference of State Legislatures (https://www.ncsl.org).
Downloaded June 2020.

Figures 8.2 and 8.3 distinguish convenience voting measures from those that ease the registration barrier. Recall the former tends to be utilized most by those already apt to vote, while the latter cuts into the turnout gaps along lines of race, ethnicity, and social class.

Figure 8.2 scores allocate one point each for early voting, mail-in option for all, and no-excuse absentee ballots. Massachusetts has but one in place as of June 2021—provisions for early voting, though only in statewide biennial elections. Nineteen states and DC rank higher than Massachusetts in terms of adopting a greater mix of these policies. Twenty-three states, including Massachusetts, have only one convenience voting policy in place, while another eight states employ no convenience voting measures.

FIGURE 8.2. Convenience Voting Measures in Place by State, 2020

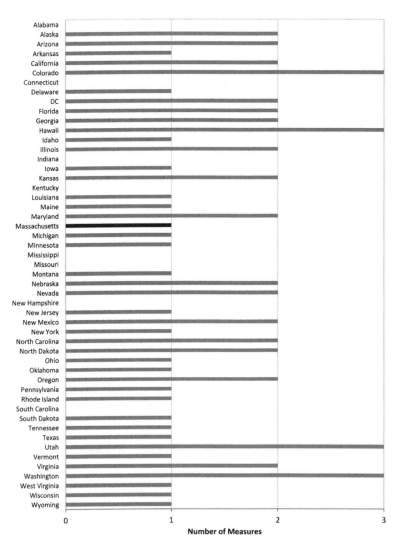

Data from Ballotpedia (https://ballotpedia.org) and the National Conference of State Legislatures (https://www.ncsl.org). Downloaded June 2020.

Figure 8.3 turns to policies that ease the registration barrier known to be so cumbersome for turnout in the United States (Piven and Cloward 2000). The four policies tabulated include a voting registration deadline fifteen days or less, same-day voter registration, online voter registration, and automatic voter registration. The higher the score, the easier it is to register to vote and cast a ballot.

FIGURE 8.3. Policies That Ease Voter Registration Barriers by State, 2020

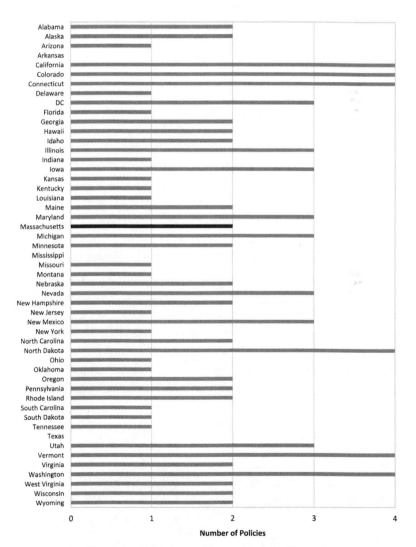

Data from Ballotpedia (https://ballotpedia.org) and the National Conference of State Legislatures (https://www.ncsl.org). Downloaded June 2020.

That the commonwealth went from zero to two on this scale since 2014 is encouraging and can help explain why some of the gaps in voter turnout by race and ethnicity have declined in Massachusetts. Nevertheless, same-day voter registration does not exist, and the registration deadline is twenty days for "any election or town meeting" (Galvin 2020c). Massachusetts employs only automatic voter registration and online voter registration. A four out of four score would prove advantageous for further narrowing *all* racial and ethnic gaps.

Fourteen states and DC do better than Massachusetts in having adopted all, or three-fourths, of the policies that mitigate the registration barrier. Eighteen states, including Massachusetts, adopted half of the policies, and the remaining have either one or none of them in place. Thus, on these measures, Massachusetts is in the middle of the pack among the fifty states.

A place where Massachusetts has resisted national trends is on voter ID laws. Primarily in the 2010s and into 2020, photo ID requirements, commonly referred to as "voter ID laws," proved tremendously controversial. Republicans have claimed that they curtail voter fraud, and Democrats have cast them as ways to keep minorities and lower-income voters from the polls. Research has tested these explanations, finding that partisanship and increases in minority turnout are the best predictors of whether states adopt photo ID requirements and other punitive measures (Bentele and O'Brien 2014). Nevertheless, voter ID laws remain a potent political symbol in many states and popular among mass publics—especially Republicans (Gronke et al. 2019).

Massachusetts has largely resisted the photo ID urge. In the electoral reforms of 2014, Massachusetts Republicans in the legislature put forth a voter ID amendment that failed by a large margin. As of February 2020, Massachusetts is one of only seventeen states and the District of Columbia that require no form of voter ID (NCSL 2020b). Massachusetts voters can be asked to show ID under several conditions: if it is the first time they are voting in a federal election, if they were inactive voters, if the poll worker has "reasonable suspicion," or if one is casting a provisional ballot (Galvin 2020b). The secretary of the commonwealth clarifies, "Acceptable identifi-cation must include your name and the address at which you are registered to vote. Examples of acceptable identification include: a driver's license, state-issued ID card, recent utility bill, rent receipt, lease, a copy of a voter registration affidavit, or any other printed identification which contains the voter's name and address." The description makes clear that on the rare occasions a voter may be asked for an ID, Massachusetts election policy does not require that it be a photo ID.

Placing Massachusetts in the context of the fifty states provides a clear takeaway: considerable improvement in terms of ease of casting a legal ballot. Other states, however, are leaders in electoral policy. Massachusetts is at the front of the class but not valedictorian.

Conclusion

This chapter likely confirmed some hunches readers had about voting and voter access in Massachusetts while uncovering some surprises. Yes, Massachusetts residents identify far more as Democrats than Republicans—but just over half prefer to not declare allegiance to either political party. Registration and turnout rates fall short of the expectations set by high levels of socioeconomic status among Massachusetts residents. Racial and ethnic gaps in registration and turnout are substantial, if declining for Asians and Hispanics while more election contingent for Blacks.

The place where Massachusetts has proved exceptional is in the rapid recent changes to voter access policies. Since 2014 the commonwealth has revamped its election laws, and it responded nimbly to the COVID crisis. As the title of the chapter indicates, Massachusetts has moved from "laggard to leader" in the state rankings. This is directly attributable to legislative changes. The Massachusetts resident who wanted to cast a ballot in 2010 and the resident who wanted to do so in 2020 faced drastically different circumstances. Beginning in 2014, policies like online voter registration, early voting, and preregistration of sixteen- and seventeen-year-olds took hold. The year 2020 saw automatic voter registration implemented. The trends unearthed in this chapter indicate that these policies have already borne fruit in narrowing the racial and ethnic gaps in turnout and registration but that real work remains, especially for Blacks in Massachusetts. The positive shifts are attributable to activists, academics, and think tanks—with the assistance of progressive lawmakers—who pushed an often-reluctant state legislature to adopt numerous voter access policies. Same-day voter registration, moving the registration deadline closer to Election Day, universal mail-in voting, as well as "souls to the polls" opportunities to vote the weekend before the election are next steps that would increase registration and turnout while narrowing socioeconomic and racial and ethnic gaps.

To the extent that the story of Massachusetts is policy innovation, an examination of voter access and turnout suggests that the commonwealth was late to the game but is now mounting a heck of an offense.

WORKS CITED

Avery, James, and Mark Peffley. 2005. "Voter Registration Requirements, Voter Turnout, and Welfare Eligibility Policy: Class Bias Matters." *State Politics and Policy Quarterly* 5, no 1: 47–67.

Bentele, Keith, and Erin O'Brien. 2014. "Jim Crow 2.0? Why States Consider and Adopt Restrictive Voter Access Policies." *Perspectives on Politics* 11, no. 4: 1088–16.

Colman, Justine. 2020 "Massachusetts Governor Signs Bill Giving All Residents Vote-by-Mail Option." *Hill*, July 6, 2020. https://thehill.com/homenews/state-watch/506110 -massachusetts-governor-signs-bill-giving-all-residents-vote-by-mail.

Commonwealth of Massachusetts. 2020. "Automatic Voter Registration." https://www.mass .gov/service-details/automatic-voter-registration.

DeCosta-Klipa, Nik. 2020a. "Massachusetts Has Passed New Emergency Changes for Voting in the New Year's Elections. Here's How They Work." *Boston.com*, July 7, 2020. https:// www.boston.com/news/politics/2020/07/07/massachusetts-early-mail-in-voting -changes-coronavirus.

———. 2020b. "Massachusetts Officially Breaks Turnout Record by Nearly 300,000 Votes." *Boston.com*, December 4, 2020. https://www.boston.com/news/politics/2020/11/19 /massachusetts-2020-turnout.

Election Performance Index (EPI). 2018. "Methodology Report." MIT Election Data and Science Lab. https://elections-blog.mit.edu/sites/default/files/2020-08/2016-epi-meth odology.pdf.

———. 2020. MIT Election Data and Science Lab. https://elections.mit.edu/.

Franko, William, Nathan Kelly, and Christopher Witko. 2016. "Class Bias in Voter Turnout, Representation, and Income Inequality." *Perspective on Politics* 14, no. 2: 351–68.

Galvin, William. 2020a. "Absentee Voting." Secretary of the Commonwealth. https://www .sec.state.ma.us/ele/eleabsentee/absidx.htm.

———. 2020b. "Identification Requirements." Secretary of the Commonwealth. https://www .sec.state.ma.us/ele/eleidreq/idrequirementsidx.htm.

———. 2020c. "Registering to Vote." Secretary of the Commonwealth. https://www.sec.state .ma.us/ele/eleifv/howreg.htm.

———. 2020d. "Voter Turnout 2016, 2020." Secretary of the Commonwealth. https:// electionstats.state.ma.us/elections/search/year_from:2012/year_to:2020/office_id:1 /stage:General.

Green, Avi, and Erin O'Brien. 2014. "Will Massachusetts Finally Pass Reforms to Make Voting Easier and More Equitable?" Scholars Strategy Network, Basic Facts Brief, Cambridge, MA.

Gronke, Paul, William Hicks, Seth McKee, Charles Stewart III, and James Dunham. 2019. "Voter ID Laws: A View from the Public." *Social Science Quarterly* 100, no. 1: 215–32.

Herron, Michael, Enrijeta Shino, and Daniel Smith. 2021. "Race and the Reduction of Early in-Person Voting in Georgia." Working paper. https://electionsmith.files.wordpress .com/2021/03/georgia_2020_early_votes.pdf.

Horwitz, Sari. 2016. "Getting a Photo ID So You Can Vote Is Easy. Unless You're Poor, Black, Latino, or Elderly." *Washington Post*, May 23, 2016. https://www.washingtonpost .com/politics/courts_law/getting-a-photo-id-so-you-can-vote-is-easy-unless-youre -poor-black-latino-or-elderly/2016/05/23/8d5474ec-20f0-11e6-8690-f14ca9de2972_story .html.

Jacobson, Louis. 2013. "Was Chief Justice John Roberts Right about Voting Rates in Massachusetts, Mississippi?" *PolitiFact*, March 5, 2013. https://www.politifact.com/factchecks/2013/mar/05/john-roberts/was-chief-justice-john-roberts-right-about-voting-/.

LeBlanc, Steve. 2021. "Massachusetts Senate Approves Bill to Expand Voting Rights." AP News, October 6, 2021. https://apnews.com/article/coronavirus-pandemic-business-bills-election-2020-voter-registration-7e4fa9f412972015f3fb7198304ce8c8.

Leighley, Jan, and Jonathan Nagler. 2013. *Who Votes Now? Demographics, Issues, Inequality, and Turnout in the United States*. Princeton, NJ: Princeton University Press.

Massachusetts Trial Court. 2014. "Election Reform Bill Signed into Law to Allow Early Voting and Online Voter Registration." *Massachusetts Law Updates: Official Blog of the Massachusetts Trial Court*, June 13, 2014. https://blog.mass.gov/masslawlib/legal-topics/election-reform-bill-signed-into-law-to-allow-early-voting-and-online-voter-regist ration/.

McDonald, Michael P. 2020. "2020 November General Election Turnout Rates." United States Elections Project, December 4, 2020. http://www.electproject.org/2020g.

National Center for Education Statistics. 2018. "Table 104.85. Rates of High School Completion and Bachelor's Degree Attainment among Persons Age 25 and over, by Race/Ethnicity and State." https://nces.ed.gov/programs/digest/d17/tables/dt17_104.85.asp.

National Conference of State Legislatures (NCSL). 2020a. "Automatic Voter Registration." https://www.ncsl.org/research/elections-and-campaigns/automatic-voter-registration.aspx.

———. 2020b. "Voter Identification Requirements, Voter ID Laws." https://www.ncsl.org/research/elections-and-campaigns/voterid.aspx#Details.

Peters, Guy. 1999. *American Public Policy: Promise and Performance*. New York: Chatham House.

Pierson, Paul. 2000. "Increasing Returns, Path Dependence, and the Study of Politics." *American Political Science Review* 94, no. 2: 251–68.

Piven, Francis Fox, and Richard Cloward. 2000. *Why Americans Still Don't Vote: And Why Politicians Want It That Way*. Boston: Beacon Press.

Rigby, Elizabeth, and Melanie Springer. 2011. "Does Electoral Reform Increase (or Decrease) Political Equality?" *Political Research Quarterly* 64, no. 2: 420–34.

Schoenberg, Shira. 2014. "Massachusetts Gov. Deval Patrick Signs Early Voting into Law." *MassLive*, May 22, 2014. https://www.masslive.com/politics/2014/05/massachusetts_gov_deval_patric_32.html.

Stout, Matt. 2021. "Massachusetts House Passes Measure Making Mail-in Voting Permanent." *Boston Globe*, June 10, 2021. https://www.bostonglobe.com/2021/06/10/metro/massachusetts-house-consider-making-mail-in-voting-permanent/.

Verba, Sidney, and Norman Nie. 1972. *Participation in America: Political Democracy and Social Equality*. Chicago: University of Chicago Press.

World Population Review. 2020. "Median Household Income by State, 2020." https://worldpopulationreview.com/state-rankings/median-household-income-by-state.

CHAPTER 9

THE MASSACHUSETTS INITIATIVE
AND REFERENDUM PROCESS

Jerold Duquette and Maurice T. Cunningham

In 2002 Harvard public health policy professor and former state legislator John McDonough evaluated the political value of the Bay State's initiative and referendum (I&R) process. His review led to a cautiously optimistic "two cheers, instead of three" appraisal. Eighteen years later, we are a bit less optimistic.

McDonough's thoughtful and thorough, yet concise, primer on the history, mechanics, and political pros and cons of the initiative and referendum process, laid out in Article 48 of the state constitution, led him to the following conclusion:

> With its elaborate checks and balances, Article 48 has proven itself a resilient tool to resolve conflict among varied interests—right, left, and center—when the Legislature can't or won't act. If it becomes primarily an instrument for corporate interests and rich guys to win new laws on the cheap, and if the Legislature becomes increasingly brazen in undermining or manipulating the process, we may see something unprecedented since 1917: serious discussion of reforming a vehicle that, if treated with proper respect, is in no need of reform. (2002)

In this chapter, we will update McDonough's primer, reassessing the condition of the state's initiative and referendum process at the beginning of the twenty-first century's third decade, just two years after its centennial on the books. Key to McDonough's positive assessment was that the indirect procedural hurdles of Article 48, which distinguish the Massachusetts initiative and referendum process from all others, prevent the kinds of imprudent policy making that most concern critics of direct democratic procedures. We find that the explosion of unregulated independent expenditures in electoral politics since McDonough's assessment, unleashed by the U.S. Supreme Court's landmark *Citizens United* decision in 2010, has added credibility to criticisms

The authors thank Anya G. Cunningham for considerable research assistance.

that the initiative and referendum process is particularly susceptible to the unfair manipulation by and influence of special interests. Today, "corporate interests" have a greater capacity to use the process to gain or maintain (or both) unfair regulatory advantages than they did twenty years ago. We argue that Massachusetts ballot measure history is almost two separate histories—the period covered and largely found open to citizen action by Professor McDonough and the nearly two decades since.

After briefly reviewing the procedural routes to the ballot box laid out in Article 48 of the state constitution, we will describe the twentieth-century history of initiative and referendum politics in the state (McDonough 2002; Gray and Kiley 1991; Friedman and Thody 2011).[1] Then we will discuss the politics and consequences of ballot measure campaigns conducted between 2002 and 2020, a period when moneyed interests' ability to exploit the initiative and referendum process using paid signature gathers and unregulated "dark" money has increased dramatically, while efforts to use ballot questions to make Beacon Hill politicians more accountable to the public have all failed.

We believe the ways and means of twenty-first-century American politics make it necessary to consider modifying this early-twentieth-century contribution to Massachusetts government and politics in ways more fitted to the legal, technological, and strategic realities of twenty-first-century American politics.

Article 48 Process and Procedures

Just as we have observed on other matters in this volume, the Massachusetts initiative and referendum process too reflects the pluralistic democratic values of America's constitutional framers more than any other state's, despite the fact that it was created by early-twentieth-century progressives whose much more participatory democratic values represented a distinct break from the framers' view. Even the most direct form of what is often called "direct legislation" in the commonwealth is "checked" multiple times before voters' professed public policy preferences can be enacted at the ballot box. This

---

1   Three sources stand out in the description and analysis of Article 48's twentieth-century history and mechanics. All three were instrumental to the writing of this chapter. Professor McDonough's assessment (2002) has provided us with both a great deal of background information, as well as a framework for our analysis. The *Law Review* article cited by McDonough as the "definitive legal treatise on Article 48" (Gray and Kiley 1991) was also very useful. Finally, the work of Lawrence Friedman, the author of chapter 6 of this volume, and Lynnea Thody (2011) was also invaluable in our efforts here.

exceptionally cautious approach, inspired at the time and preserved since by the state's centuries-old political culture, makes the Bay State's initiative and referendum process stand out, but not necessarily in a good way.

There are four routes available to Massachusetts citizens who wish to use the ballot to circumvent the state's elected lawmakers:

1. an initiative petition for a law
2. a referendum petition (to repeal an existing law)
3. an initiative petition for a constitutional amendment
4. a legislative constitutional amendment

Nonbinding advisory questions can also be placed on the ballot in Massachusetts. Local elected officials can be circumvented by citizens as well by placing measures on local ballots, though such measures may be subject to preapproval by state officials.

The *initiative petition for a law* is the most direct option. It requires ten or more registered voters to submit a proposed initiative to the state attorney general by the first Wednesday in August, fifteen months prior to the next statewide election. The attorney general then must certify that the proposal meets all the constitutional requirements for initiatives to appear on the statewide ballot. These requirements are not insubstantial, and they are part of the reason the Massachusetts initiative and referendum process is considered the most indirect of the twenty-four states that allow initiative and referendum. The attorney general must certify that a petition is not "substantially the same as any measure submitted in the last two statewide general elections" and that it does not include "excluded matters," which is to say matters that are not allowed by Article 48 of the state constitution. Excluded matters include anything that relates to religion, the judiciary, or the governance of particular cities or towns in the state or anything that requires "a specific appropriation of money from the state's treasury." The attorney general must also certify that the proposed initiative would not violate anyone's state constitutional rights, which include freedoms of speech, press, assembly, trial by jury, protection from unreasonable search and seizure, and just compensation for private property taken for public use. However, the attorney general is not permitted to deny certification to an initiative that threatens to violate citizens' due process or equal protection rights. Such matters are left to postenactment court challenges, if need be. While this last point may seem to illustrate greater respect for the will of voters, it is actually a way to ensure that such weighty constitutional determinations are made by judges, not elected attorneys general or voters (Mass.gov n.d.).

Initiatives certified by the state attorney general are returned to the petitioners with a summary of the proposed law. Petitioners then file their initiative proposal, and the attorney general's summary, with the Office of the Secretary of the Commonwealth who prepares the formal petitions that must be signed by at least 3 percent of the number of registered voters who voted in the previous gubernatorial election. No more than 25 percent of these signatures can come from voters residing in the same county. If enough signatures of registered voters are obtained, certified by local registrars of voters, and filed with the secretary of the commonwealth by the first Wednesday in December (just two months after initial submission to the attorney general's office), an initiative proposal is referred to the state legislature for their consideration. The legislature and governor have six months to enact the proposed initiative as written. The legislature also has the power to place a competing legislative proposal on the same ballot as a certified initiative. If the legislature and governor fail to enact the proposed measure and a majority of the original ten petitioners want to amend it before sending it to the voters, they may do so as long as the attorney general certifies that such amendments do not constitute "material changes" to the substance of the proposal. After legislative consideration, only the signatures of registered voters equaling or surpassing half of 1 percent of the number who voted in the previous gubernatorial election stand between the petitioners and the appearance of their initiative on the next statewide ballot (Gray and Kiley 1991).

Piece of cake, right?

In order to repeal a law enacted by the legislature, a *referendum petition* must be filed by at least ten registered voters with the secretary of the commonwealth within thirty days of the law's enactment. After the attorney general transmits a summary of the law petitioners seek to repeal to the secretary of the commonwealth, he or she has fourteen days to prepare the referendum petitions for voters' signatures. Referendum petitions with respect to laws dealing with matters "excluded" from the initiative and referendum process (detailed above) are not allowed. The signature requirements for repealing a law at the ballot box, however, are not the same as they are for enacting ballot initiatives. If referendum petitioners want the law they are targeting to be suspended until voters render their verdict at the ballot box, they must obtain signatures equaling or surpassing 2 percent of the number who voted in the last gubernatorial election. If they are willing to seek repeal without suspending the law, only the signatures of 1.5 percent of the number who voted in the last gubernatorial election are required, though, as with initiative petitions, no more than 25 percent of these signatures can come from voters residing in the same county.

Two requirements for referendum petitions further hint at the designed checks on direct, or plebiscitary, democracy that make the state's process for ballot measures less friendly to petitioners than any other state's. First, for the passage of a referendum to count, at least 30 percent of the voters who cast ballots in the election must have voted for the repeal of the existing statute. The second requirement that is unfriendly to petitioners is the language of the referendum itself. Instead of being asked if they approve of repealing an existing statute, Massachusetts voters are asked if they approve of the statute that petitioners are trying to repeal. This means that voters must vote "no" in order to affirm their agreement with the referendum petitioners, while a "yes" vote actually serves as a rejection of the petitioners' proposal. At a time when disinformation can so easily be spread by campaigns, special interests, and even foreign governments, semantics aren't really just semantics anymore.

The third route around the legislature and governor for Massachusetts citizens is the *initiative petition for a constitutional amendment.* This route requires the same initial procedures, filing, and signature requirements and precludes the same "excluded matters" as an initiative for a law but gives the legislature considerably more power to kill or substantially change constitutional amendments initiated by citizens. Although getting initiative amendments on the ballot requires the support of only one-fourth of the representatives and senators sitting jointly in two successive sessions, the presiding officer of these so-called constitutional conventions, the state senate president, can choose to not allow a vote on a proposed initiative amendment not favored by legislative leaders. Given the exceptionally top-down power structure and uncompetitiveness of state legislative elections (described in chapter 4 of this volume), it should be no surprise that voter-initiated constitutional amendments are exceptionally rare. In 2002 proponents of an initiative petition to amend the state constitution to define marriage as a union between one man and one woman were thwarted by Senate President Tom Birmingham's decision not to allow it to be voted on in the 2002 constitutional convention at which it was set to be considered. Only three voter-initiated constitutional amendments have ever reached the ballot. The last one to reach the ballot was a proposal to create a graduated income tax in 1994. It was defeated by a margin of more than two to one. Of the three that have made the ballot, only two were enacted, and one of those was annulled twelve years later by a legislative petition for constitutional amendment.[2]

A *legislative petition for a constitutional amendment* originates in the legislature and must be passed by majority vote in a joint session of the Massachusetts House and Senate in two successive elected legislatures in order to reach the state ballot. Only sixty-three legislative amendments have ever reached the state ballot. Fifty-three of them passed. Comparison of this record to that of the citizen-initiated amendments discussed above provides powerful evidence of the legislative supremacy in Massachusetts described in several chapters of this volume.

There is one additional way for voters to weigh in on statewide public policy at the ballot box in Massachusetts. A *public policy petition* is a nonbinding "yes or no" question about a public policy issue. In theory these petitions, which require the signatures of at least twelve hundred registered voters in a state senatorial district and two hundred registered voters in a state representative district, are designed to make elected officials aware of their constituents' wishes regarding a public policy issue. Though these nonbinding or "advisory" questions must be approved by the attorney general, and no more than three such questions may appear on the same district ballot, they are not subject to nearly the same level of scrutiny as initiatives and referendums. They are understood to be instructions to the state legislators in whose districts they appear. Advisory questions are often used by interested actors to gauge the public mood before committing to a potentially politically risky policy proposal. Before the state legislature repealed the voter-passed Clean Elections Law in 2003, opponents were able to get enough signatures in every state senate district to put a nonbinding advisory question on the statewide ballot in 2002 designed to demonstrate that voters in 1998 had been tricked into supporting the public campaign finance law by its title. But for the title, this advisory question was the same as the 1998 initiative. Instead of "clean elections" in 2002, voters were asked if they would support "taxpayer funding for political campaigns." As its petitioners hoped, voters overwhelmingly opposed the idea (Duquette 2002). This result cleared the way for the state

---

2 The three citizen-initiated constitutional amendments that have made the ballot in Massachusetts were as follows. The first was a 1938 amendment, which passed, converting annual legislative sessions and the annual state budget process to biennial undertakings. Twelve years later, in 1944, this amendment was repealed by a legislative amendment. In 1974 a citizen-initiated amendment was passed requiring the use of highway tax revenue for mass transit. And in 1994, a citizen-initiated amendment calling for a graduated income tax was soundly rejected at the ballot box.

legislature to confidently repeal the measure they had refused to fund since its enactment in 1998, which they did in June 2003 (*New York Times* 2003).

Massachusetts citizens also have the right to petition for initiatives and referendum to appear on local ballots. Cities and towns use ballot measures to adopt or amend home-rule charters (explained in chapter 2) and to pass or repeal local ordinances. Some cities and towns have also petitioned the state and been granted the power to use local ballots to recall local elected officials. As a result of the highly controversial property tax limitation statute passed by initiative in 1980, so-called Proposition 2½ Override questions regularly appear on local ballots asking residents if they support setting aside the statute's limitation in order to increase city or town revenue enough to cover vital services endangered by the 2.5 percent property tax levy limit. In general, cities and towns can propose new ordinances and seek to repeal existing ordinances on local ballots without preapproval of state officials.

Massachusetts Initiative and Referendum in the Twentieth Century

While direct democracy has been a core value in the birthplace of the town-meeting form of government from the beginning, its modern statewide incarnation dates back only to 1918 when the forty-eighth amendment to the state constitution added initiative and referendum procedures. Passed by the elected delegates to the 1917 state constitutional convention and ratified by the voters in the 1918 statewide general election, the initiative and referendum process was the product of the same forces propelling progressive notions of democracy and good government across America at the time—the same forces discussed in chapter 5 of this volume that successfully augmented the formal powers of governors and presidents in the interests of increasing both government effectiveness and accountability in the decades following what Woodrow Wilson had derisively dubbed the era of "congressional government" in America, by which he meant legislatively controlled government that put patronage and party machine politics before principle and the public interest.

Progressive reformers of the early twentieth century did not pass Massachusetts by, but they did confront considerably more powerful resistance in the Bay State than elsewhere to their theoretical and practical reinterpretation of the framers' understanding of representative democracy. The complicated design of Article 48 reflects that resistance as much as it does the democratic aspirations of Progressive Era reformers who shepherded it through.

Around the turn of the twentieth century, populists, progressives, and socialists in the state were agitating for the adoption of direct democratic measures that included ballot initiatives and referendum. In 1912 an organization called the *Massachusetts Direct Legislation League* campaigned across the state for the adoption of initiative and referendum with the support of Progressive and Democratic Party members eager to enlist popular support they could use against Republicans in the 1912 elections (Initiative and Referendum Institute n.d.). "In 1915, Governor David I. Walsh, a Democrat and the first Irish Catholic elected to statewide office in Massachusetts, formed the *Union for a Progressive Constitution* to push for a state constitutional convention to consider various reforms, with I&R as a priority" (Initiative and Referendum Institute n.d.). Democratic Party support for progressive reform in Massachusetts at the time was more a practical partisan strategy than an ideologically motivated pursuit. Nonetheless, Democratic support for reform helped move voters at the ballot box in 1916 to ratify the legislative proposal for the state constitutional convention in 1917 that would approve Article 48, itself ratified by voters at the ballot box in 1918.

In 1917 opponents of the proposed initiative and referendum process focused heavily on perceived incompatibilities between lawmaking at the ballot box and the handiwork of America's (and Massachusetts') constitutional framers. They warned of the danger of majorities trampling upon minority rights whose only safeguard is constitutional protection, the insufficient knowledge of voters, the rigidity and antideliberative nature of up or down votes that afford no opportunity for amendment or compromise, and they claimed that the majority of voters were not even interested in having this power (Massachusetts Constitutional Convention 1918). Ultimately, these objections helped opponents win major compromises in the final version of Article 48, "compromises that even today make the Massachusetts initiative procedure one of the nation's most cumbersome and complicated" (Initiative and Referendum Institute n.d.). The impressive durability of these objections is reflected in the fact that they very closely mirror those leveled by critics of initiative and referendum processes more than a century later.

Between 1920 and 1948, seven ballot measures were passed by voters. In 1920 opponents of prohibition successfully convinced voters to reclassify hard cider and beer as "nonintoxicating" in order to exempt them from the Volstead Act. In 1928 the power of ballot measures to impact election turnout and the balance of political power in state politics was tested by an initiative to allow sporting events on Sundays. At the time, the only states with Major League Baseball teams that did not allow sporting events on Sundays were Massachusetts and Pennsylvania. Despite spirited opposition from the then dominant Republican Party establishment in the state, as well as an opposition organization made up of civic and religious leaders called the *Save Our Sundays Committee*, Irish Catholic and Democratic turnout for the presidential candidacy of Al Smith on Election Day was enough to make Pennsylvania the last MLB state without games on Sundays. The initiative passed 50 percent to 29 percent and provided a powerful political lesson for Democrats eager to weaken Republican Party control on Beacon Hill (Menendez 2007). The successful repeal of the state's version of Prohibition, the so-called Baby Volstead Act two years later in 1930, was powered by similar political forces and partisan ambitions. These successes helped Bay State Democrats begin to identify and consolidate the electoral coalition that would allow them to end Republican domination of Beacon Hill over the following three decades.

In 1948 the power of ballot measures for Democrats was again on display, and Republicans hoping to use ballot measures for their own partisan purposes got a rude awakening. Professor McDonough explains:

> The watershed year for Article 48 was 1948. President Harry Truman was an underdog to Republican challenger Thomas Dewey, while Democrat Paul Dever had an uphill climb to unseat Republican Gov. Robert Bradford. Four ballot questions turned the election. Corporate interests sought to reverse labor union gains in the 1930s by placing three anti-union questions on the ballot: prohibiting the "union shop," requiring annual union elections, and limiting strikes. Meanwhile, the Planned Parenthood League promoted a question to permit physicians to prescribe contraceptives for married women. These ballot initiatives stirred a backlash by labor and the Catholic Church–core Democratic constituencies–and a turnout effort that generated the largest voter turnout in the Commonwealth's history up to that time. All four questions were soundly defeated, Truman and Dever both won, and Democrats seized control of the Massachusetts House of Representatives (122–118) for the first time, electing Thomas P. O'Neill Jr. of Cambridge as their Speaker. (2002)

During the 1960s and 1970s, many of the arrangements described in several chapters of this volume were enacted by voters at the ballot box. In the 1960s, voters took away the statutory power of the Governor's Council, leaving that body with confirmation power over judicial appointments only. All the statewide constitutional executive officers' elective terms were expanded from two to four years. Separate elections of governors and lieutenant governors, a situation that had produced several split party arrangements, was eliminated in 1966. In that same year, voters gave the governor the reorganization authority necessary to create cabinet departments and gave cities and towns a home-rule statute.

In the 1970s, voters twice lowered the voting age, from twenty-one to nineteen in 1970 and nineteen to eighteen in 1972. The number of seats in the state house of representatives was reduced from 240 to 160 in 1974, where it remains today. Two years later, voters ratified a legislative initiative eliminating life tenure for the state's judges, replacing it with mandatory retirement at age seventy (McDonough 2002).

In 1980, Bay State voters did their part to advance the tax revolt sweeping the nation by passing the local property-tax limitation statute known as Proposition 2½, a measure that has since frustrated local government officials, greatly assisted antitax activists, and tamed the programmatic ambitions of Beacon Hill Democrats. Many observers and analysts see Proposition 2½ as a laudable example of citizen democracy in action. Despite being "badly outspent" by "the combined forces of government and labor," the group *Citizens for Limited Taxation* was able to prevail (McDonough 2002). The measure also forced the state "to dramatically increase support for public education—reducing reliance on the unfairest major tax of all, the property tax" (McDonough 2002). Critics, on the other hand, see the measure very differently. In 2010, the Center on Budget and Public Policy Priorities published a study of Proposition 2½ detailing the "hidden consequences" of the measure. The report concluded that the law "arbitrarily constrained local governments' ability to raise revenue without any consideration of the actual cost of providing services; made local governments heavily dependent on state aid, which tends to fluctuate with economic cycles and state policies; exacerbated disparities between wealthier communities and poorer ones in access to quality local services [and] resulted in cuts to valued services rather than simply calling forth greater efficiency from local governments" (Oliff and Lav 2010).

The state's experience of Proposition 2½ since McDonough's positive review in 2002 has more clearly exposed the measure's unintended negative consequences, consequences made much more difficult to remedy because the law was overwhelmingly passed by voters at the ballot box and remains popular. Nearly four decades after its passage, the measure remains a sacred cow on Beacon Hill. A 2019 *Boston Globe* article about a proposal "nestled deep within the educational funding bill" requiring the governor to analyze the impact that "Proposition 2½ has had on municipal budgets and potentially make recommendations to mitigate those constraints" reflects well the disinclination of state legislative leaders to pay the political price of fixing the damage (Chesto 2019). McDonough highlighted the democratic virtues of Proposition 2½, but government effectiveness too must be taken into consideration. Four decades of experience with Proposition 2½ reveals that its popularity, nurtured by antitax interest groups and backed by anonymous billionaires, is preventing policy makers from repairing the damage the voter-enacted law has done to local governments' ability to function effectively.

The final two decades of the twentieth century saw fifty-one binding ballot measures brought to the ballot box in Massachusetts. Most of these were initiatives being advocated by "grass-roots citizen organizations, from the Massachusetts Public Interest Research Group, Mass. Fair Share, and the Tax Equity Alliance for Massachusetts on the left to Citizens for Limited Taxation and the Small Property Owners Association on the right" (McDonough, 2000). The fact that "grass-roots citizen organizations" from across the political spectrum were making use of the initiative and referendum process is undoubtedly part of the reason Professor McDonough's 2002 assessment of the state's I&R process was largely positive. Voters' preferences on a wide array of public policy matters were increasingly registered at the ballot box in the 1980s and '90s, but that has not been the case in recent years. During the first two decades of the present century, the degree to which the process has insulated well-connected and well-funded political and economic "insiders" and prevented needed reforms has increased, suggesting the need for serious reconsideration of the way Massachusetts makes public policy at the ballot box.

The Role and Impact of Money
in Twenty-First-Century Ballot-Measures Politics

Two matters that scholars saw as emerging in the early 2000s deserve attention. First, the concern that big money was taking over ballot questions, posing the danger that the regular citizens who were supposed to be served by ballot measures (as opposed to the moneyed interests that prevailed in the legislature) would come to be ignored by ballot campaigns, seems to have materialized. Second, the concern was that the ability of well-off interests to pay for qualifying signatures to be gathered would further tilt the process toward the powerful few, which also seems to have come to pass.

We examined a database provided by the Massachusetts Office of Campaign and Political Finance of more than seventy ballot committees registered with the OCPF from 2008 through 2018. In addition, we added ballot committees that formed for possible 2020 contests, including the four committees that faced off over two questions that made it to Election Day 2020. Twenty-two questions appeared on the Massachusetts ballot from 2008 to 2020, including twenty-one initiatives and one question seeking to determine if voters approved of Massachusetts' transgender rights law in 2018. Eleven of the initiative petitions prevailed, and voters overwhelmingly approved of the transgender rights law.

In the years we studied, eighteen questions were won by the higher spending side (in some cases one side or another was supported by more than one ballot committee; all spending by a side has been counted). There is little parity in spending. Almost uniformly when one side can outspend the other, it does so in spectacular fashion—two to one, ten to one, and even twenty to one.

Perhaps the most extreme example of how ballot questions have become contests between big-money interests occurred with Question One of 2020, a contest over access to wireless mechanical data featuring national auto-parts corporations against automobile makers. The *Right to Repair Committee,* purporting to advocate for local automobile repair shops, spent about $25 million. The *Committee for Safe and Secure Data,* which ran a wild scare campaign about data falling into the hands of criminals, spent more than $26 million. Question One set a new state record for spending. *Right to Repair* raised about $6,000 in state. The *Safe and Secure Data* committee raised about $2,000 from four Massachusetts donors.

In 2020 Question Two on ranked-choice voting saw an enormous spending imbalance, but the low spending side prevailed. In 2016 two questions were won by the side that spent less; in 2014 the less resourced side of one question prevailed. These outliers have their own stories, which highlight the limits of issues that can overcome the financial resources of well-financed interests at the state's ballot box.

EXCEPTIONS THAT PROVE THE RULE

In 2020 the *Ranked Choice Voting Committee 2020* spent nearly $10 million to modify the state's voting procedures. The measure's opponents raised and spent less than $4,000. There were various reasons offered for the defeat of ranked-choice voting, including that the measure confused voters who were reluctant to accept change. Proponents also conceded that the proposal's reliance on funding from out-of-state billionaires, including John and Laura Arnold of Texas and Rupert Murdoch's daughter-in-law, may have turned off voters (Stout 2020). Another reason ranked-choice voting was defeated is that Beacon Hill Democratic leaders were conspicuously absent on the issue. While virtually every statewide elected Democrat endorsed ranked-choice voting, neither the house Speaker nor the senate president took a position on the measure. This silence translated to relative silence among Democratic state legislators. Had the Speaker and senate president wished to, they could have deployed their Democratic members to great effect on behalf of ranked-choice voting. They didn't do so because the reform would have increased the competitiveness of state legislative elections, disrupting a very advantageous status quo for Democratic leaders in the legislature.

The proponent of Question One in 2016 was the *Horse Racing Jobs and Education Committee,* and it sought passage of an initiative to allow the state Gaming Commission to license one additional slots parlor in the city of Revere. The committee spent over $3.7 million, and its opponents, including Wynn Resorts, spent only about $71,000. There simply was no public support at all for another slots parlor—the mayor of Revere was opposed, and no one of any consequence endorsed the proposal. The proponents were out-of-state (in fact, offshore) gambling interests with no foothold in Massachusetts. They were badly beaten, 69 percent to 31 percent.

Question Two on the 2016 ballot smashed spending records in the state. The proponents, several ballot committees led in spending by *Great Schools Massachusetts,* were pursuing an increase of twelve charter schools per year in the commonwealth. They spent more than $25 million. Their opponents, the *Save Our Public Schools Committee,* spent $15 million, most of which came from teachers' unions. Most of the money flowing into *Great Schools Massachusetts* came from *Families for Excellent Schools of New York* and was dark money—the true donors could not be traced (it turned out to be a handful of billionaires and near billionaires from Massachusetts). There were also out-of-state wealthy supporters of charter schools like Michael Bloomberg of New York and John Arnold (again) of Texas. Although outspent by $10 million, the unions had great advantages: about one-third of voters reported having discussed the question personally with a teacher, and the public holds teachers in high regard. And the unions had the support of key figures in communities of color, who were among the leaders of the opposition and did grassroots organizing in their communities (Walters 2019). The opposition prevailed, 62 percent to 38 percent.

In 2014 the *Committee to Tank the Gas Tax* campaigned to repeal a law passed by the legislature to index gas-tax increases yearly. The opposition outspent the proponents $2.7 million to $115,000, but sentiment against the tax hikes was real, and the measure passed 53 percent to 47 percent. This was one instance where the citizenry really did rise up against the legislature and elites to change public policy. The 2014 defeat of the gas tax and defeat of ranked-choice voting in 2020 were two very inexpensive wins for the state's beleaguered conservatives.

PAID "VOLUNTEERS"

The notion that gathering signatures on petitions would exclude frivolous issues from the ballot while empowering citizens also sees little support among the twenty-two ballot questions appearing between 2008 and 2020. Many of the committees relied on professional signature-gathering firms, not primarily volunteers, to gather the required signatures. In most cases, this meant hundreds of thousands of dollars in fees to the firms. For instance, when the Massachusetts Nurses Association was pushing a question to limit the number of patients per nurse in 2018, it spent more than $565,000 on signature gathering. (The MNA proposal lost despite a $12 million campaign. They were outspent two to one by the Massachusetts Health and Hospital Association and its allies.) In 2016 *Great Schools Massachusetts* made a display of having parents of color present reams of signed petitions to Governor Baker, but it paid $414,000 to secure the needed signatures (Great Schools Massachusetts 2016). In some cases, volunteers collect signatures, but it is clear that in most cases the usually populist-sounding ballot committees need to pay for signatures.

That makes the achievement of the few committees that spend little or nothing on signature gathering even more impressive. The *Keep Massachusetts Safe Committee,* which sought a vote in opposition to Massachusetts law protecting transgender rights, spent only $3,800 to gather signatures. It was badly outspent and outorganized during the fall campaign, and transgender rights gained the support of 68 percent of voters. The *Committee to Tank the Automatic Gas Tax Hikes* recorded only about $1,000 in signature-gathering expenses and won handily over a much better-resourced opposition. According to former state representative Geoff Diehl, who led the campaign, signature gathering was accomplished by a handful of organizers and a hundred volunteers who set up tables at malls and community events, supplemented by hundreds of others who requested signature petitions and returned them to the committee.[3] Interestingly, the two ballot committees that spent minimally on signatures were both conservative efforts.[4]

There are more than fifty ballot committees that formed from 2008 to 2020 that never resulted in a ballot contest. Many were not well funded and fell by the wayside; several had substantial resources but dropped out. A few had the financial backing, usually from labor or business, to move forward. In those cases, opposition committees sometimes were formed and a legislative compromise was worked out, short-circuiting the process. In 2018, for example, business interests primarily in the retail industry and the union-backed social justice group *Raise Up Massachusetts* faced off over three possible initiatives. *Raise Up* wanted to advance initiatives for a $15 minimum wage and paid sick leave toward the ballot. Retailers acting as the *Massachusetts Main Street Fairness Coalition* were pushing a sales-tax decrease and tax-free weekend to a November vote. The legislature reached a compromise that gradually increased the minimum wage, ensured paid medical and family leave, eliminated premium pay for Sunday and holiday workers, and institutionalized the sales-tax holiday weekend. The matters did not appear on the ballot. Another union-backed proposal, for a fair-share tax to increase taxation on incomes exceeding $1 million per year to support education and transportation, got its needed signatures but was struck from the 2018 ballot by the Massachusetts Supreme Judicial Court for covering excluded content (Miller and Stout 2018).[5]

In reviewing the remaining ballot committees from 2008 through 2020, one fact stands out: few of them were able to spend any significant sum on signature gathering and thus make the ballot or position themselves to forge a legislative solution. Take the efforts of a group called *Massachusetts against the Individual Mandate,* for example. That committee formed in 2011 to attempt to repeal the individual health-insurance mandate under Romneycare (in fairness to the former governor, he vetoed that section, but the legislature overrode him). John McDonough was sure the question would reach the

---

3   Geoff Diehl, email exchange with Maurice T. Cunningham, August 13, 2020. In 2015 the American Association of Political Consultants awarded the *Committee to Tank the Gas Tax* its award for ballot measure of the year, a "POLLIE."

4   Two committees could not be reliably analyzed due to reporting anomalies.

5   The 2018 millionaire's tax initiative was deemed unconstitutional by the court, but reintroduced as a constitutional amendment that was certified for the 2022 state ballot.

ballot. The campaign spent about $16,000 on signature gathering and had the backing of *Massachusetts Citizens for Life,* a repeat and successful player at getting to the ballot. But the committee failed to get the signatures, in part out of political considerations, in part because it could not raise enough funds to continue paying a signature-gathering firm (McDonough 2011).

The lesson here is that getting onto the ballot is now largely a tool for well-resourced interests and not to uphold some ideal of an engaged citizenry rising up against elites.

DARK MONEY CORRUPTS THE PROCESS

In 2016 a unique set of circumstances arose in Massachusetts ballot questions. Of the four questions that appeared on the November ballot, one side on three of them was financed with dark money—large sums that cannot be traced to their true sources. About $20 million of the $25 million raised and spent by the pro–charter schools side of Question Two was dark money, much of it from *Families for Excellent Schools.* Nearly all of the $3.7 million plus deployed by the *Horse Racing Jobs and Education Committee* was dark money from overseas accounts tied to individuals who were also attempting to expand their gambling enterprises in Maine with dark money. One reason for keeping the true sources hidden in this case was that one individual had ties to a partner with criminal issues and could not get licensed in Maine.[6] A third dark money operation, *Strong Economy for Growth,* donated in favor of charter schools and Governor Baker's other priority, Question Four in opposition to legalization of marijuana. The governor's chief money person also ran fund-raising operations for *Strong Economy for Growth.* All three dark money–supported ballot questions lost at the polls, and many citizens voted with little information about the true interests involved. But readers of the *MassPoliticsProfs* blog were well aware of the likely true sources (Ravitch 2020).[7]

After Election Day in 2016, the dark money edifice began to crumble. The Massachusetts Office of Campaign and Political Finance was watching. The OCPF quietly commenced investigations and determined that three dark money organizations organized under Section 501(c)(4) of the Internal Revenue Code had acted as ballot committees under state law and needed to register with OCPF and disclose their true source donors. *Strong Economy*

---

6   "Commission on Governmental Ethics and Election Practices of the State of Maine, in the Matter of: York County Casino Initiative Campaign," December 21, 2017.

7   Followers of the *MassPoliticsProfs* blog saw frequent posts regarding the likely true sources behind the charter-school dark money, and those posts were proven to be accurate. The information proved crucial to the defeat of Question Two.

for Growth, Horse Racing Jobs and Education Committee, and *Families for Excellent Schools* all were required to file their true donors with OCPF. All did, and all soon went out of business.

It seems that OCPF's enforcement was taken seriously. The flow of dark money into candidate and ballot campaigns since 2016 has slowed to a trickle.

Twenty-First-Century Court Decisions Undermine Article 48, Grapple with Dark Money

In the last quarter of the twentieth century there was an "explosion" of statutory initiatives from grassroots citizen organizations on both the Right and the Left. But in the past twenty years, the ballot measure process has become a forum for interest group battles and the playground of the well-heeled rather than a wellspring of citizen action.

This is not the fault of the design of Article 48 but a result of court decisions, especially from the Supreme Court of the United States but also from the state's Supreme Judicial Court. As McDonough notes, in *First National Bank v. Bellotti* (1978), national banking associations and corporations wanted to spend money to oppose a referendum that would authorize the legislature to pass a graduated income tax. The Supreme Court struck down the Massachusetts statute on First Amendment free-speech grounds, holding that corporations could not be limited in their spending on ballot issues. In other decisions, the Supreme Court struck down regulations from other states attempting to regulate signature-gathering firms, and a decision of Massachusetts' own high court buttressed the signature-gathering industry as well, in McDonough's estimation (2002). Then in 2010 came *Citizens United v. Federal Election Commission.* That decision opened the way for independent expenditure committees to spend unlimited sums, and the subsequent appeals-court decision in *SpeechNow v. Federal Election Commission* (2010) made clear that unions, corporations, and individuals can contribute unlimited amounts to independent expenditure committees. These decisions were also rendered on First Amendment grounds. Shortly thereafter, savvy political professionals realized they could take advantage of Internal Revenue Service regulations to ensure anonymity to wealthy donors, and the dark money revolution was under way.

Note that each of these Supreme Court decisions has enhanced the power of the wealthy and made citizen action more imposing. That has been the story of the past twenty years. However, the *Citizens United* Court left federal disclaimer and disclosure of donations laws intact. Massachusetts also has disclaimer and disclosure laws. Disclaimer refers to language on an advertisement taking responsibility for the ad and for identifying top donors. Disclosure requires that political committees report the true source of donations to regulators. Following the 2016 dark money campaigns, the state's Office of Campaign and Political Finance acted decisively to uphold the state's disclaimer and disclosure laws, forcing dark money organizations organized under Internal Revenue Code (501c)(4) to register as ballot committees and reveal their true source donors. The citizenry then discovered that the tens of millions of dollars were not from shadowy organizations with civic-sounding names but from a handful of Massachusetts oligarchs, a few national billionaires, and overseas gambling interests.

The OCPF's decisions present a substantial deterrence to the dark money that tilts influence in ballot campaigns. Still, Massachusetts citizens learned all this months after casting their ballots. What if any of the measures passed after all the illegal spending? Perhaps the state should consider, for ballot measures at least, authorizing the OCPF to conduct investigations and order disclosure during the campaign before voters go to the polls. An Idaho court did this in 2012, stating: "The voters have a right to the most full, most accurate information they can get in spite of the many obstacles placed in their way by those who would prefer to hide behind catchy vague names. Voters are entitled to know who is hiding behind the curtain" (*Secretary of State Ben Ysura* 2012).

The OCPF could act because it found that a group like *Families for Excellent Schools* was acting as a ballot question committee "which receives or expends money or other things of value for the purpose of favoring or opposing the adoption or rejection of a specific question or questions submitted to the voters" (Massachusetts General Laws, Part I, Title VIII, Chapter 55, Section 1). The statute could be broadened to cover all groups that spend a substantial amount on politics, even if they accept donations and spend not expressly for the purpose of a specific campaign. Disclosure should be extended to organizations that donate to spender organizations, blunting the "Russian nesting doll" situation of hiding donations behind a series of dark money operations. All these opaque organizations should be required to put forth the name of the person who has final responsibility for the organization's political spending (Lee et al. 2016). This should extend to the use of limited liability corporations to hide donors as well.

Will these and similar reforms restore the balance to a century-old reform meant to empower the people over the powerful? Certainly not, not so long as the nation's highest court favors the property of the wealthy few over the democratic prerogatives of the people. But as the victory of the 2014 Tank the Gas Tax campaign and the defeat of the oligarch-funded *Great Schools Massachusetts* effort in 2016 show, citizen grassroots action is not dead, though it needs all the help it can get.

Conclusion

Idealists amended the state constitution more than a hundred years ago in the hopes that the power of citizens could overcome an unresponsive legislature and pass legal measures to meet the people's needs. They would probably be pleased with the first eighty years of reform and aghast at the last twenty.

Following voter approval of Article 48 in 1918, the people were slow to avail themselves of their new tool. From 1920 to 1948, only seven ballot measures were passed. But 1948 was an important year as ballot fights over contraception and labor rights spiked turnout among Catholics and labor, not only bringing victory to those groups but a new Democratic Party majority to the Massachusetts House of Representatives. In the 1960s and 1970s, measures concerning how state government is structured and with voting rights made the ballot. The year 1980 brought yet another thunderclap to the political establishment with passage of the property-tax limitation measure Proposition 2½, which has anchored the commonwealth's tax structure for forty years. For the next twenty years, grassroots groups from the Right and the Left pitched many of their policy battles through the Article 48 process. In the past twenty years, however, the grassroots is barely hanging on. It has been replaced by interest-group battles featuring the wealthy against labor as in the charter-schools fight, corporations opposing labor as in 2018's nurse-to-patient ratio question, and corporations against corporations typified by 2020's right-to-repair contest.

In 2002 McDonough regarded the Article 48 process as in danger of being overtaken by corporations and wealthy individuals, thus perhaps setting up the need for constitutional reform. But Article 48's design is not necessarily problematic. A political structure created by the Supreme Court that has money, not people, at its center is clearly a problem, however. It is corporations and the wealthy who set the political agenda and (with some exceptions) dominate the political process.

Over the past two decades, while moneyed interests were using the state's ballot as an alternative dispute-resolution service, efforts to use ballot questions to make Beacon Hill politicians more accountable to the public have all failed. The legislature's repeal of the voter-passed public campaign financing system known as the Clean Elections Law in 2003 and the rejection of the ranked-choice voting initiative in 2020 serve as bookends illustrating the degree to which Beacon Hill leaders have insulated themselves from competition and accountability, a situation that seems to cry out for a more direct route between voters and the enactment of public policy in Massachusetts. On the other hand, the state legislature's exceptional control over the Bay State's initiative and referendum process has very likely helped the commonwealth avoid some of the worst partisan abuses of ballot initiatives by forces who marshal financial and high-tech muscle, exploiting voters' ignorance and racial and cultural prejudices, to enact divisive and harmful measures that would never have survived the conventional legislative process (Hosang 2010).

WORKS CITED

Chesto, Jon. 2019. "A New Review Is Coming for an Old Law, Prop 2½." *Boston Globe*, November 26, 2019. https://www.bostonglobe.com/business/2019/11/26/new-review-coming-for-old-law-prop/AFAolawdlVIOj1q6z6UF5K/story.html.

Citizens United v. Federal Election Commission, 558 U.S. 310 (2010).

Duquette, Jerold. 2002. "Campaign Finance Reform in the Bay State: Is Cleanliness Really Next to Godliness?" In *Money, Politics, and Campaign Finance Reform Law in the States*, edited by David Schultz, 155–88. Durham, NC: Carolina Academic Press.

First National Bank of Boston v. Bellotti, 435 U.S. 765 (1978).

Friedman, Lawrence M., and Lynnea Thody. 2011. *The Massachusetts State Constitution*. New York: Oxford University Press.

Gray, Alexander G., and Thomas R. Kiley. 1991. "The Initiative and Referendum in Massachusetts." *New England Law Review* 26, no. 1: 27–110.

Great Schools Massachusetts. 2016. "#GreatSchoolsMA Delivers 25,000 Signatures to Governor Charlie Baker." Posted January 25, 2016. YouTube. https://www.youtube.com/watch?v=ceaunHOthw&ab_channel=GreatSchoolsMassachusetts.

Hosang, Daniel Martinez. 2010. "Genteel Apartheid." Introduction to *Racial Propositions: Ballot Initiatives and the Making of Postwar California*, 1–12. Berkeley: University of California Press.

Initiative and Referendum Institute. n.d. "Massachusetts." State I&R. http://www.iandrinstitute.org/states/state.cfm?id=14.

Lee, Chisun, Douglass Keith, Katherine Valde, and Benjamin T. Brickner. 2016. "Secret Spending in the States." Brennan Center for Justice, June 26, 2016. https://www.brennancenter.org/our-work/research-reports/secret-spending-states.

Mass.gov. n.d. "Constitutional Requirements for Initiative Petitions." Filing Initiative Petitions. https://www.mass.gov/service-details/constitutional-requirements-for-initiative-petitions.

Massachusetts Constitutional Convention. 1918. *Debates in the Massachusetts Constitutional Convention, 1917–1918*. Vol. 2, *The Initiative and Referendum*. Boston: Wright & Potter.

McDonough, John E. 2002. "Taking the Laws into Their Own Hands: The Bay State's Referendum Process Lets Voters Take Control . . . Sometimes." *CommonWealth Magazine*, November 15, 2002. https://commonwealthmagazine.org/politics/taking -the-laws-into-their-own-hands/.

———. 2011. "Dept. of Dodged Bullets—No Individual Mandate Repeal on 2012 Ballot." *Health Stew: John E. McDonough on Health Care Policy, Politics, and More* (blog), November 12, 2011. https://archive.boston.com/lifestyle/health/health_stew/2011/11 /dont_bet_against_the_ma_indivi.html.

Menendez, Albert J. 2007. "The Battle for Sunday Baseball." *Liberty Magazine* (September– October). https://www.libertymagazine.org/article/the-battle-for-sunday-baseball.

Miller, Joshua, and Matt Stout. 2018. "Legislature Passes 'Grand Bargain' on Minimum Wage, Paid Leave, Sales Tax Holiday." *Boston Globe*, June 20, 2018. https://www.bostonglobe. com/metro/2018/06/20/legislature-vote-quickly-grand-bargain-for-min-wage-hike -paid-leave-and-sales-tax-holiday/uhQGjnee5Kutd5cD1cCATK/story.html.

New York Times. 2003. "Massachusetts Legislature Repeals Clean Elections Law." June 21, 2003. https://www.nytimes.com/2003/06/21/us/massachusetts-legislature-repeals-clean -elections-law.html.

Oliff, Phil, and Iris J. Lav. 2010. "Hidden Consequences: Lessons from Massachusetts for States Considering Property Tax Cap." Center on Budget and Policy Priorities, revised May 25, 2010. https://www.cbpp.org/research/hidden-consequences-lessons-from -massachusetts-for-states-considering-a-property-tax-cap.

Ravitch, Diane. 2020. *Slaying Goliath: The Passionate Resistance to Privatization and the Fight to Save America's Public Schools*. New York: Alfred A. Knopf.

Secretary of State Ben Ysura v. Education Voters of Idaho, Inc., CV-OC- 2012–19280. 2012. "Order Granting Injunctive Relief as Requested by the Secretary of State of the State of Idaho." District Court of the Fourth Judicial District of the State of Idaho, in and for the County of Ada, October 29, 2012.

SpeechNow.org v. Federal Election Commission, 599 F.3d 686 (D.C. Cir. 2010).

Stout, Matt. 2020. "How Did Ranked-Choice Tank with Massachusetts Voters?" *Boston Globe*, November 4, 2020. https://www.bostonglobe.com/2020/11/04/nation/how-did -ranked-choice-tank-with-massachusetts-voters/.

Walters, Kyla. 2019. "Fighting (for) Charter School Expansion: Racial Resources and Ideological Consistency." In *Race, Organizations, and the Organizing Process*, edited by Melissa E. Wooten. Somerville, MA: Emerald.

PART IV

Diversity in
Massachusetts Politics

CHAPTER 10

LATINX IN
MASSACHUSETTS POLITICS

Luis F. Jiménez

This chapter looks in detail at the political context for Latinx in Massachusetts. It first outlines the demographic picture, which has changed dramatically in the past fifty years and has accelerated in the past twenty. It then describes the poor electoral showings Latinx have in relationship to their numbers and why this is the case. It shows that Latinx electoral success has been most widespread at the local level, but it has been slow and halting. Finally, the chapter looks at the specific ways the state has responded in some key policy areas, such as housing, education, and immigration, despite Latinx still lacking a critical mass of elected officials. In effect, the lack of descriptive representation has not precluded policies Latinx have demanded, but the state's responsiveness has been uneven; its most successful policy initiatives have been barely adequate. This chapter puts Massachusetts within a regional and national scope and documents where the commonwealth is in relationship to those parameters. The challenges are similar to what they face in the rest of the country, but how and why Latinx have succeeded to the extent that they have is more unique to Massachusetts. For Latinx, there is a long path to go, but change seems to be accelerating; politicians simply cannot afford to ignore them.

Latinos in Massachusetts

Over the past fifty years, the Latinx population in Massachusetts has exploded. As a percentage of the population, it has increased tenfold, going from a measly 1.2 percent in 1970 to 12.3 percent in 2019.[1] This rate of growth has been faster than the country as a whole and has accounted for a vast part of the overall growth in the commonwealth. Without Latinx, the state would be close to experiencing flat or decreasing levels of population. This gain in numbers, however, has not been accompanied by a concomitant level of

---

1 The 1970 Census did not ask whether a person identified as Latino, but instead used the term *Spanish origin*. All subsequent numbers come from the U.S. Census unless otherwise noted.

political power, and, although this has begun to change in the past decade, it remains far from what one might expect from population figures alone. This chapter examines these demographic developments in more detail, looks at how these shifts compare to the rest of New England and the country at large, and delves into the ways Latinx have engaged politically and why as a group they still punch below their weight class. It will also review prominent policies that are important to Latinx such as housing, education, and immigration and how the state has responded to these issues. It shows that electoral success has been slow and halting, but even without a critical mass of Latinx elected officials, Massachusetts has not been completely unresponsive.

The Demographic Picture

In 2019 there were roughly 854,000 people in Massachusetts who called themselves Hispanic, Latino, or a variation thereof to the U.S. Census—the equivalent of 1.41 percent of the 67 million people who identified that way nationwide. They have an uneven distribution in the state, with large concentrations in Hampden, Suffolk, and Essex Counties, where they make up 26.3, 23.3, and 22.2 percent of the overall population, respectively. Indeed, about a third of the Latinx population lives in just five cities: Boston (107,917), Springfield (59,451), Worcester (37,818), Lynn (29,013), and Chelsea (21,855). Locations where they have a sizable percentage of the population rather than just places with high absolute numbers have not changed much—they are

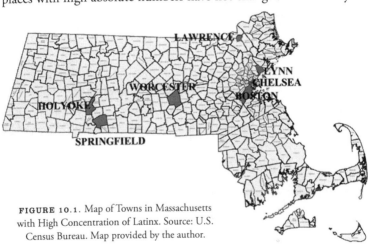

FIGURE 10.1. Map of Towns in Massachusetts with High Concentration of Latinx. Source: U.S. Census Bureau. Map provided by the author.

Lawrence (80.3 percent), Chelsea (66.9 percent), Holyoke (52.1 percent), Springfield (44.7 percent), and Lynn (41.5 percent).

As can be seen in detail in figure 10.2, the past fifty years have seen a dramatic increase in the number of Latinx in Massachusetts. And while as a percentage of population it still lags the United States as a whole (12.3 percent to 18.3 percent), it has grown at a faster rate and has also outpaced the rest of New England (12.3 percent to 10.64 percent). This trend is expected to continue. Granberry and Mattos (2019) project that the Latino population in the commonwealth will peak in 2035 at around 1.15 million, the equivalent of 15.3 percent of the overall state's population. According to the report, "The Latino population is projected to grow more from national [and] domestic migration than international migration" (9), meaning that unanticipated, sudden international migratory pressures—such as those from COVID-19—could very well push these numbers even higher than projected.

FIGURE 10.2. Latinx Population Compared over Time

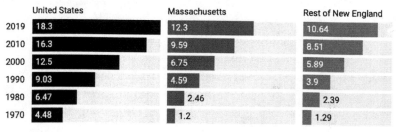

Source: Figures for population using U.S. Census Bureau, "Massachusetts Quick Facts."

One of the reasons for the continued growth is that the Latinx population in the state retains a relatively younger profile compared to other groups and to the country as a whole. The median age for Massachusetts in 2018, for instance, was 28.1. That is in contrast to a median age of 42.8 for whites, 36.3 for Native Americans, 34.0 for Asians, and 32.8 for Blacks. The equivalent numbers for the United States were 29.2 for Latinx, 40.8 for whites, 33.5 for Native Americans, 37.3 for Asians, and 34.4 for Blacks. Figure 10.3 shows that although the Latinx population in the state has gotten slightly grayer, nearly a third of it remains under eighteen—one of the reasons schools have long been of particular importance to the group (Krogstad 2016).

FIGURE 10.3. Age Struture of Latinx Population
in Massachusetts over Time

Source: U.S. Census, U.S. Hispanic Population by State, 1980, 1990, 2000, 2010,
American Community Survey Massachusetts Quick Facts, 2019, 2010.

As the number of Latinx in the state has grown, their ancestry or country of origin has not remained static. This is important because one of the preconditions for collective action is for people to feel that they are part of a group, and although the terms *Hispanic* or *Latino* might be convenient groupings for social science, they mask differences in race, culture, and even use of language, not to mention social class and familiarity with American society, all of which can be exacerbated in turn by affinity to preexisting national identities. Indeed, these terms themselves are contested by Latinx and non-Latinx. Often, one individual with ties to a particular nation-state will call herself Latina, another Hispanic, another Black, another Chicana, while still another a national from that particular country. *Latinidad* is complicated.

So how has the demographic breakdown among Latinx changed over time in Massachusetts? In 1970 the largest group by far was Puerto Ricans who had come to Massachusetts en masse for the first time in the 1950s and settled disproportionately in Boston, Holyoke, and Springfield (Carvalho 2015). They made up nearly a third of the entire Latinx population, while Cubans and Mexicans—the other two sizable Latinx groups in the country at the time—barely amounted to 14.1 percent combined. As can be seen in figure 10.4, by 2018 this had changed somewhat, mostly in the diversification of national groups, although *Boricuas* were still the largest single group—a larger one in fact, constituting nearly 40 percent of the total Latinx population. The biggest growth came from Dominicans whose migration to the United States had been occurring in substantial numbers since the assassination of Rafael Trujillo in 1961 but had concentrated mostly around New York City. They did not make Massachusetts their primary destination until the 1980s (Granberry and Valentino 2020). Originally attracted to places like Lawrence because of the remaining manufacturing jobs, Dominican migration was then sustained by familial ties and the attraction of a "smaller, safer city [than New York]" (Barber 2018) so that by 1990 they constituted more than 10 percent of the overall Latinx population in Massachusetts, and by 2018 their numbers had grown to 19.8 percent. The other newcomers arriving in considerable numbers were Central Americans (Guatemalans and Salvadorans in particular) and most recently Colombians and Venezuelans, the latter of which have more than doubled their percentage of the Massachusetts population in the past decade (0.62 percent to 1.4 percent). Migrant networks also brought these groups, as did economic opportunities; for the past twenty-five years, Massachusetts has had a consistently lower unemployment rate compared to the United States as a whole, with only a few exceptions (U.S. Bureau of Labor Statistics 2021a, 2021b).

FIGURE 10.4. Specific Origin of Latinx Population Compared, 2018

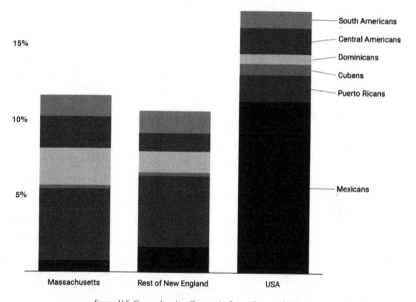

Source: U.S. Census, American Community Survey Customizable Tables
"Place of Birth for the Foreign Population in the United States" and "Latinos in Massachusetts."

This picture is very different from that of the country as a whole. Massachusetts is one of eleven states where Mexicans are *not* the largest origin group for the Latinx population—a comparable situation with the rest of New England.[2] Whereas in the United States, Mexicans represent 11.3 percent of the overall population, in the commonwealth they

---

2   The others are Connecticut, Florida, Maine, Maryland, New York, New Hampshire, New Jersey, Pennsylvania, Rhode Island, and Virginia.

barely register at 0.74 percent. The opposite is true of Puerto Ricans and Dominicans, who combined represent 2.4 percent of the population as a whole in the country, while in the state they are 7.19 percent of the population. Regionally, Massachusetts is quite comparable to the rest of New England, with slightly more Dominicans and Central Americans and fewer Mexicans and South Americans.

Naturally, an assortment of national groups this varied is going to mask all sorts of diversity—including levels of affluence. Nonetheless, as a group Latinx are more likely to have lower incomes and wealth accumulation than others. For example, at the national level, the median income for a household led by a Latinx person is $51,404, while a household led by a white person earns $67,937, but in Massachusetts those numbers are $43,789 and $86,087, respectively—making the gap in Massachusetts three times that of the United States as a whole. This disparity has not changed much over time. In 2010, taking inflation into account, the nationwide figures were $46,252 for Latinx and $62,378 for whites so that the gap in the country as a whole was slightly reduced from 2010 to 2018. The equivalent numbers in Massachusetts in 2010 were $35,740 for Latinx and $77,190 for whites—so that in the period 2010–18, the gap increased by $848.[3]

Wealth numbers are even worse. In richer parts of the state like Boston, the gap becomes a chasm and manifests itself differently within the Latinx community. For instance, Puerto Ricans and Dominicans tend to be more disadvantaged than other Latinx groups (Muñoz et al. 2014). Part of the reason is that one of the main ways for wealth to accumulate in the United States is through home ownership, and on that score Latinx in Massachusetts rank particularly poorly. Consider figure 10.5. In 2018 Latinx had a 25.3 percent ownership rate in comparison to whites at 69.3 percent. In 2000, nearly twenty years earlier, the equivalent numbers were 21.8 percent for Latinx and 66.8 percent for whites—a gap that basically has not changed at all. There is a white-Latinx gap nationwide, as well, but in 2018, in the country as a whole, Latinx enjoyed nearly twice the home-ownership rate compared to those in Massachusetts—47.5 percent—so that the nationwide gap was 22.1 percentage points narrower than in Massachusetts.

---

3   These are 2018 inflation-adjusted numbers for comparative purposes. The actual numbers in the Census were $31,036 and $66,960 for Massachusetts and $40,165 and $54,168 for the United States.

FIGURE 10.5. Latinx Homeownership Compared over Time

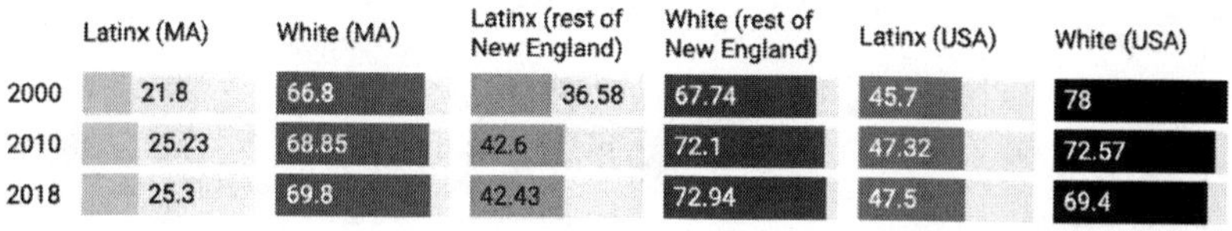

	Latinx (MA)	White (MA)	Latinx (rest of New England)	White (rest of New England)	Latinx (USA)	White (USA)
2000	21.8	66.8	36.58	67.74	45.7	78
2010	25.23	68.85	42.6	72.1	47.32	72.57
2018	25.3	69.8	42.43	72.94	47.5	69.4

Source: U.S. Census, American Community Survey, "Household Ownership Selected Characteristics Customizable Tables."

Even when considered only regionally, Massachusetts ranks abysmally. In 2018 the average home-ownership rate for Latinx was 25.3 percent, while in the rest of New England it was 42.4 percent. And although this was buoyed by rural states like Vermont and Maine where housing is cheaper and more accessible for Latinx, it still was worse than Connecticut (33.91 percent) and Rhode Island (31.94 percent). Perhaps more depressing is that if one examines just the top three cities with the largest absolute numbers of Latinx in the state—Boston, Springfield, and Worcester—the home-ownership rates are outright scandalous—18.2, 24.76, and 16.49 percent, respectively.

Not only are Latinx as a group more likely to earn less and accumulate less wealth and income than other groups at the regional and national levels, they also remain disproportionately poor and face all sorts of economic instability in the state. In 2018, as figure 10.6 shows, Latinx represented 21.6 percent of those below the poverty line in the commonwealth, while nationwide the equivalent number was 16.1 percent. To Massachusetts' credit, that gap was much larger almost forty years ago when the equivalent numbers were 36.4 percent and 25.1 percent. Thus, while the state has been successful in cutting the percentage of those below the poverty line and the gap has narrowed steadily, the fact that it remains at all is evidence of how far we still have to go. Regrettably, the number of those below the poverty line grew as a result of COVID-19. Latinx people have been hit hard by COVID-19; they have seen a disproportionate rate of positive cases, hospitalizations, and deaths (CDC 2020). These medical inequities get compounded by the disproportionate economic fallout from COVID-19 for the Latinx population. At the time of this writing, the specifics are unclear, but the trend lines are well known: Latinx are taking a disproportionate medical and economic hit from the virus.

FIGURE 10.6. Latinx Population
below the Poverty Line over Time

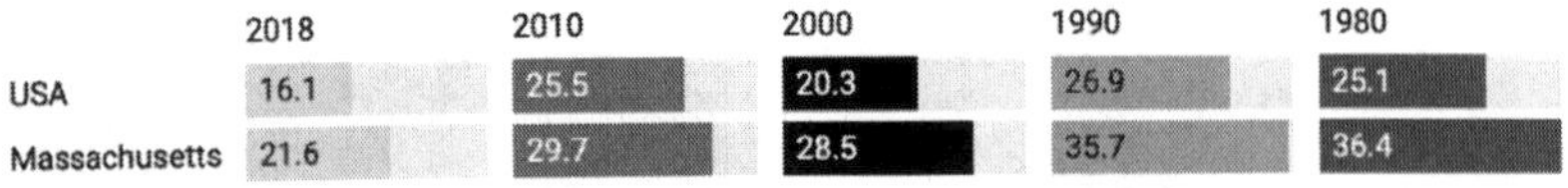

	2018	2010	2000	1990	1980
USA	16.1	25.5	20.3	26.9	25.1
Massachusetts	21.6	29.7	28.5	35.7	36.4

Source: U.S. Census, American Community Survey Customizable Tables,
"People below the Poverty Line by State Selected Characteristics."

Part of the problem is that even in circumstances where individuals are most likely to face precariousness, compared to other groups, Latinx are worse off. For example, Census data shows that 37.5 percent of all households led by single Latina mothers are below the poverty line, while the equivalent for single white mothers is 17.2. Nationwide these numbers are 33.1 percent and 20 percent, respectively, so the gap is much bigger in Massachusetts—4.4 and 2.8, respectively. In fact, the disparity is so substantial that the state ranks forty-second in the country on that measure. In New England, though, this white-Latinx disparity is roughly within the regional range. Rhode Island, New Hampshire, and Maine suffer an even larger gap, while Connecticut's is only slightly smaller.

The other variable that explains the disparity in Latinx wealth is that, to the extent that education provides one of the sturdiest paths for social mobility, the rate of educational attainment for Latinx has been lower than the rates of other groups at both high school and college levels, as can be seen in figure 10.7. This translates into a lifetime of lower earnings so that the above income and wealth disparities will not be solved easily. To its credit, Massachusetts ranks quite high in the number of Latinx with college degrees. In fact, at 21.2 percent, it is the eleventh-highest rate in the country. Unfortunately, there is a massive gap between them and other groups. The equivalent numbers for whites is 47.4, Asians is 63.5, and Blacks is 29.2. Massachusetts' white-Latinx gap in the attainment of college degrees is so large that only three states—California, Connecticut, and Colorado—exhibit more substantial ones.

High school numbers are even worse. Massachusetts sees only 70.5 percent of Latinx graduate, while 94.2 of whites, 86.7 of Blacks, and 86.6 percent of Asians earn high school diplomas. Nor have these numbers changed much over time. Ten years ago, the equivalent numbers were 66.7 percent for Latinx, 92.1 for whites, 83.3 for Asians, and 83.0 for Blacks. If one compares 2018 figures to the country as a whole, it is just above the national average, but it does worse than every other state in New England—the closest is Connecticut, and its graduation rate is 3 percent higher. Thus, although

FIGURE 10.7. School Attainment for Latinx Compared, 2018

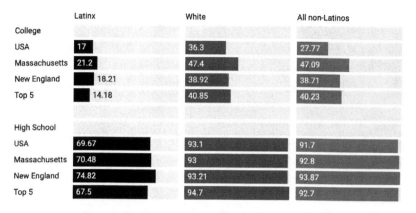

Source: U.S. Census, American Community Survey Customizable Tables,
"People below the Poverty Line Selected Characteristics Educational Attainment."

the state has one of the highest numbers of college-educated Latinx in the country, it is clear that a significant percentage were trained elsewhere or Latinx residents of Massachusetts do not have access to higher education at rates comparable to other racial and ethnic groups in the commonwealth, or both. Massachusetts can attract Latinx college graduates; it just has a much harder time educating them.

The Electoral Picture

Latinx political leadership at all political levels in Massachusetts is lacking, but it is particularly glaring in state government and above. No Latinx person has ever run for a Massachusetts government executive branch position as a nominee of either one of the two major parties, let alone won, though sitting Democratic state senator Sonia Chang-Díaz announced her candidacy for the governorship in the summer of 2021.[4] Long shots have appeared in primaries from time to time—John Bonifaz, an Ecuadorian immigrant who was a candidate for secretary of the commonwealth in 2006 would be an example—but even those have been extremely rare. Massachusetts has also

---

4   If one used the term *Hispanic* and not *Latinx*, perhaps Jay Gonzalez, the Democratic nominee in 2018 and son of a Spanish immigrant, would qualify.

never sent any Latinx to the U.S. Congress.[5] The closest it came in the Senate was during the 2013 special election when Republican Gabriel Gómez, a Colombian man, lost by 10 percentage points to Democrat Ed Markey. On the House side, the closest a Latinx individual has come to winning a seat was in 2018 when Juana Matías, a Dominican immigrant, came in fourth in the Massachusetts Third Congressional District Democratic primary.

The state legislature has been more fertile ground, but success took decades. The first Latinx candidate for state representative was Alex Rodríguez in 1968, a Puerto Rican born in New York City who aspired to represent Boston's South End but who ultimately failed (Matos Rodríguez 2005). The first Latina to do the same—Carmen Pola—tried in 1980, but she also lost. The loss was close enough, however, that it "pushed the area's representative to be more responsive to his Latino constituents," according to a prominent Latino activist from that time (Hardy-Fanta and Gerson 2002, 54). It took until 1988 and roughly thirty years from the time *Boricuas* started to arrive in substantial numbers in Massachusetts for the first Puerto Rican (and Latino) to be elected to a position in state government. That person was Nelson Merced, a very progressive candidate who rode a broad multiracial coalition to two terms in the house.[6] The senate took much longer; Jarrett Barrios, the son of Cuban immigrants, won the first seat in 2003.

Since then, some progress has been made, but not nearly enough. If one were to use proportion of the population as the relevant measure, Latinx people should hold at least 19 of the 160 seats in the Massachusetts House of Representatives. Instead, there are only 8 Latinx representatives—that includes Danillo Sena, the first Brazilian-born state representative in the United States.[7] In the senate, there are only 2 out of a potential 40 seats—Sonia Chang-Díaz and Adam Gomez—2 less than a proportional allocation based on Latinx numbers would indicate. Their tenure is recent, so state leadership remains elusive because seniority is usually central to achieving these posts. In 2017 Latinx finally had one of their own in the state leadership in the person of seven-term representative Jeffrey Sánchez, but he unexpectedly lost in the

---

5   The official congressional website includes Lori Trahan, a Portuguese American woman, under its list of Hispanic members. For another example of why the term is contested, see here: https://history.house.gov/Exhibitions-and-Publications/HAIC/Historical-Data/Hispanic-American-Representatives-and-Senators-by-State-and-Territory/.

6   For details see chapter 2 in Hardy-Fanta and Gerson's *Latino Politics in Massachusetts: Struggles, Strategies, and Prospects.*

7   Danillo is in the Black and Latino caucus and identifies as such, but not all Brazilians do. The 12.3 percent figure would not include many of those who opted not to identify that way. If it had, it would be closer to 13.7 percent and thus 21 equivalent seats in the house.

very next election. In 2020 Frank Moran was named the Third Division chair, one of four positions in the lower chamber that act as go-betweens between the rank and file and house leadership.

Although there have been some genuinely impressive electoral wins, such as Jon Santiago's beating Byron Rushing, a thirty-five-year incumbent who served as the assistant majority leader in the house, the lack of seniority matters. In theory the Speaker of the house or senate could appoint anyone for leadership positions, but the likelihood increases with seniority; at the time of this writing, the person in the leadership with the fewest years in office is Frank Moran. He was elected in 2013. This means that although Latinx representatives are becoming more common, their access to the legislative corridors of power is still limited.

The picture is much brighter at the local level, although progress has also been slow and halting. The first Latinx person to be elected to public office in Massachusetts was Grace Romero—a Black Panamanian who won a seat on the Boston School Committee in 1983. It should be noted that this early victory occurred because "she emphasized her African-American rather than Latino heritage," which in turn meant that "most of her support [came] from African-American voters" and that her campaign "did not gather much enthusiasm or support in the Latino community" (Hardy-Fanta and Gerson 2002, 54). That might explain why this milestone was short-lived, as she lasted a single year, and no other Latinx person was ever elected to the committee.[8]

More sustained electoral victories at the local level have materialized in areas Latinx have dominated numerically, although this also took decades. Two cities with high concentrations of Latinx have had representation in city government since the early 1990s. In Holyoke the first Latinx council member was elected in 1992. In Lawrence it was 1993. In both cases, Latinx had been running for office and losing for many years, especially in Holyoke where Puerto Rican candidates had been running since the 1970s despite little chance of success. Other places took much longer. Worcester, Springfield, Boston, and Lowell elected their first Latinx city council members in 2000, 2002, 2003, and 2006, respectively, while it took Cambridge until 2013; Chelsea, Haverhill, and Waltham until 2015; and Easthampton until 2017. Yet other cities, like Lynn and Revere, whose Latinx population exceeds 20 percent, have yet to have anyone elected, although they have had several Latinx candidates run.

---

8   An important reason for this is that the Boston School Committee transitioned to a mayor-appointed system in 1992. At the time of this writing, there are two Latinas serving.

Latinx mayors are rare in Massachusetts. Lawrence, the first majority Latinx city in the state, is the only place to have had Latinx leadership in the mayor's office. The first occurred in 2001 when Marcos Devers, a Dominican immigrant, became an acting mayor after the previous mayor accepted an appointment as a judge. William Lantigua, the second to sit in the mayor's chair and first to be popularly elected, also of Dominican background, gained office in 2010. Meanwhile, Boston, Springfield, and Holyoke have all had candidates in the 2010s, but none of the candidates have come close to the mayor's office, though Puerto Rican Jon Santiago, a physician and current Democratic state representative, was among six top-tier candidates in the 2021 Boston mayoral contest. Cambridge also elected a Latino vice mayor, Dennis Benzan, in 2013. However, given Cambridge's city-manager type of government, this position has little executive power.

Among elected officials, there has also been a persistent gender gap. Historically, Latinas have been the backbone of the group's activism, "mobilizing the community around felt needs" (Hardy-Fanta 1995, 230). And although they have run at comparable rates to men for public office and have held public office in roughly similar percentages, their electoral success has been nearly always limited to the municipal level (CWPPP 2017). Between 1984 and 2017, for instance, fifty-eight Latinas held public office. Of these, 55.2 percent were school committee members and 39.7 percent were elected city councilors (CWPPP 2017). In 2020, of the ten Latinx representatives in state government, only one is a woman—Sonia Chang-Díaz.

How does this record compare with other states in New England? It is not stellar. The other two states with comparable populations—Connecticut and Rhode Island—have more Latino elected officials in higher positions. For instance, proportional to their Latinx population, Connecticut and Rhode Island have a higher number of state senators, state representatives—three senators and ten representatives for Connecticut and three senators and nine representatives for Rhode Island—and also elected Latino mayors in Hartford and Providence, both capital cities that are larger than any Latinx-run cities in Massachusetts. They also currently have more Latinas in state government, two state representatives in Connecticut and six in Rhode Island.

Even worse, this advantage in Latinx representation in Connecticut and Rhode Island over Massachusetts is not new—it has prevailed for at least thirty years (Cruz 1995). The successes among Massachusetts' neighbors are also broader across Latinx subgroups. While Puerto Ricans and Dominicans have dominated elected offices in Massachusetts, Connecticut has had Peruvian,

Ecuadorian, Central American, and Cuban representatives. Rhode Island has also succeeded where Massachusetts and Connecticut have failed. Nellie Gorbea, a Puerto Rican woman, won statewide as secretary of state. Rhode Island gubernatorial races have also featured multiple Latinx candidates—though no wins.

The other three states in New England—Maine, New Hampshire, and Vermont—have only three sitting state representatives combined as of 2020; Maine has none and has never elected a Latinx state legislator. In fact, in the entire state, as of 2019, there were five total Latinx elected officials, the highest ranked of whom was a city council member in Portland. New Hampshire's and Vermont's numbers were four and three, respectively, a smaller number but in higher levels of government.

So why have Latinx in Massachusetts not been as successful in achieving the political representation that their numbers might suggest? The reasons are similar to what Latinx face in nearly every other state and can be divided into obstacles on the demand and supply sides of the political ledger. On the demand side, we can include the complexities around *Latinidad,* the high levels of voting noneligibility among Latinx population, the many hurdles associated with voting in the United States, and the disproportionate levels of poverty, which creates demand for representation but makes it harder for Latinx candidates to run. On the supply side, the issues become the lack of political know-how necessary to create quality candidates and the high cost of running for office. Let us consider each one in more detail.

As a simple matter, sharing a Census classification with others does not mean experiencing identity in the same way. As already discussed, rather than some pan-ethnic sense of self, for many Latinx, nationalities come first. In places with a high concentration but diverse group of Latinx, this can divide as much as unite. For instance, rivalry between Dominicans and Puerto Ricans in Lawrence, Massachusetts, had to be bridged before they could have some electoral success. That is partly the reason places like Lynn and Revere—where Puerto Ricans and Dominicans share the city with significant numbers of Guatemalans, Salvadorans, and even Colombians—lack Latinx leadership despite their numerical advantage. Weak shared identity also means that even if no national rivalries exist, Latinx might not prioritize *descriptive* representation around an umbrella demographic categorization. A common narrative from candidates across Massachusetts is that no matter the position, being Latinx does not guarantee the vote of other Latinx by any means (Russell 2020). Hence, one of the paradoxes of Latinx political power is that, although many shared interests exist, the shared identity that would make mobilization easier is often lacking (Beltran 2010).

The noneligibility issue is massive. A significant percentage of Latinx are noncitizens, which makes them ineligible to vote. With the exception of Puerto Ricans and everyone born in the United States who become citizens at birth, the remaining Latinx must follow a naturalization process. Many, of course, do not have that option at all because their immigration status makes them ineligible to gain citizenship. As a result, 21.5 percent of all Latinx in the state are noncitizens and therefore are not permitted to vote—a figure that is slightly higher than the rest of New England. This makes any campaign targeting Latinx as a base doubly costly, as even unanimous support in the community would mean roughly a fifth would be unable to make it official at the ballot box. That explains, in part, why places like Holyoke and Springfield have a more sustained Latinx political footprint than comparable places elsewhere in the state—having Puerto Ricans as the main group has the double benefit of universal voting rights within the electorate and group cohesiveness.

FIGURE 10.8. Non-eligible to Vote Latinx Population, 2018

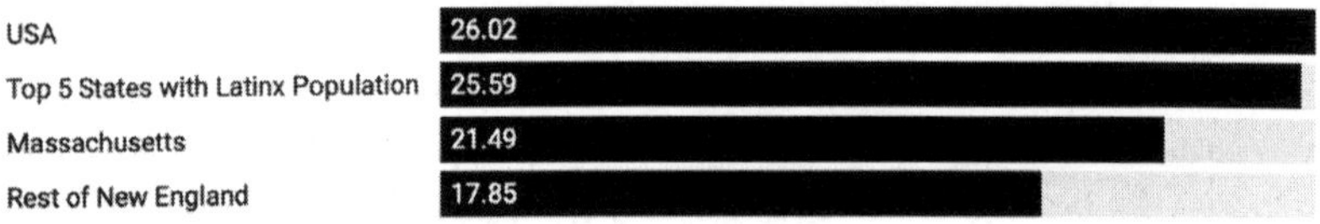

USA	26.02
Top 5 States with Latinx Population	25.59
Massachusetts	21.49
Rest of New England	17.85

Source: U.S. Census, American Community Survey Customizable Tables, "Foreign Born Population by State" and "Latino Population in Massachusetts Selected Characteristics."

The third issue is one not limited to Latinx but to any minority or disadvantaged group. The most important variables associated with voting are wealth and education (Brady, Verba, and Schlozman 1995), both of which, as we have seen, Latinx disproportionately lack. This combination exacerbates whatever underlying voter apathy might exist. It is much harder to convince people who lack education that voting matters at all or that there could be meaningful differences between candidates as nonengaged voters deem politicians in general to be the same. If we add the other usual obstacles—need to register, elections on a weekday, and local elections on off-cycle years in Massachusetts—the result is an electorate that votes at dismal rates with very gradual improvement over the years. Campaigns, already facing lower payoff from targeting Latinx because of ineligibility, see a disengaged electorate and opt to look elsewhere for support. This contributes to a vicious cycle. Poor past voting turnout means campaigns do not engage Latinx, and present neglect means future meager voting rates.

On the supply side—candidates running for office—the political training and know-how required for political campaigns, and the social networks one needs to cultivate, are disproportionately lacking among the Latinx population compared to other groups, especially whites. The majority of Latinx candidates tend to be activists or business owners as opposed to aides or appointees of elected officials.[9] It is another vicious cycle. Fewer Latinx get involved in electoral politics because few Latinx are in electoral politics. This, combined with the high cost of running for office at the state level, which usually requires thousands of dollars to compete, means that a candidate must have enough disposable income or be a talented fund-raiser. These factors underscore two necessary elements that are disproportionately missing among Latinx: wealth and political experience. All of the aforementioned political difficulties could be tempered with institutions that cut across social cleavages—churches, unions, cultural organizations, and so on. Such institutions could help reinforce group cohesion, provide important social connections, and mobilize opportunities for potential candidates. Unfortunately, each has weaknesses of its own. Numbers of regular church attendees have dropped precipitously, and membership does not cut across social class as much as it used to; union membership has been stagnant in Massachusetts and lower for Latinx than other groups, and cultural organizations are perennially underfunded.

The one thing that does seem to bridge some of these differences is time. *Latinidad* has a fundamental racialized component, so younger generations and people with more familiarity with American society are more likely to see themselves as Latinx and not individual members of a national (or other) group. This identification occurs both because ties to their countries of origin become weaker and because they are more likely to recognize shared interests with other Latinx. As U.S.-born generations of Latinx multiply, this aspect might be what fundamentally realizes their potential for political power.

The Overall Political Picture and the State Response

Of course, elections are only one way to engage in politics, and a small part of what Latinx are doing politically in Massachusetts. Activism long predates

---

9   In the Massachusetts legislature, for instance, only four out of nine Latinx elected officials had any kind of connection to previous politicians, including internships.

electoral victories, and, indeed, there are numerous triumphs. For instance, in Holyoke, community organization against arson and infant mortality that began in the 1970s and 1980s succeeded in stopping the former and in unlocking government resources to fight the latter (Borges-Méndez 1994). Similarly, a lawsuit in 1981 from the Hispanic Parents Advisory Council versus the city of Holyoke secured an accord to provide bilingual education and other special education measures to the Latinx community; this was later replicated in Lowell in 1987 to stop school segregation with similar success. Likewise, in Lawrence, after riots consumed the city in 1984, Latinx used the opportunity to push the city to improve schools, rehabilitate housing projects, and hire more Latinx in city jobs.[10] Even in places like Cambridge where the small numbers of Latinx and the high cost of living have made Latinx electoral victories rare, organizations like Concilio Hispano succeeded in "pressuring the legislature to require recording of court proceedings so that abuses could be challenged, demanding the Elections Commission guarantee Puerto Ricans the right to vote, exposing police harassment, and lobbying local universities . . . to provide the community with more jobs at better pay" (Hernández 2006, 156). Though incomplete, especially in Lawrence, which continued in a steady economic decline through the 1990s and where Latinx precariousness barely improved, this small subset of successful Latinx community activism shows that they have not been powerless even in the face of meager political representation. Currently, there are many community organizations that advocate and work with the state to improve the lives of Latinx. Among the largest groups we can include La Alianza Hispana and Sociedad Latina. Both Boston based and women led, they were founded in the 1960s and 1970s, respectively, and beyond educational and workforce programs they also concentrate on matters of civic engagement. Two other important organizations are Centro Presente and MIRA (Massachusetts Immigration Refugee Advocacy Coalition), both of which specialize in migration matters important to Latinos. While MIRA is not specifically Latinx staffed and led, as is Centro Presente, and its goals are not limited to Latino concerns, it does have Latinx membership and prioritizes those interests.

STATE RESPONSE ON HOUSING, EDUCATION, AND IMMIGRATION

So how has the state responded to the needs of Latinx? Consider three broad policy areas of import to Latinx in the state—housing, education,

---

10   For a detailed history of the city and how Latinos have changed it, see Barber 2017.

and immigration. Improving the affordability of housing is difficult to tackle because unlike most states, Massachusetts is one of the few where land use is decided by municipalities with little state or regional oversight (Modestino et al. 2019). In turn, disproportionately older and wealthier residents tend to rise in opposition to any multifamily developments (Levine Einstein, Palmer, and Glick 2019). Consequently, insufficient housing supply has plagued the region for decades, which in turn makes demand difficult to meet and the cost of housing go up. Attempts at using legislation to reduce the supermajority requirement for zoning in the various towns in the commonwealth to a simple majority have been unsuccessful. As a result, the government's main tools have been to strategically develop unused or underutilized commonwealth properties, to offer grants and technical assistance to encourage towns to build more affordable housing, and to employ Chapter 40B—a law that permits the overriding of some zoning laws to build affordable housing. This has had some success in places like Boston and Chelsea (Levine Einstein, Palmer, and Glick 2019), and as a result minority segregation diminished between 2010 and 2017 (Chiumenti 2020), but the need to do more remains vast. COVID-19 exacerbated the problem, so the governor has looked into using funds from the American Rescue Plan Act of 2021 for housing, but this remains a point of negotiation with the legislature. Lack of affordable housing will be a major issue for the foreseeable future.

The record on education is similarly mixed. Massachusetts is one of the better states with regard to education spending—it does a good job of using more resources on poorer districts than rich ones and is far better on this point than any other New England state (Baker, Di Carlo, and Weber 2019). From 2015 to 2017, early in the Baker administration, the ratio spent on the 30 percent of poorest school districts in the commonwealth—the ones most likely to have Latinx students—compared to those with zero poverty went up slightly from 1.09 to 1.11 (Baker, Di Carlo, and Weber 2019). This contributed to a sizable dropout reduction in districts with the highest numbers of Latinx students in Massachusetts—Holyoke, Lawrence, and Springfield (Williams 2017). Beyond more strategic use of resources, the Baker administration attempted to make college more affordable for Latinx and other minorities. For instance, they created Boston Bridge, a tuition-free program for low-income students attending a number of community colleges in the Greater Boston area.

One of the most important pieces of legislation of interest to Latinx in recent years was the passage of the LOOK Act in 2017. Bilingual education in the state had been severely restricted as a result of the 2002 referendum officially known as Massachusetts English in Public Schools Initiative, which required all schoolchildren to be taught all subjects in English. The purported intent of the law was to accelerate language acquisition for English-language learners, which the bilingual education model at the time supposedly impeded. Fifteen years later, it was clear the referendum's model did not work (Larkin 2017). Subsequently, a broad coalition of Latinx activists, teacher organizations such as MATSOL (Massachusetts Association of Teachers of Speakers of Other Languages), and other pressure groups like MABE (Multistate Association for Bilingual Education) pushed to change it. It finally did under the leadership of Representative Jeffrey Sánchez and Senator Sonia Chang-Díaz as the Massachusetts General Court passed legislation that provided the flexibility necessary for school districts to design the language-acquisition program that best suited their needs. As a result, the state currently has forty-seven bilingual programs of some kind. Out of these, thirty-five are Spanish, and an additional one has a Spanish-Portuguese dual curriculum. Unfortunately, a problem that remains is that "there is a severe nationwide shortage of bilingual teachers."[11]

On immigration-related issues, Massachusetts' record is worse than on the other two from the perspective of Latinx communities. Since the 2010s, activists have been pushing for two specific policy changes—in-state tuition and driver's license access for undocumented people. Neither has succeeded. Governor Baker's threatened veto for in-state tuition and his support of a 2016 bill that made it unlawful for the state to issue a driver's license to anyone with irregular immigration status set the tone. Consequently, the commonwealth lags behind other states in New England and many more throughout the United States. Regionally, Connecticut and Vermont permit undocumented individuals to obtain a driver's license, while Connecticut and Rhode Island have extended in-state tuition to all residents regardless of immigration status. Nationally, there are an additional sixteen states and the District of Columbia for the former and seventeen states for the latter. Massachusetts does provide in-state tuition for students granted Deferred Action for Childhood Arrivals status—a program first begun under Governor Deval Patrick in 2012. Unfortunately, because of the Trump administration's hostile treatment of DACA recipients, which often led to refusals to renew their status or to consider initial claims even in the face of legal orders to the contrary, this program is not as effective for DACA recipients in Massachusetts as it might seem.

---

11   Email communication with Helen Solorzano, executive director of MATSOL.

Conclusion

The Latinx population continues to grow in Massachusetts, and so do the needs of the community. Massachusetts ranks dismally in providing Latinx with affordable housing, educating Latinx children, and closing the wealth gap that has developed between Latinx and whites. Unfortunately, some of the same structural causes that make Latinx life precarious in the commonwealth also shape the lack of Latinx elected representation in the state and federal delegations. Another major obstacle to the accruing of political power is that the Latinx grouping is a complicated and contested one. Because there are many forms of identity flattened by the moniker, individuals that might be understood to be part of the group might or might not necessarily see themselves as such and might or might not see the need for descriptive representation; additionally, political interests might differ dramatically from one issue to another within the group. This increases the difficulty of organizing for both insiders and outsiders, leading to an unfortunate feedback loop. Candidates pay less attention to Latinx because they vote in meager numbers, and Latinx vote in meager numbers because candidates are less likely to court their support.

Yet, despite the many obstacles, Latinx have found ways to organize and improve their communities; they are quickly increasing their political power in the state, and despite lacking a critical mass, elected officials have succeeded in forcing the leadership in the state to pay attention to their needs. Numbers have not gained them concomitant power, but they have made it impossible for politicians to ignore them. The path to solving many of these problems remains a long one, but the number of Latinx will continue to increase, needs will not simply disappear, and undoubtedly new Latinx leadership in the state will arise. The new generation seems to be further along in solving some of the difficulties in organizing Latinx. We will see if they are up to the task, but there is reason for hope.

WORKS CITED

Baker, Bruce, Charles Di Carlo, and Mark Weber. 2019. School Finance Indicators Database, Albert Shanker Institute. https://schoolfinancedata.org/researchers/.

Barber, Llana. 2017. *Latino City: Immigration and Urban Crisis in Lawrence, Massachusetts, 1945–2000.* Chapel Hill: University of North Carolina Press.

———. 2018. "This Would Be a Ghost Town: Urban Crisis and Latino Migration in Lawrence." *Historical Journal of Massachusetts.* 46, no. 1: 61.

Beltran, Cristina. 2010. *The Trouble with Unity: Latino Politics and the Creation of Unity*. Oxford: Oxford University Press.

Borges-Méndez, Ramón. 1994. "Urban and Regional Restructuring and Barrio Formation in Massachusetts: The Cases of Lowell, Lawrence and Holyoke." Master's thesis, Massachusetts Institute of Technology.

Brady, Sidney, Kay Lehman Schlozman, and Henry Brady. 1995. *Voice and Equality: Civic Voluntarism in American Politics*. Cambridge, MA: Harvard University Press.

Carvalho, Joseph III. 2015. "The Puerto Rican Community of Western Massachusetts, 1898–1960." *Historical Journal of Massachusetts* 43, no. 2: 34–62. http://www.wsc.ma.edu/mhj.

Center for Disease Control (CDC). 2020. "Risk for Covid-19 Infection, Hospitalization and Death by Race and Ethnicity." https://www.cdc.gov/coronavirus/2019-ncov/covid-data/investigations-discovery/hospitalization-death-by-race-ethnicity.html.

Center for Women in Politics and Public Policy (CWPPP) at the University of Massachusetts–Boston. 2017. "Latina Political Leadership in Massachusetts." http://scholarworks.umb.edu/cwppp_pubs/53.

Chiumenti, Nicholas. 2020. "Recent Trends in Residential Segregation in New England." New England Public Policy Center Regional Briefs. https://www.bostonfed.org/publications/new-england-public-policy-center-regional-briefs/2020/recent-trends-in-residential-segregation-in-new-england.aspx.

Cruz, José E. 1995. "Puerto Rican Politics in the United States: A Preliminary Assessment." *New England Journal of Public Policy* 11, no. 1: article 13. https://scholarworks.umb.edu/nejpp/vol11/iss1/13.

Granberry, Philip, and Trevor Mattos. 2019. "Massachusetts Latino Population, 2010–2035." Gaston Institute Publications 241. https://scholarworks.umb.edu/gaston_pubs/241/.

Granberry, Philip, and Krizia Valentino. 2020. "Latinos in Massachusetts: Dominicans." Gaston Institute Publications 250. https://scholarworks.umb.edu/gaston_pubs/250/.

Hardy-Fanta, Carol. 1995. "Latina Women and Political Leadership: Implications for Latino Community Empowerment." *New England Journal of Public Policy* 11, no. 1: article 13. https://scholarworks.umb.edu/nejpp/vol11/iss1/14.

Hardy-Fanta, Carol, and Jeffrey Gerson. 2002. *Latino Politics in Massachusetts: Struggles, Strategies, and Prospects*. New York: Routledge.

Hernández, Deborah Pacini. 2006. "A Quiet Crisis: A Community History of Latinos in Cambridge, Massachusetts." In *Latinos in New England*, edited by Andrés Torres, 149–70. Philadelphia: Temple University Press.

Krogstad, Jens Manuel. 2016. "The Economy Is a Top Issue for Latinos and They're More Upbeat about It." Pew Research Center. https://www.pewresearch.org/fact-tank/2016/07/15/the-economy-is-a-top-issue-for-latinos-and-theyre-more-upbeat-about-it/

Larkin, Max. 2017. "Why Mass Is Making a Third Attempt at Reforming English Language Ed." WBUR, August 9, 2017. https://www.wbur.org/edify/2017/08/09/english-language-learning-bills

Levine Einstein, Katherine, Maxwell Palmer, and David M. Glick. 2019. "Who Participates in Local Government." *Perspectives on Politics* 17, no. 1: 1–19.

Matos Rodríguez, Felix V. 2005. "Saving the Parcela: A Short-History of Boston's Puerto Rican Community." In *Puerto Rican Diaspora: Historical Perspectives*, edited by Carmen Whalen and Victor Vázquez Hernández, 200–226. Philadelphia: Temple University Press.

Modestino, Alicia Sasser, Clark Ziegler, Tom Hopper, Calandra Clark, Lucas Manson, Mark Melnik, Carrie Bernstein, and Abby Raisz. 2019. "The Greater Boston Housing Report Card: Supply, Demand and the Challenge of Local Control." Boston

Foundation. https://www.tbf.org/-/media/tbf/reports-and-covers/2019/gbhrc2019
.pdf?la=en&hash=6F5C3F0B829962B0F19680D8B9B4794158D6B4E9.

Muñoz, Ana Patricia, Marlene Kim, Mariko Chang, Regine O. Jackson, Darrick Hamilton,
and William Darity. 2014. "The Color of Wealth in Boston." Federal Reserve Bank of
Boston, Duke University, and the New School. https://www.bostonfed.org/-/media/
Documents/color-of-wealth/color-of-wealth.pdf.

Russell, Jenna. 2020. "Tough Race for Latino in Springfield: Mayoral Hopeful Can't Count
on Ethnic Vote." *Boston Globe*, November 5, 2011. https://www.bostonglobe.com
/metro/2011/11/05/tough-race-for-latino-springfield/XHvai83jpIUbNiAmFcKLDJ
/story.html.

Stout, Matt, and John Chesto. 2021. "Baker, at Odds with Legislature Looks to Spend Half
of $5B Stimulus Windfall with a Focus on Housing." *Boston Globe*, June 17, 2021.
https://www.bostonglobe.com/2021/06/17/business/baker-looks-spend-half-states-5b
-stimulus-windfall-quickly-with-housing-topping-priority-list/.

U.S. Bureau of Labor Statistics. 2021a. "Unemployment Rate." Retrieved from FRED, Federal
Reserve Bank of St. Louis, June 17, 2021. https://fred.stlouisfed.org/series/MAUR.

———. 2021b. "Unemployment Rate in Massachusetts [MAUR]." Retrieved from FRED, Federal Reserve Bank of St. Louis, June 17, 2021. https://fred.stlouisfed.org/series/MAUR.

Williams, Michelle. 2017. "Dropout Rate Down More than 50% in Holyoke, Lawrence,
Springfield in Five Year Period." *MassLive*, February 28, 2017. https://www.masslive
.com/news/2017/02/dropout_rate_down_more_than_50.html.

CHAPTER II

WOMEN, WOMEN OF COLOR IN MASSACHUSETTS POLITICS

Not So Exceptional

Erin O'Brien

This volume is organized around the theme of "Massachusetts exceptionalism" in both politics and public policy. When it comes to electing women, Massachusetts is best described as "exceptionally poor" in New England and "exceptionally average" among the fifty states.

Huh?

National and international audiences certainly know Massachusetts senator Elizabeth Warren and her ultimately unsuccessful fight for the 2020 Democratic presidential nomination. Congresswoman Ayanna Pressley rose to national prominence in her successful 2018 campaign to unseat a fellow Democrat, Congressman Michael Capuano, to represent the Massachusetts Seventh Congressional District. She is prominent in American political consciousness as she, along with her fellow "squad" members of second-term elected congresswomen of color, remains a favorite foil for former president Trump as well as a policy agenda setter. Congresswoman Katherine Clark of the Massachusetts Fifth is notable among House political observers as she is in leadership and, as of January 2021, became the number-four House Democrat, winning the post of Assistant Speaker. These women, along with the four (of six) women who serve within statewide constitutionally elected offices are bright exceptions to Massachusetts norms: women currently hold about 30 percent of the seats in most elected positions. Despite the commonwealth being comparatively rich in conditions that usually advance women in elected office, Massachusetts is in the middle of the pack in electing women to the state legislature and last in New England, with the latter pattern generally holding for almost a hundred years. The state's record for electing women of color is dismal.

This chapter explores these trends. It begins with the current status of women in Bay State elected offices and then leverages the most comprehensive

---

The author thanks Allyson Bachta and Jane JaKyung Han for dedicated research assistance. Dr. Marija Bingulac tagged in with technical acumen when I was at my wit's end. Thank you all. These diverse women made this project immeasurably better.

longitudinal dataset of New England state legislators ever compiled (1921–2021) to uncover the development of women in Massachusetts elected offices as well as how this compares to that of regional neighbors and U.S. averages. An almost fifty-year examination of women of color (WOC) in the state legislature provides more dreary layers: the gains women have made in the state legislature are almost exclusively enjoyed by white women, and the gap between the percentage of women of color in the state and in the Massachusetts state legislature is more than ten points. It is a puzzling state of affairs: the progressive hotbed of Massachusetts is average in electing women, especially women of color, and regularly falls short of the other New England states.

The second half of the chapter unpacks this puzzle. Massachusetts excels in state conditions linked to seeing women elected to office. For instance, it has the second-highest percentage of women with a bachelor's degree or higher nationally and is ranked the highest in the region (Institute for Women's Policy Research 2017). The commonwealth is third nationally and again first in the region for percentage of women in the workforce who are in managerial or professional occupations (Institute for Women's Policy Research 2015). Religiosity, state educational rates, and women's earnings all similarly suggest Massachusetts should be leading both New England and most of the country for electing women. It does not. The chapter concludes with similarly comparative analyses to answer this riddle. Factors implicated are intuitive—child care, elder- and dependent-care policies, and their associated costs in Massachusetts. A surprising finding of this research is the role that single-party Democratic dominance plays.

Documenting Women in Massachusetts' Elected Offices

CURRENT STATUS OF WOMEN IN MASSACHUSETTS ELECTED OFFICE

It is usually the case that the lower the office, the more likely one is to see a woman occupant (Sparks 2014). Not that women necessarily dominate in lower-level positions, but it is the case that the lower the prestige, the more likely that the numbers of women will be higher (Dolan, Deckman, and Swers 2020, 154). Having women in these lower-level offices alters the policy agenda in these cities and towns (Beck 2001; Boles 2001) and provides women in these offices the skills, experiences, and networks facilitative for higher office runs. They are often pipeline or "feeder" positions.

As table 11.1 illustrates, Massachusetts does not follow this pattern. It provides the number and percentages of women in Massachusetts elected offices from town select board to Congress.[1] When we look to town select boards, three hundred of the twelve hundred members are female—25 percent. City council members are 29 percent female (Colarusso 2019). Only fourteen of forty-seven (29 percent) Massachusetts mayors are women. It was not until March 2021 that Boston, the economic and cultural hub of the commonwealth, saw a female occupy the mayor's office. Acting mayor Kim Janey ascended from the city council when the previous mayor, Marty Walsh, took a cabinet position in the Biden administration. She made history as the first women and the first person of color to hold that office in Boston. The field aiming to take her spot featured five debate-eligible candidates—all of color, with four of the five being women—with Michelle Wu winning the contest and, thus, becoming the first popularly elected female mayor in Boston's history. Yet of the top-ten most populous cities in Massachusetts, only two—Boston and Cambridge—are led by a female as of 2021. Mayor Sumbul Siddiqui of Cambridge, Massachusetts' first Muslim mayor, was elected in 2019.

TABLE 11.1. Women in Massachusetts Elected Positions, 2021

	TOTAL	PERCENTAGE
TOWN SELECT BOARDS	300/1200	25
CITY COUNCILORS	176/603	29
MAYORS	14/48	29
STATE LEGISLATURE	62/200	31
CONSTITUTIONAL OFFICERS	4/6	67
CONGRESS	4/11	36

Data from: Town Select Boards and city councilors for 2019: WGBH News; mayors: Massachusetts Municipal Association; and legislature, constitutional officers, and Congress: CAWP 2021.

Since the mid-1990s, the percentage of women in the state legislature has hovered around 25 percent, with small gains in recent years. Up until 2018, the percentage of women remained at a quarter, but then increased to 28.5 percent in 2019. As seen in table 11.1, it increased to 31 percent in 2021. The uptick nonetheless places Massachusetts a mere twenty-fourth among the

---

1   Figures for select boards and city councilors are from 2019 as updated data was not available as of June 2021. All other figures are for 2021.

fifty states and dead last in New England. By comparison, Rhode Island ranked second, Maine sixth, Vermont eighth, New Hampshire twelfth, and Connecticut seventeenth in the nation (CAWP 2021). When it comes to state legislative leadership, the senate president, Karen Spilka, is female. However, there have been only three female senate presidents, and the first was elected only recently, in 2007. Despite a history dating all the way back to 1644 with the Massachusetts Bay Colony, the house Speaker has never been a woman.

Current constitutional officeholders (governor, lieutenant governor, attorney general, secretary of the commonwealth, treasurer, and auditor) and the congressional delegation fare better for gender equity, though this is a recent development—and neither saw changes between 2019 and 2021. Four of the six statewide elected positions are held by women—lieutenant governor, attorney general, treasurer, and auditor. Massachusetts has had one female governor, Jane Swift, who assumed the office from her post as lieutenant governor in April 2001 as the previous governor stepped down for an ambassadorship. She briefly campaigned to win election to the position but withdrew from the race when Mitt Romney, a fellow Republican, announced he would be (successfully) entering the race. Her time in office was April 2001–January 2003. In the history of the commonwealth, only ten women have held statewide offices (CAWP 2021e).

The 2019 Massachusetts congressional delegation saw the highest percentage of women in the Bay State's history—36 percent—and this figure remains in 2021. On this regional comparison, Massachusetts places third in New England. Both New Hampshire (75 percent) and Maine (50 percent) surpass Massachusetts for percentage of women in their 2021 congressional delegations. Connecticut's congressional representatives are 28 percent female, and both Vermont and Rhode Island have no women in their respective congressional delegations. The gains in Massachusetts, however, are recent. Only eight women have ever served in Congress from the state, and no women served for significant stretches in the modern era, 1983–2006 (CAWP 2019). It was not until 2013, when Elizabeth Warren (D) successfully challenged then sitting senator Scott Brown (R), that Massachusetts elected a female senator. Congresswomen Ayanna Pressley, the first woman of color Massachusetts sent to Congress, and Katherine Clark are joined by Lori Trahan in the House. Both Pressley and Trahan first won in 2018. Pressley is the only woman of color to have ever served in the state's congressional delegation, and no woman of color has ever served in a statewide constitutional position.

A top-to-bottom accounting of the current percentages of women in Massachusetts elected office indicates that only in constitutional offices do women have a majority, and, even there, the top spot is occupied by a man and has been so for all but twenty months in Massachusetts' history. Significant gains have been made in the congressional delegation, though it remains but one-third female. Approximately 30 percent of elected faces are women on town select boards and city councils, in mayors' offices, and in the state legislature.

ELECTED WOMEN OVER TIME: STATE LEGISLATURES

How do these numbers and state comparisons stack up over time? Perhaps 2018 and 2020 were politically unique election cycles. After all, some political observers heralded 2018 as another "year of the woman," as Democratic women rallied to run for office following Trump's election and the Kavanaugh Supreme Court nomination hearings. The 2020 election to potentially oust Trump saw significant gender appeals in campaigning, and the electorate was both highly polarized and voting during a pandemic. To answer this question, we turn to an in-depth analysis of women in New England state legislatures over time along with comparisons to U.S. state legislative averages. State legislature compositions are advantageous cases for comparison, as all fifty states have similar bodies[2]—as opposed to, say, various forms of local government. State legislatures are comparable objects across all cases (the states) and not burdened by the low numbers inherent in comparing New England congressional delegations—which range from three to eleven. In New England, only Massachusetts sends double digits to Congress. State legislative positions are usually more professionalized than local town representatives and serve as pipeline positions to higher office.

The data for Massachusetts and the other five New England states was compiled from the Center for American Women and Politics (CAWP) at Rutgers University. For the years 1921–73, the searchable database provided the raw number of female state senators and state representatives by state. From this, a longitudinal dataset was built. Each woman was coded too for their party affiliation, also recoverable via filters in the CAWP database. For the years 1975–2021, CAWP provides summary fact sheets reporting the percentage of women serving by state for each session. These percentages were entered directly into the longitudinal dataset. The summary fact sheets, however, did not provide partisanship breakdowns for years 1975–79. For these additional considerations, we returned to the searchable database. For race and ethnicity, each state was searched separately using the CAWP database. All women who served and were coded by CAWP as "multiracial," "Black/African American,"

2   Nebraska is the unicameral state legislature in 2021. Georgia, Pennsylvania, and Vermont were originally unicameral, but each switched to bicameral by 1830 (Minnesota Reference Library 2020).

"Hispanic/Latina," "Asian/Pacific Islander," "Middle Eastern/North African," "Native American," or "other" were entered into the longitudinal dataset. They were eventually combined for comparative state analyses because the *n* was so low across New England states in each singular category.

The resulting longitudinal data set provides the most comprehensive accounting of women and women of color serving in New England state legislatures since women won the right to vote.

WOMEN IN THE MASSACHUSETTS STATE LEGISLATURE OVER TIME WITH NEW ENGLAND AND U.S. COMPARISONS

Figure 11.1 provides the percentage of women among state legislators in Massachusetts from 1921 to 2021. The graph begins in 1921 because that is when women won the right to vote in all elections. Interestingly, though, Massachusetts did not concurrently grant women the right to vote and run for office as per the state attorney general's interpretation of the Nineteenth Amendment (Cox 1996, 151–52).[3] The state legislature did affirm the right to run by legislative decree in May 1921, officially sanctioning Massachusetts women to run for office in 1922. Two women did so and won. Among New England states, only Maine and Massachusetts did not immediately allow women to run for any elective office following ratification of the Nineteenth Amendment.

As is immediately evident from figure 11.1, women are almost nonexistent in the Massachusetts state legislature until the early 1970s. Substantial upward growth corresponds with the rise of second-wave women's organizing (Costain 1992). The period from the early and mid-1990s to 2017 is best described as stagnant, with small but substantively important increases in 2019 and 2021. Nonetheless, the fact remains that in the past approximately twenty-five years Massachusetts has held steady with between 25 and 31 percent of the legislature being female. Claims of steady and inevitable modern rise toward equity are unsubstantiated.

---

3 School committees were somewhat of an anomaly regarding the ability to run for office. The New England Women's Club pursued "a campaign to win representation for women on the Boston School Committee. In 1873, Abby May and Lucretia Crocker were elected to the Committee (by men only). The Committee, however, refused to allow them to take their seats after a challenge based upon their sex. In 1874 a special act of the legislature opened membership to women, and Abby May and five other women were elected. She was re-elected to a three-year term in 1875 but defeated in 1878. Her defeat may have been the stimulus in 1879 for reform action to win for women the right to vote in elections for members of school committees throughout Massachusetts." The ability to run and be seated was hard won, though it is also of note that women's service on school committees is not nearly as challenging to the cult of femininity as serving in the state legislature. See http://www.herhatwasinthering.org/biography.php?id=4205.

FIGURE 11.1. Percentage of Female State Legislators in Massachusetts, 1921–2021

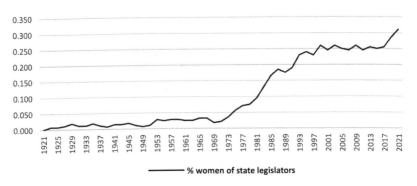

This trend line does not mask substantial or uneven gains in the Massachusetts House or Senate in the modern era. Figure 11.2 reveals that women disproportionately gained house seats through the turn of the new century. House seats are less prestigious, easier to win, and feeder positions to the more coveted senate seats, so this is not particularly surprising. However, figure 11.2 makes evident that this pattern flips in the late 1990s. Women make up a higher percentage of the state senate (hence not necessarily more positions) than in the house for most of this period, leveling to near parity between the two chambers in 2021.

FIGURE 11.2. Percentage of Female Legislators in Massachusetts House and Senate, 1921–2021

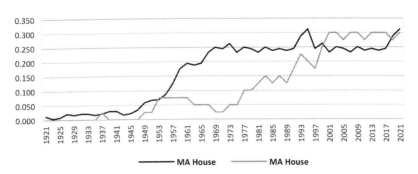

The 2021 figures that opened this chapter indicate that the current Massachusetts legislature is twenty-fourth among the fifty states in seating women and last in New England. But do these patterns hold over time? The answer is yes.

Let us compare the percentage of women in the Massachusetts legislature to the average percentage of women in the other forty-nine state legislatures. As figure 11.3 makes evident: Massachusetts and the U.S. state legislative averages are near mirror images. In 2021 they are both 31 percent. Massachusetts has been in the middle of the pack for electing women since the adoption of the Nineteenth Amendment. Although Massachusetts has significant abolitionist history (Ruchames 1955) and has been at the forefront of issues like national health care (Belluck 2006), gay marriage (Pew Research Center 2015), and transgender rights (Creamer 2018), when it comes to electing women to office, it has consistently been unexceptional.

FIGURE 11.3. Percentage of Women in the Massachusetts Legislature and U.S. State Legislative Average, 1921–2021

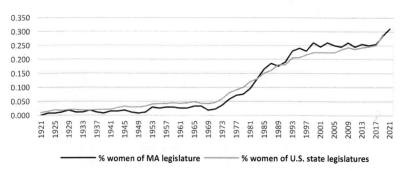

A regional comparison only underscores this conclusion. The fifty states differ widely in political culture, demographics, and party identification. Regional comparisons can help hold factors like political culture and values relatively constant. There are differences between the six New England states in political culture, of course, but they are far less pronounced than, say, between Massachusetts, Ohio, Hawaii, and Louisiana.

Massachusetts is currently last in New England for electing women to the state legislature. Figure 11.4 provides the data to determine whether this pattern holds over time. The X axis again begins at 1921 because it was on August 20, 1920, that the Nineteenth Amendment was ratified, providing women the right to vote (Terborg-Penn 1998).

FIGURE 11.4. Percentage of Female State Legislators across New England (1921–2021)

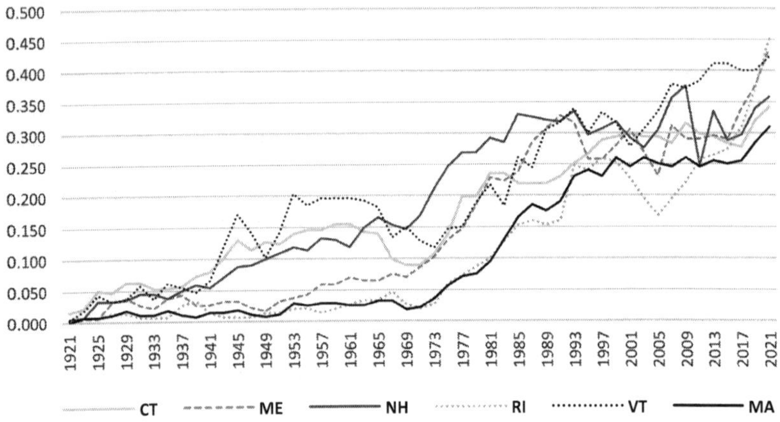

So is Massachusetts regionally wanting over time? Yes. Massachusetts, in solid dark black, vies only with Rhode Island over the hundred-year time span for "worst in show." Rhode Island, though, shifted dramatically to lead the New England region in 2021, while Massachusetts remained back of the pack. Nonetheless, figure 11.4 shows that differences between Massachusetts, Rhode Island, and the other four states over the one-hundred-year span are often dramatic. It is only in 1999 that the percentages come close to aligning. For our purposes, the major takeaway is that the 2021 Massachusetts snapshot is not an aberration. The Bay State is like the Red Sox of old—perpetually at the bottom of the division. Massachusetts is the regional laggard but reflective of the national average.

CURRENT STATUS: WOMEN OF COLOR

An intersectional perspective highlights the fact that women's experiences are far from the same in the United States (Davis 2001; Orleck 1995; Pharr 1988). When it comes to voting, political participation, and political opportunity, the story of the United States is that women of color have not enjoyed the material resources and voice won by the waves of women's organizing to the same degree as white women (O'Brien 2004). In the modern era, Black women in particular are the most loyal Democratic constituency (Akin 2018), but this loyalty at the polls has not translated to promotion in office proportionate to their turnout (CAWP 2019). Does Massachusetts follow this pattern?

The data says yes. In 2021 a mere 4.5 percent of Massachusetts state legislators were women of color. Parity does not necessarily mean equal percentages across all racial and ethnic categories in each state, as states differ in their degree of demographic diversity (McCann 2019). However, the distance between percentage of women of color in the legislature and percentage of women of color in the Massachusetts population is sizable: 4.5 percent versus 14.9 percent. The gap is a dramatic 10.4 percent.

Another illuminating cut on the data is to compare the percentage of women of color in the Massachusetts legislature with the percentage of WOC *among those women serving*. Even if the former is low, in the abstract, it is possible that the latter is high—that women of color constitute a substantial proportion of those women elected to serve.

This is not the case in Massachusetts.

Just 14.5 percent of the female state legislators serving are women of color. These are dismal statistics, indicating that the gains that have been made for electing women in the legislature are disproportionately enjoyed by white women.

Table 11.2 provides the Massachusetts figures cited above as well as the New England comparisons for 2021. Column 1 provides the best approximate percentage of women of color in each state's population. Column 2 lists the percentage of women of color among *all* state legislators. The stark takeaway in comparing the two columns is that all New England states woefully underperform in reflecting the proportion of WOC in their respective states at the state legislature level. However, Connecticut (-12.7) and Massachusetts (-10.4) stand out in the relative severity of their double-digit shortfalls. A potentially fair point is that Maine (-3.1), New Hampshire (-3.7), and Vermont (-2.6) have far smaller shortfalls, but these states are less diverse to begin with, making the substantive proportionate gaps just as important. Rhode Island is helpful in teasing out the Massachusetts implications. Rhode Island's diversity in the population is similar to Massachusetts and Connecticut—women of color make up between 14 and 17 percent of each state. Rhode Island's gap between WOC in the population and WOC in the legislature is but 5 points, though both Massachusetts and Connecticut at least double that shortfall. All New England states are wanting, but Massachusetts and Connecticut, as diverse states, are particularly behind.

TABLE 11.2. State Legislative Offices
and Women of Color, 2021

	WOC IN POPULATION (%)	WOC IN LEGISLATURE (%)	WOC OF FEMALE LEGISLATORS (%)
MASSACHUSETTS	14.9	4.5	14.5
CONNECTICUT	17.5	4.8	14.1
MAINE	3.6	.5	1.2
NEW HAMPSHIRE	5.1	1.4	3.9
RHODE ISLAND	14.7	9.7	21.6
VERMONT	3.7	1.1	2.6
UNITED STATES	20.3	7.5a	25.5a

Data from: Figures for computing WOC in state population data from: US Census Bureau QuickFacts. WOC in legislature obtained using CAWP "women elected officials by race/ethnicity" database. WOC as percentage of female legislators: database results divided by total women serving via CAWP.

a Summary statistic is as of December 31, 2020.

The last row in table 11.2 provides the average for U.S. state legislatures. In 2021 the U.S. population was approximately 20.3 percent women of color, but only 7.5 percent of state legislators fell into this broad category. The 12.8 percent gap generally reflects the Massachusetts gap of 10.4 and Connecticut's 12.7-point deficit. Massachusetts is second to last in New England and slightly better than the U.S. average.

The third column of data provides the percentage of women of color *among the women elected to each state's legislature.* Here again, the results are alarming. Only in one state, Rhode Island, are more than 20 percent of the women who serve of color. We can gain further illumination through a comparison of the data in column 3, that is, percentage of WOC *among women in the legislature,* with the percentage of women of color who reside in the state, that is, column 1. Compelling arguments can definitely be made that WOC should be overrepresented in the legislature *and among women in the legislature* given the historical legacies of discrimination, bias, and differential material reward from women's organizing. Only Rhode Island meets the latter metric—14.7 percent of the population is WOC, while 21.6 percent of the women in the state legislature are WOC. Using the more conservative benchmark that WOC's representation *among women serving* should reflect the proportion of women of color in the state, all other New England states fall short. The percentage of WOC living in Massachusetts is 14.9 percent, while the percentage of WOC *among women in office* is 14.5 percent. Vermont (-1.1), New Hampshire (-1.2), Maine (-2.4), and Connecticut (-3.4) follow in sequential order. Thus, while the differences between WOC in the population and legislature are dramatic, and especially so in Massachusetts and Connecticut, when we look the WOC as a percentage of women serving, Massachusetts and the New England states—especially Rhode Island—fare better.

Turning again to the final row of table 11.2, which provides the U.S. comparisons, we see that women of color are drastically underrepresented as a percentage of all state legislators versus numbers in the U.S. population (7.5 percent versus 20.3 percent). However, *among female legislators serving*, WOC make up a *higher* percentage than they do of the U.S. population—25.5 percent of women serving versus 20.3 percent of the population. Thus, Rhode Island mirrors the overrepresentation on this metric, while all other New England states fall short of the U.S. average.

The major takeaway is that WOC are not represented proportionate to their numbers within New England state legislatures. This is layer one of representational bias. Massachusetts and Connecticut are neck-and-neck as the region's biggest offenders. Layer two of representational bias is that among the already depleted percentage of women in the legislature, women of color now make up almost the same percentage of women serving as they do in the Massachusetts population. The small deficit in Massachusetts is a bitter pill considering that based on the U.S. average, WOC are overrepresented as a percentage of women serving in state legislatures.

WOMEN OF COLOR, 1973–2021: MASSACHUSETTS AND THE NEW ENGLAND LEGISLATURES

Comparisons over time do little to complicate these takeaways. Figure 11.5 compares the percentage of female state legislators in Massachusetts (the gray line) to the percentage of WOC in the whole of the Massachusetts state legislature (the black line). The graph begins in 1973 as this is the first year Massachusetts elected a woman of color. Doing so punctuates the 2021 cross-sectional findings. The gains that have been made over time in women's representation have been enjoyed almost exclusively by white women in Massachusetts. The gap largely gets worse as the years progress, showing no evidence of significant modern narrowing.

FIGURE 11.5. Percentages of Women and WOC in
Massachsetts' Legislature, 1973–2021

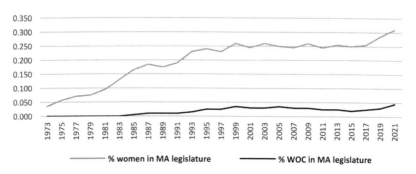

The dismal picture for representation of women of color in New England, and Massachusetts in particular, looks bleaker through a longitudinal lens. Figure 11.6 provides this perspective. At no point in the forty-eight years under review has any New England state reached even 10 percent of the legislature being WOC. The all-time high is in Rhode Island in 2021—with 9.7 percent of legislators. No other state, including Massachusetts, ever cracks 5 percent.

FIGURE 11.6. Percentage WOC in
New England State Legislatures, 1973–2021

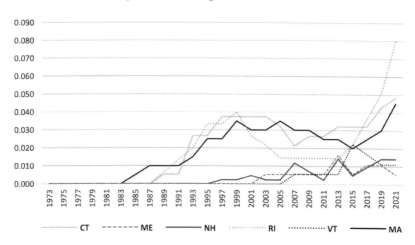

SO WHAT HAVE WE LEARNED?

It is easy to get bogged down in all the statistics and data. Stepping back, what conclusions can we draw about how exceptional Massachusetts is in electing women to office? First, the good news: substantial gains have been made in the number of women serving in the Massachusetts congressional delegation and in statewide constitutional offices. In 2021 both of these delegations offer the most gender diversity in the commonwealth's history, though they remain stagnant from 2019. The first woman of color elected to the Massachusetts congressional delegation occurred in 2018. Attorney General Maura Healey, elected in 2014, is the nation's first openly gay attorney general (Johnson 2014).

Yet it took until 2018 to elect a woman of color to Congress, and Massachusetts only recently elected their first female senator in 2013. A woman has never been popularly elected to the governorship, and none of the 2021 statewide elected constitutional officers are women of color. These facts hint at the more prevailing takeaway from a full review of the evidence. When it comes to electing women to office, Massachusetts is not exceptional and can best be described as average among the fifty states and poor among the New England states.

Why Is Massachusetts So Average?

If you go to a physician who tells you that your health is about average but way worse than your neighbors, you are apt to be concerned. You want a diagnosis, an explanation, a way to fix it. The second half of this chapter offers just that. What follows is an explication of what political science suggests could be to blame for Massachusetts' lackluster record in electing women, why these explanations actually provide little insight for the commonwealth, and the subsequent reasons comparative state analysis indicates that Massachusetts actually performs poorly.

POTENTIAL CAUSES: POLITICAL SCIENCE EXPLANATIONS
FOR WHY FEWER WOMEN SERVE IN OFFICE

Political science scholarship offers ample explanations for why American women are elected to office less frequently. The explanations are often mutually reinforcing—they work together to explain why U.S. women trail men in office. As we will see, the scholarship is well developed but wanting in its explanation for why Massachusetts is at the back of the New England pack. In fact, it suggests that Massachusetts should lead the region and the nation.

But first the explanations. They include sex-role stereotypes and discrimination, family responsibilities, leaky pipelines, and an ambition gap between young men and women.

Sex-role stereotypes are exactly what you think. These are long-held American cultural expectations that women are best tasked in the private realm where they are thought to naturally thrive. The "softer sex" is nurturing—more caretaker than leader. Stereotypes of men are that they are best suited to the public realm—where politics resides—as they are natural leaders, competitors, and outward facing. The rigidity of stereotypes has certainly lessened in the last forty years, but, consciously or not, voters and party leaders are still socialized to them (Sigel 1996). Male candidates thus start with the cultural expectation that they belong in politics, whereas female candidates are more likely to need to prove they are "tough enough" for office while taking into account that they are more likely to receive attention for "likability" and ability to balance a family with political office. Even in the 2016 presidential contest, analysis of news coverage revealed that then candidate Trump was more likely to be covered as an expert and in terms of dominance than Secretary Clinton (Duerst-Lahti and Oakley 2018). Sometimes these stereotypes can boost female candidates, but, more often, they come with larger drawbacks: "Research shows that voters historically give women . . . a virtue advantage, but then the other side is that they punish [women] for any real or manufactured infraction" (Astor 2019). Female candidates negotiate murkier expectations as to their fitness for office, what criteria make them fit for office, and what factors they weigh when considering a run because of sex-role stereotypes (Fox, Lawless, and Feeley 2001). Stereotypes make it harder for women to conceive of themselves running while encouraging both men and women to default to male names when thinking of who should be recruited to run.

Differential family responsibilities flow from sex-role stereotypes so that, as a simple matter of time, women have less of it to run for office. Major changes, however, have occurred in American public opinion in terms of endorsing equitable division of family responsibilities (Luker 1996; Sigel 1996). Strong majorities of men and women agree, but agreement is not necessarily action. Time-budget analyses and polling still indicate that women take on a much larger share of family responsibilities in married heterosexual relationships (Parker 2015a; Bianchi et al. 2012). The subsequent time constraints leave many women to run later in life (Mariani 2008), making it harder for them to reach the top spots and gain equity with male officeholders (McGlen el al. 2010).

Sex-role stereotypes and discrimination deplete the pipeline of women who consider running, and disproportionate family responsibilities present real hurdles to these women who, consequently, are more apt to drop out of the race than men (Carroll and Sanbonmatsu 2013, 28–33). This is true despite the fact that women are now more likely than men to graduate college and enroll in graduate school (DiPrete and Buchmann 2013)—which would seemingly up the pool of eligible women who are considered viable candidates. Time away from paid work to raise children and disproportionate family responsibilities, nevertheless, produce those pesky leaks in the candidate pipeline. Women are also more likely to need to be asked to run—meaning they are less likely to "naturally" think they are candidate material (Lawless and Fox 2010). This too shrinks the pool of female candidates.

Political socialization produces a marked difference in political ambition between young men and women (Fox and Lawless 2014). In high school, boys and girls are equally likely to report they would be willing to run for office, but, by the end of college, women are 50 percent less likely than men to consider running (Fox and Lawless 2014, 500). This ambition gap persists and helps explain why the pool of female candidates is not on a rapid ascent.

POLITICAL SCIENCE'S DIAGNOSES JUST DON'T FIT MASSACHUSETTS

The trouble with all these well-documented reasons that women run for elected office less frequently is that they just do not do a good job at explaining Massachusetts. To return to our metaphorical doctor's visit, it is as if the doctor ran all the right lab work to discern why you are the sickest in the neighborhood, *but* the results suggest you should be an Olympian. Said differently, Massachusetts runs hot with the very factors predicted to elevate women to elected office. It then follows that Massachusetts should be clear and away the regional leader for percentage of women in the state legislature and well atop the American states. This just is not the case.

Table 11.3 provides the New England state rankings for degree of religiosity, educational attainment, women with a bachelor's degree or higher, women's median earnings, and women in full-time managerial or professional positions. These rankings provide empirical evidence for the disjuncture between factors that typically impede women in office and the realities in Massachusetts.

TABLE 11.3. New England State Rankings on Factors
Associated with Electing Women

	MA	CT	ME	NH	RI	VT
LEAST RELIGIOUS	1 (tie)	3	2 (tie)	1 (tie)	15	2 (tie)
EDUCATIONAL ATTAINMENT	1	6	20	8	17	7
WOMEN, BA OR HIGHER	2	5	22	8	16	6
WOMEN, MEDIAN EARNINGS	3	5	22	13	7	18
WOMEN IN MANAGERIAL/ PROFESSIONAL	3	6	21	5	19	10

Data from: Religiosity: Pew Charitable Trusts, "Religious Landscape Study," November 2015. Educational attainment: "America's Most and Least Educated States." September 2018. Women-specific factors: Institute for Women's Policy Research, state fact sheets, 2017 release, 2015 data.

Take sex-role stereotypes, for example. Looking at the state's data, we see Massachusetts is one of the two least religious states, ranks first for overall educational attainment, and ranks second for women's higher educational attainment. It is third among the fifty states, and first in New England, for both women's median earnings and percentage of women in full-time managerial or professional jobs. All this does not make Massachusetts residents immune from experiencing or endorsing sex-role stereotypes, but higher educational attainment and lower religiosity are associated with challenging them (Cassese and Holman 2016; McGinn and Oh 2017). Women with professional jobs and earnings to match actively reject many of those stereotypes and model the same to others. Commonwealth residents *see* this day to day. All of New England does well on these marks, but Massachusetts excels. Yet it is comparatively poor at electing women.

Family responsibilities still fall disproportionately on women, but higher education rates are correlated with rejecting this idea as the "proper" state of affairs (Sigel 1996). The relationship between social class and family roles is complicated, but women with higher earnings, with higher education, and in professional roles have more disposable income to hire out for help. Professional women still do more of the inflexible family work, emergencies, and child care (Parker 2015b; Cohen 2017), but they are more resourced when doing so. They can stay on the job. So it is not that Massachusetts is a woman's panacea for shared household management. It is just that compared to other states, women are in a political culture that promotes equity and are better resourced to negotiate their disproportionate responsibilities. This should translate to more rapid gains in elected office. It has not.

The rankings in table 11.3 would also suggest that pipeline challenges and ambition gaps would be at their lowest levels in Massachusetts. Again, women in the commonwealth are second in the United States for obtaining higher education (first in New England) and third in the percentage who work in professional positions (first in New England). This should build a pipeline of ambitious candidates. To the extent religiosity is associated with traditional feminine norms that curtail women's ambition for higher office, being the least religious state should bolster the desire to run and run earlier—perhaps while having kids and not after.

State rankings, of course, are blunt indicators. But combined, they paint a compelling picture. Compared to other states, Massachusetts seemingly has all the right ingredients to be a leader in electing women not only regionally but also nationally. Deciding to both run and then subsequently winning is always a complicated equation, but, in Massachusetts, key variables seem uniquely hospitable for women entering office.

SO WHAT GIVES, MASSACHUSETTS? PARTY POLITICS AND CARE WORK

So what gives? What explains the puzzle of why Massachusetts underperforms? Two explanations emerge. The first is fairly intuitive and harks back to family responsibilities. The second will be counterintuitive to many readers who know that the Democratic Party currently far outpaces the Republican Party in electing women and that Massachusetts has been dominated by Democrats since the 1950s. Though counterintuitive, it is precisely this dominance that is to blame.

First, family responsibilities. Table 11.4 below replicates the prior state rankings but with two vital additions—child care and elder/dependent care. Both are drawn from the Institute for Women's Policy Research 2015 report "The Status of Women in the States." The child-care index captures the average annual cost of full-time infant care in a child-care center and the cost of infant care as a percentage of women's full-time, year-round median annual earnings. The elder and dependent care encapsulates how expansive policy supports are for elder and dependent care as well as the amount of assistance home health-care aides can offer.[4]

---

4   Specifically, the child-care index includes whether unemployment insurance covers family care, if dependent-care credits are limited to child care, and whether the dependent-care credit is refundable. The elder- and dependent-care index includes the maximum monetary dependent-care credit and the number of long-term support services that can be delegated to a home health-care agency worker.

TABLE 11.4. Care Work and the New England State Rankings

	MA	CT	ME	NH	RI	VT
CHILD-CARE INDEX	49	37	27 (tie)	42	40	27 (tie)
ELDER- AND DEPENDENT-CARE INDEX	37	27	7	14	33	8
LEAST RELIGIOUS	1 (tie)	3	2 (tie)	1 (tie)	15	2 (tie)
EDUCATIONAL ATTAINMENT	1	6	20	8	17	7
WOMEN, BA OR HIGHER	2	5	22	8	16	6
WOMEN, MEDIAN EARNINGS	3	5	22	13	7	18
WOMEN IN MANAGERIAL/ PROFESSIONAL	3	6	21	5	19	10

Data from: Religiosity: Pew Charitable Trusts, "Religious Landscape Study," November 2015. Educational attainment: "America's Most and Least Educated States," September 2018. Women-specific factors: Institute for Women's Policy Research, state fact sheets, 2017 release, 2015 data. Elder- and child-care indices: Institute for Women's Policy Research, "The Status of Women in the United States, 2015," methodological appendix.

My, how the mighty have fallen. New England as a whole fares poorly, but Massachusetts is abhorrent. No other New England state performs as poorly on either metric—adding credence to chapter 9's conclusion that Massachusetts is slipping as a policy innovator. For child-care affordability, Massachusetts is forty-ninth among the fifty states as well as last in New England for elder and dependent care. Maine, Vermont, and New Hampshire are all in the top fifteen for elder and dependent care, while Massachusetts is a dismal thirty-seventh in the nation. The child-care index—which measures child-care affordability, in part, as a percentage of women's median earnings—for Massachusetts is particularly striking. Massachusetts is third in the nation with respect to women's median earnings, but child-care costs far exceed the strength of those earnings.

We have already reviewed how men and women express support for the equal sharing of family responsibilities but not how these responsibilities, in reality, fall disproportionately on women in heterosexual relationships. Whatever the positives of Massachusetts' political culture, the fact that earnings are uniquely overtaken by child-care costs suggests that the day-to-day lived experience of women with kids in the commonwealth is not conducive to running for office. Resources are stretched thin, and, for many potential candidates, the costs are too prohibitive. Leaving the paid labor market, or taking a break from it, constricts the pipeline and induces many potential candidates to delay running for office.

The elder- and dependent-care ranking tells a similar story. On this index too, Massachusetts women experience the most burdensome terrain in New England. They do far more paid and unpaid care work than men and suffer under inhospitable policies while doing so (Albelda et al. 2010). The time and stress of coordinating this work and actually providing it fall disproportionately on women in the commonwealth. This too draws women out of the pipeline and away from political ambition—no matter the other advantages in professional experience, higher education, and median earnings. In no other New England state is the context so dire for child care, elder care, and dependent support. It is easy to see how this directly impacts women's ambition and ability to run for office in the Bay State.

The second explanation for underperformance, Massachusetts party politics, requires some unpacking. The National Conference of State Legislatures documents that Republican women accounted for 32.3 percent of state legislators in 2021. This is up from 31 percent in 2019 but still trails the 38 percent indicative of 2018. The Republican Party's modern weakness in advancing women to state legislative office extends beyond this temporal snapshot (Carroll and Sanbonmatsu 2013) and level of office (Astor 2019). Though Republican women saw gains in Congress during the 2020 election cycle, "women make up a much bigger share of congressional Democrats (38%) than Republican (14%). Across both chambers, there are 106 Democratic women and 38 Republican women in [2021]. Women account for 40% of House Democrats and 32% of Senate Democrats, compared with 14% of House Republicans and 16% of Senate Republicans" (Blazina and DeSilver 2021).

Democrats currently excel at electing women, and they dominate Massachusetts in both the electorate and elected office. In 2021 Massachusetts voters registered Democratic over Republican to the tune of three to one (Galvin 2021). The entire congressional delegation is Democratic. Democrats enjoy supermajority status in the state house and senate. Even in heavily Democratic New England, as table 11.5 shows on the left-hand side, Massachusetts stands out. Along with Connecticut and Rhode Island, Democrats enjoy filibuster-proof majorities, with Massachusetts and Rhode Island having the greatest partisan imbalance.

TABLE 11.5. Relative New England Democratic Party Strength

	STATE PARTY BREAKDOWN, 2021			LEGISLATIVE PARTY SHIFTS SINCE 1959
	House (D/R/I/L/P)	Senate (D/R)	Governor	
MASSACHUSETTS	129/30/1	37/3	R	0
CONNECTICUT	97/54	24/12	D	12
MAINE	80/66/4/1	22/13	D	14
NEW HAMPSHIRE	186/212a	10/14	R	12
RHODE ISLAND	65/10	33/5	D	0
VERMONT	92/46/5/7	21/7	R	8

a Two vacancies as of June 2021.

Furthermore, this dominance is no anomaly—chapter 7, on political parties and elections, and chapter 4, on the state legislature, drive home this point. A Republican last served in the House of Representatives from Massachusetts more than twenty years ago, and Republican senator Scott Brown shocked the country by winning a special election in 2010 only to lose in 2012. Before that, the last Massachusetts Republican U.S. senator left office in 1979. Democrats have controlled both chambers of the state legislature since 1959. The right-hand side of table 11.5 shows how, again, only Massachusetts and Rhode Island are so solidly blue. This column measures party shifts in the state legislature—times since 1959 when either chamber flipped parties (from D to R or R to D). Connecticut has seen eight such shifts from 1959 to 2021. Maine has seen fourteen, New Hampshire twelve, and Vermont eight. The dominance extends to the electorate as well. At least since 1948, when voter registration data is first available, Massachusetts voters have registered as Democrats over Republicans. The margin first reached two to one in the late 1960s and has fluctuated around three to one since 1984 (Galvin 2021).[5]

This party dominance has meant that when women win in Massachusetts, they are almost exclusively Democrats. Since 1999 more than 80 percent of women in the legislature have been Democratic. In 2021 it is at 90 percent. But proportions can conceal important phenomena. The black line in

---

5 In 2019, unenrolled voters made up more than half of the electorate.

FIGURE 11.7. Percentage of Massachusetts Female Legislators Who Are Democrats, 1975–2021

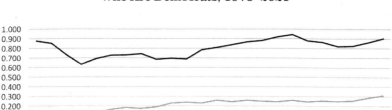

figure 11.7 represents the percentage of Democratic women serving in the Massachusetts legislature among all women serving beginning in 1975, as this is the first year women were over 5 percent of Massachusetts legislators. The gray line reminds of the vital context that Massachusetts women are making slow overall gains—last in New England.

Single-party dominance over time shoulders much of the blame for that gray line. Yes, Democrats do better than Republicans in electing women in Massachusetts, but if they were tightly vying with one another at the polls, both parties would do better at forwarding female officeholders. Foundational work on political parties understood that electoral competition encourages parties to expand their electoral base by mobilizing new constituencies (Key 1949; Schattschneider 1942; Schattschneider 1960, 95; Rosenstone and Hansen 1993). So, when Democrats and Republicans are evenly matched, they fight to expand their base with untapped constituencies.[6] Running more diverse faces is a popular strategy for doing so (Sanbonmatsu 2002). Party competition shakes up *both* parties.

This is hardly the case in Massachusetts, as we have just seen. Democrats and Republicans have not been tightly matched for generations in either electoral or legislative contexts. Yes, Republican governors enjoy success in Massachusetts, but they are the anomaly. The point is that the Democratic Party has not had to reinvent itself in decades. Old dogs do not learn new

---

6   A contrasting view suggests that tight electoral competition encourages demobilization of the other party's core constituencies (Piven, Minnite, and Groarke 2009; Piven and Cloward 1988; Keyssar 2011). With Keith Bentele, I have uncovered this empirically elsewhere (Bentele and O'Brien 2014). The mobilization or demobilization question, however, agrees that sans electoral competition, the dominant party will not look to innovate their base.

tricks—unless, in the case of parties, electoral vulnerability forces them to. As we saw in chapter 1, interviews with Massachusetts political observers and candidates, especially female observers and candidates, regularly emphasize that the Democratic Party is an "old boys' club" (Colarusso 2019). Empirical evidence indicates that strong party structures undermine women's presence in the state legislature (Sanbonmatsu 2002). Democratic Party dominance in Massachusetts began in 1959—hardly an era of women's empowerment. The party apparatus that has been so electorally successfully developed and matured as the Republican Party withered. Without competition, expanding the pool of candidates lagged on both sides of the aisle: same old, same old, without any pressure to change.

Here a return to table 11.5 is helpful. Only Massachusetts and Rhode Island have seen zero party shifts within the legislature since 1959. These states are the only ones with supermajorities in both chambers. And, from 1959 on, these two New England states are most wanting in the representation of women (and highest in corruption) for all but three terms. Massachusetts is among the bottom two in all cycles but one and remains last in 2021.

Party threat breeds creativity—the shaking of norms. The men who have long dominated Democratic Party circles in Massachusetts have largely felt neither. Even the good news of increased representation of Massachusetts women in congressional and executive offices bolsters the thesis. Among the most celebrated are Congresswomen Pressley and Attorney General Healey. Both ran primary contests against white men backed by the state's Democratic establishment—Michael Capuano and Warren Tolman, respectively. The women now celebrated for advancing the status of women in Massachusetts politics did so by challenging the party apparatus. They won *despite* the old boys' club. Thirty-two-year Democratic Massachusetts congressman Barney Frank (1981–2013) illustrated the hostility institutional Democrats voiced when Pressley challenged Capuano in the Democratic primary. At the time, he argued that it was a "fight that is being generated by personality and ego, with zero issues. The last thing liberals need at this point is to have fights. . . . When Mike Capuano retires, it would be very good for other people to run" (Lips 2018).

Astute readers will note that while Rhode Island has been a longitudinal laggard, fates changed dramatically in 2019 and, especially, 2021. Rhode Island topped New England for women in the legislature in 2021 and is the only New England state where the percentage of WOC among female legislators outpaces the percentage of WOC in the state. Does this undermine the single-party thesis? Not a bit.

A deep dive into Rhode Island politics reveals that since 2016 the Ocean State has seen a de facto party challenge between the Democratic Party establishment and well-organized progressive challengers. The dramatic uptick in women's representation, and WOC, in Rhode Island followed the 2020 cycle where various progressives ran, and regularly won, primary challenges. The Rhode Island Political Cooperative "founded by veteran Ocean State lefties," the local Sunrise Movement, Reclaim Rhode Island "made up of former Bernie Sanders organizers," the Democratic Socialists of America, and the Working Families Party all recruited candidates and provided valuable infrastructure to challenge the "party establishment." They faced "nearly two dozen insurgents challenging establishment politicians" (Grim 2020). So, consistent with the thesis, Rhode Island legislators became more diverse when interparty competition became a realized threat. No such statewide well-funded, well-organized interparty threat with primary challengers has come to the Massachusetts state legislature.

Single-party dominance is thus a major barrier to seeing more women in elected office in the Bay State. It produces inertia in each party. This explanation does not delve into the policy debate as to whether a Democrat or a Republican in office is better for women writ large. Rather, it focuses on the very centered, and important, question of why Massachusetts trails in electing women, locating the cause in the inherent problem associated with extended party dominance. Typically, looking beyond existing candidate-selection processes transpires in response to electoral competition over time, which Massachusetts Democrats have largely not experienced.

Conclusion

In 1858 Oliver Wendell Holmes wrote that the "Boston Statehouse is the hub of the solar system. You couldn't pry that out of a Boston man, if you had the tire of all creation straightened out for a crowbar." As any New Englander not living in Massachusetts will tell you, Bostonians and Massachusetts residents still believe, and embrace, the city's nickname of "the HUB," understanding themselves as the leaders of New England. Ironically, the actual hub Holmes referred to, the Massachusetts State House, is the Jupiter of New England—outer rung, dead last for electing women.

Yes, as this chapter has shown, there have been gains in Congress and statewide constitutional offices. But with respect to all other positions, women make up but 25–31 percent of those elected. When women make inroads at the State House, these gains are concentrated among white women. These trends hold over time. And though Massachusetts would seem fertile ground for electing women, the high costs and comparative policy burdens of child care, elder care, and dependent care undermine the pipeline of women who may run. More surprisingly, the dominance of Democrats has hurt too. Most women in Massachusetts' elected offices are Democrats, but the lack of party competition between Republicans and Democrats has stymied both parties from reinventing themselves with women at the electoral fore.

So how can Massachusetts improve? Leadership and candidate training schools are a good start, and, thankfully, many exist in Massachusetts. Policy changes that address the exorbitant cost of child care and lessen difficulties of care work would keep women in the pipeline. Relationships that both endorse and act to truly share care responsibilities would too. And though Democratic women and men might feel ambivalent, a Republican Party that is a threat at the ballot box would help substantially.

From the perspective of leadership among the states, Massachusetts needs a kick to become exceptional for electing women.

WORKS CITED

Akin, Stephanie. 2018. "Black Voters Propelled Blue Wave, Study Finds." *Roll Call*, November 19, 2018. https://www.rollcall.com/2018/11/19/black-voters-propelled-blue-wave -study-finds/.

Albelda, Randy, Mignon Duffy, Nancy Folbre, Clare Hammonds, and Jooyeoun Suh. 2010. "Placing a Value on Care Work." *Federal Reserve Bank of Boston* (Winter): 6–10.

Astor, Maggie. 2019. "'It Can't Be Worse': How Republican Women Are Trying to Rebuild." *New York Times*, July 9, 2019. https://www.nytimes.com/2019/07/09/us/politics /republican-women-congress.html.

Beck, Susan Abrams. 2001. "Acting as Women: The Effects and Limitations of Gender in Local Governance." In *The Impact of Women in Elected Office*, edited by Susan Carroll, 49–67. Bloomington: Indiana University Press.

Belluck, Pam. 2006. "Massachusetts Set to Offer Universal Health Insurance." *New York Times*, April 4, 2006. https://www.nytimes.com/2006/04/04/us/massachusetts-set-to -offer-universal-health-insurance.html.

Bentele, Keith, and Erin O'Brien. 2014. "Jim Crow 2.0? Why States Consider and Adopt Restrictive Voter Access Policies." *Perspectives on Politics* 11, no. 4: 1088–1116.

Bianchi, Suzanne, Liana Sayer, Melissa Milkie, and John Robinson. 2012. "Housework: Who Did, Does or Will Do I, and How Much Does It Matter?" *Social Forces* 91, no. 1: 55–63.

Blazina, Carrie, and Drew DeSilver. 2021. "A Record Number of Women Are Serving in the 117th Congress." Pew Research Center, January 15, 2021. https://www.pewresearch.org/fact-tank/2021/01/15/a-record-number-of-women-are-serving-in-the-117th-congress/.

Boles, Janet. 2001. "Local Elected Women and Policy-Making: Movement Delegates or Feminist Trustees." In *The Impact of Women in Elected Office*, edited by Susan Carroll, 68–86. Bloomington: Indiana University Press.

Carroll, Susan, and Kira Sanbonmatsu. 2013. *More Women Can Run: Gender and Pathways to the State Legislatures*. New York: Oxford University Press.

Cassese, Erin, and Mirya Holman. 2016. "Religious Beliefs, Gender Consciousness, and Women's Political Participation." *Sex Roles* 75, nos. 9–10: 514–27.

Center for Women in American Politics (CAWP). 2021a. "Facts: Women in State Legislatures." Eagleton Institute of Politics, Rutgers University, Rutgers, NJ.

———. 2021b. "Facts: Women of Color in Elective Office." Eagleton Institute of Politics, Rutgers University, Rutgers, NJ.

———. 2021c. "State Fact Sheet—Connecticut."

———. 2021d. "State Fact Sheet—Maine."

———. 2021e. "State Fact Sheet—Massachusetts."

———. 2021f. "State Fact Sheet—New Hampshire."

———. 2021g. "State Fact Sheet—Rhode Island."

———. 2021h. "State Fact Sheet—Vermont."

Chan, Tackey (Rep). 2016. "First Asian American Caucus Formed in Mass. House of Representatives." *Patriot Ledger*, May 21, 2016. https://www.patriotledger.com/opinion/20160521/rep-tackey-chan-quincy-first-asian-american-caucus-formed-in-mass-house-of-representatives.

Cohen, Patricia. 2017. "Why Women Quit Working: It's Not for the Reasons Men Do." *New York Times*, January 24, 2017. https://www.nytimes.com/2017/01/24/business/economy/women-labor-force.html.

Colarusso, Laure. 2019. "'Original Old Boys' Club.'" WGBH, March 24, 2019. https://www.wgbh.org/news/original-old-boys-club.

Costain, Anne. 1992. *Inviting Women's Rebellion: A Political Interpretation of the Women's Movement*. Baltimore: John Hopkins University Press.

Cox, Elizabeth. 1996. *Women and State Territorial Legislators, 1895–1995*. Darby, PA: Diane.

Creamer, Lisa. 2018. "Mass. Votes 'Yes' on Question 3 to Keep Law Protecting Transgender People in Public Accommodations." WBUR, November 6, 2018. https://www.wbur.org/news/2018/11/06/question-3-transgender-ballot-yes-wins.

Davis, Angela. 2011. *Women, Race, and Class*. New York: Vintage Books.

DiPrete, Thomas, and Claudia Buchmann. 2013. *The Rise of Women: The Growing Gender Gap in Education and What It Means for American Schools*. New York: Russell Sage Foundation.

Dolan, Julie, Melissa Deckman, and Michele Swers. 2020. *Women and Politics: Paths to Power and Political Influence*. Lanham, MD: Rowman and Littlefield.

Duerst-Lahti, Georgia, and Madison Oakley. 2018. "Presidential Elections." In *Gender and Elections*, edited by Susan Carroll and Richard Fox, 15–47. Cambridge: Cambridge University Press.

Fox, Richard, and Jennifer L. Lawless. 2014. "Uncovering the Origins of the Gender Gap in Political Ambition." *American Political Science Review* 108, no. 3: 499–519.

Fox, Richard, Jennifer L. Lawless, and Courtney Feeley. 2001. "Gender and the Decision to Run for Office." *Legislative Studies Quarterly* 26, no. 3: 411–35.

Galvin, William. 2021. "Massachusetts Registered Voter Enrollment, 1948–2021." Secretary of the Commonwealth of Massachusetts. https://www.sec.state.ma.us/ele/eleenr/enridx.htm.

Grim, Ryan, 2020. "Rhode Island's Progressive Wave Was Four Years in the Making." *Intercept.* September 11, 2020. https://theintercept.com/2020/09/11/rhode-island-democrat-primary-progressive-wave/.

Institute for Women's Policy Research. 2017. "The Status of Women in the States—2015." https://statusofwomendata.org/references/.

Johnson, Akilah. 2014. "Maura Healey Setting Her Course as Attorney General." *Boston Globe,* November 12, 2014. https://www.bostonglobe.com/metro/2014/11/12/maura-healey-will-nation-first-openly-gay/80FGXxzaV6RKssW5jktmjL/story.html.

Key, V. O., Jr. 1949. *Southern Politics in State and Nation.* New York: Alfred A. Knopf.

Keyssar, Alexander. 2011. "How Americans Vote." *Election Law Journal: Rules, Politics, and Policy* 10, no. 4: 471–73.

Lawless, Jennifer, and Richard Fox. 2010. *It Still Takes a Candidate.* Cambridge: Cambridge University Press.

Lips, Evan. 2018. "Barney Frank on Boston City Councilor's Bid to Primary Capuano for Congress." *NewBostonPost,* March 8, 2018. https://newbostonpost.com/2018/03/08/barney-frank-on-boston-city-councilors-bid-to-primary-capuano-for-congress-politics-at-its-most-egotistical/.

Luker, Kristin. 1996. *Dubious Conceptions: The Politics of Teenage Pregnancy.* Cambridge, MA: Harvard University Press.

Mariani, Mack. 2008. "A Gendered Pipeline? The Advancement of State Legislators to Congress in Five States." *Politics & Gender* 4:285–308.

McCann, Adam. 2019. "Most and Least Diverse States in the United States." *Wallethub,* September 17, 2019.

McGinn, Kathleen, and Eunsil Oh. 2017. "Gender, Social Class, and Women's Employment." *Current Opinion in Psychology* 18:84–88.

McGlen, Nancy, Karen O'Connor, Laura van Assendelft, and Wendy Gunther-Canada. 2010. *Women, Politics, and American Society.* 5th ed. Boston: Longman.

Minnesota Reference Library. 2020. "Minnesota Issues Resource Guides: Unicameral Legislatures." https://www.leg.mn.gov/lrl/guides/guides?issue=uni.

National Conference of State Legislatures. 2011. "Annual versus Biennial Legislative Sessions." https://www.ncsl.org/research/about-state-legislatures/annual-vs-biennial-legislative-sessions.aspx#:~:text=The%20biennial%20system%20affords%20legislators,and%20to%20campaign%20for%20reelection.&text=timely%20and%20orderly-,5.,brought%20together%20twice%20as%20often.

Nelson, Albert J. 1991. *The Emerging Influentials in State Legislatures: Women, Blacks, and Hispanics.* Westport, CT: Praeger.

O'Brien, Erin. 2004. "The Double-Edged Sword of Women's Organizing: Poverty and the Emergence of Racial and Class Differences in Women's Policy Priorities." *Women & Politics* 26, nos. 3–4: 25–56.

Orleck, Annelise. 1995. "Common Sense: New York City Working Women and the Struggle for Woman Suffrage." In *Common Sense and a Little Fire: Women and Working Class Politics in the United States, 1900–1965,* 87–113. Chapel Hill: University of North Carolina Press.

Parker, Kim. 2015a. "Despite Progress, Women Still Bear Heavier Load than Men in Balancing Work and Family." Pew Research Center. https://www.pewresearch.org/fact-tank/2015/03/10/women-still-bear-heavier-load-than-men-balancing-work-family/.

———. 2015b. "Women More than Men Adjust Their Careers for Family Life." Pew Research Center. Last modified October 1, 2015. https://www.pewresearch.org/fact-tank/2015/10/01/women-more-than-men-adjust-their-careers-for-family-life/.

Pew Research Center. 2015. "Same-Sex Marriage, State-by-State." Last modified June 26, 2015. https://www.pewforum.org/2015/06/26/same-sex-marriage-state-by-state/.

Pharr, Suzanne. 1988. "The Effect of Homophobia on Women's Liberation." In *Homophobia: A Weapon of Sexism*, 27–43. Berkeley, CA: Chardon Press.

Piven, Frances Fox, and Richard Cloward. 1988. *Why Americans Don't Vote*. New York: Pantheon.

Piven, Frances Fox, Lorraine Minnite, and Margaret Groarke. 2009. *Keeping Down the Black Vote: Race and the Demobilization of American Voters*. New York: New York University Press.

Rosenstone, Steven, and John Mark Hansen. 1993. *Mobilization, Participation, and Democracy in America*. New York: Macmillan.

Ruchames, Louis. 1955. "Race, Marriage, and Abolition in Massachusetts." *Journal of African American History* 40, no. 3: 250–73.

Sanbonmatsu, Kira. 2002. "Political Parties and the Recruitment of Women to State Legislatures." *Journal of Politics* 64, no. 3: 791–809.

Schattschneider, E. E. 1942. "Party Government." *National Municipal Review* 31, no. 4: 220–42.

———. 1960. *Semi-sovereign People: A Realist's View of Democracy in America*. Boston: Cengage Learning.

Sigel, Roberta. 1996. *Ambition and Accommodation: How Women View Gender Relations*. Chicago: University of Chicago Press.

Sparks, Sarah, 2014. "Women's Voices Lacking on School Boards: Women Tend to Just Listen." *Education Week*, August 26, 2014. https://www.edweek.org/ew/articles/2014/08/27/02schoolboard.h34.html.

State Library of Massachusetts. 2017. "Black and Latino Legislators in the Massachusetts General Court, 1867–Present." https://archives.lib.state.ma.us/handle/2452/48905.

Terborg-Penn, Rosalyn. 1998. *African American Women in the Struggle for the Vote, 1850–1920*. Bloomington: Indiana University Press.

CONCLUSION
MASSACHUSETTS POLITICS
Exceptional? It's Complicated

Jerold Duquette and Erin O'Brien

The chapters in this volume offer a comprehensive description of Massachusetts politics as well as nuanced analysis of the most Massachusetts of questions, "How special are we?" Said more diplomatically, "Is Massachusetts exceptional?" John F. Kennedy certainly thought so, saying in his 1961 Farewell Address to the Massachusetts legislature that the "enduring qualities of Massachusetts" are "an indelible part of my life, my convictions, my view of the past, and my hopes for the future." In Massachusetts, he reasoned, "we do not imitate—for we are a model to others." Lily Geismer's scholarly take makes clear that this consideration of Massachusetts exceptionalism has a "long mythology" in the Bay State "dating back to the Puritans christening of Boston as 'the city on the hill' and claims that the city was the 'birthplace of liberty' during the American Revolution and extending to the recent invocation of the 'Massachusetts liberal' label" (2015, 7). Michael Barone summarized, "Massachusetts . . . has always assumed it has a lot to teach others" (Barone and Cohen 2007, 783), while Geismer affirms that Massachusetts "residents have frequently adopted various elements of the state's history and even appropriated criticisms as a means to distinguish themselves from the rest of the nation" (2015, 15).

This volume showed that Massachusetts is well set up for exceptionalism—for being a worthy model to the other forty-nine states. After all, as chapter 1 demonstrated, the commonwealth features the most educated populace among U.S. states, a subsequently thriving knowledge economy, high marks for household median income, and relatively low poverty rates. The history of the Bay State is well known to American schoolchildren, as Professors Jenkins and Ubertaccio note in chapters 2 and 3, respectively, so much so that early Massachusetts history *is* U.S. history (sorry, Virginia). Beyond Provincetown, Plymouth, and Pilgrims, sparks for both the Revolutionary War and the Civil War took hold in Massachusetts. The Boston Massacre, Boston Tea Party, Battles of Lexington and Concord, as well as the abolitionist movement all feature prominently, exceptionally, in early American history. Massachusetts leadership on the national stage is not limited to the 1600s, 1700s, and 1800s, though—as Professor Ubertaccio also documents in chapter 3. National political leaders continue to be drawn disproportionally from the Bay State. Yes, that includes four American presidents, but also consistent leadership in the U.S. Congress and serious candidates for president on both sides of the aisle. Lodges and Kennedys begot Tip O'Neal, Katherine Clark, Richie Neal, Mitt Romney, Deval Patrick, Elizabeth Warren, Seth Moulton, and Bill Weld. National agenda setters like Ayanna Pressley and Maura Healey represent the Bay State too, and the connections to Massachusetts among President Biden's top circle outnumber those of any other state (O'Connell 2021).

Massachusetts' defining governmental structures remain a model for much of the federal government. In chapter 6, Professor Friedman proclaims, "It is no idle boast to claim as exceptional both the Massachusetts Supreme Judicial Court and the constitution it is chiefly responsible for interpreting. The SJC remains 'the oldest court in continuous service in the hemisphere, operating under the oldest still functioning written constitution anywhere.' . . . And while the Massachusetts Constitution of 1780 was not the first postrevolutionary charter, few state constitutions have proved to be as influential." In chapter 5, Professor Duquette explores how the design of the modern presidency finds its roots in the administrative arrangements of the Massachusetts executive as well as how the collegial relationship between the governor and state legislature provides aspiration in our current time of national discord. Even that participatory ideal, the town meeting, still defines more than 70 percent of municipal governments in Massachusetts (chapter 2). Massachusetts does have fertile ground then for exceptional leadership among the fifty states—relative prosperity, educated workers who can drive a knowledge economy, influential historical legacies, and institutional designs replicated within the federal government.

Fertile ground does not always yield an exceptional harvest. Several chapters, but especially chapters 1 and 2, document how the economic boom of Massachusetts is better understood as a Greater Boston boom. Southern, central, and western Massachusetts have seen neither the same climbing economic fortunes nor the population gains of Greater Boston. These areas lack the public transportation serving Greater Boston (itself often lacking) and do not enjoy the same gains in population or racial and ethnic diversity.

The cost of living is so great in Massachusetts that the state's high median income does not proportionally cover the expense of being a Massachusetts resident. Housing is out of reach for many, and the state has one of the highest levels of wealth and income inequality. Chapter 1 too revealed how vulnerable elements of the knowledge economy are to economic downturn. COVID-19 exposed how those in positions that support knowledge workers—restaurant workers, daycare workers, and those in entertainment spaces—were devastated by the disruption. The same chapter demonstrated that Massachusetts' poor reputation on racial politics remains, and Black residents in particular suffer systemic racism when it comes to wealth, income, residential segregation, educational experiences and outcomes, as well as disproportionate incarceration. Those foundational institutional structures? Blueprints for American democracy? Professor O'Brien finds in chapter 11 that the state legislature is last in New England when it comes to having women and just middle of the pack compared to the other forty-nine states. In chapter 10, Professor Jiménez describes a diverse Latinx population in Massachusetts but one where demographic representation in electoral office has not kept pace. Professor Jenkins notes the unusually high amount of corruption in the General Court (state legislature) as well as how it remains deeply hierarchical—"exceptionally old-school," as her chapter 4 names it. Turns out that foundational in structure does not always produce favorable results. "The old boys' network" remains formidable in Massachusetts political culture and in at least two branches of Massachusetts government. Yet, importantly, in chapter 5 Professor Duquette finds that the commonwealth's exceptional structural fidelity to the framers' intentions insulates Massachusetts governance from the culture war chaos and partisan gridlock sowing dysfunction nationally.

So, then, is Massachusetts exceptional? The whole of this volume indicates that the question might be more precisely phrased as "When and how is Massachusetts exceptional, and is this for the democratic good or bad?" It is for the reader to weigh the evidence and findings from the eleven empirical chapters to decide how they answer this more precise question. Nevertheless, themes emerge by which one may weigh the evidence.

In chapter 5, Professor Duquette summarizes, "Massachusetts' reputation for exceptionalism owes quite a bit to the fact that the state's founders, the designers of its form of government, were also at the epicenter of America's founding and the design of America's exceptional form of government." We see this theme in all three branches of government. Chapters 4 and 5, on the General Court and governor, respectively, both emphasize how legislative supremacy defines the relationship between Beacon Hill and the corner office. This arrangement of legislative dominance is a far better mirror of the framers' original conception of how the executive and legislative branches should coexist. Professor Friedman's treatment in chapter 6 of the Massachusetts Constitution and Supreme Judicial Court too shows how the "Massachusetts model" exerts continual and significant influence beyond the borders of the Bay State.

The relationship between the executive and legislative branches is not unique for legislative supremacy alone. This deep-blue state, as Professors Cunningham and Ubertaccio uncover in chapter 7, regularly votes to place a Republican in the governor's office. Divided government is nothing new, but it is fairly unique for a state whose congressional delegation is composed entirely of Democrats and where the state legislature, especially the senate, is almost comically lacking in elected Republicans. Even more exceptional, as chapters 4 and 5 explicate, is that modern Republican governors and the Democratic senate president and house leader typically have excellent working relationships, better, in some ways, than Democratic governors and legislative leaders. The partisan dysfunction of congressional-presidential relations is not replicated in Massachusetts. The key difference? Legislative supremacy in Massachusetts versus the imperial presidency in DC.

Governor aside, single-party dominance is the norm. Professors Cunningham and Ubertaccio (chapter 7) remind that this was not always the Democratic Party—Federalist, Whig, and Yankee Republicans too had their day. But in the modern era, Democrats dominate local government (chapter 2), the General Court (chapter 4), and the Massachusetts congressional delegation (chapters 7 and 8). Single-party control is central for understanding the unusual amount of corruption in state government (chapter 4) and the slow diversification of all layers of Massachusetts government (chapters 10 and 11). Women, women of color, Black, Asian, and Latinx populations have made gains, as Professors O'Brien (chapters 1 and 11) and Jiménez (chapter 10), respectively, demonstrate, but these gains run far behind other states and fall short of their percentage of these groups in the Massachusetts population.

Single-party dominance is not just the story of political institutions in the Bay State. Professors Cunningham and Ubertaccio (chapter 7) and Professor O'Brien (chapter 8) each draw forth the not so surprising fact that Democratic Party identification far outpaces that of Republican Party identification. However, and more surprisingly given the institutional dominance of Dems, "unenrolled" is the most popular self-categorization in Massachusetts. Republicans are a distant third, but unenrolled voters ("independents" elsewhere) have outpaced Democrats since 1990.

Other surprising rankings merit summary attention as well. We saw in Professor O'Brien's chapter 8 that when Massachusetts wants to become a policy leader, it does. Since 2014 Massachusetts has made truly remarkable gains in terms of voter access. The state went from not having online voter registration to implementing that reform as well as early voting, preregistration of sixteen- and seventeen-year-olds, and automatic voter registration. It adjusted nimbly to the challenges of the 2020 cycle with mail-in voting for both the primary and the general elections. Professor O'Brien's chapter 1 and Professor Jiménez's chapter 10 also demonstrate how Massachusetts is diversifying. Neither contribution has on rose-colored glasses as to the ways Massachusetts has sometimes responded to increased diversity, especially residential and racial diversity. But it is the case that Massachusetts is becoming more diverse, and, while slower than many states, descriptive representation commensurate to proportions in the population is improving, though as Professor Jiménez emphasizes in his chapter on Latinx politics, critical mass has not been achieved.

One reason that gains in descriptive representation remain slow is the hierarchical "wait your turn" culture of Massachusetts politics (chapters 1, 4, 5, and 7). Professor Jenkins shows in chapter 4 how this concentrates legislative power in the hands of the house Speaker and senate president. Ironically, when deference combines with concentrated power, legislative outcomes are regularly more conservative than the "deep-blue" numerical reality would suggest. In chapter 1, Professor O'Brien shows how the expectation to "wait one's turn" is perceived by many politicos to elevate the "old boys' club" at the expense of new voices in Massachusetts politics—particularly women and women of color. Chapter 7 is but one place where the exceptions to the rule emerge—Ayanna Pressley's successful primary challenge to a fellow Democrat for a congressional seat is most prominent. Congressman Seth Moulton too challenged the party, and, before becoming President Biden's labor secretary, then sitting Boston mayor Marty Walsh faced two quality challengers from inside the Democratic Party—both women of color and Boston city councillors, Andrea Campbell and Michelle Wu.

Hierarchical political culture too adds quite a kick to the role of single-party control in Massachusetts' corruption stew. Numerous examples throughout this text provide colorful illustrations of the place of corruption in Massachusetts political culture. William Bulger serving as senate president while his brother Whitey sat at number two on the Federal Bureau of Investigation's "Ten Most Wanted List" was rich fodder for Hollywood movies. Fairly or not, these depicted a senate president who knew where his brother was and peddled some additional clout on Beacon Hill as a result of the familial association. In real life, three consecutive house Speakers were indicted and forced to resign for infractions including kickback schemes, extortion, giving false testimony, federal obstruction of justice, mail and wire fraud, and felony tax convictions. Yet "Massachusetts has a long history of canonizing the corrupt. During his fourth term as Boston's mayor, James Michael Curley was convicted of mail fraud and sent to his second term in federal prison. His bronze likeness stands near Boston's Faneuil Hall. In 1919, the U.S. House of Representatives ejected John 'Honey Fitz' Fitzgerald, a Curley nemesis and grandfather of President John F. Kennedy, after discovering that voter fraud had elected him in 1918. Boston later named its main highway artery (since disassembled) in his honor" (Flynn 2011).

In chapter 9, Professors Duquette and Cunningham remind us that corporate corruption need not be illegal to have negative consequences for representation and public policy. They argue that the ballot initiative and referendum process in Massachusetts may once have advanced democratic norms but, since at least the *Citizens United* Supreme Court decision in 2010, has too often provided conduits for dark money to advance corporate interests dressed up as participatory democracy. Duquette and Cunningham conclude that the ballot initiative and referendum process effectively insulates the state's entrenched political and economic "insiders" diminishing the prospects of needed reforms that might threaten Beacon Hill incumbents or the interests of well-financed special interests in the state.

This volume thus provides the data, themes, and full considerations to determine the degree to which Massachusetts' politics is exceptional and to what ends in a democratic polity. The authors of this volume believe Massachusetts' politics exceptional, but our exact conclusions about how, where, and to what ends differ substantially. We handle this healthy debate in the most Massachusetts of fashions—with humor intended to make our take reign supreme and a pint (or two).

WORKS CITED

Barone, Michael, and Richard E. Cohen. 2007. *The Almanac of American Politics, 2008.* Washington, DC: National Journal Group.

Flynn, Daniel. 2011. "Bay State Bums: Massachusetts House Speakers and Their Many Convictions." *City Journal*, Summer 2011. https://www.city-journal.org/html/bay-state-bums-13406.html.

Geismer, Lily. 2015. *Don't Blame Us: Suburban Liberals and the Transformation of the Democratic Party.* Princeton, NJ: Princeton University Press.

O'Connell, Sue. 2021. "Exploring Massachusetts' Connections to the Biden Administration." New England Cable News, January 5, 2021.

CONTRIBUTORS

MAURICE T. CUNNINGHAM recently retired as an associate professor of political science at the University of Massachusetts Boston. Professor Cunningham is a recognized expert on Massachusetts government and dark money in politics. His work exposing the dark money behind a ballot question to increase charter schools in Massachusetts in 2016 has been recognized as contributing to the defeat of that question. His accomplishments in this arena led to prestigious awards from the Massachusetts Association of School Committees and the Massachusetts Teachers Association. Professor Cunningham is a proud native son of Massachusetts and a cofounder of and senior contributor at the popular blog *MassPoliticsProfs*. His most recent book is *Dark Money and the Politics of School Privatization* (2021).

JEROLD DUQUETTE is a cofounder and senior contributor at *MassPoliticsProfs* and an associate professor of political science at Central Connecticut State University. A western Massachusetts native, Professor Duquette earned degrees from the Catholic University of America (BA), George Washington University (MPA), and the University of Massachusetts at Amherst (MA, PhD). He is the author of *Regulating the National Pastime: Baseball and Antitrust* (1999) and has published articles and book chapters on a wide variety of topics related to American and Massachusetts politics. Professor Duquette lives in Longmeadow, Massachusetts, with his wife, retired Marine Lieutenant Colonel Kara Duquette, and their four children. Thanks to his one term on the Longmeadow School Committee and the fact that the Baseball Hall of Fame library owns his book, Duquette boasts (frequently) that he has never lost an election and is in the Baseball Hall of Fame.

LAWRENCE FRIEDMAN teaches constitutional law, privacy law, and national security law at New England Law | Boston. He has written widely about state constitutional law and the Massachusetts Constitution in particular. He is the author of *The New Hampshire State Constitution* (2nd edition, 2015), coauthor of *The Massachusetts State Constitution* (2011), and coeditor of *State Constitutional Law: Cases and Materials* (5th edition, 2015).

SHANNON JENKINS is the associate dean of the College of Arts and Sciences at the University of Massachusetts Dartmouth and a professor in the Department of Political Science, where she served as chair from 2012 to 2018. Her primary research focuses on decision making in state legislatures, with a specific focus on the role of political organizations and gender in shaping outputs in these institutions as well as women's political engagement. She also researches the effect of engaged learning pedagogies on college students' political interest and engagement; she was awarded the Manning Prize for Teaching Excellence in 2019 in recognition of this work. She is the author or coauthor of three books and has received two Fulbright Awards, one in China in 2012 and one in Japan in 2019. She received her PhD in political science from Loyola University in Chicago in 2003.

LUIS F. JIMÉNEZ is an associate professor in the Political Science Department at the University of Massachusetts Boston. His main research interests are Latin American politics, immigration, and U.S.–Latin American relations. He has published in *PS: Political Science & Politics* and *Social Science Quarterly*. In addition, he has just published a book titled *Migrants and Political Change in Latin America* (2018) on the impact that Latin American migrants have in their home countries. Using quantitative and qualitative methods, he demonstrated the ways that migrants are shifting the political behavior and politics of Mexico, Colombia, and Ecuador. He is currently working on a second book exploring the reasons the United States and Latin America have followed such different development paths.

Since 2007, ERIN O'BRIEN is a proud "Bostonian with Buckeye flair." She earned her PhD in 2003 from American University in Washington, DC, and is associate professor of political science at University of Massachusetts Boston. O'Brien is the author of two prior books, *The Politics of Identity: Solidarity Building among America's Working Poor* (2009) and *Diversity in Contemporary American Politics and Government* (2009). She publishes in top journals in the field, including the *American Journal of Political Science*, *Perspectives on Politics*, *Political Research Quarterly*, and *Women & Politics*. O'Brien is a nationally sought-out political voice who leverages her political science lens for outlets including the Associated Press, the *Economist*, the *New York Times*, NPR's *Marketplace*, the *Wall Street Journal*, and the *Washington Post*. Locally, she appears frequently for Boston25, the *Boston Globe*, NBC-10

Boston, GBH NPR, and New England Cable News. Come summer, you can find her *hoping* to dodge sharks in open-water swims along the South Shore and Cape Cod. Come fall, you can find her rooting for THE Ohio State Buckeyes.

PETER UBERTACCIO is the vice president for academic affairs at Caldwell University in Caldwell, New Jersey, and the former dean of arts and sciences and an associate professor of political science at Stonehill College in Easton, Massachusetts. He is a cofounder of *MassPoliticsProfs*. Professor Ubertaccio's scholarly work has been featured in the *American Political Science Review, Routledge Handbook of Political Management, Winning Elections with Political Marketing*, and the *Routledge Handbook of Political Marketing*. The author of two career guides for undergraduates studying politics, he received his PhD in politics from Brandeis University, lives on Cape Cod, and serves as the chair of the board of directors of the JFK Hyannis Museum Foundation.

INDEX

Page numbers followed by a *t* indicate a table.